Pittsburgh Series in

Composition, Literacy, and Culture

Fragments of
Rationality

---

*Postmodernity
and the Subject of
Composition*

LESTER FAIGLEY

University of Pittsburgh Press

PITTSBURGH AND LONDON

Published by the University of Pittsburgh Press, Pittsburgh, Pa., 15260
Copyright © 1992, University of Pittsburgh Press
All rights reserved
Manufactured in the United States of America
Third printing, 1995

Library of Congress Cataloging-in-Publication Data
Faigley, Lester, 1947–
        Fragments of rationality : postmodernity and the subject of
composition / Lester Faigley.
            p.   cm. — (Pittsburgh series in composition, literacy, and culture)
        Includes bibliographical references and index.
        ISBN 0-8229-3717-4   ISBN 0-8229-5492-3 (pbk.)
        1. English language — Composition and exercises—Study and
teaching. 2. English language — Rhetoric —Study and teaching.
3. Postmodernism.   I. Title.   II. Series.
PE1404.F35   1992
808'.042'07—dc20   92–5701
                                                                        CIP

A CIP catalogue record for this book is available from the British Library.
Eurospan, London

Sections of chapters 3 and 5 appeared in "The Study of Writing and the Study of
Language," *Rhetoric Review* 7 (1989): 240–59. An earlier version of chapter 4 was pub-
lished as "Judging Writing, Judging Selves," *College Composition and Communication* 40
(1989): 395–412. The first transcript in chapter 6 was previously analyzed in
"Subverting the Electronic Workbook: Teaching Writing Using Networked
Computers," in *The Writing Teacher as Researcher: Essays in the Theory and Practice of Class-
Based Research*, ed. Donald A. Daiker and Max Morenberg (Portsmouth, N.H.:
Boynton/Cook, 1990). All are reprinted with permission of the publisher. Two stu-
dent essays that appear in William E. Coles, Jr., and James Vopat, eds., *What Makes
Good Writing Good* (Lexington, Mass.: Heath, 1985) are reprinted with permission of
D.C. Heath and Company.

For my parents,

V. V. and Madaline R. Faigley

Face it, Dad. You're totally out of it.
Your last good year was 1976, the year you had me.
—Ian Faigley

Contents

Preface

LATELY MANY BOOKS have been published that consider the relationship of postmodern theory to various disciplines, in particular to an array of new disciplines such as women's studies, cultural studies, African-American studies, Latino-American studies, and various other ethnic and Third World studies, whose emergence is sometimes described as a postmodern phenomenon. This book examines the relationship of postmodern theory to another relatively new discipline, composition studies, that is rarely considered among the disciplines mentioned above. The alleged beginnings of the "disciplinary period" in composition studies in 1960s coincides with what other cultural analysts have claimed as the onset of postmodernity, when in the United States pop art, acid rock, street theater, the civil rights movement, the black activist movement, the feminist movement, the Native American movement, the gay/lesbian movement, the environmental movement, the free speech movement, the anti-Vietnam movement, and a general euphoria about technology all arose in the same decade. But while composition studies is concurrent with some characterizations of an era of postmodernity, it has by and large resisted the fragmentary and chaotic currents of postmodernity, and it has remained in many respects a modernist discipline, especially in its prevailing conceptions of the subject. The disruptions of postmodern theory that have caused major upheavals in other disciplines in the humanities and interpretative social sciences have had far less effect on composition studies.

Even though composition studies might seem a peculiar choice for a disciplinary case study of the impact of postmodern theory, I find that the conservatism of composition studies in the face of postmodern theory is precisely what makes it interesting to study. The intimate relationship of theory to the classroom practice in teaching of writing enacts theoretical debates by constructing subjectivities that student writers are expected to occupy. Composition studies as a discipline relies upon *disciplinary* technologies of the sort

Foucault describes—technologies that are committed to the molding of docile bodies. Many of the practices in the contemporary teaching of writing follow from an ongoing debate within composition studies that restages a long debate within modernism, a debate between those who wish to preserve the rational, coherent subject of the Enlightenment and those who advocate the self-expressive subject of Romanticism.

By the 1980s both conceptions of the subject came under attack for positioning the writer as an autonomous, "free" individual and thus placing the writer within the dominant ideology of patriarchal capitalism. These critiques pointed out that the teaching of writing carries many assumptions about subjectivity. I extend these critiques to show why in spite of the efforts of many writing teachers to promote social equality through education, their belief in the writer as a "free" individual often undercuts their efforts. The question of the subject, however, leads to many other relations involved in the teaching of writing, and much of this book is devoted to exploring those relations, which include the contradictory location of composition studies with respect to other disciplines and the larger culture, as well as the impact of electronic technologies on conceptions of the subject. Finally I consider how composition studies might be an important site for working through what some have called the "impasse" of postmodern theory—a sense that the critiques of postmodern theory are so powerful that no principled position can stand in their wake. If composition studies becomes such a site, then it will become one of the primary venues of critical pedagogy.

Acknowledgments

I AM EXTREMELY grateful to those I imposed on to read sections of this book while they were in progress. These friends include Julie Allen, Phyllis Artiss, Jim Berlin, Linda Brodkey, JoAnn Campbell, Andrew Cooper, Beth Daniell, Mara Holt, Carolyn Miller, Thomas Miller, Neil Nehring, Rick Penticoff, Wayne Rebhorn, Jack Selzer, John Schilb, Mary Trachsel, John Trimbur, Keith Walters, and Steve Weisenburger. As reviewers of the manuscript, Patricia Bizzell and James Slevin gave me thorough and insightful readings. I thank the series editors, David Bartholomae and Jean Ferguson Carr, for their good counsel and encouragement, and Jane Flanders, for her meticulous attention in preparing the final manuscript. I also appreciate the contributions of many students whose voices are represented directly and indirectly in this book.

The University Research Institute at the University of Texas at Austin supported my work by granting me leave for a semester. The greatest support came from my family, who remain skeptical about "pomo" but gave me the space to finish the project.

Fragments of
Rationality

Introduction

IN AN INTERVIEW with Don DeLillo that was first published in *Rolling Stone* in 1988, the interviewer, Anthony DeCurtis, asked: "There's something of an apocalyptic feel about your books, an intimation that our world is moving toward greater randomness and dissolution, or maybe even cataclysm. Do you see this process as irreversible?" DeLillo answered: "This is the shape my books take because this is the reality I see. This reality has become part of all our lives over the past twenty-five years. I don't know how we can deny it." DeLillo's date for the beginning of our current era of randomness and dissolution is 1963, the year of John F. Kennedy's assassination that is the subject of DeLillo's novel, *Libra*. DeLillo says that "what's been missing over these past twenty-five years is a sense of manageable reality. . . . We seem much more aware of elements like randomness and ambiguity and chaos since then."

This growing awareness of randomness, ambiguity, and chaos since the 1960s is expressed not only in the work of novelists like DeLillo, but also in the work of many other artists, musicians, choreographers, film makers, and architects, and even in the productions of advertisers, fashion designers, sports promoters, and politicians. It is often referred to as *postmodern*. Postmodern is also used to describe a general movement in philosophy and cultural criticism identified most prominently with French intellectuals of the past three decades— Roland Barthes, Jacques Derrida, Michel Foucault, Julia Kristeva, Jean-François Lyotard, Jean Baudrillard, Gillès Deleuze, and Félix Guattari—but also with Americans such as Fredric Jameson, Richard Rorty, and many others. Critics of postmodernism are fond of pointing out the disparities of usage in the term and that any concept of postmodernism is itself contradictory. Both caveats should be kept in mind. There is no way of working quickly through the contradictions described in discussions of postmodernity as a cultural condition, nor is there any satisfactory definition of postmodernism. Indeed, the assertion that there is no satisfactory definition of postmodernism is a positive expression of postmodernism. When it can be defined, the provocativeness of postmodernism will have long since ended.

Yet even those such as Andreas Huyssen and David Harvey, who survey developments called postmodern with a skeptical eye, still claim that there has been a sea change in cultural, artistic, political, and economic practices during the past three decades, and while Huyssen, Harvey, and others heavily qualify such claims by noting the unevenness of change and the contradictory relationship of postmodernism to modernism, they still maintain that there has been a major shift in what they call "the structure of sensibility." These theorists argue that what is new about postmodernity is not the awareness of the fragmentary, the ephemeral, and the contingent; such awareness was always a part of modernism. The key difference is that modernism posited a tension between the transient and the eternal, between low culture and high culture, between the vernacular and the elite, while in postmodernism this tension is lost. Harvey says that "postmodernism swims, even wallows, in the fragmentary and the chaotic currents of change as if that is all there is" (44).

Architecture has been one of the most important discourses for theories of postmodernism because it is easy to demonstrate a disjuncture between the modern and postmodern. When I was a student in architecture in the late 1960s, Le Corbusier, Mies van der Rohe, and Frank Lloyd Wright were still spoken of as deities, and the ideal society would give the architect control over planning what buildings should be built, how they should be built, and how land should be used. The architect as urban planner was still thought capable of solving the many problems cities presented—slums, congestion, sprawl, the waste of land and resources, and general ugliness. Our teachers inspired us with grand schemes for redesigning old cities and erecting new ones devised by planners in the 1950s and 1960s. If some of the realized grand schemes had not worked as well as planners had hoped, the glitches were attributed to unforeseen factors such as the heat of Brasilia that made ordeals out of the treks between widely separated buildings in its architectural sculpture garden. Oscar Niemeyer's grand scheme for Brasilia typified the large-scale, design-from-high-above perspective of urban planning that dominated the modernist era in architecture.

By the end of the 1960s, however, city dwellers began to voice strong resistance to planners as they watched their cities pulled down around them. Urban riots in the United States raised doubts about the motives of "urban renewal," and in Britain planners were accused of causing more damage to British cities than the bombers of Hitler's Luftwaffe. The most prominent recent example of the failure of comprehensive planning was Nicolae Ceausescu's thwarted plan to bulldoze the picturesque country villages in Romania and replace them with uniform blocks of housing flats. David Harvey observes that today it is "the norm to seek out 'pluralistic' and 'organic' strategies for approaching urban development as a 'collage' of highly differentiated spaces and mixtures, rather than pursuing grandiose plans" (40).

The rejection of comprehensive urban planning is an example of what Harvey and others mean by a shift in the structure of sensibility. Out of the failure of modern planning with its faith in rational design came a new appreciation of the variety of urban life. Writing of Jonathan Raban's *Soft City*, an exuberant account of life in London in the 1970s, Harvey says,

> Raban depicts as both vibrant and present what many earlier writers had felt as a chronic absence. To the thesis that the city was falling victim to a rationalized and automated system of mass production and mass consumption of material goods, Raban replied that it was in practice mainly about the production of signs and images. He rejected the thesis of a city tightly stratified by occupation and class, depicting instead a widespread individualism and entrepreneurialism in which the marks of social distinction were broadly conferred by possessions and appearances. (3)

Rather than viewing the city as a lost but longed-for community as did Jane Jacobs in her analysis of New York City, Raban represents the city as a labyrinth full of diverse and intertwined paths of social interaction without necessary relation to each other, incapable of being understood according to any architectonics. The city is like a huge theater that offers the possibility of playing many different roles but at the same time is extremely stressful and vulnerable to random violence. For Raban the city is held together not by government or by planners but by highly conventionalized semiotic systems which, because of their plasticity, are always in danger of breaking down, throwing the city into chaotic violence and totalitarian nightmare. This deeply contradictory response to urban living—the experience of simultaneous exhilaration and terror—is Harvey's embodiment of postmodern sensibility.

Postmodernism, Postmodern Theory, and Postmodernity

If we cannot define postmodernism, we can at least describe generally how the term is being used today and how the notion of a postmodern sensibility is articulated. Since postmodernism is applied to everything from Andy Warhol's multi-image paintings, the music of John Cage, and the novels of William Burroughs to Disneyland, fast food, and MTV, it would seem as fragmented and chaotic a term as the qualities it describes. I am going to follow the suggestion of Stephen Best and Douglas Kellner to sort discussions of postmodernism into three metadiscourses: (1) aesthetic discussions of *postmodernism*; (2) philosophical discussions of *postmodern theory*; and (3) sociohistorical assertions that Western nations, if not indeed all the world, have entered an era of *postmodernity*. This classification is not altogether satisfactory because theorists like Lyotard and Jameson are involved in all three discourses, but it does help to distinguish the scope of claims in discussions of postmodernism.

First, *postmodernism* began to be used in literary criticism in the late 1950s to describe a dwindling in the energy of modernism—authors weren't writing novels like *Ulysses* anymore. In the 1960s and early 1970s more favorable views of contemporary literature were advanced, and many of the general characteristics of aesthetic postmodernism were identified by Susan Sontag, Leslie Fiedler, and Ihab Hassan. Sontag's essays of the 1960s proclaimed a "new sensibility" of style and "erotics" in fiction that opposes the modernist emphasis on meaning. Fiedler noted a blurring of the distinction between high and low culture, which led to a movement to study popular culture as something other than barbarism or ideological deception. Hassan wrote extensively on postmodernism during this time, describing in *The Dismemberment of Orpheus* (1971) the nonlinear quality of postmodern literature and its pastiche of names and quotations.

In the 1970s discussions of postmodernism proliferated and came to be applied to art, theater, film, and architecture, where the ruptures with modernism were more dramatic and more evident than in literature. For instance, Charles Jencks popularized the use of *postmodern* to describe a trend in architecture that cannibalizes elements and styles from many periods and defies the modernist prescription of form following function. But it was Robert Venturi's essays and books, especially *Learning from Las Vegas* (1972), written in collaboration with Denise Scott Brown and Steven Izenour, that announced the rejection of modernist functionalism. Venturi, Brown, and Izenour described the Las Vegas strip as the emergence of a new urban form, one "radically different from that we have known; one that we have been ill-equipped to deal with and that, from ignorance we define today as urban sprawl" (xi). In the energy and eclecticism of Las Vegas, they found proof that the modernist revolution in architecture had failed by forgetting the social symbolism of architecture. Las Vegas gave people symbols on the scale of cathedrals, which Venturi and Brown irreverently pointed out were not so very different from casinos in their complex symbolic development. The major difference is that Las Vegas, unlike Rome, was built in a day.

There is a great divergence in discussions of aesthetic postmodernism on where the break occurs between modernity and postmodernity and whether there is really a "break" rather than merely an exhaustion of modernism. In architecture the break can be documented with specific buildings. While modern architects attacked the clichés of traditional genres, they did so by affirming rationality and technological progress, and they thus allied themselves with what has become known as the project of modernism. Modern art and literature, on the other hand, was questioning rationality and technological progress before the end of the nineteenth century. A central problem in aesthetic discussions is what to do with figures like the avant-garde artists of Dada and surrealism, Gertrude Stein, or the Joyce of *Finnegans Wake*, who from the perspective of the 1990s all look postmodern.[1]

Jameson argues that what makes a monument of high modernism like *Finnegans Wake* different from the novels of contemporary postmodern writers is not so much its content but how the novel takes its place against the culture of its time. Works of the artists and writers of modernism were part of an oppositional movement that attacked bourgeois culture, and the bourgeoisie often responded with vitriolic condemnation of works like *Ulysses*, Stravinsky's *The Rite of Spring*, and Picasso's cubist paintings. Today, the modernist movement has become a canon of "dead classics," and postmodern art has lost the oppositional stance that distinguished modernism. Jameson charges that postmodern artists have become part of a general production of commodities for consumers that expect "fresh waves of ever more novel-seeming goods . . . at ever greater rates of turnover," and thus postmodern culture "assigns an increasingly essential structural function and position to aesthetic innovation and experimentation" (*Postmodernism* 4–5). Don DeLillo sums up the predicament of the contemporary artist in *Mao II*, when the reclusive writer, Bill Gray, remarks, "Years ago I used to think it was possible for a novelist to alter the inner life of the culture. Now bomb-makers and gunmen have taken that territory. They make raids on human consciousness. What writers used to do before we were all incorporated" (41).

The aesthetic discourses on postmodernism entered philosophical discourses when at the end of the 1970s *postmodern* was taken up by French philosophers, notably Julia Kristeva and Jean-François Lyotard, who extended its domain to include not only the ongoing poststructuralist critique of the foundations of Western philosophy but also a major transformation in Western thought. Needless to say, this development has a long, complex history, and here I shall note only that *postmodern theory* now is used to refer to common lines of philosophical critique. A summation of the main targets of critique in postmodern theory is offered by Jane Flax. Flax writes that postmodern discourses "throw into radical doubt beliefs still prevalent in (especially American) culture but derived from the Enlightenment," of which she lists the following:

1. The existence of a stable, coherent self.
2. Reason and its "science"–philosophy–can provide an objective, reliable, and universal foundation for knowledge.
3. The Knowledge acquired from the right use of reason will be "true"–for example, such knowledge will represent something real and unchanging (universal) about our minds and the structure of the natural world.
4. Reason itself has transcendent and universal qualities. It exists independently of the self's contingent existence.
5. There are complex connections between reason, autonomy, and freedom. All claims to truth and rightful authority are to be submitted to the tribunal of reason. Freedom consists of obedience to laws that conform to the necessary results of the right use of reason.
6. By grounding claims in the authority of reason, the conflicts between truth, knowledge, and power can be overcome. Truth can serve power without distortion; in turn, by utilizing knowledge in the service of power, both freedom and progress will be assured. Knowledge can be neutral.
7. Science, as the exemplar of the right use of reason, is also the paradigm of all true knowledge.
8. Language is in some sense transparent. (41–42)

If I can generalize even further from Flax's list, the key assumption that motivates each of these lines of critique is that there is nothing outside contingent discourses to which a discourse of values can be grounded–no eternal truths, no universal human experience, no universal human rights, no overriding narrative of human progress. This assumption carries many radical implications. The foundational concepts associated with artistic judgment such as "universal value" and "intrinsic merit," with science such as "truth" and "objectivity," and with ethics and law such as "rights" and "freedoms" suddenly have no meaning outside of particular discourses and are deeply involved in the qualities they are alleged to be describing objectively.[2]

The radical critiques of knowledge and the sign in postmodern theory fold back on the modernist conception of the subject and for some commentators represent the culmination of several nineteenth- and twentieth-century critiques of the modernist subject. The modernist conception of the subject is frequently traced to Descartes and is characterized as the final reduction of the corporeal, ethical self of classical philosophy to the state of pure consciousness detached from the world. Since the nineteenth century, that conception and its corollary assumption–that language provides an unproblematic access to reality–have undergone repeated critiques. Marx reinterpreted the autonomous subject as a collective entity located in a historical teleology, Freud explored the desires of the unconscious and found that representation involves repression, and Nietzsche saw the Cartesian subject as a will to domination. More recently, many feminist scholars have shown how the self-knowing

Cartesian subject is a gendered construct and a product of patriarchal culture. Postmodern theory decisively rejects the primacy of consciousness and instead has consciousness originating in language, thus arguing that the subject is an effect rather than a cause of discourse. Because the subject is the locus of overlapping and competing discourses, it is a temporary stitching together of a series of often contradictory subject positions. In other words, what a person does, thinks, says, and writes cannot be interpreted unambiguously because any human action does not rise out of a unified consciousness but rather from a momentary identity that is always multiple and in some respects incoherent. If consciousness is not fully present to one's own self, then it cannot be made transparent to another.

The debate over the identity of the subject might seem relatively unimportant if it concerned only the academics who participate in these discussions, but in the third metadiscourse on postmodernism, discourses that propose an era of *postmodernity*, the dislocations of postmodern theory are claimed to be indicative of a more general cultural condition. Unlike the metadiscourses on aesthetic postmodernism and philosophical postmodern theory, which are predominantly housed in the academy, the metadiscourse on postmodernity is widespread, extending from academic philosophers like Lyotard to novelists like DeLillo to media theorists like McLuhan to "futurologists" like John Naisbitt and Alvin Toffler to popular media uses of "postmodern," such as a program on MTV called *Postmodern MTV.* Discourses on postmodernity also run across the political spectrum from right to left. Similar to the critiques of postmodern theory, discourses on postmodernity often speak of the fragmentation of the subject, the loss of faith in science and progress, and a rising awareness of irrationality and chaos, but they attribute these effects to major economic and cultural shifts.

Nearly all who theorize a disjuncture between modernity and postmodernity locate the break after World War II, with the most usual date somewhere between the late 1950s and the early 1970s.[3] The conservative cultural historian Daniel Bell speaks of the advent of a "postindustrial society" or an "information society" in the United States brought about by a shift from the manufacture of traditional economic products to the production and distribution of knowledge ("Social Framework"). Bell's postindustrial society was popularized by John Naisbitt in *Megatrends* and Alvin Toffler in *The Third Wave*, both of whom envision a high-tech world where smokestacks and poverty have disappeared, robots perform the routine jobs previously done by people, computers run households, and advanced telecommunications technology removes the need for being physically present at a job and allows access to data bases worldwide. Unlike the postindustrial utopias of Naisbitt and Toffler, however, in Bell's the foundations of contemporary capitalism are built on the privileging of self-gratification and hedonism to keep the economy expanding. Without the balancing constraints of religion, Bell sees free-market capitalism eventually undermining traditional authority and promoting an "anything goes" ethic of individual fulfillment at the expense of the social fabric.

Cultural historians on the left make analyses similar to Bell's in theorizing that capitalism has entered a new stage. The best known of these analyses in the United States is Fredric Jameson's claim that postmodernism reflects a new "cultural dominant" where cultural production has become integrated into commodity production. This claim is advanced in "Postmodernism, or The Cultural Logic of Late Capitalism," a much discussed essay published in *New Left Review* in 1984, and in a 1991 book with the same title that supplements the essay. Jameson adapts the argument of Ernest Mandel in *Late Capitalism* that there have been three periods in capitalism, "each one marking a dialectal expansion over the previous stage. These are market capitalism, the monopoly stage of imperialism, and our own, wrongly called postindustrial, but what might better be termed multinational, capital" (*Postmodernism* 35). Jameson connects the trajectory of capitalism with the artistic movements of realism, modernism, and postmodernism through a mediation that would explain postmodernism as a new cultural logic. Jameson links postmodern styles of art, architecture, literature, and music to the larger culture when he cites the correspondences between the flatness, decenteredness, and fragmented quality of contemporary art with the lack of depth, unity, and coherence in contemporary life. Jameson is least explicit, however, in his characterization of multinational capitalism itself.

British theorists have been more thorough in analyzing the advent of multinational capitalism, describing the effects of a transition from "Fordism" to "post-Fordism."[4] "Fordism" is a summary term for the system of mass production consolidated by Henry Ford in the early decades of this century.[5] Fordism required elaborate central planning to standardize tasks and parts, to analyze discrete tasks, and to arrange tasks in a sequence on an assembly line, and Fordism used an authoritarian hierarchical management structure to ensure that the plan was followed. After its initiation in the United States (Ford installed the assembly line in his Dearborn factory in 1913), Fordism soon spread to other industries and to other nations. Probably the most committed convert to Fordism was Lenin, who based Soviet industrialization on the Fordist principles of central planning, hierarchical organization, and large-scale production.

Because establishing an assembly line and mechanizing part of that line requires a large initial commitment of capital, Fordism is predicated on mass consumption in order to be profitable. Mass consumption in turn requires elaborate systems of distribution and an economic climate that produces steady demand. For Fordism to flourish, nations had to build infrastructures and manage markets with a degree of hierarchical control similar to that used by corporations to manage workers. Large variations in consumer demand, such as the slackening of demand during the 1930s, could be catastrophic for Fordist industries. It was not until the application of Keynesian economics following World War II that the Fordist economic era realized its potential. The United States and other Western governments actively managed the national economies to promote stable economic growth that enabled ongoing mass consumption of mass-produced goods.

The triumph of Fordism proved to be short-lived. By the 1960s the Fordist model began to be eroded by transnational competition and by more diversified and volatile markets. West Germany and Japan grew to be major forces in the world's markets, and multinational corporations began to shift production overseas in search of cheap labor. The Keynesian solution of increasing the money supply brought inflation that threatened steady economic growth. These weaknesses in Fordism were exposed in the sharp economic downturn caused by the OPEC oil embargo following the Arab-Israeli War in 1973. Many old-style factories of the Rust Belt in the United States closed in the 1970s, and economic growth was concentrated in the Sun Belt and in areas where high-tech, computer-based companies were located such as the Route 128 corridor around Boston. Those industries that remained were forced to become more sensitive to consumer demand following the lead of retailers.

Market researchers developed new ways of analyzing of patterns of consumption, and markets became divided into numerous specialized niches according to income level, age, household type, and locality, each to be "targeted" with particular products and stores. Manufacturers also reorganized their mode of production, following a model developed in Japan by Toyoda, the founder of Toyota, who computerized production and quality control. This systemization of production not only allows stocks of supplies to be reduced and items assembled far more quickly, but also changes the organization of the work force so that fewer workers control assembly and more of the routine tasks are shifted to subcontractors. As a consequence, the work force has become divided into knowledgeable core work groups and low-paid peripheral contract workers.

The term for this development in the discourse of business management is *flexibility*. In post-Fordism the work force becomes flexible in several senses: (1) core workers are flexible since they are trained to do varied tasks, including some assigned to supervisors in Fordist management; (2) peripheral workers are flexible because their numbers can rise and fall according to the specific needs of a company; (3) the entire work force becomes geographically flexible as production is dispersed across regions and national boundaries;

(4) production becomes flexible as it responds to specific consumer demands. Besides shifting the work force away from manufacturing to service occupations in Western nations, thus eliminating many high-paid working-class jobs and creating many low-paid jobs, post-Fordism has also shifted many of the risks of capitalism onto these low-paid contract workers, who have few benefits and little job security.

Accompanying the transition from Fordism to post-Fordism has been the breakup of mass culture as it was constituted in the United States throughout much of this century into a pluralization of tastes, styles, and practices. The formerly common experiences of popular culture—reading Look, Life, and the Saturday Evening Post, listening to and later watching the programs of the three major broadcast networks, eating similar foods, wearing similar fashions, and living in similarly structured male-headed families—were closely tied to Fordism. Look, Life, and the Saturday Evening Post have long since ceased publishing as mass circulation magazines, replaced by hundreds of specialized magazines devoted to hobbies, fashion, interests, and occupations. Many former viewers of the major networks have been diverted to the multitude of television channels available on cable or by satellite dish or they watch thousands of movie titles available on video. Even in small provincial cities, exotic items for consumption are becoming commonplace: clothing from Africa, South America, and Asia, restaurants featuring food from India to the Caribbean, luxury cars from Europe and Japan, and collectible items from many parts of the world. The expansion of leisure time has led to numerous new social movements ranging from Tai Chi and Kung Fu to jogging and aerobics to yoga and massage to gourmet cooking and wine making to amateur magic and computer hacking. The world has become a bazaar from which to shop for an individual "lifestyle." If traditional religion doesn't inspire, New Age religion encourages you to make up your own, selecting beliefs and practices from a smorgasbord of Western religions including Christianity and Judaism; Oriental imports including Islam, Buddhism, Vedanta, Hinduism, Zen, Sufism, and other Eastern teachings; religions of native Americans, astrology, paganism, Satanism, witchcraft, and numerous new religions ranging from science fiction writer L. Ron Hubbard's Church of Scientology to Rastafarianism.

Like postmodern theory, theories of postmodernity also describe the fragmentation of the subject, but they work from a different line of reasoning that associates the fragmentary subject with the desires of consumption that Daniel Bell feared would result from unrestrained capitalism. In The Society of the Spectacle, Guy Debord observed that what is consumed in contemporary Western societies is not so much objects but images of objects, through which consumers imagine themselves as consuming subjects. Acts of consumption thus close the gap between subject and object, but open the gap within the subject. Because living consumers can never be self-identical with the imaginary consuming subject, the desires of the consuming subject are never completely fulfilled. The desire to consume is predicated on the lack of a stable identity. Purchasing and using a consumer object is a temporary and unstable attempt to occupy an imagined identity provoked by an image.

Jameson would see the decentered subject of postmodern theory as a kind of epiphenomenon of the fragmented social subject of post-Fordism or what he calls "multinational capitalism." Jameson is one of the theorists who describes the breakdown of links between signifiers in postmodernity as a kind of cultural schizophrenia. In "Postmodernism and Consumer Society" he writes that the schizophrenic "is condemned to live in a perpetual present with which the various moments of his or her past have little connection and for which there is no conceivable future on the horizon. In other words, schizophrenic experience is an experience of isolated, disconnected, discontinuous material signifiers that fail to link up into a coherent sequence" (119).

The experience of flipping across television programming approximates the consciousness of the schizophrenic living in the intense, eternal present. The viewer watches a series of spectacles from around the world—"smart" bombs exploding buildings, sports heroes in the elation of victory, royal marriages, plane crashes, assassinations, rock concerts, ranting dictators, shuttle launches, hurricanes, scandals, earthquakes, revolutions, eclipses, and international terrorism—all issued in an economy of images competing for attention. Jameson proposes that if "theory" (he does not make the distinction I am making between postmodern theory and theories of postmodernity) is to have a political project, then it will be to provide "cognitive maps" so that "we may again begin to grasp our positioning as individual and collective subjects and regain a capacity to act and struggle which is at present neutralized by our spatial as well as our social confusion" (*Postmodernism* 54).

Composition Studies in Postmodernity

This book examines the peculiarly North American discipline of composition studies in light of claims that Western culture has taken on a new structure of sensibility. Composition studies has only recently considered itself as a discipline, and it is an interesting coincidence that several scholars who have written about the beginnings of composition studies as a discipline also use DeLillo's date, 1963, as a point of embarkment. (See Schilb "Composition.") Robert Connors, Lisa Ede, and Andrea Lunsford in *Essays on Classical Rhetoric and Modern Discourse* (1984) and Steven North in *The Making of Knowledge in Composition* (1987) speak of the papers given at the 1963 Conference on College

Composition and Communication as the outset of the "modern" discipline of composition. Richard Braddock, Richard Lloyd-Jones, and Lowell Schoer's survey of research on writing published in 1963 is also frequently cited as the beginnings of a research community that would give composition a distinct method of academic inquiry. In these estimates, at least, the disciplinary era of composition studies comes with the era of postmodernity described by DeLillo, Jameson, and Huyssen (Harvey begins postmodernity in the early 1970s). But if composition studies coincides with the era of postmodernity, there is seemingly little in the short history of composition studies that suggests a postmodern view of heterogeneity and difference as liberating forces, and there are very few calls to celebrate the fragmentary and chaotic currents of change.

In terms of the three metadiscourses—postmodernism, postmodern theory, and postmodernity—composition studies is variously situated. If examined from the perspective of aesthetic discussions of postmodernism, composition studies has maintained a modernist tension between form and chaos, coherence and fragmentation, and determinancy and indeterminancy, consistently privileging the former over the latter. For example, in "The Culture of Postmodernism" Ihab Hassan describes artistic and literary postmodernism as a reaction to modernism by listing a series of oppositions, which he is careful to qualify as unstable and representing a much more complex structure of feeling (123). Below are the first seven oppositions in Hassan's list:

modernism	postmodernism
romanticism	paraphysics
form (conjunctive, closed)	antiform (disjunctive, open)
purpose	play
design	chance
hierarchy	anarchy
mastery/logos	exhaustion/silence
art object/finished work	process/performance/happening

Except for the last opposition, the conception of a "good" student text lines up squarely on the side of modernism. The postmodern qualities of antiform, play, chance, anarchy, and silence are those associated with "free writing" and early drafts—the disorganized materials that the writer shapes into the purposeful design of the end product, a design that achieves closure. Even in the last opposition—"art object/finished work" versus "process/performance/happening"—composition studies tilts toward modernism because while composition studies has professed to value process, it is not process for its own sake but rather the process of teleological development toward a product.

Composition theory is more contradictorily situated in relation to postmodern theory, oscillating between positions that might be referred to as "modern" and "postmodern." In the 1980s much of composition theory came to assume that knowledge is socially constructed and rhetorical in nature, a development attributable to the impact of postmodern theory. The work of Richard Rorty, Thomas Kuhn, and Clifford Geertz is widely influential in composition studies and has led to a conception of knowledge as a set of shifting interpretations and agreements among members of a community. But even this "social" conception of knowledge shortly came to be contested. By the end of the 1980s, critiques of notions of community and "normal discourse" raised issues of politics and attacked beliefs that knowledge and language are neutral. Representation of any kind came to be viewed as implicated in social and political relations. Where composition studies has proven least receptive to postmodern theory is in surrendering its belief in the writer as an autonomous self, even at a time when extensive group collaboration is practiced in many writing classrooms. Since the beginning of composition teaching in the late nineteenth century, college writing teachers have been heavily invested in the stability of the self and the attendant beliefs that writing can be a means of self-discovery and intellectual self-realization.

While it is possible to generalize about contemporary composition teaching in relation to the issues in postmodern aesthetics and postmodern philosophical theory, it is less easy to make generalizations about the effects of postmodernity on composition studies beyond the well-documented claim that an "information society" increases dramatically the amount and kinds of writing done by people in occupations that require a college education.[6] With the dispersal of employees of multinational corporations to many sites around the world, the increase of people in service occupations related to government, banking, tourism, research, transportation, health care, and finance, and the introduction of computer technologies that give many people access to data bases, word processing programs, and electronic mail, it is not surprising that the transition from Fordism to post-Fordism would place new demands on writing in the workplace. But it is more difficult to connect the claim that we live in an age of fragmentation, multiplicity, drifting, plurality, and intensity to how writing is taught in the United States today. One could point to the present diversity of college writing courses, but much current teaching maintains practices in place by the end of the last century. College writing teachers in introductory courses still require "themes"–short nonfiction texts which they annotate and return to the students. The required topics of themes then as now are often based on personal experience rather than on academic investigations (Connors, "Personal"). Both the writer and potential readers are removed from any specific setting and are represented as living outside of history and having no investment in particular issues. The curriculum then as now is organized by rhetoric textbooks, which include advice on methods of development that bear a direct lineage to the "modes" of discourse and urge conformity with "standard" English. These textbooks are often supplemented by collections of readings from well-known authors that serve as examples.

Ferreting out the residual modernism in the teaching of writing, however, risks missing the obvious. A significant scholarly discourse in composition studies seemingly came out of nowhere in the 1960s, and that discourse has been enlarging and dividing into increasingly specialized subdiscourses ever since. If much in the teaching of writing remains in the rut of current-traditional rhetoric, the enormous expansion of scholarly discourse concerning writing suggests that the teaching of writing as a profession has greatly changed.[7] Aside from claims for the continuity of rhetoric from classical times to the present, scholarship in composition studies has not had at any point a stable canon of texts at its center, and the young discipline has experienced not only rapid growth but also rapid consumption of theory so that what seemed at the cusp a decade ago now is regarded as little more than shards from a distant and superseded past. The quick-changing fashions of thought within composition studies and the continuous searching for new discourses about writing and ways of representing writing might be considered as part of a postmodern sensibility that delights in ephemerality and the commodification of culture.

But if the proliferation, fragmentation, and rapid consumption of scholarship in composition studies reflects postmodern chaos, it is chaotic like the weather—a phenomenon difficult to predict but one that follows certain regularities at particular sites, and one of the chief sites, if not the primary site, for scholarly debates is the subjectivity of the student writer. Discussions of the subjectivities that student writers occupy are often confusing because two related notions of the *individual* are frequently conflated.

The first notion of the individual is the subject of high modernism: a coherent consciousness capable of knowing oneself and the world. In the works of the famous authors and thinkers of high modernism (for example, Goethe, Rousseau, Baudelaire, Dostoevski), the world is no less fragmented and transitory than in descriptions of the postmodern condition, but the individual is granted the possibility of being able to critique that social formation from a distanced viewpoint and to discover a potential course of human emancipation. The second notion of the individual is the postmodern "free" individual of consumer capitalism: one who can change identities at will because identities are acquired by what one consumes. This conception of the free individual is at the foundation of the dominant American ideology because it promises to empower individuals through their choice of consumer goods and thus justifies the existing social order. Because the individual is said to be free to choose her or his "lifestyle," politics, religion, and occupation, as well as which brand of soap to use, the poor are alleged to choose to be poor, or as Ronald Reagan said of the homeless, "They've brought it on themselves."

The argument that runs through this book is that many of the fault lines in composition studies are disagreements over the subjectivities that teachers of writing want students to occupy. In the 1960s and 1970s many writing teachers opposed the second notion of the individual with the first. In the 1980s both notions of the individual were criticized, and a communitarian notion of the subject was advanced that locates the subject in terms of the shared discursive practices of a community. It would be convenient to label these divisions within composition scholarship as either "modern" or "postmodern" in orientation and to locate politically progressive teaching in one of these terms. Postmodern theory, however, is suspicious of this sort of dichotomous categorization, and it works to unravel existing categories rather than to reify them.

Take, for example, the tripartite division of theories of composing that James Berlin proposes in "Rhetoric and Ideology in the Writing Class" (1988), a scheme similar to the one I set out in 1986 in "Competing Theories of Process: A Critique and a Proposal," which in turn draws on Berlin's earlier work (*Writing Instruction*, 1984). I argue that conceptions of writing as process position themselves in three overriding views of composing: an "expressive view" that emphasizes the qualities of integrity, spontaneity, and originality from romantic expressivism, a "cognitive view" that emphasizes the rational working of the individual mind, and a "social view" that considers an individual writer as a constituent of a culture. Berlin identifies three rhetorics—expressionistic rhetoric, cognitive rhetoric, and social-epistemic rhetoric—that he claims occupy distinct positions in relation to ideology ("Rhetoric" 478). Berlin's notion of ideology follows from Göran Therborn's "postmodern" interpretation of Althusser, which abandons Althusser's distinction between science and ideology and thus the possibility of "truth" outside of ideology.

Berlin sees expressionistic rhetoric as extending the modernist dualism between the transcendent individual and the dehumanizing and fragmenting forces of modern society. Proponents of expressionistic rhetoric hold out that the main goal of writing is to probe one's sense of selfhood and that it is possible to convey authentic selfhood through original language. Donald Stewart, one of the principal advocates of "authentic voice" pedagogy, makes the connection explicit between expressionistic rhetoric and the artistic triumphs of high modernism in "Collaborative Learning and Composition" (1988), an article that attacks social constructionist philosophy and collaborative learning pedagogy. Stewart raises concerns that were often voiced in the 1950s by associating anything "social" with conformity and totalitarianism. He allows along with Daniel Bell that capitalism can run amok, but the fault is not with individualism: "Individualism under capitalism is not a bad thing per se; it is bad when it gives free rein to greed, power-seeking, and vicious and unethical competitiveness" (74).

Stewart uses the artists and thinkers of high modernism as his chief examples in attacking social constructionism, singling out Richard Rorty's notion of "abnormal discourse" to account for exceptional creativity. Stewart writes of Rorty:

> The person who has learned the conversation of mankind, we are told, learns how to challenge the status quo, to sniff out the stale and no longer viable. How? This is a completely unsatisfactory explanation of Mozart's ability to transcend the influence of Haydn, of Beethoven's to transcend Mozart, of Brahms' to transcend Beethoven. (67)

The privileging of the unified individual consciousness that Stewart advocates has been called into question by many contemporary philosophers and other writers. For example, bell hooks in *Talking Back* describes experiences in college creative writing classes where she was told by white teachers and peers that she was using her "'true,' authentic voice" when she wrote in a particular southern black dialect. She says she was troubled by these comments because she was aware that black poets were capable of speaking in many voices. She then remarks: "The insistence on finding one voice, one definitive style of writing and reading one's poetry, fit all too neatly with a static notion of self and identity that was pervasive in university settings" (11). Hooks gives a powerful example of how the belief in unified subjectivity collapses differences into singular categories of substance—that a black writer's "authentic" voice could be rendered only in a black English dialect.

But hooks's answer is not to try to remove voice from her writing but rather to problematize it. To develop a voice for her writing, she draws on memories of black women speaking in the homes of the southern community where she grew up. Like other feminists she is deeply critical of the separation of public and private, and she writes that it is crucial to be open about "personal stuff" in order to oppose ongoing practices of domination. The position adopted by hooks is consistent with those of postmodern theorists like Foucault and Lyotard, who insist that political resistance can be staged only at the micro level. It also makes the issue of locating expressive writing in terms of "modern" versus "postmodern" highly problematic. To give an example within composition studies, Mara Holt, a scholar identified with collaborative learning, writes, "Personal expression needs defending now . . . because it is politically important" (Holt and Trimbur 53).

Cognitive rhetoric is similarly fissured in terms of modernity versus postmodernity. Cognitive rhetoric might seem to be unequivocally modern with its emphasis on orderly operations of reason. Berlin accuses the prevailing model of cognitive rhetoric described by Flower and Hayes of replicating the structures of Fordist management by dividing composing into discrete units and representing the mind in terms of a rational hierarchy. He writes that Flower and Hayes's "entire scheme can be seen as analogous to the instrumental method of the modern corporation" (483). However, had Berlin considered the cognitive model that Mike Rose uses in *Writer's Block: The Cognitive Dimension* (1984), he might have had to qualify his characterization of cognitive rhetoric. Rose takes issue with the hierarchical character of goal-oriented composing in the Flower and Hayes model and turns instead to a cognitive model developed by Barbara and Frederick Hayes-Roth based on "opportunism." Rose's model of composing is more analogous to the decentralized, post-Fordist corporation with its dispersed, horizontal organization. Cognitive rhetoric is neither distinctly modern or postmodern. Berlin's main complaint against cognitive rhetoric—that it never questions the values of the goals it enables—is also a frequent complaint from both the Right and the Left against the alleged absence of values in postmodernity.

My "social view" and Berlin's "social-epistemic rhetoric" would seem more compatible with postmodern theory, since most of the composition scholars who have proposed social theories extend interpretative social science theory and poststructuralist theory to issues of student writing. Once again, however, it is often hard to distinguish what is "modern" from what is "postmodern," and the political implications of each are matters of contention.

An example of a modern/postmodern debate within the larger social perspective may be found in an exchange between John Schilb and James Berlin published in *College English* (November 1989). Schilb attacks Berlin's article for lumping together fourteen theorists of different persuasions under the category "social-epistemic rhetoric" and then claiming that their theories "inevitably" support democracy (769). He then faults Berlin for upholding Göran Therborn's postmodern notion of ideology but then praising the pedagogy of Ira Shor, whose *Critical Teaching in Everyday Life* (1980), according to Schilb, presents ideology as "false consciousness" in the "vulgar" (modernist) Marxist tradition. Berlin answers these charges by accusing Schilb of misrepresenting his position. Berlin adds that "a more serious objection is the political position Schilb endorses, a matter of much greater consequence" ("Response" 774). Berlin alleges that "the political consequences of the kind of skeptical [postmodern] critique Schilb offers . . . result in a paralyzed acquiescence in the status quo" (777).

This sharp exchange between scholars who share much in common is perhaps unfortunate, but not unexpected. I see both Berlin and Schilb in their recent work attempting to find space for political agency in light of postmodern theory. This effort is extremely difficult because of postmodern theory's strong resistance to "grand narratives."[8] Postmodern theory offers an ongoing critique of discourses that pretend to contain truth and serve to justify practices of domination, but it does not supply a theory of agency or show how a politics is to arise from that critique. For these absences postmodern theory has been often attacked, especially by Marxists and feminists who hold that any attempt to end domination requires a theory of positive social action.

The "Impasse" of Postmodern Theory

In spite of the appeal of postmodern theory and theories of postmodernity in offering some insights into the extraordinary changes going on around us, many find postmodern theory frustrating because it offers so few possibilities for redirecting those changes. In a review of *Profession 88*, a collection of essays published by the Modern Language Association written in response to E. D. Hirsch's proposals for cultural literacy, Patricia Bizzell speaks to the dilemma caused by the power of postmodern critique. Bizzell notes that seven of the eight essays in the volume oppose Hirsch, but none of them offers a way to regain a national political discourse. Bizzell calls this abandonment of the possibility of public discourse an act of "pedagogical bad faith" ("Beyond" 670). "To take the next step," Bizzell argues, "we will have to be more forthright about the ideologies we support as well as those we attack, and we will have to articulate a positive program legitimated by an authority that is nevertheless non-foundational" (671). The sticking point is in the notion of "a positive program legitimated by an authority that is nevertheless non-foundational." How is such a program to be constructed? Is it possible to develop a "positive program legitimated by authority" without reference to some sort of metanarrative? What conception of the subject will this program offer?

This "impasse" of postmodern theory has been around long enough for a reaction to set in, and a self-questioning of postmodern theory has begun. Conferences held by the Institute of Contemporary Arts in London have been one of the main venues for international discussions of postmodernism, and the ICA conference held in December 1990 on "Values" is indicative of this reaction.[9] The conference announcement claimed that postmodern theory is paralyzing in its deconstruction of all "principled positions" and stated that the purpose of the conference was "to assess whether there is now a gradual shift away from these manifestations of postmodernity, towards a reassertion of value, and to look at the implications and effects of this shift across a spectrum of cultural, aesthetic and political fields" (Soper 120). This reflexive questioning has redirected attention once again to the subject as the site where ethics enters postmodern theory.

The reappraisal of postmodern critique begins by examining the motives for engaging in critique. Kate Soper argues that it is not by accident that postmodern theory attacks the discourses claiming the status of knowledge and truth. She asks:

> Why, for example, lend ourselves to the politics of "difference" if not in virtue of its enlightenment—what it permits in the way of releasing subjects from the conflations of imperializing discourse and the constructed identities of binary oppositions? Why lend ourselves to the deconstruction of liberal-humanist rhetoric if not to expose the class or racial or gender identities it occludes? . . . Why call science into question if not in part because of the military and ecological catastrophes to which the blind pursuit of its instrumental rationality has delivered us? Why problematize the artistic canon and its modes of aesthetic discrimination if not to draw attention to the ways in which art can collude with the values of the establishment and serve to reinforce its power elites? (124)

Soper's point is that it makes no sense to be asking such questions unless one is willing to argue for certain ethical values and political principles. By selecting a politically and ethically motivated set of issues, postmodern theorists can be accused of inconsistency, but the alternative is cynicism as a means of adjusting to the ugliness, starvation, grotesque violence, and environmental degradation of our times. Soper is not the only theorist who finds in the midst of postmodern skepticism a desire to understand the world and change the world on the basis of that awareness.

Like Soper I am ambivalent about postmodern theory. I am also ambivalent about claims that we have entered an era of postmodernity. The mention of *postmodern* is too often a license for hyperbole, and claims for a "condition of postmodernity" too often move toward quick conclusions when the notion is exploratory. The brief analysis of Berlin's and my categories is intended to illustrate that postmodern theory and theories of postmodernity are not especially valuable for classificatory purposes, even though there is a great rush to attach to various cultural objects and phenomena the label of postmodern.

Yet in spite of the fact that the term *postmodern* has been spread so widely that it can be applied to nearly anything, I am persuaded by Jameson's argument that even if there is no way to define *postmodernism*, to begin to understand what has happened over the past three or four decades, "for good or ill, we cannot *not* use it" or some concept like it (*Postmodernism* xxii). Applying the critiques of postmodern theory and considering the claim that Western culture has radically changed over the past thirty years gives us different ways of reading and different ways of thinking about recent history. This book uses postmodern theory and theories of postmodernity to attempt to understand some of what has happened in composition studies since the 1960s and to address what I see as the most vexed question in composition studies—the question of the subject.

The first two chapters examine why the question of the subject is central today. These chapters chart parallel and related upheavals that have severely disrupted composition studies as it enters the 1990s. I examine in chapter 1 the entry of postmodern theory into composition studies. When composition studies first encountered postmodern theory as deconstruction and social constructionism, it appeared that composition studies would accommodate postmodern theory without major upheavals. But by the end of the 1980s, however, more troublesome interpretations of postmodern theory were used to critique fundamental assumptions in the teaching of writing. As a result, many in composition studies have abandoned the modernist privileging of individual expression and mental processes and have turned to the examination of meanings and practices linked with certain discourses that are historically produced. This attention to the politics of writing has led to examinations of what systems of power are implicated in particular discursive practices and what exclusions are necessary to maintain these practices and meanings.

The theory crisis in composition studies I describe in the first chapter would not have occurred, or at least not with the same magnitude, without large-scale changes in American society that have affected attitudes toward and expectations of literacy education. In chapter 2 I argue that the lingering influence of the "back-to-basics" movement, the heightened emphasis on education for economic productivity, the cuts in funding for public education, and widening gap between haves and have-nots in the United States have forced teachers to consider the role of literacy instruction in reproducing social inequality. This shift in attitudes about literacy is associated with a post-Fordist shift to the right among Western nations. At the beginning of the 1990s composition studies has gained the status of a major subfield within English studies, but at the same time often finds itself at odds with conceptions of literacy education held by much of the public and many in the academy.

In chapters 3, 4, and 5, I investigate how subjectivity has been conceived in composition studies and the consequences of those formulations. In chapter 3 I explore how an alternate conception of the subject might have developed within composition studies had linguistics had remained a major influence in the discipline throughout the 1980s. Scholars might have approached issues of ideology and power very differently had discussions more fully explored issues surrounding the linguistic agent; however, the restriction of linguistic analysis to the text makes any linguistic analysis severely limited for investigating questions of ideology and subjectivity.

In chapter 4 I take a different approach by examining the subjectivities privileged in writing instruction. I contrast the assumptions about what constitutes "good" writing in a 1931 report reviewing student essays written for a 1929 college entrance examination with assumptions set out in a 1985 collection of "best" student essays. While the assumptions in the 1931 report stand out more clearly given the perspective of six decades, the assumptions in the 1985 collection are nonetheless identifiable. The 1985 collection suggests that the belief that "good" writing is "honest" or "authentic" writing is more widespread than the professional literature of the 1980s would indicate and that teachers who claim to value what they describe as "honesty," "authenticity," "sincerity," and "truth" in writing privilege certain kinds of self-reflection. The practice of writing about the self in college composition might be viewed as part of a much larger technology of confession for the production of truth in Western societies—witness Foucault's description of the frequency of confession in legal, medical, and educational practice as well as in family and love relations and even in the popular media. Foucault argues that this production of truth is deeply embedded within relations of power where teachers are receivers of confessions as part of the institutional exercise of power.

In chapter 5 I develop further the Foucauldian critique of the rational, unified subject in composition pedagogy by beginning with the question: why are writing textbooks that advocate coherence themselves so often incoherent? After presenting examples of incoherent prose in prominent textbooks, I advance three possible explanations: that the authors themselves are poor writers, that textbooks represent accumulations of "lore," and that textbooks replicate the contradictions within capitalism. Each of these explanations is rejected as incomplete. Instead, I argue that the production of a student subject is a chief outcome of a course in composition. The molding of these subjects results not so much from the imposition of power from above as from the effects of an array of discourse practices, which in part are set out in textbooks and which serve to justify and perpetuate the discipline of composition.

In chapter 6 I turn to how electronic communications technologies are further destabilizing texts and subjects. I examine how discursive relations are altered when a college writing course is taught in a classroom equipped with networked computers allowing everyone to "talk" at once by sending written messages that are immediately posted on everyone else's screens. This technology radically alters the authority of the teacher in a traditional classroom and might be viewed as the culmination of the movement toward the "student-centered" classroom. While this technology greatly increases the participation of those most likely to be silenced in a traditional classroom, it also allows students to use discourses forbidden in many classrooms such as the discourses of racism, sexism, and homophobia. The issue of student "empowerment" thus becomes problematic in the networked classroom and exhibits many of the contradictions inherent in Lyotard's description of the postmodern condition.

My discussion of the implications of postmodern theory for the teaching of writing continues in chapter 7, where I consider Jameson's analysis of postmodernity in more detail and contrast it with Jean Baudrillard's vision of postmodernity. Neither version of postmodernity is comforting for a teacher of literacy; indeed, Baudrillard insists that academics are among the few people in America who remain oblivious to the triumph of the image. Baudrillard's position is so extreme that it is easy to dismiss, except that students often sound very much like him. Jameson suggests that while postmodernity is complex and contradictory, it still can be theorized. Nonetheless, his vision of postmodernity is also apocalyptic and suggests that historical awareness has collapsed into a nostalgia for past styles. I find both positions overstated. From examples of student writing I argue that college students are not merely "switching centers" for various media and that at least a few can make historical analyses of popular forms and locate resistance within the popular.

Finally, in chapter 8 I argue that the rejection of the individual-versus-community dichotomy for conceiving the subject and the recognition of heterogeneity and unassimilated otherness establish ethics as the central concern for postmodern subjectivity. While postmodern theory does not supply an agenda for social agency, it does uncover networks of relations of power, how these relations are constituted, and how we do and do not think about them. If theory does not point to the direction that change should take beyond resistance to domination, it does locate spaces where change occurs and refocuses attention on the politics of knowledge and practice.

1

In the Turbulence of Theory

IN MAY 1968 I remember watching images of the student revolution in the streets of Paris on the CBS *Evening News* with friends who were active in protesting the Vietnam War. Although we had seen American demonstrations reach violent intensity at Berkeley and Columbia, we realized that the barricades across the streets in the Latin Quarter represented a much more serious challenge to the established order. Some of us had been to Europe the year before, we had talked with students there, and we thought the causes of student unrest were similar to our own. It was obvious we were wrong.

While radical French students despised the hypocrisy of their government, which condemned American aggression in Vietnam while refusing to allow the tribunal on war crimes chaired by Bertrand Russell to convene in Paris, their causes for revolution were different from ours. They reacted against an outdated, hierarchical, and authoritarian educational system that served as a machine for social selection. As the students battled in the streets of Paris, for a few days thousands of workers went on strike throughout France. The coalition between students and workers threatened to topple the French government and send an 1848-like shock through the rest of Europe. But this last storm of revolutionary fervor in Western Europe quickly dissipated, partly because it threatened the establishment Left as well as the Right. The leaders of organized labor and the French Communist party were as scared of the prospect of a "people's union" government as the Gaullists, and they took a law-and-order stance against the students. When police ejected the last of the students from the Sorbonne on June 16, few outcries were heard. The students' strongest allies among the workers—the striking metalworkers at Renault—returned to their jobs the next day (Schnapp 395). The revolution was over.

The immediate effects of the May revolution were small outside of France, but the long-term effects of the revolution on academic disciplines have been

25

enormous. The May revolution denounced the content of the academy as well as its structure. The revolution did not begin among elite students at the Sorbonne but among students in the social sciences at Nanterre, a new "concrete jungle" university in the Paris suburbs. The students were dissatisfied with a curriculum that made them, in their words, into "stuffed geese." In a pamphlet titled "Why Sociologists?" distributed in the spring of 1968, Daniel Cohn-Bendit and other student leaders at Nanterre charged, "The study of society has managed the *tour de force* of depoliticizing all teaching—that is to say, in legitimating the existing politics" (Schnapp 118). The students found that what was called knowledge and technical progress in the university was "subordinated to the struggles between firms for profit (or, which is the same, for monopolistic hegemony), and to the military and economic confrontation between East and West" (119). They concluded, "The hypocrisy of objectivity, of apoliticism, of the innocence of study, is much more flagrant in the social sciences than elsewhere, and must be exposed" (120).

The students' challenges to the traditions of "objective" scholarship in the university came at the end of a decade when French philosophy and, more generally, the foundations of Western thought were undergoing a radical questioning by a diverse group of theorists who later came to be known in Britain and in North America as *poststructuralists*. The May revolution intensified this intellectual agitation by forcing theorists to confront social practices, leading to more broadly construed critiques combining the analysis of knowledge with social practice. The most discussed shift of attention to practice came in the work of Michel Foucault, who in his "genealogical" period of the 1970s (*Discipline and Punish; Power/Knowledge; History of Sexuality*, vol. 1) focused on the rationalized practices of systems of social control and their complicity with discursive formations. Opposed in many respects to his pupil Foucault, Louis Althusser in the aftermath of the May revolution also reinterpreted his structuralist Marxist position in his important essay, "Ideology and Ideological State Apparatuses," that rejects the older epistemological notion of ideology as "false consciousness" in favor of one that explains how ideology offers ways of being.

The work of Roland Barthes and Jacques Derrida also changed after the May revolution, and a generation of new theorists appeared including those more identified with postmodern theory—Jean Baudrillard, Jean-François Lyotard, Gillès Deleuze, and Félix Guattari—and the "new" French feminists Julia Kristeva, Hélène Cixous, and Luce Irigaray.[1] By the end of the 1970s, poststructuralist theory penetrated literature departments at British and American universities, and during the 1980s postmodern theory spread across disciplines and diverged. The new theory exploded: feminist theory divided into feminisms, Marxist theory became various neo-Marxisms and post-Marxisms,

Freudian theory was reinterpreted once again, African-American, gay/lesbian, and postcolonial theory appeared, and new theories were advanced that we have entered an era of postmodernity.

There have been so many accounts of this explosion of theory that it now has the contour of a boulder that has tumbled a long way down a mountain stream, grinding off its edges until it has become as smooth as an egg. For example, David Lodge began a talk in 1986 ("After Bakhtin") with the story polished down to two sentences:

> We are all familiar with the story, and with its sequel, when the Saussurean model of the linguistic sign, and the serene, deductive logic of the structuralist enterprise which it supported, began to be undermined or deconstructed by the critiques of the two Jacques, Lacan and Derrida. Thus was ushered in the era of post-structuralism, which we now inhabit, a noisy and crowded bazaar in which many different, competing voices are to be heard, peddling their wares. (89)

The outline of the story is so familiar that Lodge can portray the "wares" as characters in his novels, "wares" that elicit recognizing smiles from his academic readers. But if the story of the rise of poststructuralism among Parisian intellectuals has become a familiar one, there is also an increasing realization that in spite of its French cast of leading players, poststructuralism, as it has become incorporated into a more general movement of postmodern theory, is more hybrid and nativized than most Anglo-American commentators acknowledge.[2]

Several recent versions of the spread of poststructuralism have focused on how poststructuralist theory altered as it crossed national boundaries rather than how it developed in response to structuralism, hermeneutics, and phenomenology within France. Anthony Easthope, for example, explores why British and North American poststructuralisms took on such different characters, with British poststructuralism proceeding initially from Althusser and Foucault, and North American poststructuralism from Derrida. Easthope attributes this difference in reception of French poststructuralism to differences in the ways theoretical discussions were housed and conducted in Britain and North America. The larger political implications of poststructuralism were more strongly felt in Britain, where a consensus about national culture was breaking up during the 1970s and where there was an active tradition of Left scholarship. Poststructuralism was introduced into an ongoing political opposition within the academy in Britain. In the United States, by contrast, poststructuralism appeared on the scene as deconstruction in elite English departments, stimulated in large part by Paul de Man's appropriation of the pre-1968 work of Derrida for the reading of literature.[3] By 1980, when Colin MacCabe was being fired from his lectureship at Cambridge and denounced in the British press for his radical poststructuralist views, the "Yale School" critics—Paul de Man, Geoffrey Hartman, and J. Hillis Miller—brought deconstruction to the forefront of literary studies in the United States.[4]

During the 1980s the labels *poststructuralism* and *deconstruction* became too restrictive to describe a vast international and multidisciplinary enthusiasm for theory which I refer to as postmodern theory, and while there is no shortage of overviews of this spread, the pretense of offering a comprehensive overview is becoming more and more difficult to assume.[5] In recognition of the diversity and multiplicity of postmodern theory, more local narratives of the coming of postmodern theory are being written for specific disciplines, including disciplines such as literary studies and anthropology, where there has been a major rethinking of the foundations of the discipline, and disciplines such as economics, which are only beginning to consider the degree to which scholarship relies on tactics of persuasion (McCloskey).

Composition studies now stands somewhere between literary studies and economics in terms of the magnitude of the impact of various lines of postmodern theory and may be only at the beginning of major dislocations and reformulations. The coming of postmodern theory to composition studies is too much a phenomenon in progress to attempt an overview that would be out of date before it could be printed. What I am more interested in addressing is the paradoxical situation in which composition studies now finds itself: why when composition studies rests on much more secure institutional foundations at the beginning of the 1990s than at the beginning of the 1980s—witness many new graduate programs, conferences, journals, book series, and other signs of scholarly activity—and why when "rhetoric" has been proposed by many as a conceptual framework that might bring the many factions of English studies into conversation, the intellectual foundations of composition studies are more disputed and its future course more difficult to predict.[6] The circumstances of this paradox are complex, but certainly the turbulence that postmodern theory has brought to architecture, the visual arts, dance, film, literature, and philosophy is beginning to be felt strongly in composition as well.

Postmodern Theory Comes to Composition Studies

Some perspective on how much the scope of theory has changed for composition studies in less than a decade might be gained by comparing a book and two essays that were published in 1982: Jonathan Culler's *On Deconstruction*, a popular introduction to Derrida for literary studies; Maxine Hairston's "The Winds of Change: Thomas Kuhn and the Revolution in the Teaching of

Writing," a proclamation of the triumph of the process movement in composition studies; and Patricia Bizzell's "Cognition, Convention, and Certainty: What We Need to Know about Writing," which anticipated the trajectory much theory in composition studies would follow during the 1980s. Culler's *On Deconstruction* and Hairston's "The Winds of Change" serve today as high-water marks for deconstruction and writing as process, the two revolutions that were surging through American English departments simultaneously in the late 1970s without reference to each other.

Culler's *On Deconstruction* is a more ambitious book than its title suggests because Culler does more than discuss Derrida and his applications to literary study; he attempts a general survey of new developments in theory, including reader-oriented criticism, feminist criticism, and psychoanalytic criticism, and he relates how each of these developments shares certain concerns of deconstruction. The heart of the book is a careful elaboration of the philosophical critique in deconstruction and why that critique invites charges of both anarchism and conservatism—the former because of the subversive potential of deconstruction, the latter because it remains implicated in the system it criticizes.[7]

Culler raises several issues in Derrida's writings that would become as salient for composition studies as for literary studies by the end of the decade. Perhaps most important is Derrida's critique of intentions in texts. His reversal of the hierarchical opposition of speech and writing exposes and challenges "the metaphysics of presence," the belief that the intentions of a self-present writer can be expressed in a text and can be identified by competent readers of that text. The deconstruction of other oppositions such as thought/language, meaning/expression, literal/figural, central/marginal, and clarity/obscurity exposes the extent to which the teaching of college writing is tied to logocentric hierarchies that privilege the first term in these binary oppositions.

Maxine Hairston's "The Winds of Change," published in *College Composition and Communication*, also surveys new developments, but Hairston is much more confident that a new consensus has emerged in composition studies than Culler is for literary studies. She describes the shift in the teaching of writing from an emphasis on the product of writing, especially form, style, and usage, to an emphasis on the mind of the individual writer—a shift Hairston places as analogous to the paradigm shift from a Copernican to a Ptolemaic model of the solar system.[8] Adherents of the traditional paradigm for teaching writing, according to Hairston, "believe that competent writers know what they are going to say before they begin to write; thus their most important task when they are preparing to write is finding a form into which to organize their content" (78). This critique of the traditional paradigm would seem to be leading in the same direction as deconstruction in questioning the unity of a writer's intentions, but Hairston, like most other advocates of writing as process, stops well short of allowing a text inevitably to exceed a writer's intentions.[9] Instead, the new paradigm, which Hairston says is informed by cognitive psychology and linguistics, emphasizes strategies for helping student writers to discover their intentions. The strategies are to be based on a profile of the strategies of effective writers abstracted from research in the composing process.

Hairston looked back on a decade of research on composing beginning with Janet Emig's 1971 monograph, *The Composing Process of Twelfth Graders*, that redefined the process movement from a pedagogical trend to a research agenda. By the end of the 1970s much cognitive theory was imported into composition studies, especially cognitive-developmental theory by researchers such as James Britton and Barry Kroll and problem-solving theory in the work of Linda Flower and John R. Hayes. Anticipating another fruitful decade in process research, Hairston speculates that "we are beginning to find out something about how people's minds work as they write, to chart the rhythm of their writing, to find out what constraints they are aware of as they write, and to see what physical behaviors are involved in writing" (85). In Hairston's vision of the new paradigm, instructors use this knowledge to "intervene in students' writing during the process," and they "evaluate the written product by how well it fulfills the writer's intention and meets the audience's need" (86).

The very different notions of writing and reading proffered by Culler and Hairston suggest how far apart were the scholarly front ranks in composition studies and literary studies in 1982. Three years later, Hairston angrily denounced the neglect of composition studies by those in literary studies in her chairperson's address at the Conference on College Composition and Communication. In this speech she compares the relations between the two camps to an abusive marriage and urges the "female" partner, composition studies, "to make a psychological break with the literary critics who today dominate the profession of English studies" ("Breaking" 273). She cites as a sign of disciplinary insecurity those in composition who would turn to scholarship in deconstruction and semiotics: "By bringing in the magic names—Cullers [sic], Fish, Hartman, and Derrida—they signal that they have not abandoned the faith" (274). Theorists are in her view the enemy: "The politically active literary critics . . . are 'full of passionate intensity' and have an effect that belies their numbers. If we are going to hold our own against them, the question we must face . . . is 'How can we rally our forces against this intimate enemy?'" (276–77).

But even in 1982 when Hairston was confidently predicting a consolidation of a new process paradigm, other scholars in composition studies began introducing the new lines of theory that had led to vehement controversies in literary studies. The "intimate enemy" was perhaps even closer than Hairston realized. At the margins of composition studies in the then obscure journal, *Pre/Text*, Patricia Bizzell's review essay, "Cognition, Convention, and Certainty" begins with the question: "What do we need to know about writing?" Bizzell contrasts two kinds of answers to that question: one kind from "inner-directed" theorists such as Flower and Hayes who "seek to discover writing processes that are so fundamental as to be universal" (215); the other from "outer-directed" theorists who believe that "thinking and language use can never occur free of a social context that conditions them" (217).

Bizzell uses "outer-directed" theory to demonstrate the shortcomings of cognitive "inner-directed" theory that Hairston claimed as the basis of the new process paradigm for teaching writing. Because "inner-directed" theorists seek to isolate the "invariant" thinking processes involved in composing, Bizzell claims that "inner-directed" theorists consider the *how* of composing at the expense of asking *why* writers make certain decisions. Answers to the latter question, Bizzell insists, must come not from the mind of the individual writer but from the ways of making meaning in a particular community. She concludes that when students have difficulties in writing, they should not be assumed to be cognitively deficient, but rather their difficulties "should be understood as difficulties with joining an unfamiliar discourse community" (227). Bizzell mentions the work of Stanley Fish, one of the theorists on Hairston's "enemies list," as one example of how the ethical and political dimensions of writing instruction might be explored.

Bizzell was not the first person to criticize the aims of the cognitive research program, but she was prescient in sensing a turn in composition studies away from the modernist focus on the autonomous individual and toward understanding writing as operating within socially and historically produced codes and conventions.[10] The shift in research methodology that Bizzell anticipated in composition studies was already well under way in the social sciences in what Paul Rabinow and William Sullivan described in 1979 as the "interpretive turn." A number of anthropologists, sociologists, and social psychologists had abandoned the ideal of objective science and recognized that for the human sciences both the object of investigation and the tools of investigation are inextricably bound up in webs of meaning. By the mid-1980s several lines of scholarship in composition studies developed that investigated the situatedness of writers within webs of meaning.

First, the desire to explore in more detail the contexts for writing led a number of researchers to use ethnographic methodology as a means for understanding the cultural practices of classroom writing and writing in the workplace. The popularity of Shirley Brice Heath's insightful ethnography of literacy and schooling in three southern communities, *Ways with Words*, augmented the considerable interest this line of inquiry had gained and inspired many dissertations employing ethnographic methodology.[11] Heath's active participant role in the sites where she observed exemplifies the interpretive turn that denies privileged status to the researcher as detached onlooker.

At the same time, genre analysis emerged as a major topic of study, with some scholars developing genre theory (for example, Carolyn Miller; James Slevin, "Genre Theory"), while others were busy studying the writing of academic disciplines, combining interpretive social theory with rhetorical analysis. In the latter endeavor Charles Bazerman ("Scientific Writing") and Greg Myers ("Social Construction") drew on work in the sociology of science for studying writing in the sciences, Gay Gragson and Jack Selzer brought reader-oriented literary theory to scientific texts, while Jeanne Fahnestock ("Accommodating Science") used traditional rhetorical concepts for analyzing how scientific discourse is adapted for nonspecialist audiences. Such efforts became the scholarly companion of the writing-across-the-curriculum movement in college classrooms, and they have been followed by considerable work taking a variety of theoretical perspectives on writing in academic disciplines and in other professions.[12] The discourse of composition studies itself became an object for study in Stephen North's self-reflexive examination of the methodological communities in composition research.

Besides opening new territory for scholarship in composition studies, the influence of social constructionist theory and antifoundationalist theory led to a broad reinterpretation of notions of the writer and writing. One influential effort was Kenneth Bruffee's claims for collaborative learning pedagogy as representing the social nature of knowledge. Bruffee gained much acclaim in composition circles during the 1970s for training peer tutors to cope with the large numbers of students entering the City University of New York through the policy of open admissions. The success of peer tutoring led him to develop a method of writing instruction based on student interaction called "collaborative learning." In the 1980s Bruffee interpreted collaborative learning as acting out the philosophical position that knowledge and authority are socially negotiated, and he advanced the metaphor of conversation for the production of knowledge through writing ("Collaborative Learning"; "Liberal Education"). Bruffee uses the neopragmatist philosophy of Richard Rorty, in particular Rorty's notion that to learn something requires a shift in a person's relations with others, to explain the workings of a collaborative classroom.

Other scholars offer differing interpretations of the social nature of writing. Marilyn Cooper ("Ecology") and Linda Brodkey ("Modernism") critique writing pedagogy that reproduces traditional images of the literary artist working alone; Gregory Clark argues for Bakhtinian dialogue as the practice of democratic rhetoric; and Karen Burke LeFevre asks writing teachers to consider a "collective" view of invention based on a recognition that acts of writing are social acts taking place in a particular culture. Lisa Ede and Andrea Lunsford in Singular Texts/Plural Authors also examine the social nature of invention, using their own collaboration as an important source of data in addition to historical and theoretical scholarship and empirical research to argue for a model of collaborative writing that is dialogic and relational. "Scenes of writing," they maintain, "are peopled, busy—full of the give-and-take of conversation and debate" (42).

Beyond inspiring these new lines of scholarship, theory emphasizing that acts of writing occur in ongoing streams of discourse came to influence conceptions of teaching writing among rank-and-file instructors. The university was described as an unfamiliar discourse community that students seek to enter—a notion that provided an alternative to explanations of cognitive deficiency for students judged to be poor writers. Rather than being assessed as lacking in certain cognitive processes, students came to be viewed as foreigners in an established discourse community, and the writing teacher's job was reinterpreted as a guide to the customs and conventions of that community. Even though the assumption that the academy constitutes a single community was quickly contested, the metaphors implied by a notion of community proliferated in discussions of writing pedagogy.[13] These metaphors came to influence classroom practice through the rapid expansion of the use of writing groups in writing classrooms. (See Gere, Writing Groups.)

By the end of the 1980s some were announcing that another major transformation had occurred from the consensus on process that Hairston describes to a consensus based on social constructionist theory. Donald Stewart writes that "the era of the cognitive psychologists is waning; the era of the social constructionists is just beginning" (58). Geoffrey Chase observes, "We have watched the emphasis in composition studies swing from product to process. . . . Now another shift seems to be underway, one toward an emphasis on discourse communities" (13). And Martin Nystrand notes, "there has been a shift in perspective from things cognitive to things social" ("Social-Interactive Model" 67). None of these articles, however, exudes the confidence and enthusiasm of Hairston's celebration of the process movement; indeed, Stewart regrets the fading of the process movement, charging social constructionists with neglecting the individual.[14]

For those commentators who look more favorably than Stewart on the move toward social constructionism, the predicament has been that no single theory or even two or three theories of the social have become widely embraced by writing teachers. Consequently, what is meant by "social" and "social construction" differs from theorist to theorist. Because of the lack of a dominant theory of the social, the notion of a "discourse community" became a way of acknowledging of the social quality of writing, but that notion has proven inadequate. In examining the use of the term *community* in composition studies, Joseph Harris writes that "recent theories have tended to invoke the idea of community in ways at once sweeping and vague: positing discursive utopias that direct and determine the writings of their members, yet failing to state the operating rules or boundaries of these communities" ("Idea of Community" 12). The vagueness, Harris claims, results from conflation of the "speech community" of linguistics—referring to speakers living in close geographical proximity—and the notion of an "interpretive community" from literary theory in which dispersed readers share certain assumptions about particular kinds of texts.

Similar complaints have been made about the use of *social* in relation to writing. James Reither and Douglas Vipond argue that the ambiguity in the use of the term in discussions of writing is unresolvable (856). C. H. Knoblauch is even more skeptical in his remark,

> When roving, and normally warring, bands of cognitive psychologists, text linguists, philosophers of composition, historians of rhetoric, Marxist critics, poststructuralists, and reader-response theorists all wax equally enthusiastic about 'the social construction of reality,' there is a good chance that the expression has long since lost its capacity to name anything important or even very interesting. ("Some Observations" 54)

What Harris finds wrong with the notion of community in composition studies is that it often presents the language and conventions of writing as unproblematic and cohesive, minimizes or ignores competing discourses, and glides over the question of how membership in a discourse community is defined. Bizzell anticipates these problems in "Cognition, Convention, and Certainty" where she sees the suppression of political and ethical issues in an allegedly neutral pedagogy applying to both individual and community conceptions of teaching writing. She points out that schools transmit many assumptions from the larger culture that some refer to as the "hidden curriculum" and that students who are assigned to remedial classes known as "basic writing" often have different cultural backgrounds from those in regular sections.

The displacements forced upon students entering the discourses of the academy are examined in detail by David Bartholomae, who observes that basic writing students are not so much trapped in a "writer-based prose" of personal language as they are aware of the privileged discourses of the university but unable to control these discourses. Bartholomae brings a poststructuralist perspective in describing acts of writing as always taking place in relation to previous writing and writers' selves as always shaped by the selves of other writers. He argues that becoming an "insider" in a privileged discourse community "is not a matter of inventing a language that is new" but rather "a matter of continually and stylistically working against the inevitable presence of conventional language" ("Inventing the University" 143).[15]

Other scholars used theory concerning the workings of ideology to expose the politics of discourse communities. In "Reality, Consensus, and Reform" (1986), Greg Myers questioned Kenneth Bruffee's goal of consensus in collaborative learning from a Marxist perspective. Myers asserts that privileging the notion of reality as a social construct without giving students any means of examining the structure of this construct risks reproducing the inequalities of the existing social order.

More extensive critiques of the ideologies implicit in the teaching of writing are made by John Clifford and John Schilb, James Berlin, and Linda Brodkey. Clifford and Schilb discuss the implications of Terry Eagleton's claim in *Literary Studies: An Introduction* that the center of English studies should be rhetoric. Schilb also examines how political questions are suppressed in composition research ("Ideology"). In an essay discussed in the introduction, "Rhetoric and Ideology in the Writing Class," Berlin shows that rhetorics contain ideological assumptions about what exists, what is good, and what is possible. Berlin advocates placing the questions of rhetoric and ideology at the center of a writing class.[16]

In "On the Subjects of Class and Gender," Brodkey analyzes issues of writing and social class in letters exchanged between white middle-class teachers and students enrolled in an adult basic education class. She finds that the teachers were unable to acknowledge differences of class and fell back into an educational discourse that denies the existence of class, and (by extension) race, ethnicity, and gender. Brodkey makes clear that the teachers in this study had good intentions, but in spite of their energy, dedication, and commitment to universal education, they could not admit that their lives were very different from those of their correspondents because there was no space in their discourses for the subjectivities that their working-class correspondents presented.

Feminist theory added another dimension to theories of ideology by focusing on antagonisms within communities. During the 1970s and 1980s different lines of feminist theory challenged the assumption that acts of writing are similar for men and women. Radical feminists such as Mary Daly and Adrienne Rich argued that women's experience is distorted by language that purports to be objective and disinterested. Language in their view does not merely name inequality, it reproduces it. In a frequently reprinted essay, "Taking Women Students Seriously," first delivered in 1978, Adrienne Rich speaks of the connections between feminist theory and the teaching of writing as a result of her experience as a teacher in the SEEK program at the City College of New York in the late 1960s, a program that was a forerunner to the open admissions policy made familiar to those in composition studies by Mina Shaughnessy's *Errors and Expectations* (1977). Rich sums up eloquently the challenge these nontraditional students presented for writing teachers: "How can we connect the process of learning to write well with the student's own reality, and not simply teach her/him how to write acceptable lies in standard English?" (239). Rich continues that when she later began teaching at a women's college, she found striking parallels to teaching the so-called disadvantaged minority students in New York, since even at the women's college the educational system was set up to "indoctrinate women to passivity, self-depreciation, and a sense of powerlessness" (240).

But in spite of the burst of feminist writing and theory, in the introduction to a collection titled *Teaching Writing: Pedagogy, Gender, and Equity* (1987), Cynthia Caywood and Gillian Overing write, "[When] we began to search for scholarship on the relationship between feminist theory and the teaching of writing, . . . we discovered it was a relatively unexplored area" (xi). Elizabeth Flynn makes a similar observation in "Composing as a Woman" (1988) about the scarcity of feminist critiques in composition. The situation has changed rapidly since then.[17] One example of how feminist theory has affected composition studies is Andrea Lunsford and Lisa Ede's account of how their own view of collaboration has changed. In "Rhetoric in a New Key" (1990), they write:

> In the six years since we began what we originally thought of as a fairly straightforward data gathering project, we have come to situate the issue of collaborative writing in a much broader historical, political, and ideological context and to contemplate the ways in which our society locates power, authority, authenticity, and property in an autonomous, masculine self. (234)[18]

A second generation of feminist scholarship in composition studies has now begun to appear that emphasizes politics. Susan Jarratt notes that some feminists in composition have rejected argument as being inherently patriarchal in its aspiration to dominance ("Feminism"). These feminists align themselves with proponents of "expressivism" such as Donald Murray and Peter Elbow because both positions seek to provide a supportive environment that suppresses conflict and encourages narrations of personal experience. Jarratt points out that Elbow himself recognizes the affinity between his "believing game," which invites listening with acceptance and compliance, and feminist theory that rejects conflict. Jarratt praises both the feminist rejection of argument and the expressivist conception of writing as process for shifting power from teacher to students, but she faults both for ignoring the differences of gender, race, and class that exist among teacher and students. Jarratt writes: "Demanding that our female students listen openly and acceptingly to every response from a mixed class can lead to a discursive reenactment of the violence carried on daily in the maintenance of an inequitable society" (110–11). By foregrounding differences rather than pretending they are suspended within the space of a classroom, Jarratt believes that students can come to identify how their personal interests are implicated in larger social relations and, as a result, they will be better able to develop a public voice as well as a private one.

The entrance of deconstruction into composition studies meanwhile followed a path similar to other lines of postmodern theory, where after initial enthusiasm the political stresses soon came to be felt. By the beginning of the 1980s, a few informed members of English departments recognized that both deconstruction and writing as process undermined the fixed, authoritative text and that literary theorists and composition scholars were in some respects allied against traditional literary critics, even if they rarely acknowledged their shared positions. Both revolutions attacked the privileging of the written product.

Deconstructionists held that while what is written is apparently fixed, its meaning is open to a "big bang" of ever spreading readings, while process theorists subverted the fixed text from the other direction by emphasizing that a text can be endlessly revised; a text is never finished, but at some point the writer decides to quit. In 1984 Edward White observed that composition teachers welcomed "poststructuralism as if it were an old friend" (186).[19] White says of deconstruction that "once we strip away the jargon," it "has an almost eerily familiar sound" (190). He sees the insights of recent literary theory as describing "with uncanny accuracy our experience of responding with professional care to the writing our students produce for us" (191). White advises that writing teachers should be pleased that literary theorists support their insights, but writing teachers shouldn't expect to be outraged or astonished when they read theory.

A similar view on composition and deconstruction can be found in the introduction to *Writing and Reading Differently* (1985), a collection of essays on deconstruction and the teaching of composition and literature. The editors, G. Douglas Atkins and Michael L. Johnson, acknowledge that they "run the risk of dulling and weakening what deconstructionists sometimes regard almost as a finely honed intellectual and even political weapon" (10), but they argue that "deconstruction *is* teaching as well as an interventionist strategy" (11), implying that politics and teaching are somehow separate and thus erecting a boundary while seeming to demolish one.

By the end of the decade, more disturbing versions of deconstruction had come to composition studies, questioning the advice given in composition textbooks to use thesis statements, topic sentences, headings, and other cues to the reader. Such advice, from a Derridean perspective, gives writers a false sense of confidence that their meanings can be readily intelligible, and, more insidiously, teaches them to ignore other meanings and other perspectives. In an essay in *Reclaiming Pedagogy: The Rhetoric of the Classroom* (1989), Nina Schwartz points to the paradox that arises "when we direct our students to read complicatedly but to write clearly. . . . How can we invite students to see so much but to say so little?" (63).

In another chapter in the same volume, Randall Knoper explains how this theoretical sleight-of-hand is accomplished. The magic act of applying deconstruction to composition while maintaining "product" as usual is achieved by equating deconstruction with invention. Interpreting deconstruction in this way also suits the containment of process theory to how students write rather than to *what* they write. Knoper compares this view of invention to "a contractor's litter, |which| is cleaned up and hidden before the final, balanced, centered edifice is presented to view" (131).

Other scholars in composition studies, however, have not sought to contain deconstruction by cleaning up the litter of oppositions in a text, but instead, as John Schilb proposes in "Deconstructing Didion," to use deconstruction to make students "increasingly conscious of how contemplating the act of writing might involve grappling with philosophical issues germane to their own lives" (283–84). Jaspar Neel and Sharon Crowley have used deconstruction to critique the assumption in both traditional and process-oriented writing pedagogy that writing begins with an originating author. The hope of Neel's call for liberating composition studies from philosophy ("the notion of the forever-absent truth toward which discourse moves" 203) or Crowley's call for shifting attention away from authors and toward language is to recognize the role of rhetoric in a participatory democracy ("Derrida").[20]

The Habermas-Lyotard Debate

For those who have followed this succession of theory in composition studies, the situation is not much different from that of other disciplines which have come to view all forms of cultural representation, whether high art or mass media, literary or nonliterary, visual or aural, as actively involved in political and social relations and as thus politically invested.[21] This turn in composition studies is a recognition of the mutuality of theory and practice—a recognition that, as Foucault argues in a conversation with Gillès Deleuze reprinted in *Language, Counter-Memory, Practice*, "Theory does not express, translate, or serve to apply practice, it is practice" (208). This revised notion of theory situates the practices of composition textbooks that encourage the orderly application of reason in a long theoretical tradition of the advancement of reason dating from the Enlightenment (see chapter 5). Much of the work of Foucault explores how the Enlightenment conception of rationality is inextricably bound up in the exercise of power, and it presents a strong challenge to the commonplace assumption that society has progressed as the result of the development of rational knowledge.[22] Foucault chronicles a double movement of liberation and domination in the reforms of prisons, schools, hospitals, and asylums brought about by the humanitarian ideals of the Enlightenment. Enlightenment ideals inspired numerous disciplinary technologies that shape individuals through continuous observation, supervision, and training.[23]

Postmodern theory has not produced, however, a broad theory of agency that would lead directly from these critiques to political action. Indeed, the incisive critique in much of postmodern theory is inimical to such efforts, viewing them as a way of closing off critique too quickly and short-circuiting its radical potential, even replacing old structures of domination with new ones. There is deep suspicion of theory among postmodern theorists, who question any effort toward universal description and especially attempts to regulate on the basis of such descriptions.

In *The Postmodern Condition: A Report on Knowledge* (*La Condition postmoderne: Rapport sur la savoir*, 1979), Jean-François Lyotard defines *modern* as discourses that legitimate themselves with reference to the *grands récits*. He argues that these grand narratives are no longer capable of even legitimating themselves, and that, moreover, we have lost our nostalgia for these narratives. By grand narratives Lyotard refers to the overarching narratives of history such as Enlightenment humanism, scientific progress, and Marxism, each characterized by a belief in reason and science and a faith that we are advancing toward human emancipation. Because grand narratives deny their own historical production of first principles in their aspiration for universality, Lyotard claims that they inevitably become oppressive. They deny their status as narratives in their aspiration to represent themselves as universal truth. For Lyotard such totalizing truth entails closure, and the striving for the certainty of reason brings about authoritarianism. Lyotard sees the autonomous, rational subject of liberal humanism and the collective subject of the proletariat theorized by Marx as not only outmoded but even sinister concepts because over the past two centuries they have been used to justify wars, arsenals of nuclear weapons, concentration camps, gulags, social engineering, assembly lines, and other forms of centralized social control. Lyotard concludes *The Postmodern Condition* with a cry of outrage against the suffering caused in the name of truth: "The nineteenth and twentieth centuries have given us as much terror as we can take. We have paid a high enough price for the nostalgia of the whole and the one. . . . Let us wage war on totality" (81–82).

The gap between postmodern critique and a theory of agency was raised prominently in the 1980s in what is now referred to as the "debate" between Jürgen Habermas, a philosophy professor at Johann Wolfgang Goethe University in Frankfurt-on-Main, and Lyotard, now professor emeritus of philosophy at the University of Paris VIII. The "debate" was not a debate but an exchange of critiques, of which the most prominent examples are Lyotard's 1984 afterword to *The Postmodern Condition* and Habermas's Adorno Prize address, "Modernity versus Postmodernity" (1981), in which Habermas defended reason and the project of modernity from the critiques of the French. In the early 1980s Habermas continued his attack on postmodern theory in lectures that formed the basis of *Der philosophische Diskurs der Moderne: Zwölf Vorlesungen* (1985), translated as *The Philosophical Discourse of Modernity* in 1987. The work presents a philosophical history of the critique of reason and places the postmodernists in a tradition of philosophers who have rejected modernity, most notably Nietzsche and Heidegger. For Habermas the postmodernists are actually antimodernists, and he refers to them as "neoconservatives."

Habermas is the recognized heir of the Frankfurt School of critical theory following from Theodor Adorno and Max Horkheimer.[24] But Habermas's defense of enlightened rationality is a significant revision of Adorno's move toward aesthetics, which many take as the Frankfurt School position. Throughout his career Habermas has argued that a just society must be based on a comprehensive notion of reason, which he identifies as the project of modernity. In "Modernity—An Incomplete Project" he sees this movement consolidating in the eighteenth century:

> The project of modernity formulated in the 18th century by the philosophers of the Enlightenment consisted in their efforts to develop objective science, universal morality and law, and autonomous art according to their inner logic. . . . The Enlightenment philosophers wanted to utilize this accumulation of specialized culture for the enrichment of everyday life—that is to say, for the rational organization of everyday social life. (9)

Contrary to the French postmodernists, who view the Enlightenment belief in reason as a project that came to disaster in the twentieth century, Habermas sees the Enlightenment as a great unfinished project. Habermas admits that "Foucault did indeed provide an illuminating critique of the entanglement of the human sciences in the philosophy of the subject" (*Philosophical Discourse* 294). But Habermas faults Foucault for following the exhaustion of the philosophy of consciousness to its dead end. Habermas finds the underlying cause for the massive and extensive kinds of institutional oppression in the twentieth century not to be the excesses of reason, as Foucault contends, but rather the insufficiency and abandonment of reason. Habermas accuses the French postmodernists of giving up the fight.

Habermas feels that the postmodern critique of modernity is made at the expense of any beneficial concept of reason. By rejecting general standards of truth and goodness, postmodern theorists leave no basis for a social formation other than the struggles of antagonistic groups—a situation according to Habermas that invites the rise of fascist governments in the name of restoring order. Habermas would preserve some standard of truth and goodness, and he continues to insist on the emancipatory potential of modernity. But the foundation Habermas builds on is not that of liberal humanism. His defense of rationality is not a call for the return of the autonomous, rational subject, but instead he relocates rationality in the potential for communicative action. In his two-volume *Theory of Communicative Action*, Habermas separates what he calls "instrumental reason," the insidious rationality of bureaucratic power that Foucault describes, from the possibility of "communicative rationality," which allows people to question the claims of others in a movement toward consensus. Habermas would preserve the project of the Enlightenment by shifting rationality from the unified, self-present subject to the pragmatics of language use. True rationality is claimed to be achievable in the ideal speech situation, which is a precondition for a genuinely emancipated society. Even in less than ideal conditions, social reproduction to some extent depends on the ability of individuals to negotiate consensus over competing claims.

In *The Postmodern Condition*, Lyotard allows that Habermas's goals are worthy but his method and analysis misguided. He says that what Habermas requires is a grand theory of human experience, one that would "bridge the gap between cognitive, ethical, and political discourses, thus opening the way to a unity of experience" (72). Lyotard strongly questions the wisdom of attempting to homogenize the heterogeneity of language games into a "soft imperialism." He attacks Habermas's argument for its goal of rational consensus and accuses Habermas of attempting to stifle what is most liberating in postmodern culture—the splintering of culture into a multiplicity of differences. Lyotard asks:

> Is legitimacy to be found in consensus obtained through discussion, as Jürgen Habermas thinks? Such consensus does violence to the heterogeneity of language games. And invention is always born of dissension. Postmodern knowledge is not simply a tool of the authorities; it refines our sensitivity to differences and reinforces our ability to tolerate the incommensurable. Its principle is not the expert's homology, but the inventor's paralogy. (xxv)

This statement expresses the argument of *The Postmodern Condition* in miniature. Lyotard disputes the assumptions underlying Habermas's goal of a universal consensus in a dialogue of argumentation. First, Lyotard argues that

Habermas assumes a unified rational discourse is possible when discourses are emphatically heterogeneous, employing different sets of pragmatic rules. Second, Lyotard faults the goal of dialogue as consensus, which he maintains is but a temporary condition in discourse and not its end. Lyotard argues that the result of discourse is not consensus but paralogy and a "multiplicity of finite meta-arguments" (65). Consensus is precisely what we should not strive toward because it leads to the suppression of difference and particularity. Instead, Lyotard urges that we should celebrate dissensus and listen to the voice of the Other rather than trying to merge it into our own voice. Invention, he insists, is born of dissension, not of consensus.

Composition Studies in the Aftermath of Postmodern Theory

Some of the issues in the Habermas versus Lyotard debate have also been raised in discussions of collaborative learning and the ensuing debate over the politics of consensus. In "Consensus and Difference in Collaborative Learning" (1989), John Trimbur addresses Greg Myers's criticisms that collaborative learning occludes social conflicts in its goal of consensus. Trimbur maintains that consensus "can be a powerful instrument for students to generate differences, to identify the systems of authority that organize these differences, and to transform the relations of power that determine who may speak and what counts as a meaningful statement" (603). If collaborative learning is to move beyond a more efficient means of locating students within existing social structures, Trimbur claims that a rhetoric of consensus must be defined in relation to a rhetoric of dissensus. Consensus would come to be based "not so much on collective agreements as on collective explanations of how people differ, where their differences come from, and whether they can live and work together with these differences" (610). Trimbur cites Habermas's distinction between consensus as an empirical condition and consensus as an aspiration to organize a conversation outside relations of domination. Habermas thus conceives of consensus much differently from Bruffee and Rorty in their empirical descriptions and redefines consensus as a utopian project, which according to Trimbur would "tap the impulses toward emancipation and justice in the utopian practices of Habermas's 'ideal speech situation'" (615).

In a comment on Trimbur's essay appearing a year later, Kenneth Bruffee defends the "success orientation" of instrumental reason that Habermas, Trimbur, and Lyotard reject. Bruffee says that instrumental control and rational efficiency is "not entirely a bad thing; . . . the question is not how to avoid or sabotage instrumental control and rational efficiency. The question is how to teach other people how to exercise it and thus give them genuine access to it" ("Comment" 694). Trimbur responds, "What Habermas calls 'instrumental control' and 'rational efficiency' cannot be abstracted from the regime of the specialist and the expert, from professional monopolies which remove knowledge from the public sphere" ("Response" 699). Trimbur sees the "success orientation" as often restricting access rather than granting it and that consensus is forced by the more powerful imposing their will on the less powerful.

The debate over consensus and dissensus in collaborative learning offers a perspective different from those of Habermas and Lyotard. Trimbur, like Habermas, explores what constitutes an ideal speech (and writing) situation, but unlike Habermas, Trimbur does not fall back to a defense of universal rationality. Like Lyotard, Trimbur contests the autonomous, rational subject of the Enlightenment and instead would use arguments of historical situatedness to uphold the Enlightenment's value of civility and consensus. By relocating the debate over consensus versus dissensus to actual classroom discussion, Trimbur suggests indirectly that both Habermas and Lyotard overstate their positions. Trimbur gives the example of a typical use of collaborative learning in a literature class where students are expected to come to a consensus that the meaning is neither contained in the text nor is it entirely arbitrary, but derives from the authority of the interpretive community. Such a use of collaborative learning, Trimbur argues, accepts as a given the enterprise of interpretation. Instead, Trimbur would call into question the goal of interpretation by asking students to consider the division between literature and nonliterature—why some reading is "good for you" and other reading is "fun." The purpose of such a discussion is not to manipulate students into reaching agreement about what counts as literature but to make students aware that literature depends on a rhetoric of dissensus between what literature is and what literature is not.

Habermas, Lyotard, Trimbur, and Bruffee share many assumptions. All posit a socially constructed reality, all believe in the notion of a just society (Lyotard is unusual among postmodern theorists in this respect), and all propose discursive means toward achieving justice. All, I think, would support Trimbur's conclusion "to turn the conversation in the collaborative classroom into a heterotopia of voices—a heterogeneity without hierarchy" ("Consensus and Difference" 615).

Yet there are major differences among these theorists about how we are to achieve democracy through discourse. These differences in methodology underscore a paradox of postmodern theory: the power of critique is made problematic by how action is to result from critique. This power to fold language back on itself makes postmodern theory at once an extremely powerful means for exposing the political investments of foundational concepts, but the same power prevents postmodern theorists from making claims of truth or emancipatory value for this activity. Postmodern theory can resemble a terrorist bomb that demolishes bystanders and even its maker as well as the target. Few of the postmodern theorists are of much help in formulating what should be the appropriate politics for a particular writing classroom. Foucault's response is to turn away from formal theorizing that might grow out of critique. The incisive analysis of prisons in *Discipline and Punish*, for example, does not lead to proposals for prison reform. Foucault distrusted any global political theory of resistance because he believed it would inevitably reproduce what it set out to eliminate. Baudrillard more directly dismisses political efforts as fruitless continuations of modernism that seek to find some direction and order in a directionless and disorderly world (see chapter 7). His answer is to plunge into the chaos. But the binge of hyperconsumption in the 1980s was a plunge into the chaos, and it has left us with a cynical generation of young people who are pessimistic about the future.

The utopian hope of many who were in college in the late 1960s, both as students and teachers, was to create a nonracist, nonsexist, ecologically responsible, participatory democracy. Social reformers of the 1960s, however, failed to understand that history was not necessarily on their side. They believed in a metanarrative of human progress, and they believed that the desire for freedom is part of the human essence. The ending of racism and the aspiration for nonviolence, therefore, was understood as a cultural evolution toward a more enlightened humanity. What many social reformers did not appreciate fully was that the victories of the civil rights movement and the movement against the Vietnam War were fought and won rhetorically in public space. The 1980s were an ongoing demonstration that discourse is a means of power to be seized as the political Right redefined the social consensus of what is good and possible for America. Today, the goals of 1960s reformers are discredited as producing a new "McCarthyism" of "political correctness." In widely selling and quoted books, Allan Bloom, Roger Kimball, and Dinesh D'Souza have sounded the alarm that radicals from the 1960s have taken over the teaching of humanities in college, aiming at nothing less that the destruction of the West.

How our situation now differs from the late 1960s might be appreciated by examining the basis for radical claims in the 1960s. I want to return not to Paris but to Miami Beach in April 1969, where the Conference on College Composition and Communication held its annual meeting. The Miami Beach convention was probably the most politically active in the history of CCCC. The Executive Committee took a public political stand by voting to move the 1971 convention, which had been scheduled for Chicago, to another city as a protest against police violence against demonstrators at the 1968 Democratic Convention. A statement was prepared by a subcommittee to explain this action, which was mailed to the CCCC membership later in the month. The paragraph from the statement that justifies the Executive Committee's action reads:

> Since the summer of 1968 Chicago has become a symbol of much that is wrong with a society in trouble. What is wrong with Chicago, what is wrong with our society is its expression of values. As teachers of English, we are in the business of trying to improve our society's expression of values. Therefore, we choose not to meet in Chicago—gesture though this may be—in order to rededicate ourselves to our belief in just language. In doing so we state our opposition to the language of the nightstick, and we restate our commitment to the language of words in their auspicious places. (Roth 270)

At this same meeting in Miami, a group called the New University Conference Caucus of CCCC was much in evidence. The NUC was a broader radical movement within the academy, and it had disrupted the Modern Language Association convention the previous December. The NUC succeeded in covertly inserting a series of proposals into the CCCC convention program at Miami Beach, and it raised these proposals for discussion in an extended scheduled session, as well as in meeting rooms assigned to the NUC and at tables in the lobby of the main convention hotel.

In the "Counterstatement" section of the October 1969 *College Composition and Communication*, the NUC responded to the Executive Committee's statement. The NUC applauded the committee's decision not to meet in Chicago, but it criticized the explanation sent to the membership for concentrating on the expression of values rather than the values themselves. The conclusion of the NUC response is worth quoting at length:

> This concentration on "expression" and forms seems to avoid the facts of our situation in the U.S. Can we deny that evil *values* are the primary problem and not the *way* in which those values are expressed? That is, the Daley and police rhetoric, both of words and nightsticks, reveals despicable values, but the rhetoric is not the source of the evil. Thus our effort should not stop at criticizing the expression, the symptoms of evil. Rather, we should look beyond these superficial symptoms of wrong to the more fundamental problem of inhumane goals (e.g., the desire to impose U.S. interests on Viet Nam or Latin American countries). . . . Let us not spend too much time and effort with the problem of "society's expression of values." Let us work primarily to foster humane values themselves as the rhetoric in college catalogs and elsewhere asserts we are doing. This requires even more action than the gesture of not going to Chicago. It requires organizing ourselves to foster change, fundamental change, in the country. (New University)

The NUC's response speaks to our situation today. Many would agree that it is not enough to focus on expression of values but that teachers should enable students to become agents for social change. Few, however, are saying now that fostering humane values will necessarily result in social change. Indeed, the discourse on values was appropriated in critiques of education from the Right in the 1970s and 1980s. With the substitution of references to Chicago, U.S. imperialism, and humane values expressed in college catalogs with ones concerning sexual permissiveness, patriotism, and the Bible as authority, this critique could have come from religious fundamentalists. Appeals to the kind of humane values expressed in college catalogs now come from defenders of the status quo like Allan Bloom.

Postmodern theory offers a sustained critique of a unified discourse of humane values by revealing how such a discourse results from a dichotomy between what is held to be universal and what is is particular and contingent. A unified discourse of human values follows from the ideal of impartial moral reason, where from a disinterested and detached standpoint the particularities of different social contexts can be abstracted into universals.[25] Claims for universality depend on what Theordor Adorno calls the "logic of identity" or what Jacques Derrida in On Grammatology calls "the metaphysics of presence." The logic of identity attempts to merge different things into a single unity. By theorizing underlying principles that unite different things, the logic of identity becomes "totalizing." It denies difference by denying the particularity of situations. It denies feelings by establishing dichotomies of subjective/objective and private/public. Instead, it posits a universal subjectivity that all reasoning people are expected to occupy.

The ideal of impartiality, however, has been used over and over to justify asymmetries of power by locating reason in European men and denying reason in others. The humane values described in the Declaration of Independence, for example, did not extend to Native Americans and slaves. Postmodern theory in its many varieties emphasizes the multiplicity of subjectivities and resists the impulse to speak for the Other and to turn the Other into the same person as the speaker. "Humane values" are argued to be heterogeneous rather than homogeneous, highly nuanced according to particular situations and the particular of people in those situations. More important, heterogeneity is increasingly the social situation of North America. In states like Texas and California and in most major cities in the United States, where now over half the students in public schools are African-American, Hispanic, or Asian-American, appeals to a single, unified discourse of humane values, no matter how well-intended they might be, run dangerously against the social conditions of education.

In the next chapter I construct a narrative of the relations of composition studies to political changes in the United States. I argue that composition studies has entered a very different political landscape concerning assumptions about literacy than when it emerged in the 1960s and that the theoretical disruptions described in this chapter are related to this changing landscape.

2

The Changing Political Landscape
of Composition Studies

A FREQUENT SUBJECT of hallway talk at the Conference on College Composition and Communication is the extent the convention has come to resemble the Modern Language Association convention with groups of scholars in many different rooms holding conversations that are mutually uninteresting and verge on being mutually unintelligible. In the introduction I suggested that the MTV-like speed in which scholarship in composition studies is produced, consumed, and discarded may in itself be a phenomenon of postmodernity. It is also a sign of its disciplinary success.

Composition studies now contains the many divisions characteristic of other mature disciplines. In some departments we now find scholars studying topics ranging from pre-Socratic rhetoric to interactive computer networks, and, given such diversity, composition studies is not exempted from the theoretical debates raging in other disciplines. For those interested in a comprehensive framework for composition studies, the question is no longer what sort of theory might unite all who teach and study writing, but rather, to adapt Gerald Graff's challenge for literature professors, "How can the many kinds of things [we] do . . . be so organized as to begin providing a context for one another and take on a measure of corporate existence in the eyes of the world?" (251).[1] Scientists have long ago given up the concern for disciplinary unity because specialization has produced the visible results that give science its popular legitimacy. But, as Graff implies, the humanities are expected to be relatively stable and conceptually unified "in the eyes of the world," or at least in the eyes of those who support the humanities. During the 1980s many composition scholars were busy upholding this belief by making claims for disciplinary paradigms and advancing proposals for bringing together literature and composition as well as warring factions within composition.

Just as composition studies was expanding, diversifying, and debating its disciplinary foundations, a global political change was under way that began with a shift to the right in the United States, Canada, the United Kingdom, and other European nations during the 1970s and 1980s, followed by the abandonment of communism in Eastern Europe in 1989–1990, and climaxed by the remarkable breakup of the Soviet Union at the end of 1991. What is now clear from the perspective of the early 1990s is that this shift to the right involved more than the popularity of Reagan or Thatcher. For different reasons, many people in many nations lost faith in the ability of the state to represent their interests, and the Left became identified with the bureaucratic state that is unresponsive to desires of individuals and restricts choices.

The ascendancy of the Right in the United States, Britain, and Canada was not a return to "conservatism" but instead an attempt to radically restructure society. The Right exploited the decline of Fordism to argue for a "free-market" philosophy and a resurgence of competitive individualism. The Right represented social organization as a simple dichotomy between sovereignty of individualism and the ill-founded attempts of the state toward collective actions. Society is reinterpreted as neutral space where individuals are set against each other in competitive relations and rise and fall according to their abilities and motivation—a conception that not only promises the individual a great deal of power but also frees the individual from a sense of social responsibility. When money becomes the universal language, the new source of social identification is the level of consumption one displays. Money allows individuals to redefine themselves according to what they consume if they have enough money to spend.

The turn to the right also brought major shifts in cultural attitudes. The Right was broadly successful in the 1980s because it assembled several discourses that addressed anxieties as well as consumer desires. Appeals to individualism were couched in nostalgic images of the patriarchal family, rural or small-town life, and national identity. The images appealed to an imagined stability in the past and blamed the problems of the present on the "enemy within," those who would deny the truth and goodness of the old orders.

In education, these appeals were built on fears of "permissiveness" and calls for getting "back to basics" and to "return" to the strict standards of the past. This chapter traces the trajectory of the process movement—the engine of disciplinary success that gained academic respectability and institutional standing for composition studies—against the background of political change in the United States. It might seem that from the beginning the process movement, with its deemphasis of errors and its validation of students' experience rather than traditional authority, would have been at odds with the Right's call for a return to standards, and these movements did collide early over the issue of what is "correct" English. But the political terrain that composition studies has occupied has never been so clearly ordered. While the "back-to-basics" movement brought mandatory standardized testing and prescriptive curricula to the schools, it initially benefited college composition because it created widespread interest in the teaching of college writing that helped to open new faculty positions and new sources of funding. Only at the end of the 1980s and in the early 1990s has the process movement began to be viewed by some in composition studies as having run out of steam and, more dangerously, as obscuring the politics of composition instruction for those who teach writing.

This chapter concludes with the present situation in composition studies, where there are a number of efforts to join the teaching of writing with a larger movement to engage the discourse of the humanities with democratic public life. These efforts have stirred much enthusiasm, but they have also provoked enraged condemnations both from within composition studies and in the national media. Although the current debate over literacy can be mapped in terms of Right versus Left, the fears about the teaching of critical literacy among people who call themselves liberals suggest that the narrative of Right versus Left may be misleading for understanding the present. Thus, while the current political crisis in composition studies in part reflects a clash of narratives about literacy, it may also reflect an exhaustion of those narratives.

The Turn to the Right

Throughout most of its history, composition studies maintained a narrative about literacy that was consolidated when the discipline emerged in the 1960s. This narrative has deep roots both in American history and in the immediate circumstances of the 1960s—the last years of America's geopolitical and economic dominance following World War II. By 1960 Japanese and European economic recovery was well under way and America's share of world markets was quickly shrinking, but the United States was still producing 52 percent of the world's automobiles, and it supplied the world with high-technology products. Even with the increased competition, the United States still contributed over a quarter of the world's GNP.

The election of John F. Kennedy in 1960 brought a resurgence of confidence in America, a renewed sense of patriotism, and a revival of the tradition of liberalism that prevailed during the twenty years of the New Deal and Fair Deal from 1932 to 1952. Kennedy raised hopes that the affluence of America could be extended to everyone. He saw that improvement of education was necessary if the United States was to maintain leadership of the "free world," recognizing that only a major federal effort could achieve rapid change. Kennedy succeeded in overcoming longstanding opposition to federal aid to the public schools because of fears of federal control. His vision of a trans-formed America became the basis for Lyndon Johnson's ambitious legislative program known as the Great Society, which proposed to renew major cities, abolish racism, end the disgrace of poverty in a land of plenty, and offer educational opportunity to all Americans. The 1964 presidential campaign between Lyndon Johnson and Barry Goldwater became a comprehensive referendum on social issues. Goldwater argued against the increasing federal role in government, against federal legislation on civil rights, against programs to help the poor, and for a balanced budget.

The vote of the people was unequivocal. On November 3, 1964, Johnson won 61 percent of the popular vote, which remains the largest popular-vote percentage victory in presidential-election history, even surpassing Roosevelt's (1936) and Reagan's (1984) landslide second-term victories.[2] The coattail effect of Johnson's victory was equally magnified as Republican losses in the Senate and House of Representatives gave the Democrats more than two-to-one majorities in both Houses of Congress and ensured that Johnson's social legislation would be approved. While Johnson later frustrated his supporters in seeming to adopt Goldwater's policies by escalating the war in Vietnam, he held true to his campaign promise to make education the nation's "first work" by putting education first on his legislative agenda.

In 1965 Congress enacted what was called at the time an "educational revolution." Building on the Economic Opportunity Act of 1964, which had established programs such as Project Head Start for preschool children and the Job Corps for unemployed young adults, the Eighty-ninth Congress passed the Elementary and Secondary Education Act and the Higher Education Act, both of which promised to address social and economic inequality through increasing resources for and access to education. Johnson's support of education as the vehicle to equality inspired teachers nationwide and led to many community service programs.

The liberal consensus in America forged in the Kennedy and Johnson administrations was to last less than a decade. After the debacle of the Vietnam War, the economic realities of a United States in decline in relation to Europe and Japan began to be felt keenly. The liberal consensus started to fragment in the 1970s, and in the 1980s it was thoroughly rejected. The decisive victory margins of Ronald Reagan in 1984 (by 59 percent of the popular vote) and George Bush in 1988 (by 54 percent) confirmed that the ideals that inspired Johnson's Great Society, including the role of education in promoting social equality, had been largely abandoned.

In the 1980s the ruling political Right maintained that schools exist to provide a supply of trained workers for the labor market. The widely read report published in 1983, A *Nation at Risk*, charged that the U.S. educational system has failed to produce a "trained capability" adequate to compete with those of Germany, Japan, and a host of new economic rivals. While the Right's agenda for education was pushed ahead by the Reagan and Bush administrations in the 1980s and early 1990s, a reversal of the longstanding American belief that the public schools should give everyone equal opportunity to education was well under way by the time Reagan assumed power. During the decade before Reagan came to office, the public schools in major cities were declining visibly and public universities suffered deep budget cuts, causing them to raise tuition, increase class size, reduce student aid, and devote more money to research that promised to bring in outside corporate and government support. These trends accelerated during the Reagan years. Many parents who could afford to pay the high costs of private education abandoned public education, placing their children in private schools and sending them to increasingly expensive private colleges and universities.

The Reagan administration was able to consolidate widespread criticism of public education around a few themes popular with the media and large segments of the public. For the teaching of literacy, these themes stressed the importance of "basics": frequent testing of grammar and usage, upholding standard English, and a distrust of teachers' commitment to the basics. By the end of the 1980s these themes became the cornerstones of educational policy in the states, no matter whether Democrats or Republicans were in charge. This wholesale political shift has had major consequences for teachers in the United States. Teachers of writing who remain committed to progressive goals for education have yet to determine how to respond to the nation's replacement of the ideal of literacy as a means for achieving social equality with a cynical acknowledgement of education as part of the machinery for sorting people into categories of winners and losers.

Given that the social problems the New Frontier and Great Society programs aimed to eradicate thirty years ago now seem worse than ever, some teachers of writing have begun to interrogate their role in confirming the social order. Even though Richard Ohmann questioned this mission as early as 1976 in *English in America*, charging that first-year college English prepares students for a world of corporate capitalism, many writing teachers continued to think of themselves as the undervalued workers in the fields of English departments, the ones who perform the most important work of the university. John Schilb describes this belief as the "ethos of service" that pervades the teaching of writing ("Cultural Studies").

Had social, economic, and political conditions remained constant, perhaps there would have been no perceived need to rethink the enterprise of teaching writing within undergraduate education. But the social, economic, and political conditions have not remained constant, and those changes have led some to argue that the focus of rhetoric and composition must extend beyond the "ethos of service" to the critical examination of contemporary culture.

A more immediate cause is the recognition of the colonized status of writing instruction at many colleges and universities. James Slevin writes, "While undergraduate catalogs regularly speak with rapture of writing instruction's central contribution in preparing America's citizens and future leaders, such centrality is not apparent in the status of those who teach these courses" ("Depoliticizing and Politicizing" 2). He goes on to estimate that 70 percent of postsecondary English courses are writing courses, yet the large majority are taught by either graduate students or persons in nontenured or non–tenure track positions, often part-time positions. Furthermore, writing teachers have become increasingly aware that this colonized status developed very early in the teaching of college writing.[3] In this respect, composition studies anticipated a post-Fordist scheme of dividing the work force into core and peripheral workers before the consolidation of Fordism.[4] Willingly or unwillingly, many college writing teachers have been forced to consider the politics of literacy in America.

Anxieties of the Middle Class

Those in composition studies have written little about how the broad changes that have taken place in U.S. society during the years of the process movement have influenced the teaching of writing. Like most faculty members, they have assumed that today's middle-class students are similar to the middle-class students during the long Fordist postwar boom in America that lasted from 1945 to 1973. But while the middle class did not suffer to the extent of the working class and the poor from post-Fordist economic changes since 1973, they have been profoundly affected nonetheless.

These changes are the subject of Barbara Ehrenreich's *Fear of Falling* (1989), which theorizes that the "retreat from liberalism" in America since the 1960s reflects a change in the professional middle class's perception of itself. In the 1960s, middle-class America still believed in a classless society, with the inner cities and Appalachia looked upon as lingering areas of poverty soon to be brought up to the respectable standard. In the 1970s and 1980s, the professional middle class, which Ehrenreich defines as "all those people whose economic and social status is based on education rather than on the ownership of capital or property" (12), became more aware of itself as a class located between the moneyed elite above them and the workers and the poor below.[5] Unlike the children of the rich who can expect to inherit wealth, and children of the poor who with few exceptions are going to remain poor, children of the professional middle class often must go to school twenty years or more and serve an apprenticeship after that (such as an associate position in a law firm) just to achieve their parents' status.

Children of the middle class of course have enormous advantages over working-class children in negotiating the barriers of schooling, since the institutional culture of school is to a great degree an extension of middle-class culture, but in order to succeed children of the middle class still must reproduce the self-discipline and faith in deferred gratification that their parents possessed. Within the contemporary middle class is a perpetual dread of falling down the social incline. Ehrenreich sees the inner anxiety of the professional middle class as the fears Daniel Bell described in *The Cultural Contradictions of Capitalism* (1976)—the fears of losing the desire to strive and becoming soft and hedonistic. Paradoxically, the terms of success for the professional middle class exacerbate their anxiety because affluence threatens to lead to self-indulgence. The seduction of the consumer through appeals such as "fly now, pay later," promising an immediate hedonistic utopia of relaxation and pleasure, undermine the Protestant ethic of hard work and delayed gratification.

The political Right exploited the anxiety of the professional middle class during the 1970s and 1980s by blaming everything that was perceived to be wrong on permissiveness. Ehrenreich notes that the discussions of permissiveness had largely been confined to child-rearing practices until "permissiveness" became the theme of Spiro Agnew's vice-presidential campaign in 1968. Agnew blamed permissiveness for the rise of student radicals and black militants. Soon the use of permissiveness was extended to explain a host of other alleged social evils, including unorthodox sexual practices, pornography, drug use, and feminism. Ehrenreich argues that this extension was one of the chief means used by the Right to gain support for their conservative economic policies. They linked their economic agenda to working-class opposition to abortion, the Equal Rights Amendment, school busing to achieve racial integration, and gun control. Crime in the cities was blamed on giving up old-fashioned standards instead of on poverty as it had been in the 1960s, allowing the Right to accuse the poor of complicity in their own condition. The Right told the poor that their biggest problem was not their lack of money but their lack of initiative and self-discipline. The Right blamed welfare for sapping the incentive of poor people to work, while ignoring that the majority of the poor do indeed work in low-paying jobs.

The irony of this Calvinistic stance in telling the poor to work hard, save hard, and not to waste was that the middle class had in the meantime ceased to believe it. The message that Jimmy Carter preached—that resources were scarce and that America would have to learn to live on less—was not the one that the middle class wanted to hear. When the Reagan administration succeeded in cutting taxes by one-third, the middle class responded with an appetite for imported goods that ran the 24-billion-dollar merchandise trade deficit in 1980 to a deficit in excess of 152 billion dollars by 1986 (Bureau of the Census 786). The massive borrowing of the Reagan administration to underwrite a military buildup returned a sense of affluence to those positioned to take advantage of leveraged buyouts and paper financial empires. It was only when the Dow Jones average dropped 508 points on October 19, 1987, that the middle class began to suspect that the bills run up on easy credit might have to be paid. Although the October stock market crash turned out to be a short-term event, the collapse in debt markets meant the party was over for many of the newly well-off.

For the poor it was a different story. They didn't get invited to the party. Government statistics support Ehrenreich's claim that a seismic shift in the distribution of wealth took place during the 1980s. In 1985 the top fifth of American families had 43 percent of the total family income; the bottom fifth had less than 5 percent, the widest separation since the Census Bureau began keeping such statistics, and a trend made evident by the thousands of homeless people in the streets of major U.S. cities.[6] The shift in wealth had major consequences for the working class as well. Traditional blue-collar workers suffered from factory closings and the decline in real wages and benefits as manufacturers increasingly exported their jobs to the Third World, where many nations are willing to supply endless cheap labor and overlook the dangers of toxic waste. The effect on the middle class was to divide it. Within the middle class, those at the bottom (such as teachers and other government workers) struggled to remain at their current level, while many at the top (such as corporate lawyers and financial analysts) became part of the corporate elite.

Although Ehrenreich does not analyze in depth the changes in American education from the 1960s through the 1980s, she does observe that the shift in wealth had significant effects on the attitudes of college students and on the circumstances of their education. The migration of college students toward business-oriented careers accelerated during the 1970s and 1980s. Ehrenreich notes, "There had been a time when ambitious students saw corporate employment as an option for the intellectually handicapped. Now it was the professions that seemed like a dull, low-paid backwater compared to the brisk world of business" (210). The competition to get into prestigious business and law schools grew increasingly intense, and colleges of liberal arts on many campuses became holding pens for those students whose averages dropped below the minimum required for business and engineering majors. Surveys among students revealed increasing conservatism and desire for wealth.[7]

The 1960s Heritage of the Process Movement

The Right's attack on permissiveness used as its symbol the long-haired, wild-eyed student radical of the late 1960s and early 1970s. The issue of permissiveness, however, is a complex one. Before the disruptions at colleges and universities during the Vietnam period, critics of education and society in general complained about uniformity and dehumanization, and they used images similar to William H. Whyte's "organization man," a caricature of the thoroughly institutionalized bureaucrat with no identity apart from his niche in the organization, living a look-alike life in a look-alike house in a look-alike suburb.

Even at the apex of American confidence during the 1950s and 1960s, there were fears that something had gone terribly wrong, that the dreaded loss of individualism under communism had occurred in the midst of capitalist prosperity. These fears were reiterated again and again in popular books, including Eric Hoffer's *The True Believer* (1951), Sloan Wilson's *The Man in the Gray Flannel Suit* (1955), Whyte's *The Organization Man* (1956), Vance Packard's *The Naked Society* (1964), and Herbert Marcuse's *One Dimensional Man* (1964). In 1965 Edgar Z. Friedenberg asserted in *Coming of Age in America* that the core assumptions of American education are based on conformity and order rather than individualism and creativity. His portrait of the American school was that of a prison.

These critiques of the staleness and conformity of U.S. education made the first expressions of student radicalism in the 1960s, such as the "Port Huron Statement" (1962) from the Students for a Democratic Society, appear as a breath of fresh air. The SDS made critiques of American society and schooling similar to those of Wilson, Whyte, Packard, and Friedenberg (in sexist language as well as content): "Men have unrealized potential for self-cultivation, self-direction, self-understanding, and creativity. It is this potential that we regard as crucial and to which we appeal—not to the human potentiality for violence, unreason, and submission to authority" (236). SDS's criticism of their fellow students is also similar to complaints about students in the 1980s:

> Almost no students value activity as a citizen. Passive in public, they are hardly more idealistic in arranging their private lives; Gallup concludes they will settle for "low success, and won't risk high failure." There is not much willingness to take risks (not even in business), no setting of dangerous goals, no real conception of personal identity except one manufactured in the image of others,

no real urge for personal fulfillment except to be almost as successful as the very successful people. Attention is being paid to social status (the quality of shirt collars, meeting people, getting wives or husbands, making solid contacts for later on); much, too, is paid to academic status (grades, honors, the med-school rat race). But neglected generally is real intellectual status, the personal cultivation of mind. (238)

Many professors shared the SDS disdain for the political quietism on college campuses. When large-scale ferment erupted among students during the years of the Vietnam War, some faculty welcomed it as a sign of finally emerging from the intellectual stagnation of the Eisenhower years. For some it was a sign that the promise of John F. Kennedy's administration could be fulfilled, that young people could create a new national identity.

There were, of course, many professors who saw students' attempts to take control of their education as a siege of the barbarians, but many college writing teachers greeted student activism with enthusiasm. Several writing teachers saw the writing-as-process movement as an answer to students' rejection of traditional authority, and they emphasized in their pedagogy the values that their students cried out for—autonomy, antiauthoritarianism, and a personal voice. Influential early proponents of process invited students to take control of their writing as a political act. In one of the first articles calling for free writing, Ken Macrorie starts "To Be Read" (1968) with a breathless appeal to urgency: "We have a small chance to keep our students from turning our schools into the shambles remaining after revolutions in Watts, Newark, and Detroit. But it is a chance" (686). Donald Murray's first sentence in a 1969 article entitled "Finding Your Own Voice: Teaching Composition in an Age of Dissent" reads: "Student power is no longer an issue, it is a fact" (118).

A sense of the times can be gained from a remarkable alternative textbook published in 1970, Leonard Greenbaum and Rudolph Schmerl's *Course X: A Left Field Guide to Freshman English*. Greenbaum and Schmerl challenge students to create their own classroom and to meet in groups outside of class if the teacher is not willing to share authority. In the new kind of writing class that Greenbaum and Schmerl envision, "Students will experiment with skills and changes in behavior without being penalized"; "Students will continually interact with one another in ways that will lead them to make decisions"; and "The teacher will be a resource person—an authority on questions, not answers, who participates in class *actively*" (xix).

James Berlin has discussed (in "Rhetoric and Ideology") how in the 1960s and early 1970s proponents of expressionistic rhetoric were highly critical of American society and politics and saw the teaching of writing as a means of liberating students from that society. The aim of these teachers was to aid students in resisting authoritarian institutional structures by offering students experiences that challenged official versions of reality. This radical edge quickly was dulled. Berlin notes that the moderate wing of the expressionists became dominant, and they succeeded in defining power in terms of the individual, such as Peter Elbow's goal in *Writing without Teachers* (1973, vii) of allowing students to get "control over words." Much less recognized, however, is how the political activism of the 1960s and 1970s is reflected in the beginnings of cognitive research on composing.

In her influential monograph, *The Composing Processes of Twelfth Graders* (1971), Janet Emig sees empirical research as a way of changing the limited conception of writing taught in the schools. She blasts teaching practices centered around the five-paragraph theme, dismissing as a fantasy "easy to disprove" the then current claim that this form has correlates outside the classroom (97). "Much of the teaching of composition in American high schools," she writes, "is essentially a neurotic activity. There is little evidence, for example, that the persistent pointing out of specific errors in student themes leads to the elimination of these errors, yet teachers expend much of their energy in this futile and unrewarding exercise" (99). What makes this curriculum worse than inefficient in Emig's view is that it stifles opportunities for a personal voice. She sees the exclusion of expressive (what she calls "reflexive") writing as abhorrent: "One wonders at times if the shying away from reflexive writing is not an unconscious effort to keep the 'average' and 'less able' student from the kind of writing he can do best" (100).

Not all of the influences on composition studies of 1960s and early 1970s activism have been documented. A little discussed influence in the early process movement and collaborative learning is the rise of the contemporary feminist movement. By the late 1960s women began meeting across the country to discuss issues that concerned them—issues that had been suppressed in the mass media, in political discourses, and in everyday conversations. Out of these consciousness-raising groups came the political agenda of the women's movement: women should receive equal pay for equal work, women should have control over their bodies, and women should change the patriarchal structure of the family.

The spirit of this broad call for emancipation came into the process movement in both subtle and direct ways. Women in consciousness-raising groups explored alternatives to hierarchical and competitive male styles of discussion (Annas). By narrating personal experiences and listening intensely to the experiences of other women, women were better able to understand how they had been forced to occupy the subjectivities offered to them in patriarchal social structures and how with the support of other women they might challenge those structures. In articles on the teaching of writing that appeared in *College Composition and Communication* and *College English* in the 1960s and 1970s, there are few explicit connections made between the women's movement and the emerging process movement. But undoubtedly there was more mutual influence than one can find in the professional literature.

In "Collaborative Learning: Some Practical Models" (1973), Bruffee noted the relevance of consciousness-raising groups for collaborative learning (635), and independent women's writing groups frequently used Elbow's *Writing without Teachers* as a model during the 1970s. That readers should first listen to a writer in Elbow's "believing game" would have been a familiar practice for women who had participated in consciousness-raising groups. In fact, Elbow acknowledges that the believing game "invites behaviors associated with femininity: accepting, saying Yes, being compliant, listening, absorbing, and swallowing" (*Embracing Contraries* 266). The emphasis on personal journals in the early process movement also validated a form of writing that is traditionally associated with women's writing.

The turbulent 1960s spilled directly into composition studies when on April 4, 1968, during the annual CCCC meeting in Minneapolis, Martin Luther King was assassinated in Memphis. The shock felt at the convention was expressed in a letter from Richard Braddock to King's widow, Coretta Scott King, on behalf of the organization. The letter, published in *College Composition and Communication* in October 1968, describes a memorial service held at the convention where speakers "made eloquent statements about the racist sickness among Americans, including our own members, most of whom are white." Braddock continued, "It is only recently we have realized that we have been hurting ourselves by not discovering and utilizing the rich resources of our Negro members we have not known well or of non-member Negro colleagues we have not known at all. . . . After all these years, we are finally taking steps to identify and establish closer communication with all our colleagues and to broaden the representation on our Executive Committee and, very soon, among our officers." The CCCC program was broadened as well, and several sessions at the 1969 and 1970 conventions discussed issues of language and culture, particularly the language and culture of black students.

The 1968 CCCC convention is still remembered by those who attended as a somber and subdued meeting, but the mood was just the opposite at the 1969 convention held at Miami Beach, where, as described in the previous chapter, the activist New University Conference provoked intensive debate of the politics of the organization. The NUC's proposals were prominent in one session titled "Future of CCCC," where they were presented by Neal Resnikoff of Providence College. The proposals recommended teaching Black Studies for black students, banning racist textbooks, and taking positions against the grading system, the draft, the Vietnam War, and other foreign involvement. The last of six resolutions addressed students' language:

CCCC and NCTE meetings and CCCC and NCTE Executive Committees should work actively to make non-standard dialects acceptable in all schools from kindergarten on and create an active articulation between the elementary schools, secondary schools, junior colleges and universities to deal with this problem. Linguists and English teachers should concentrate not on trying to teach everyone to speak and write upper-middle-class white dialect but rather on changing the attitude of society that discriminates against other dialects. Their efforts should be devoted to teaching the truths that all dialects are effective and valuable and that no dialect is any more indicative than any other of intelligence and even language ability on the part of the speaker. ("Workshop" 265)

This resolution led to the appointment of a committee by the CCCC Executive Committee in November 1969 charged with formulating a statement on language and social attitudes. When the original committee failed to write a report, another was appointed in November 1971, and the second committee produced a resolution that was adopted by the Executive Committee a year later. The resolution restated the sentiment of the NUC position statement:

We affirm the students' right to their own patterns and varieties of language—the dialects of their nurture or whatever dialects in which they find their own identity and style. Language scholars long ago denied that the myth of a standard American dialect has any validity. The claim that any one dialect is unacceptable amounts to an attempt of one social group to exert its dominance over another. Such a claim leads to false advice for speakers and writers, and immoral advice for humans. A nation proud of its diverse heritage and its cultural and racial variety will preserve its heritage of dialects. We affirm strongly that teachers must have the experiences and training that will enable them to respect diversity and uphold the right of students to their own language.

Realizing that the resolution would be controversial, the Executive Committee appointed another special committee, chaired by Melvin Butler of Southern University, to draft a defense of the resolution. That committee's draft was discussed at the 1973 CCCC meeting in New Orleans and approved as the organization's official policy at its meeting at Anaheim in 1974. The approved statement, *Students' Right to Their Own Language*, was published as a special issue of *College Composition and Communication* that fall.

The discussion of research included as a justification for the *Students' Right* statement grew from a new direction in American sociolinguistics, which up to that time had been chiefly concerned with mapping geographical dialects using rural speakers as informants. With the work of William Labov and others, sociolinguistics moved to the cities and examined the relationship between Black English Vernacular and standard English. This research was immediately relevant to the changing student population in U.S. colleges: the removal of admissions barriers and increased financial aid extended the opportunity to attend college to many who had been previously denied it.

Students' Right to Their Own Language posed the question of dialect as a dilemma: "Shall we place our emphasis on what the vocal elements of the public think it wants or on what the actual available linguistic evidence indicates we should emphasize?" (Committee 1). The statement charges that "perhaps the most serious difficulty facing 'non-standard' dialect speakers in developing writing ability derives from their exaggerated concern for the *least* serious aspects of writing" (8).

Like Emig's 1971 monograph, the *Students' Right* statement placed much of the blame for ineffective writing instruction on handbook pedagogy, but the statement went beyond Emig's charge that the marking of errors is "neurotic activity." A section headed "What Do We Do about Handbooks?" begins with the accusation: "Many handbooks still appeal to social-class etiquette and cultural stasis rather than to the dynamic and creative mechanisms which are a part of our language" (10). The statement goes on to argue that "deviation from the handbook rules seldom interferes with communication" (11).

The sociolinguistic research that supported the 1974 *Students' Right* statement also led to the systematic investigation of errors in student writing, interpreting them as an aspect of learning an unfamiliar dialect. The landmark study in this area was Mina Shaughnessy's *Errors and Expectations* (1977), which almost on its own established basic writing as an important subfield within composition. The deemphasis of errors advocated in the *Students' Right* statement was harmonious with the new focus on the process of composing rather than on the written product. "Mechanics come last" was one of the ten principles in Donald Murray's often reprinted manifesto of process pedagogy, "Teach Writing as a Process not Product," first published in 1972. Several researchers later reiterated the claim of the *Students' Right* statement that making students excessively conscious of errors stultifies their writing process (for example, Bartholomae, "Study of Error"; Selfe, "Apprehensive Writer").

Back to Basics

The magnitude of the difference between writing teachers' optimistic visions of literacy leading to social equality and the attitudes of much of the public soon became apparent. Shortly after the *Students' Right* statement was published, the "vocal elements" to whom the statement alludes became quite shrill. A countermovement to educational pluralism known as the "back-to-basics" movement began in the popular media following the publication of "Why Johnny Can't Write" in *Newsweek* in 1975, an article that sounded the alarm of a "literacy crisis." The article cited declining Scholastic Aptitude Test scores as evidence that U.S. schools are "spawning a generation of semiliterates" (Sheils 58), and it singled out the *Students' Right* statement as an example of what was wrong in our schools.

At first, English teachers were not alarmed by calls for getting "back to the basics" because senior members of the profession had heard it all before: complaints that students don't write as well as they used to are frequent in the history of English departments.[8] Furthermore, the results of standardized test scores combined with data from the National Assessment of Educational Progress were inconclusive, with gains in some areas offsetting declines in others. While the much publicized SAT Verbal scores went down, scores on the English Composition Achievement Test went up between 1967 and 1976. Considering the increased number and diversity of students taking the tests, the evidence could have been interpreted positively.[9] The mood of the middle class in America, however, was receptive to proclamations that a literacy crisis was at hand.

Beginning in 1973, the long ride of postwar prosperity and confidence in the United States' ability to lead the rest of the world came to an end. The last American troops left Vietnam on March 29, concluding the most costly and humiliating military defeat in American history. On June 25, John Dean, a top presidential aide, told Senate hearings that Richard Nixon and his staff had covered up the Watergate break-in. The scandal proved to be a fatal wound for the Nixon presidency, leading to impeachment articles and Nixon's resignation in 1974. On October 10, Vice-President Spiro Agnew resigned after pleading no contest to charges of evading taxes on payments made to him by Maryland contractors.

On October 19, the cartel of oil-exporting nations (OPEC) imposed an oil embargo that lasted until the following March, causing a panic in the United States that led to long lines at gas pumps and gasoline rationing, eventually driving up prices nearly 250 percent. Investors lost confidence in the stock market, which dropped precipitously in 1973–1974 and didn't regain its 1972 level again until 1982.

With the economy remaining precarious for the remainder of the 1970s, a legion of government scandals from the Nixon era brought to trial, fights over school busing in the streets of Boston, and memories of the disruptions of the 1960s fresh in mind, the middle class was ready to believe that American education had veered off course and that a "golden age" of education had existed in the not-too-distant past. The list of villains proposed as causes for the literacy crisis—too little grammar, too little homework, too little discipline, too much freedom, too many electives, and of course too much television—supports Ehrenreich's argument that the middle class feared its children were losing their drive and initiative.

The anxiety of the middle class, now translated into charges of a national failure to keep up with Western Europe and Japan, has set the tone for discussions of U.S. education and educational policy in the last quarter of the twentieth century. Unlike most educational fads that leave the status quo intact after the controversy fades, the tempest over the literacy crisis produced long-term effects. The back-to-basics movement fueled the accountability movement that had begun in the early 1970s when states started to require schools to publish achievement test scores (Spring 321). Several state legislatures in the mid-1970s passed laws requiring exit exams and frequent performance testing while state education boards orchestrated the new requirements by implementing curricula by objectives that directed teaching toward the exams. Mandated "reforms" passed in the name of "excellence" came as measures against teachers' independence in the classroom, forcing them to follow in step the drills-and-skills curriculum packages supplied by textbook publishers. The net result was that making testing the driving force of the curriculum shifted power away from teachers, local schools, and local school boards. It created a power elite of distanced educational "experts" working in conjunction with politicians who recognized educational "reform" as a hot campaign issue.

Within the public schools, the back-to-basics movement reduced the opportunities students had to write extended discourse, which were few enough even before the "reforms" took hold. In a number of school districts, teacher-led movements did manage to oppose this trend. In particular, the National Writing Project has been an important force in introducing process pedagogy into the schools and in supporting teachers who encourage students to write. In many other school districts, however, the conglomerate of state education agencies, opportunistic politicians, test makers, and textbook publishers was too powerful to overcome as teachers got the message of what was expected of them.

A survey of English teachers in fifty high schools published in 1977 found that "despite their doubts about the validity of [college entrance] tests, teachers in our sample are doing what they can to increase students' chances of improving their scores. They are, for example, giving more instruction in grammar and usage, instruction of a type that they feel will help students perform better on the CE tests" (Tibbetts 15). Arthur Applebee's research team found in the early 1980s that in terms of encouraging more writing in high schools, the national impact of the process movement was disappointing (*Writing in the Secondary School; Contexts for Learning to Write*). In 1981 Applebee reported that only 3 percent of the lesson time in the classroom and only 3 percent of homework assignments were devoted to producing texts of a paragraph or more (*Writing*). Teaching writing as a process does not suit the typical use of writing for evaluation, and it is far too unwieldy to fit into the drills-and-skills curriculum.

College English teachers, at least those who taught writing at public institutions, also felt some of the hostility that had closed off possibilities for teaching writing as process in the schools. The backlash of the Right on language issues is expressed in John Simon's *Paradigms Lost* (1980). Simon set out the critique of language that would be often repeated by the Right in the 1980s. The English language, according to Simon, is on a "downhill course" caused by

> the four great body blows: (1) the student rebellion of 1968, which, in essence, meant that students themselves became the arbiters of what subjects were to be taught, and grammar by jingo (or Ringo), was not one of them; (2) the notion that in a democratic society language must accommodate itself to the whims, idiosyncrasies, dialects, and sheer ignorance of underprivileged minorities, especially if these happen to be black, Hispanic and, later on, female or homosexual; (3) the introduction by more and more incompetent English teachers, products of the new system (see items 1 and 2 above) of even fancier techniques of *not* teaching English . . . ; and (4) television. (xiv)

Simon takes special delight in denouncing English teachers as a threat to English, describing the NCTE as "a body so shot through with irresponsible radicalism, guilt-ridden liberalism, and asinine trendiness as to be . . . one of the major culprits—right up there with television—in the sabotaging of linguistic standards" (45). He calls the *Students' Right* statement a product of "democratic, egalitarian frenzy" and declares that every sentence in it "pullulates with logical and moral errors" (166). He mocks the committee members who wrote the report—"one of their number, Jenefer Giannasi (whose Christian name reads rather as if she didn't know how to spell it)"—and the research they cite as support.

Simon makes no bones about what is at stake. Teachers should be in the business of maintaining fences and making them higher, not tearing them down. And Simon doesn't mince words either about who should be kept on the other side of the fence. He writes: "As for 'I be,' 'you be,' 'he be,' etc., which should give us all the heebie-jeebies, these may indeed be comprehensible, but they go against all accepted classical and modern grammars and are the product not of a language with roots in history but of ignorance of how language works" (165–66). Simon goes on to make personal racist attacks by deriding the people of color who spoke at the 1978 NCTE convention held in New York. He labels Geneva Smitherman's speech "a piece of black rabble rousing" and says, "I must admit that her English showed few, if any, traces of . . . capitalist intimidation."

Elsewhere in the book Simon rails about the loss of the suffix *-ess* as an indicator of gender. He pretends to be unaware of the nonsexist alternative *flight attendant* when he asks, "If *stewardess* is out, should we write, 'The stewards wore blue skirts,' implying that they were Scottish or transvestites?" (33–34). Simon insists that "Negress and Jewess are not pejorative" (35), even when the linguistically conservative *American Heritage Dictionary* had noted in 1969 that both terms are considered offensive.

Yet reviews of *Paradigms Lost* overlooked the racism and sexism, and they tended to repeat William F. Buckley's cover blurb that Simon's "sensitivity to language is demonstrated with stunning virtuosity." Carole Cook in *Saturday Review* called Simon a "great stylist" and said of the book, "It's all in good fun." Joseph Barbato in *Change* assessed the book as a "vigorous defense of discriminating usage, written with the same intelligence, wit, and invective that characterize his film and theater reviews." Hugh Kenner wrote in *National Review* that "whole chapters of *Paradigms Lost* deserve circulation as schoolroom pamphlets" (1272). The receptiveness to Simon's rage against teachers, editors, and politicians who (to use Simon's word) would "lionize" the intellectually inferior suggests that a large segment of the American middle class believed that linguistic markers of class distinction were being blurred. When the realization sank in after 1973 that sharing the economic pie would mean a smaller piece for themselves, many in the middle class like Simon got the "heebie-jeebies" about the prospect of increasing educational equality.

Attacks like those of *Newsweek* and *Paradigms Lost* that made English teachers scapegoats for middle-class anxieties for the most part went unanswered. There were few opportunities for English teachers to reach the readership that Simon could address, because the mass media gave its space almost exclusively to the critics of education from the Right. The "Why Johnny Can't Write" article included quotes from S. I. Hayakawa, Jacques Barzun, Karl Shapiro, and Ronald Berman, head of the National Endowment of the Humanities, who saw the young people of America descending down the evolutionary scale to the level of intellectual invertebrates. The professional journals in composition studies did give brief prominence to the back-to-basics movement, the unfriendly reaction to the *Students' Right* statement, and the institution of "competency" examinations in literacy (for example, Crew's 1977 critique of the Georgia Regents' Composition Examination in *College English*). But shortly *College English* and *College Composition and Communication* moved on to other subjects, and sustained published discussion of competency testing and other language issues affected by public policy was left principally to CLAC, a newsletter that reached a few hundred readers.[10]

The one occasion when the issues regained prominence in the profession came when CCCC leaders appointed the Committee on the Advisability of a Language Statement for the 1980s and 1990s to consider revising or rescinding the *Students' Right* statement, but after a small uproar the committee eventually decided to take no action. (See Sledd "In Defense"; Zemelman.) James Sledd was one of the few even to remark about the silence of the profession on public language issues. In characteristic biting style, he commented in 1985 that "English teachers have never been the public's darlings; and today there is more than usually widespread suspicion that those who can't write teach, that those who can't teach teach writing, and that those who can neither teach nor write teach the teaching of writing. It is therefore understandable that the educated layman seldom reads addresses to the educated layman from the National Council of Teachers" ("Layman and Shaman" 327).

English teachers weren't the only academics missing from larger public debate. In the 1980s it seemed an entire generation of intellectuals disappeared from public view. Unlike the 1960s, when dissenting opinion in the academy challenged the structure of institutions and often reached at least some sectors of the public, radicalism within disciplines during the 1980s was channeled safely within established formats—professional journals, professional books, and scholarly conferences—where Marxism became one more species of theory to be paraded across the academic stage. Even within these cautious limits, young faculty members were often turned down in tenure decisions when their work was perceived as too far out of the scholarly mainstream.[11] Given the marginalized status of many writing teachers, it is not surprising that most shied away from taking public political stands even when they disagreed with prevailing attitudes toward literacy.

There was another important reason why most writing teachers remained silent during the mid-1970s furor over the "literacy crisis" and have seldom challenged public attitudes toward literacy since then. Unlike secondary teachers, many college writing teachers benefited from the "literacy crisis." In the September 1976 *Harper's*, Gene Lyons offered an explanation of how the college-level literacy crisis favored writing teachers and anticipated the literature versus composition debate that would develop over the next decade. Lyons accuses college English departments of grossly neglecting their social responsibility to teach reading and writing. He concludes, "The business of the American English department is not the teaching of literacy; it is the worship of literature" (34). From the viewpoint of perceptive students, Lyons continues, English teachers are not so much "dedicated practitioners of their disciplines [as] . . . persons whose good fortune it has been to convince the government or the trustees to underwrite their hobbies. And what students are learning from these teachers is that learning to write is simply not important" (36). Articles on the "higher illiteracy" in magazines like *Harper's* expressed a growing discontent among employers and professional schools over the writing abilities of college graduates, and complaints from these groups brought pressure on college administrators to improve the teaching of writing.

These complaints came just as researchers in composition studies were becoming increasingly critical of what Richard Young called in 1975 the "current-traditional paradigm." Young's essay was published in the NCTE volume *Research on Composing: Points of Departure* (1977), which called for changing the focus of writing research from pedagogy to how students compose. While the public and writing researchers differed in their analyses of what ailed the teaching of writing in the United States, writing researchers took external criticisms of writing as validating their own critique. The literacy crisis gave an air of urgency to curricular reform. Soon provosts and deans began creating positions for writing specialists. New sources of funding became available to launch innovative undergraduate programs and support graduate students in newly formed graduate rhetoric programs. Furthermore, the attention to writing in the university community helped to spread writing instruction across disciplines, and on many campuses writing became central to the conception of the undergraduate curriculum, although the intensive labor of teaching writing almost inevitably caused slippage from these ambitious designs.

In spite of the continuous skirmishing between literature and composition factions in English departments at public universities during the 1970s and 1980s, the institutional conditions at many schools favored the development of writing programs. If there were often snarling colleagues in traditional literary fields, there were also smiling deans and vice-presidents. Professional schools were eager to improve the writing abilities of their graduates, and as students became more career-oriented, they began to recognize that writing would be important to their future. Even the stance of many English departments moderated when they realized that elevating the status of composition would not turn them into service departments and that large writing programs could underwrite many of their traditional activities. Process pedagogy was extraordinarily valuable during this period of rapid growth of writing instruction because it proved widely adaptable across many kinds of writing courses. Similarly, process research developed a professional discourse that earlier diverse efforts to improve writing had lacked. Even as the interests of writing scholars diverged into new areas, writing as process remained the acknowledged center of the young discipline of rhetoric and composition.

Disillusionment with Process

Almost from the beginning, teachers of writing as process and later researchers of composing were divided into competing camps, but it was not until the later 1980s that expressions of general disillusionment with writing as process began to be heard. The harshest critics of the process movement pointed not so much to the classroom shortcomings of process pedagogy as to the failure of the process movement to fulfill the goal of "empowering" students as part of a larger project of creating equality through education.

The liberal assumptions that had been part of the process movement from the outset came under scrutiny when it became evident that educational equality was declining. The 1980s was a decade of increasing inequality, and higher education was no exception to this trend. From 1976 to 1988, when process reigned in the teaching of college writing, the percentage of lower- and middle-class African-American and Hispanic students entering college dropped unexpectedly.[12] African-American and Hispanic students who did get to college were far less likely than their white peers to complete their degrees.

The tone for the 1980s was summed up by Reagan's first secretary of education, T. H. Bell, who charged that the schools had devoted too much attention to "bringing up the bottom" ("Bell Names Commission"). Bell claimed he was responding to "what many consider to be a long and continuing decline in the quality of American education." He declared federal efforts to improve the teaching of poor and handicapped students a success, but stated, "|Our| zeal has if anything pushed our priorities too much in that direction." In the 1980s the longstanding goal of achieving equality through education in America was replaced by calls for "quality."

To accuse process advocates as accomplices in closing the doors of colleges to African-American, Hispanic, and other underrepresented minority students grossly overstates the power of writing teachers and ignores the achievements of many teachers in working with students from the educational underclass. But as a discipline the process movement did not confront the reversal of affirmative action and open admissions in terms other than validating basic writing within the discipline. After the *Students' Right* statement was passed and forgotten, most process researchers proceeded with a typical American unconsciousness of class, race, ethnicity, and gender.

This silence about issues of difference eventually prompted response. In "The Silenced Dialogue" (1988), a review of child-centered, process approaches to education from the perspective of people of color, Lisa Delpit contends that the goal of autonomy is fine for children who are already members of the culture of power but not for those who seek entry from outside the culture of power. She accuses middle-class process advocates of hypocrisy by creating situations in which students are expected to know language conventions that they have not been explicitly taught. Myron Tuman's "Class, Codes, and Composition" (1988) launches a similar critique of process pedagogy based on Basil Bernstein's analysis of "open" education in the United Kingdom, where the "freedom" given to students in school works to the advantage of children from the middle class where authority is negotiated. Both Delpit and Tuman see the process movement as one of the ways the middle class attempts to remake the world in its own image.

A more extensive critique of the process movement is found in Susan Miller's *Textual Carnivals* (1991). Miller sees the teaching of writing as process as fulfilling a task of ideological reproduction that the teaching of literature is no longer able to fulfill. The emphasis on "process for its own sake," according to Miller, promotes "as an article of faith that he or she is 'independent' and 'free' to choose within the controls the society establishes" (89). "Process for its own sake" removes acts of writing from the circumstances in which it is produced and the results that come from its reception. Miller writes:

> It is tempting to infer that contemporary composition has gone literature one better in creating the sensitivity for its own sake that literary studies has required of students. It has, that is, removed a canon of ideologically joined works that instill ethnocentric, logocentric, or any other congruent set of values and has substituted for them an almost entirely formalistic and intransitive vision of writing. (97–98)

Miller claims that the process movement has placed students in "an infantile and solipsistic relation to the results of writing" (100).

Critics of writing as process have joined a larger questioning of the role of literacy in our society. Discussions of literacy within the academy often follow in the tradition of John Dewey, whereby one of the main goals of teaching literacy is to create more politically active citizens. The radical pedagogy of Brazilian educator, Paolo Freire, is frequently cited in these discussions, but efforts similar to Freire's in the United States to teach literacy so that people might challenge existing social and political orders have not been widely praised or supported.[13] The dominant conceptions of literacy among the public are the functional literacy perspective, which is often tied to arguments concerning the need for literate workers in an "information" economy, and the cultural literacy perspective of Allan Bloom and William Bennett, which affirms social cohesion and traditional values through reading the classic texts of Western European society.

While arguments for teaching literacy for reasons of personal growth are still often heard, especially in testimonies about the value of literacy, the resources to make this dream possible for those below the middle class have, by and large, not been provided. According to Jonathan Kozol (4–5), 25 million American adults cannot read a warning label and another 35 million have only marginal reading ability. As a result, the United States ranks forty-ninth among the 158 members of the United Nations in measures of literacy. Such figures would seem to be enough to shock the nation into supporting a massive educational initiative with the kinds of proven educational programs such as Head Start that were started in the 1960s. But it is clear that if there is genuine concern for the closing off of large segments of American society from significant economic and political participation through lack of education, there is also little national resolve to reverse the decline in educational opportunities for those who cannot afford the increasing costs of schooling. Massive illiteracy, like massive poverty, has come to be viewed as one of the inevitable conditions of life in contemporary America. Critics now even describe literacy as "a system of oppression that works against entire societies as well as against certain groups within a given population and against given people" (Stuckey 64).

By the end of the 1980s, many academics concerned with literacy began to ask how they might offer conceptions of literacy to counter the Right's reports of declining standards that had become dominant in government and in the popular media. For the first time in its history, the Modern Language Association made a sustained effort to reach beyond its membership to focus on literacy education.

The MLA sponsored two major conferences, the Right to Literacy Conference (1988) and the Responsibilities of Literacy Conference (1990), that brought together college, secondary, and elementary teachers of literacy, teachers in rural and urban literacy programs, and interested others. In their introduction to the essays produced by the 1988 conference, Andrea A. Lunsford, Helene Moglen, and James Slevin explain that the conference's title

> posits that literacy is a right and not a privilege: a right that has been denied to an extraordinary number of our citizens. It implies, therefore, that illiterate persons are not themselves dysfunctional but are, rather, the signs of a dysfunctional society. Such an assertion, while obvious, may also be misleading, for it may be interpreted as suggesting that, once all citizens have learned to read and write, justice will have been done and we will have achieved a more nearly perfect democratic society. This is, of course, not true. Literacy is not in itself a panacea for social inequity; it does, in fact, guarantee little. It will not effect the redistribution of this nation's wealth. It will not grant more influence or power to those who have been disempowered by their race, their class, their gender, their sexual orientation, or their nationality. Nor will it ensure freedom or democracy. (2)

This statement is a sober reflection on the predicament of literacy teachers at all levels. On the one hand, the statement expresses outrage over the great injustice of denying adequate schooling to millions of people in the United States, but on the other, it recognizes that lack of education is only one aspect of a large-scale system of inequality and that education may be complicit in this system of inequality.

Reinventing the Rhetoric of Democracy

The new political awareness in composition studies has influenced some members of the field to look for ways to encourage the political consciousness that was present at the beginnings of the process movement in the 1960s and early 1970s. John Trimbur asks that we "recognize the toll that the eighties has taken on our own and our students' sense of political possibility" and "how the retreat from public life has privatized experience and diffused collective energies into the atomized channels of careerism and consumerism" ("Cultural Studies" 17). Patricia Bizzell writes, "Certainly the [1988] Presidential campaign suggested that national discourse is dead . . . and that we have no way of sharing views and concerns on the challenges confronting us" ("Beyond" 674).

Trimbur and Bizzell are not the first rhetoricians to lament the diminishing participation of citizens in public life. One of the main justifications of studying historical rhetoric has been to reintroduce rhetoric as a means of fostering public discourse. Michael Halloran's research that charts a truncation of the scope of rhetoric in nineteenth-century American colleges proceeds with the aim of recovering a lost tradition of rhetoric in public life. Halloran observes that rhetoric in the classical tradition occupied a central place in the American college curriculum at the end of the eighteenth century, but by the end of the nineteenth century, this emphasis on public discourse had been lost with the rise of current-traditional rhetoric, an absence that continues to the present.

While historical studies have made us aware of how the teaching of rhetoric has shifted in scope and purpose, they should also remind us that we cannot go back to a golden age of rhetoric. American colleges at the end of the eighteenth century educated only the male ruling elite. Today over 60 percent of high school graduates undertake some form of postsecondary education. The diversity of contemporary American culture, the speed of cultural change, and the multiplicity of the mass media demand that we find new ways of studying the possibilities for rhetoric.

In some ways, process pedagogy came as a response to the complexity of new modes of communication in postwar America. By privileging process over form, process-oriented teaching worked against the teaching of writing according to correctness and fixed modes. But in other ways, process pedagogy followed current-traditional rhetoric in denying differences among writers and avoiding the social histories and consequences of particular acts of writing.

To challenge the lingering conception of the writer as ungendered, classless, and living outside of history, several scholars in composition have invited students to explore their situatedness as writers and the politics of literacy. These explorations are often aligned with a more general movement known as *cultural studies*. Much of the present disciplinary impetus of cultural studies comes from the Centre for Contemporary Cultural Studies at the University of Birmingham, where British scholars wrote extensively about the politics of popular culture and mass media in the 1970s and 1980s. When cultural studies became popular in the United States, it became more widely conceived as an interdisciplinary inquiry rather than a disciplinary formation with a specific body of knowledge.[14] The focusing assumption of this interdisciplinary inquiry is that meanings and representations are historically situated. From these situated meanings and representations, scholars work outward to their consequences. Scholars in cultural studies find that the struggles over meanings and representations do not merely reflect cultural conflicts but are the primary sites of cultural conflicts.

Inquiries concerning the historical situatedness of cultural meanings and representations are not new to composition—witness the long use of textbooks such as Donald McQuade's and Robert Atwan's *Popular Writing in America* and numerous articles on popular culture, especially those published in *College English* during Richard Ohmann's editorship that critically examined the public media. What distinguishes current work in cultural studies from earlier work in popular culture is more attention to how mass culture is produced, circulated, and consumed.[15] Earlier work tended to focus on the text itself and especially how it misleads readers and viewers. Work in cultural studies allows for more complex responses, emphasizing that people often resist and rewrite the dominant meanings of mass culture.

A cultural studies approach in a writing classroom aims at asking students to consider the histories of meanings that they take as evident. For the most part, students believe the meanings of films, television shows, music videos, magazine photographs, and other commodities to be matters of personal taste. Since the individual as consumer is proclaimed to be free to choose, one either likes the object or one does not. When students become conscious that the object is produced—even by such a simple method as having them listen attentively to the laugh track on a situation comedy—they consider the object differently and frequently can make subtle analyses of who the text calls on them to be. Much greater complexity comes when the lives of readers are taken into account because the texts of mass culture do not come to us as solitary and detached but in promiscuous saturation.

Proponents of a cultural studies curriculum such as James Berlin ("Composition Studies and Cultural Studies"), Richard Ohmann (*Politics of Letters*), and Robert Scholes (*Textual Power*) argue that it challenges the trend toward making exclusion the basis of education and defining higher education as the acquisition of narrowly specialized knowledge. They maintain that rather than setting out a content to be learned, a cultural studies curriculum explores the relations among cultural practices and the political interests of discourses. At the same time, however, the goal of reintroducing possibilities of public discourse through questioning the status quo makes the implementation of such a curriculum often difficult.

A short, informal account by a teacher at the University of Minnesota, Geoff Sirc, illustrates one kind of difficulty. Sirc discusses his efforts to analyze critically Allan Bloom's *The Closing of the American Mind* in basic writing classes. Sirc writes of his students' response to Bloom's book: "It's as if [students] are finally able to stand in front of their accuser. All the hard-luck mis-judgments they've had to labor under for years are distilled under the name Allan Bloom." Sirc then writes of an exception:

> But this past quarter [spring 1989] I had a most interesting student reaction. It was from a woman who was one of the best writers/thinkers/respondents in the class. And she was puzzled at the reaction that the rest of the class had, the contra-Bloom attitude, because she kept insisting "He's right! Don't you see? I wish my parents had raised me with the values of literacy he's talking about." And when we'd look at Bloom's style to determine class markers/audience kinds of things, all she could think of was "I wish I could write like that. I think it's too late for me to write like that." I find it very hard to shake the response of this student.

Sirc's frankness about his class gives one pause. The values of literacy that Bloom endorses are just as much signifiers of wealth and power as Rolex watches. Why shouldn't Sirc's student want to write like Bloom? The material objects of the discourses that surround her—Jaguars, Porsches, and BMWs, gourmet groceries, designer clothes, pricey restaurants, vacations to Aruba, expensive collectible items—tell her that Bloom is right. Only after she receives her degree will she learn if she will be granted all that has been promised: that you too can be a success if you go to college, work hard, and do what you're told.[16] That the median income for white and black women who hold full-time jobs and who have attended four or more years of college is less than the median income for white male high school graduates isn't one of the statistics that shows up on the color graphs of USA *Today*.[17]

Bringing cultural studies into writing classes as a means of developing critical thinking also challenges the dichotomy of a teacher-centered versus a student-centered classroom popular in discussions of teaching writing as process. Paul Smith, who now has a few years' experience teaching in a cultural studies program, explains that the contradiction remains between the teacher-centered and the student-centered classroom or, as he puts it, between "the lecturing, professional stance and the desire to have students articulate their own experience" ("Pedagogy" 42). Smith says that there is no easy way of resolving this contradiction by privileging one or the other or by calling for a dialogue between them. Instead, the contradiction has to be worked through for each set of circumstances. Just as Lisa Delpit criticizes the process movement for encouraging teachers to deny students access to the knowledge teachers possess, Smith suggests that teachers are obligated to work from their own cultural experience and knowledge to pose "a particular question or set of questions which open out beyond both pedagogical theory and classroom analysis" (42).

But acknowledging that any curriculum that might lead to social change can be uncomfortable for both teachers and students is only one of the first steps. In "Rhetoric in the American College Curriculum: The Decline of Public Discourse" (1982), Michael Halloran notes that in the colonial period both Harvard and Yale required students to debate at commencement major public issues. For example, the questions in 1770 at Harvard included "Is a government tyrannical in which the rulers consult their own interest more than that of their subjects?" and "Is a government despotic in which the people have no check on the legislative power?" (251). Needless to say, these were hardly "safe" topics. Instead, they represented the culmination of an education that prepared young men to be leaders of their society. In a much wider sense, the emphasis on rhetoric in a cultural studies curriculum aspires toward a similar goal of engaging students in the discourse surrounding major social issues, even though these issues are now understood not only to be matters of the state but also of everyday life.

Composition and "Political Correctness"

The effort to reintroduce major social concerns into rhetoric, however, has run into powerful opposition from the media and from the middle class itself. An important case in point occurred at the University of Texas at Austin during the summer of 1990, when the director of lower-division English, Linda Brodkey, and a committee of faculty and graduate students wrote a revised syllabus for the required first-year composition course, English 306, which would allow students to write about important public debates on racial, sexual, and ethnic diversity.[18] The text materials for the new syllabus were to come principally from U.S. Supreme Court cases and cases from federal courts, and the cases would include at least three arguments (the plaintiff's, the defendant's, and the court's), providing a spectrum of opinions. The course did not include a case on the volatile issue of affirmative action. The approach to argumentation taught in the course was to be based on Stephen Toulmin's *The Uses of Argument*, and the syllabus required the use of a handbook. Other than the substitution of legal cases for the usual "pro" and "con" essays in an argument reader, the proposed course would have been similar in many respects to other first-year courses in argumentation.

But before the syllabus was even finished, it came under heavy attack, both on and off campus, causing its implementation to be "postponed" for a year, apparently from pressure on the university administration, and eventually to be canceled. The Texas chapter of the National Association of Scholars ran full-page ads in the student newspaper and other campus periodicals arguing that "'multicultural education' should not take place at the expense of studies that transcend cultural differences: the truths of mathematics, the sciences, history, and so on, are not different for people of different races, sexes, or cultures."[19] George F. Will also condemned the course in his nationally syndicated weekly column with a close paraphrase of NAS materials, and shortly the course was drawn into the growing national debate of the teaching of "multiculturalism," although the irony of these charges was that the legal discourse proposed as the bulk of the readings for the course is thoroughly saturated with Western European values. It comes as no surprise that well-funded organizations on the right would seize an opportunity to discredit university professors. Charges that Marxists have infiltrated universities are old hat for the Right.[20]

The critical question is why a course that would have been in most respects a typical first-year writing course could provoke strong denunciations from those who identified themselves as liberals, both on campus and in the national press, and more generally why liberals have joined the rush to condemn "political correctness." Few who attacked the course took the time to read the syllabus and the proposed materials, but the consistent misrepresentation of the course in the media does give clues about the fears the course raised.

Richard Bernstein, writing in the *New York Times*, lamented the dropping of "literary classics" from the course, and the *Houston Chronicle* made a similar assumption in an editorial titled "Good Riddance," celebrating the canceling of the course. The editorial begins: "A University of Texas freshman English course, restructured with strong overtones of a new McCarthyism of the academic left, has died aborning. To which we add our heartfelt 'good riddance.'" It goes on to call the designers of the course "latter-day versions of the Hitler

Youth or Mao Tse-tung's Red Guards," and it concludes: "PC thinking has no place in Austin—or anywhere else for that matter. It is certainly no substitute for a survey of literary works widely regarded as forming the foundation of Western thought, which is what that UT freshman English course has long been and should remain." The last sentence suggests that English 306 was conflated with a Stanford program that had been similarly attacked when *one* of eight core tracks was revised to include works by women, minority, and Third World authors. "Literary classics" have not been taught in English 306 at Texas for decades. *Newsweek* claimed the course was being taught when no section was ever allowed to be taught at Texas, even on a trial basis.

Perhaps it is too much to expect the *New York Times* and *Newsweek* to check facts in an age when daily newspapers run stories about sightings of Elvis and people and their pets being kidnapped by UFOs. The narrative of a radical takeover of the humanities has wide appeal among journalists who portray themselves as guardians of a threatened cultural heritage. The cover of the December 24, 1990, issue of *Newsweek* ran the headline *THOUGHT POLICE* in large, ominously shadowed, concrete letters with the caption below: "There's a 'Politically Correct' Way to Talk About Race, Sex and Ideas. Is This the New Enlightenment—Or the New McCarthyism?" The cover story inside titled "Taking Offense" gives what has become the official version of the takeover of the academy.

Newsweek reports that the "generation of campus radicals who grew up in the '60s" have seized control of "the conventional weapons of campus politics: social pressure, academic perks (including tenure) and—when they have the administration on their side—outright coercion. There is no conspiracy at work here, just a creed, a set of beliefs and expressions which students from places as diverse as Sarah Lawrence and San Francisco State recognize instantly as 'PC—politically correct" (Adler 48–49). Advocates of "PC" are described as "barbarians who would ban Shakespeare because he didn't write in Swahili" (49–50) and who would subvert the First Amendment right to free speech. According to *Newsweek*, PC is a totalitarian ideology that is "Marxist in origin" and "informed by deconstructionism, a theory of literary criticism associated with the French thinker Jacques Derrida. This accounts for the concentration of PC thought in such seemingly unlikely disciplines as comparative literature" (53). Professors are accused of abandoning the great works of Western thought and spending their time producing propaganda and indoctrinating students against the evils of racism, classism, sexism, and the tradition of Western culture.

Several implications can be drawn from the controversy over political correctness beyond journalistic disregard for facts, and none is favorable to incorporation of composition studies within a broader cultural studies movement.

First, the controversy reveals that there is very little awareness of current trends of scholarship in the humanities or public knowledge of the major theoretical debates. The attacks on theory bear so little relation to what is being argued that theorists are at a loss on how to respond. Michael Bérubé writes of the attack on literary critics, "At first I thought this might not be a bad development: since academic literary critics are normally considered to be roughly as necessary to contemporary American life as catapults and moats" (32).

Controversy, however, has not brought more awareness. In most accounts of the genealogy of PC and especially in D'Souza's *Illiberal Education*, "deconstruction" is the force behind a host of evils ranging from affirmative action to revision of the canon. D'Souza claims that the texts of Marx have been granted immunity from deconstruction when in reality just the opposite is the case. Since the failure of the May rebellion in 1968, French theorists have taken special delight in flogging Marxism. Feminists in turn have strongly attacked both Marxists and French poststructuralists. Furthermore, deconstruction is little involved in canon revision, and it is inimical to universals like the concept of equality on which arguments for affirmative action are based. If there were even minimal reporting of the debates of postmodern theory, then readers of the *Atlantic*, which reprinted a long excerpt of *Illiberal Education*, might have been able to recognize that the Great Satan of deconstruction is a phantasm.

Every Tuesday the *New York Times* reports on current developments in science, and *Scientific American* has long been an important popularizer of science. But as Bérubé notes, the *New York Times Book Review* has "decided its readers are more interested in whether Hemingway really slept with Mata Hari than if new historicism or 'reception theory' constitutes a challenge to the dominant American models of literary theory and literary history" (32). There is no ongoing discussion of ideas in the humanities outside of the academy that a curious nonacademic reader might follow.

If current philosophical and literary theory appear in nonacademic forums only in extremely simplified and distorted form, composition theory is almost totally unknown. The English 306 controversy at Texas demonstrates that many in the public and in the academy think that first-year writing courses should be either about great literature or matters of grammar and mechanical correctness. In spite of nearly thirty years of scholarship in the "disciplinary" period, composition studies has not reached square one in convincing much of the public that writing should be understood as a process. Consequently, if the media represents teachers of writing doing *anything* other than teaching students the proper use of semicolons (one of the charges against the proposed syllabus for English 306), then many people will believe that something is amiss. With such a limited view of what the teaching of writing should involve, it is no wonder that many administrators continue to see the teaching of writing as work fit for part-timers and graduate students.

The controversy over political correctness also shows how strongly many feel that scholarly discourse in the humanities should be accessible to anyone who cares to pick it up 'for a casual read. In particular, James Berlin's "Rhetoric and Ideology in the Writing Class" has been singled out for censure allegedly because it contains jargon. Rachel Erlanger, in "Johnny's Teacher Can't Write Either" published in the New York Times, advocates that Berlin be required to take a course in basic writing. She finds fault in these sentences by Berlin: "More recently the discussion of the relation between ideology and rhetoric has taken a new turn. Ideology is here foregrounded and problematized in a way that situates rhetoric within ideology rather than ideology within rhetoric." Apparently it does not matter to Erlanger that Berlin takes the first three pages to explain how he is using the term *ideology* and what difference it makes to how composition studies is viewed. Not only should any scholarly work in the humanities be transparent, but any sentence taken out of context should be transparent as well. Such is not expected of scholarly writing in science, which is why the New York Times provides interpreters of scientific discourse every Tuesday, yet the discourse of the humanities should aspire to the ideal of being available to everyone who can pass E. D. Hirsch's cultural literacy test.

In larger terms, the controversy is symptomatic of an uneven reaction to postmodernity. Diminishing of spatial barriers has created a world bazaar of products to satisfy an enormous appetite for diversity in consumable form. The middle class eagerly patronizes ethnic and foreign restaurants, listens to an extraordinary range of music, watches films, and buys cars, clothing, furniture, art, and many other products from around the world. The middle class as consumers seemingly cannot get enough diversity and novelty, but the triumph of the world market economy has also changed the nature of social interaction. Lyotard writes that "the temporary contract is in practice supplanting permanent institutions in the professional, emotional, sexual, cultural, family, and international domains, as well as in political affairs" (Postmodern Condition 66). The ad slogans tell it all: "Go for the gusto"; "Make him your obsession"; "Just do it"; "Pure pleasure"; "Pure attraction"; "Life is short. Play hard"; "Why not have it all?" "Why ask why?"

The demise of stable institutions is for the middle class the dark underside of the joys of consuming. Their insatiable appetite for diversity is accompanied by fears of instability—that things are changing too fast. Many in the middle class want to believe that there are discursive realms of truth beyond the flux of politics and daily life. They cling to a notion of secure spaces, whether they are located within the individual as a right to "privacy" or in actual physical space such as the "safety" of the home. Since language has long been a site where cultural conservatives have sought to stay the tide of change, it is little wonder that writing teachers would be called upon once again to uphold standards. For centuries *language* has functioned as a cover term for an array of cultural values and identities. As I describe earlier in this chapter, the moment writing teachers began to recognize language diversity in public ways with the *Students' Right* statement in 1974, *Newsweek* and other periodicals quickly responded with alarms of a "literacy crisis" and accused writing teachers of being an "enemy within."

Current "liberal" media attacks on "political correctness" like "Taking Offense" in *Newsweek* are reminders that attempts to teach literacy in ways that encourage people to take more control over their own lives will be viewed by many as suspect and even provoke heavy-handed censorship. Attacks on such courses from within the profession indicate that they challenge not only the political, economic, and social status quo, but also the position of the writing teacher. Susan Miller argues that composition is marginalized not only by its relation to literature but also by its location within a patriarchal symbolic order. Miller finds parallels between the traditional subjectivities offered to women implied by terms such as motherhood and the complex "feminized" subjectivity occupied by the composition teacher, and she compares the subjectivity of the writing teacher with Freud's analysis of the family nurse in nineteenth-century bourgeois households. Just as the nurse was expected to discipline the child as well to provide care for it and thus became a designated "mother/power" figure, the composition teacher is expected to nurture immature attempts at extended discourse but at the same time function as a disciplinarian and keeper of standards, becoming "a sadomasochistic Barbarella version of either mother or maid" ("Feminization" 48). Miller's analysis suggests that the subordination of composition within English departments is far more complex than the asymmetrical relations of literature and composition. The location of composition within English departments also reflects negative images of student writing and composition teaching held by many members of the academy, the popular press, large sections of the public, and by many writing teachers themselves.

In the remaining chapters of this book, I explore how the subjectivities of writing teachers and student writers have been articulated and contested in the discourses of composition studies, and finally how subjectivity might be conceived in terms other than the coherent, unified subject of modernity or the fragmented, dissolved subject of postmodernity.

3   The Linguistic Agent as Subject

MAXINE HAIRSTON'S 1982 proclamation of a "paradigm shift" claimed that the two allied disciplines motivating the new process paradigm were cognitive psychology and linguistics. By the end of the 1980s, one of these forces, linguistics, apparently had vanished. A noncontroversial aspect of Stephen North's controversial survey of writing research, *The Making of Knowledge in Composition*, is the omission of linguistics as an important disciplinary subfield. North does not even include *language* or *linguistics* in the index. Another classification of writing theorists and researchers presented by Patricia Bizzell at the 1987 meeting of the Conference on College Composition and Communication (CCCC) also fails to mention linguistics as a major line of disciplinary inquiry ("Forming the Canon").

One could argue that North and Bizzell erred either by leaving out linguistics or by subsuming it under a broader heading, and in support of this argument one could assemble a formidable group of North American researchers of written language, who in the 1980s applied principles and analytical tools developed by linguists.[1] Nonetheless, one could also easily defend the position implied by North's and Bizzell's classifications—that the influence of linguistics on the study and teaching of writing in North America has dwindled to such an extent that linguistics is no longer a major contributor of ideas. The demise of the influence of linguistics results not so much from the lack of substance in recent work on written language as it does from the lack of a dominant approach within linguistics that is applicable to the study of writing. Researchers of written language do not share common goals and methodologies, nor use the same terms, nor recognize common research issues, nor even agree about the nature of language. In spite of the brilliance of certain individual studies, the whole adds up to considerably less than the sum of the parts.

The situation was much different in earlier decades of CCCC. In the 1950s linguists were leaders in the organization and published articles frequently in its journal. The major conflict within CCCC was characterized as "correctness" versus "usage," with linguistics contributing research on language variation to counter absolute judgments of "good" and "bad" English. Donald Lloyd's call for a composition course built around linguistics in 1952 reflected the newly found tolerance for usage among the liberal wing of CCCC.

Correctness again became an issue following the publication of *Webster's Third New International Dictionary* in September 1961, which set off a storm of public controversy over its practice of basing descriptions of usage and pronunciation on what people actually said rather than what experts assumed to be correct. The much vilified editor of *Webster's Third*, Phillip Gove, was a featured speaker at the 1962 meeting of CCCC. More important, however, was work in sociolinguistics arguing that dialects considered prestigious or "standard" gain their status by being identified with the wealthiest and most powerful groups in a society and not from their inherent superiority. Sociolinguists denied assumptions that speakers of "nonstandard" dialects are somehow deprived or suffer from a cognitive deficit by demonstrating that nonstandard dialects are as inherently logical as standard ones. A measure of the authority given to sociolinguistics during this time came with the 1974 *Students' Right to Their Own Language* statement discussed in the previous chapter, which lists 129 entries on dialects and the teaching of writing in an attached annotated bibliography.

The work on usage and dialects was only a part of the influence of linguistics in the 1960s and 1970s. When rhetoric and composition blossomed as a discipline in the mid-1960s, advances in rhetorical theory represented by the work of Wayne Booth, James Kinneavy, and James Moffett were paralleled by new directions in language study. By 1965, English teachers' awareness of linguistics was viewed as the most important development in the first two decades of the CCCC (Gorrell), and linguistics was proposed as the basis of a modern theory of rhetoric (Young and Becker). The most important work on written language during this period was Francis Christensen's theory of generative rhetoric, set out in a series of four articles in *College English* and *College Composition and Communication* in 1963 and 1965, later collected with two earlier articles and published as *Notes Toward a New Rhetoric* in 1967.

Christensen's stylistic analyses demonstrated that textbook advice favoring the periodic sentence ran counter to the practice of published writers who frequently use right-branching sentences often referred to as "loose" sentences. Christensen renamed these right-branching sentences "cumulative" sentences and made them the basis of his pedagogy. He assigned semantic levels to the modifiers of a main clause and devised a scheme to represent what he called "levels of generality." Christensen quoted this sentence from Sinclair

Lewis as an example of a semantically subordinate sequence of modifiers, each modifying the level above.

    1   He dipped his hands in the bichloride solution and shook them,
       2   a quick shake,
          3   fingers down,
             4   like the fingers of a pianist above the keys.

Using such examples as models, Christensen designed exercises that teach students to observe carefully and to describe accurately. He felt that practice in using nonrestrictive modifiers could generate the supporting detail that is characteristically absent from much student writing. In "Generative Rhetoric of the Paragraph," he used the cumulative sentence as a way of analyzing units of discourse larger than the sentence. Christensen believed that the paragraph is structurally a macrosentence, and he found intuitive evidence that the paragraph is structurally similar to the cumulative sentence from the fact that many of his cumulative sentence examples could easily be translated into paragraphs if the nonrestrictive modifiers were made into complete sentences.

In successive issues of *College Composition and Communication* immediately following the initial publication of "Generative Rhetoric of the Paragraph" in 1965, Alton Becker and Paul Rodgers presented alternative views of paragraph structure. Becker proposed a semantic slot conception based on tagmemics, another variety of structuralism. He criticized Christensen's model for its lack of a semantic theory adequate to explain in formal terms the relationships Christensen perceived. Becker's criticisms were on the mark because no semantic theory existed at that time (nor does one exist today) that can account for these relationships. But by the same standard Becker's tagmemic alternative also lacked an elaborated semantic theory, and it had less intuitive appeal because it presented only two basic paragraph patterns. Rodgers's criticisms of Christensen's analytical model of the paragraph were more substantial. He argued that the paragraph is not so much a·semantic unit as it is an orthographic unit. Instead of the paragraph as the basic unit of discourse, Rodgers advanced semantic units that he called *stadia of discourse* (conceptual chunks of discourse, not often coincident with paragraph divisions).

Considerable work followed in the 1970s from lines of research established in the 1960s, including the continuation of the discussion of how coherence is achieved by Ross Winterowd ("Grammar") and extensions of Christensen's ideas to the essay as a whole by Frank D'Angelo, Michael Grady, and Will Pitkin. But as these efforts grew in scope, their shortcomings became immediately apparent. Without an elaborated semantic theory, the structural classifications seemed too idiosyncratic and arbitrary, as well as too vague, to be the basis of pedagogy.

In the 1970s the energy in the language camp within rhetoric and composition passed to those interested in sentence combining, which grew out of the work of Kellogg Hunt on syntactic development in the 1960s. Like others at the time, Hunt was inspired by Chomsky's theory of generative grammar. His suggestion that sentence-combining practice would enhance the syntactic maturity of developing writers was demonstrated in several studies with junior-high age children, most notably by John Mellon, in *Transformational Sentence-Combining*, and Frank O'Hare. These findings were extended to a college population in a major study at Miami (Ohio) University conducted by Donald Daiker, Andrew Kerek, and Max Morenberg, which concluded that a sentence-combining curriculum could increase the syntactic maturity and overall writing quality of first-year college students. At first the researchers assumed that the gains were related (Daiker), but when they analyzed the extent to which syntactic factors influenced readers' judgments, they found that the measures were almost unrelated to the assessments of quality (Kerek).

The failure of researchers to associate linguistic variables with perceptions of writing quality cooled the interest in linguistics raised by pedagogical studies of sentence combining. After 1980, linguistics was no longer seen as a panacea for improving student writing, and applications of structural linguistics, Chomsky's generative linguistics, and sociolinguistics faded from composition journals. For a short time, European work on text linguistics promised to provide the comprehensive theory of discourse structure that the earlier efforts of Christensen had lacked. Teun van Dijk's theory of a semantic macrostructure underlying texts, most fully elaborated in *Macrostructures* (1980), was especially attractive for the study of structure in written discourse because it promised to resolve the ambiguity of Christensen's levels of generality.

But van Dijk's ambitious project failed to provide adequately for the contexts in which language is used, and after several attempts to augment his semantic theory with pragmatic theory, van Dijk turned his attention elsewhere. For those who continued to work in text linguistics, the scope of their inquiry became more and more restricted. Even though there has been much research on written language in the 1980s from both inside and outside composition studies, no work has inspired the enthusiasm raised by generative rhetoric and sentence combining, nor have their been any large-scale movements within the discipline based on linguistic research.

Given the abstract, theoretical direction of most North American universities' linguistics departments and the virtual absence of alternative language study within English departments, linguistics appears to have little chance of reemerging as a major disciplinary influence in composition studies. Nonetheless, a categorical dismissal of linguistics from rhetoric and composition may be premature. Questions concerning subject positions in discourse were discussed in linguistics outside of North America in the 1980s, and there is much work now being done on language and politics.

Before I begin to use postmodern theory to investigate how subjectivity is understood in composition studies, I will consider in this chapter how subjectivity has been conceived in linguistics. In particular, I examine the critical linguistics movement, which, had it been better known, might have influenced composition studies during the 1980s and led to some of its current concerns by a different path.

The Limits of Formal Linguistics

Before moving to how critical linguistics might have influenced the study of writing, I would like to reflect on why language study within composition declined so quickly. The obvious answer is that the influence of linguistics was swept away by the movement toward understanding and teaching writing as a process, but the process movement alone does not explain such a quick demise. For underlying reasons we must look to the discipline of linguistics itself. If we ask what happened within linguistics, again there is an easy answer: Noam Chomsky. Chomsky's theory of transformational-generative grammar influenced the study of language in North America as no other theory had in the past. Shortly after the publication of Chomsky's second major book in 1965, *Aspects of the Theory of Syntax*, linguists were either on board the fast Chomsky theoretical express or hopelessly behind on the slow, data-gathering local.

For those in other disciplines interested in questions concerning language and discourse, generative grammar at first appeared to be a methodological breakthrough, a way of describing the messy data of language with orderly rules that could obtain universally. These researchers, however, soon encountered the limitations that Chomsky had been careful to anticipate. Language could be orderly only if it were idealized; if actual language was used as data, the orderliness of language predicted by generative grammar soon disintegrated. Chomsky insisted that language be viewed as abstract, formal, and accessible through intuition. His goal for a theory of language was describing a human being's innate capacity for language, not how people actually use language. When asked what relevance the study of linguistics had for education, Chomsky has consistently answered: absolutely none.[2]

Gradually, those interested in studying discourse came to heed Chomsky's warnings. No matter how hard they tried, researchers could find no fruitful way of applying advances in formal linguistics for their own research programs beyond early language acquisition. Research in sentence combining as a method of teaching writing is a good case in point. Early sentence-combining experiments developed from the concept of the "kernel" sentence in Chomsky's initial presentation of transformational grammar in *Syntactic Structures* in 1957. Students were given two or more short kernel sentences and asked to combine them into one, using a particular transformation signaled in the exercise. But by the time John Mellon published *Transformational Sentence-Combining: A Method for Enhancing the Development of Syntactic Fluency in English Composition* in 1969, the first report of a major sentence-combining study, Chomsky had abandoned the notion of kernel sentences. Soon "transformational" was dropped as an adjective modifying "sentence combining," and research in sentence combining proceeded independently of later developments in syntactic analysis.

Had Chomsky's influence been restricted to language theory, linguists in North America might have remained more active in the study of writing. In some ways generative grammar turned out to be like other radical theories that for a time gain many enthusiastic supporters but quickly lose their impetus when the supporters begin to diverge into warring camps.[3] But in another way the life of the generative grammar movement was different from that of other radical theories. Generative grammar altered the disciplinary map.

Before the rise of generative grammar, linguists were scattered in departments of anthropology, English, and other modern language departments. These linguists tended to share some of the interests of members of those disciplines, and the arrangement fostered interdisciplinary cooperation. The excitement that accompanied Chomsky's theory accelerated the formation and growth of separate linguistics departments committed to the theoretical study of structure in language. The methodology of generative grammar with elaborate sets of formal rules emphasized the difference of its project from those of other humanities and social science disciplines, as well as from other schools of linguistics. Theoretical linguists dismissed the questions of other disciplines such as those of language education as applied and "uninteresting." In their view, the only truly interesting questions in the study of language concern abstract universals underlying language.

To blame Chomsky, however, for the decline of linguistics within composition studies is not merely simplistic; it is wrong. The limitations of generative grammar were demonstrated when stylistic studies aimed at analyzing the "deep structure" of style failed to produce results beyond what could be observed from surface features (for example, Ohmann, "Generative Grammars"). Nevertheless, researchers of language in written discourse did not cease working when they realized that generative grammar was not useful for their purposes. Rather, they encountered again and again a fundamental difficulty met by earlier linguists beginning with Zellig Harris, who in a boundary-breaking article in 1952 had ventured beyond the sentence.

When these linguists analyzed stretches of language larger than a sentence, they attempted to apply those criteria they had used for analyzing phonemes, morphemes, and clauses. In the tradition of American structural linguistics, they assumed that a continuum of formal correspondences exists between smaller and larger units. What many researchers in written language did not consider was that the basis of text structure might be radically different from that of sentence structure, that no one kind of structural description might be adequate to characterize text structure. Models of text structure based on a few patterns, such as those of paragraph theorists Christensen and Becker, at first were attractive but inevitably failed to account for a variety of distinctions that readers perceived among different texts. These models were confounded when readers encountered a paragraph where a topic sentence could not be readily identified, or when readers with different levels of familiarity with the subject matter of a paragraph could assign differing interpretations of what is important.

Efforts to describe text structure have all been frustrated because texts—unlike phonemes, morphemes, and clauses—are semantic rather than structural units. Semantics has been the least developed area in American linguistics, as opposed to European linguistics, partly as a result of different readings of Saussure. American structural linguistics derived from Saussure a methodology that was well suited for describing the phonology of unstudied and often quickly disappearing languages. Because U.S. linguists grew up within the dominant ideology of behaviorism in the social sciences, they continued to make empiricist assumptions about language and ignored Saussure's discussions of meaning.

European structuralists, on the other hand, explored Saussure's proposal that since language is a self-contained system, the boundaries for meaning, like those for meaningful sounds or phonemes, are largely arbitrary. Following Roman Jakobson's analysis of how differences in sound are grouped as distinct phonemes according to shared articulatory features (*Selected Writings*), several European linguists, including Louis Hjelmslev and A. J. Greimas, proposed a systematic analysis of semantics based on shared aspects of meaning. The broadening of European structuralism to questions of semantics led to an even more expansive use of structuralism to study culture as a system of signs—a pursuit also known as semiology.[4]

Most American linguists avoided such extensions. Instead, they took the advice of Leonard Bloomfield, who argued in 1933 that language can be studied scientifically only to the extent that meaning is ignored. The Chomsky revolution did not overturn this bias from structuralism. Indeed, Chomsky has frequently argued (most recently in *The Generative Enterprise*) that linguists should not be concerned with semantics (though Chomsky claims that much of semantics can be incorporated within syntactic theory). When North American theoretical linguists brushed against semantic issues, they used the same methodology devised for structural description of material features of language. Phonemes, for example, can be described in terms of their articulatory features. The English phoneme /b/ is distinguished from /p/ by vibration of the vocal cords, a feature that linguists describe as "voicing" and represent with the notation < + voice>. The logic of distinctive features was extended to semantics. The noun *man* might be described by the following distinctive features:

Man
|Noun|
|count|
(+ human)
(+ male)

Such an analysis, however, is not going to account for why a speaker today who begins a talk before an academic audience with the sentence *Every professor must deal with his students man to man*, and who continues with a pattern of male pronouns to refer to students of both genders, risks alienating a large segment of the audience. The deficiency in formal semantics cannot be corrected by adding secondary connotative features.

The problem is one that Bronislaw Malinowski identified a half century ago. Malinowski argued that language cannot be understood apart from the contexts of its use. Meaning, therefore, cannot be described adequately in terms of universal features but only in terms of specific functions in specific contexts. Meaning can never be fixed in the way that models of text structure imply they can, nor can hedges such as determining authorial intent provide the firm ground for building models of text structure. But American linguistics rejected the possibility that the basis of language is meaning and that meaning is socially constructed.

Chomsky refused to consider this position. When he attacked structuralism, he attacked the American empiricist version, staging the debate in terms of the individual mind. Chomsky argued that because language is too complicated and too creative to be learned from the behaviorist stimulus-response model (Rev. of *Verbal Behavior*), language must be innate, part of the genetic heritage of every healthy human being, needing only exposure to language to take shape much like the instant food for which you "just add water." Language from a formal linguistics perspective is complex but unproblematic.

European structuralism, however, produced an alternate definition of language, a definition that placed language outside the individual mind. From this viewpoint, language does not have to be developed either out of sensory experience or be activated from structures existing in the mind but can be *preexisting* in a culture. One of the classic statements of this position came in Roland Barthes's *Mythologies* (1957), where Barthes demonstrates that social meanings precede the perception of ordinary things. Many observers, however, trace the entry of this rich tradition of European structuralism into North American discussions of language as stemming from Roman Jakobson's paper, "Linguistics and Poetics," presented at the 1958 Indiana University Conference on Style.

The issues raised by European structuralism were not new to everyone, however. One British linguist familiar with Malinowski and well aware of developments on the continent was J. R. Firth (1890–1960), who remains relatively obscure in the United States. One of the reasons Firth has been relegated to a far branch of the linguistic family tree is that many of his essays were first given as occasional papers, and at first glance they read like afterdinner speeches with their many local references. Within these essays, however, are passages that offer insights about language that only recently have scholars of written discourse begun to accept. Firth maintained that we are born individuals but that we become persons by learning language. I will quote at length from an essay first published in 1935:

> Every one of us starts life with the two simple roles of sleeping and feeding; but from the time we begin to be socially active at about two months old, we gradually accumulate social roles. Throughout the period of growth we are progressively incorporated into our social organization, and the chief condition and means of that incorporation is learning to say what the other fellow expects us to say under the given circumstances. It is true that just as contexts for a word multiply indefinitely, so also situations are infinitely various. But after all, there is the routine of day and night, week, month, and year. And most of our time is spent in routine service, familial, professional, social, national. Speech is not the "boundless chaos" Johnson thought it was. For most of us the roles and lines are there, and that being so, the lines can be classified and correlated with part and also with episodes, scenes, and acts. . . . We are born individuals. But to satisfy our needs we have to become social persons, and every social person is a bundle of roles or *personae*; so that the situational and linguistic categories would not be unmanageable. (28)

Firth here sounds very much like Bakhtin's associate (and perhaps his pseudonym), V. N. Voloshinov, who speaks of a physical birth as an animal and a historical birth as a person (37), as well as Bakhtin's contemporary, Lev Vygotsky. While Firth's functionalist notion of the subject now has been challenged by the contradictory, decentered subject of postmodern theory, Firth did recognize that the dichotomies of individual/society and cognitive/social are false. He did not stop at theorizing but was equally concerned with the implications of a social view of language for systematic analysis. Firth believed there can be no one method of analysis adequate to explain meaning. In a later essay he wrote, "The statement of meaning cannot be achieved by one analysis, at one level, in one fell swoop" (184).

Critical Linguistics

Firth's belief that social interaction is embodied in language was taken up by his students whose work collectively came to be known either as *systemic* or *functional* linguistics or by the combination. The most notable of these students is M.A.K. Halliday, who is best known in rhetoric and composition from applications of *Cohesion in English*, which he wrote with Ruqaiya Hasan. *Cohesion in English* attempts to define the concept of a *text*, an issue that has left those who would analyze texts open for attack on the charge they could not identify their object of study.

The concept of cohesion, however, is only a small part of Halliday's larger theory. In *Language as Social Semiotic*, Halliday asks how people construct social contexts for language and how they relate social contexts to language. The key principle for Halliday and for others working in the Firthian tradition is function—how language is actually used, not how it might be idealized as an abstract system. Following Malinowski's lead, Halliday theorizes that contexts precede texts, that words come to us embedded in the contexts where they are used, and that meaning is organized according to those contexts. He considers how people in different groups develop different orientations to meaning, advancing the concept of *register* to explain how certain configurations of meaning are associated with particular situations, ranging from relatively fixed registers such as the International Language of the Air, which pilots and navigators who fly internationally must learn, to more open registers such as the discourses of medicine.

Other students of language familiar with Halliday's work were also influenced by the rise of the political Left in British universities in the 1970s, and soon they began exploring how systemic-functional theory might illuminate questions of language and politics. The manifesto for *critical linguistics*, a marriage of Marxism and systemic-functional linguistics, came in the 1979 volume *Language and Control*, written by four scholars who were then teaching at the University of East Anglia: Roger Fowler, Robert Hodge, Gunther Kress, and Tony Trew.[5] Their joint efforts proceeded from two assumptions in the Firth-Halliday tradition. First, language is functional in the sense that all language, written or spoken, takes place in some context of use. According to Halliday, "Language has evolved to satisfy human needs; and the way it is organized is functional with respect to these needs" (*Introduction to Functional Grammar* xiii). Second, language is systemic because all elements in language can be explained by reference to these functions; in other words, we should conceive of elements of language as constituting an organic whole. From these two assumptions, the East Anglian linguists inferred a third: if the relationship between form and content is systematic and not arbitrary, then form signifies content. The latter assumption brought these linguists close to the Sapir-Whorf hypothesis that language determines thought. But instead of working across languages as Sapir and Whorf did, they worked within English, linking language use directly to social structure and ideology.[6]

In the concluding chapter in *Language and Control*, Fowler and Kress claim that "ideology is linguistically mediated and habitual for an acquiescent, un-critical reader who has already been socialized into sensitivity to the significance of patterns of language" (185). They argue that if ideology is embedded in language, then "linguistics analysis ought to be a powerful tool for the study of ideological processes which mediate relationships of power and control" (186). In their view, the reason linguistic analysis has not been so employed is itself ideological. Linguistics is neutralized as an instrument of analysis when form and content are separated. In particular they fault sociolinguistics for considering the relationship between language and society as one of arbitrary correlation, accusing "mainstream" sociolinguistics as practiced by Labov and others of taking social structure as a given and then examining its influence on language.

Fowler and Kress argue that language is not simply a reflection of social structure nor is it independent. Rather, the influence between language and society is bidirectional. They write: "Language serves to confirm and consolidate the organizations which shape it, being used to manipulate people, to establish and maintain them in economically convenient roles and statuses, to maintain the power of state agencies, corporations and other institutions" (190). They call for a critical linguistics capable of analyzing the "two-way relationship between language and society" (190). The program for critical linguistics they envision is not aimed at "mining" representative structures out of language nor at isolating those features that typify a particular social group. Instead, the priority is reversed. Descriptive linguistics is used as a means for a larger social critique of unjust social relations. The project of critical linguistics is to engage in an unmasking of ideology, or what Fowler and Kress call *demystification*. In another chapter Tony Trew shows how conservative newspapers transform events potentially disturbing to their ideology into "safe" readings. When white police indiscriminately shot blacks in the former British colony of Rhodesia (now Zimbabwe), the event was reported in the *Times* as a result of "tribalism" through a series of linguistic transformations.

Another major difference between the East Anglia group of critical linguists and earlier critics of language such as George Orwell lies in the scope of critical linguistics. Where Orwell pointed to lexical items such as *pacification* as examples of deceptive language, critical linguistics extends beyond syntax to the constraints of genre, which are often taken by linguists as well as writing teachers to be ideologically innocent. While the East Anglian project for critical linguistics does not provide a set of procedures for each analysis comparable to Walker Gibson's method for distinguishing "tough," "sweet," and "stuffy" styles, it does apply many of the methods of systemic-functional linguistics for investigating the cultural assumptions involved in unproblematic readings of everyday texts. To demonstrate how the critical linguistics project employs the tools of analysis Halliday developed, I would like to examine two texts I collected while I was a senior fellow at the National University of Singapore during the 1986–1987 academic year.

Clothing and Institutions

When I began teaching in Singapore in July 1986, I received a large folder from the university administration that included the usual kinds of general information given to new staff members such as a map of campus, a description of the library, and so on. The large folder also contained an assembled collection of twenty-three memos. These memos were dated as far back as 1976 to a few months before my arrival. After reading these memos, I assumed that the reason for including them in the folder was to communicate university policy to new staff members. For example, four of the memos warned faculty not to talk with the press without prior approval from the university. One of these memos concerning the university's dress code is reproduced as figure 1. Figure 2 is a copy of a newsletter sent to me by the headmaster of United World College of South East Asia, a private school that my then fifteen-year-old son attended while we lived in Singapore. The newsletter also deals with institutional regulation of clothing, but in some respects it differs from the university memo.

Both texts are at times explicit about what kinds of clothing should not be worn. The university memo warns against wearing "Hawaiian shirts, T-shirts, singlets, shorts, and sandals." (The provision against Hawaiian shirts puzzled me, since batik shirts, which resemble Hawaiian shirts, are considered national dress and worn on formal occasions in Singapore. A veteran colleague explained to me that this provision was intended for a former member of the faculty who was particularly outspoken and fond of wearing Hawaiian shirts.) The newsletter declares that nonregulation blouses, shoes with colors other than brown, and sockless feet are illegal.

Both the memo and the newsletter also have explicit primary and sec-

NATIONAL UNIVERSITY OF SINGAPORE

KENT RIDGE • SINGAPORE 0511 • REPUBLIC OF SINGAPORE

TEL 7756666 • TELEX UNISPO RS33943 • CABLE UNIVSPORE

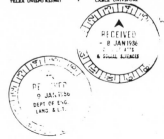

UNIVERSITY LIAISON OFFICE

REF UL/3

7 January 1986

Deans of Faculties
Directors of Schools

I shall be grateful if you will convey the following message through your
heads of departments to all academic staff and students:

FOR ACADEMIC STAFF

"In order to maintain the image of the University, all academic staff are
reminded that they should be appropriately attired when conducting
classes, be they lectures, tutorials or laboratory or workshop sessions.

Hawaiian shirts, T-shirts, singlets, shorts and sandals or slippers are
not considered appropriate attire."

FOR STUDENTS

"In order to maintain the image of the University, students are reminded
to be appropriately attired when attending lectures, tutorials and other
classes."

Peter Lim
DIRECTOR
UNIVERSITY LIAISON OFFICE

cc Vice-Chancellor
   Registrar
   Director, Personnel Department
   Student Liaison Officer

PL/pch

Heads of Departments
Faculty of Arts & Social Sciences

Dean requests that the contents of this
circular be brought to the attention of
staff and students.

HEADMASTER'S NEWSLETTER TO PARENTS

30th March 1987

Dear Parents,

UNIFORM

It has been a long, hard term and we have just enjoyed a most successful arts festival.' I will be writing at greater length next month. Before we start the Easter vacation, however, I want to clarify the College stand on school uniform in which one or two unofficial modifications have begun to appear. This letter is to give parents ample time to ensure that all students are correctly attired for the first day of the next term.

There has been no official change in the uniform requirements for boys or girls at UWCSEA during this academic year. The specifications for shirts/blouses, skirts, culottes and trousers are unchanged and only garments tailored to these specifications are acceptable. All students will wear brown footwear. All boys will wear socks.

A very few students have been in breach of these regulations as regards design of blouse and the wearing of socks. They have till 20th April to return to the orthodox. I do not wish to send a student home because his/her uniform is not correct - we all have more important things to do - but I will not hesitate to do so if this rule is not strictly observed.

This school stands for something. The uniform is a symbol of our commitment and esprit de corps. It is not a mere colour code, but a prescribed suit of clothing. Until such times as it is officially modified the specifications as set down in the Student Handbook and as supplied to the official tailors will continue to apply.

I wish all students and parents a happy Easter holiday.

Yours sincerely,

M. D. Watson
Headmaster

---

ondary audiences. Both address subordinates through intermediaries. The memo is addressed to deans, who are to inform subordinate department heads, who are to inform faculty who, in turn, are to inform students. The quotation marks suggest that the secondary transmissions from head to staff and staff to students are intended to be oral, that the memo literally attempts to place words in the mouths of department heads and staff. It is a kind of public notice that, since its contents are announced to students, cannot be ignored. Students cannot plead ignorance of it, nor can faculty, who because they have read the announcement to students, can be accountable for the definition of appropriate attire for the faculty as well. The headmaster also addresses parents as intermediaries, urging them to make sure that their children are in compliance with school rules. He too presumes a secondary oral transmission of the rules from parents to students.

But the differences between the two texts are more noticeable. The first is an internal memo from higher administration written on letterhead stationery in the formal style of other circular memos, including a reference number at the top. It bears official stamps of receipt at the dean's and department head's offices and the signed endorsement of the dean at the bottom with the directive to bring it "to the attention of staff and students." The newsletter, on the other hand, apparently is a less formal document. It is not printed on letterhead and identifies itself by a typed heading: "HEADMASTER'S NEWSLETTER TO PARENTS." The texts also differ in length. The newsletter is almost three times as long as the university memo.

More interesting to this discussion, however, are specific linguistic differences and similarities. I will start by considering what some linguists call *agency*, the match between the language of the text and the actions being described in the text. The fit of a text to the reality it depicts has been analyzed in different ways by linguists Charles Fillmore and M.A.K. Halliday. Halliday explores the phenomenon in far greater depth in his discussion of *transitivity*, a term that Halliday uses not in the traditional grammatical sense to distinguish verbs that take direct objects from those that do not, but rather a term to talk about how speakers and writers choose to represent their experience by selecting among the options available in the grammar of a language. Halliday's goal has been to explicate how ordinary language codes some extraordinarily sophisticated interpretations of experience.

In *An Introduction to Functional Grammar* Halliday assembles his extensive work on transitivity. He analyzes transitivity in a clause as consisting of three components: the *process* itself, typically coded as a verb phrase; *participants* in a process, typically coded as noun phrases, and *circumstances* associated with the process, typically coded as prepositional phrases and adverbial constructions. Halliday describes as "congruent" clauses that code agents as subjects and processes as verbs in sentences such as *Prisoners of war build the railroad to Burma*. Halliday refers to clauses such as *The railroad pushed through to Burma* or *1943 saw the railroad reach the Burmese border* as being "cross coded"; that is, something other than an agent functions as the subject or something other than the underlying process functions as the verb. He labels these clauses instances of "grammatical metaphor." The metaphor is not expressed exclusively in the personification of *railroad* or *1943* but also in the grammar, since the participants in the clause fill grammatical slots at one remove or more from an underlying semantic representation. Thus, when something other than the agent functions as the subject, the relationship between verb and process is likewise altered, creating a metaphorical displacement that changes the meaning of the entire clause.

The university memo starts with a sentence that is congruent: I *shall be grateful if you will convey the following message* . . . This opening, however, is merely a formulaic expression, as it appears verbatim in other circular memos from higher administration. The body of the letter lies in three sentences, two directed to staff and one to students. The first sentence of each of two sections begins with a phrase that serves as a justification: In *order to maintain the image of the University*. After the comma we find the subject of the sentence, which we would normally take to be the agent. In all three sentences, the agents are not present. Each sentence uses an agentless passive construction. We do not know who wishes to *remind* university staff and students that they should be properly clothed—whether it is Mr. Lim, higher administration as a collective, or some other person. Critics of bureaucratic language from Orwell onward have pointed to the use of the passive for concealing agents. Less recognized is the subtle way the agentless passive shifts responsibility to the noun occupying the grammatical subject slot—in this case, the students and staff.

Another grammatical metaphor is buried in the phrase *the image of the University*. Who sees the image? How do those viewers connect the image with the mission of the university? These questions are hidden when the underlying clause is turned into a nonfinite phrase and thematized at the beginning of the sentence. When agents are removed and actions are coded in nouns and phrases, readers can determine the relationships only through laborious digging to uncover participants and processes.

The mood of the second sentence is declarative, but the modal *should be* indicates it is a command. If it were worded as a direct command in its most unmitigated form, it would read: I *command all staff members to wear clothing that* I *consider appropriate*. The actual wording is perhaps more polite, but removing agents, disguising actions, and obscuring relationships serves a more important purpose. The decisions of individuals can be questioned and negotiated, but the policies of organizations cannot be disputed if the process of making that policy is concealed. Notice too that the sentence *Staff are reminded that they should be appropriately attired* contains a projecting clause. It doesn't say *Staff should be appropriately attired* but *Staff are reminded that they should be appropriately attired*. The use of *remind* suggests that the policy is preexisting, that staff should know about it, even though the Hawaiian shirt provision was at least a new wrinkle in the dress code.

The newsletter, by contrast, assumes a more equal relationship in power between writer and reader at the beginning. The writer starts with a topic other than the one stated in the heading "UNIFORM" at the top of the letter—presumably to gain the goodwill of the readers. He begins by announcing, *It has been a long, hard term and we have just enjoyed a most successful arts festival.* He doesn't elaborate on why he characterizes the term as *long* and *hard.* By joining the two clauses with the conjunction *and*, the headmaster forces his readers to make the connection, perhaps leading them to ascribe the Churchillian overtones of a *long, hard term* to the alleged success of the arts festival. The coding of agents in the first paragraph begins as congruent. The pronoun *we* in the first sentence includes writer and reader, since *we* refers to staff, students, and parents who attended the arts festival.

In the second sentence the headmaster promises to write again to parents. The presence of agents continues at the beginning of the third sentence: *Before we start Easter vacation, I want to clarify. . . .* But when the topic of uniforms is announced as *the College stand on school uniform,* the agents disappear.[7] The headmaster does not say, *Here's what I think students should wear,* but instead, *I want to clarify the College stand,* as if he is privy to the thoughts of some entity called *the College.* Likewise, in the next sentence he does not say that *students are wearing clothing of which I disapprove,* but instead writes that *one or two unofficial modifications have begun to appear.* The last sentence in the paragraph cleverly makes *letter* the agent and a munificent agent at that, *giving* the parents time to ensure that their child is appropriately attired. This wording is grammatical metaphor at work. If the sentence were congruent, it might read *If your child is not wearing the clothing I deem appropriate, buy her or him the proper clothes during the Easter vacation.* Like the university memo, the headmaster's language is not merely a matter of politeness. The congruent version can be analyzed, argued, and rejected much more easily than the headmaster's metaphorical sentence.

The second paragraph in the newsletter sets out the specifics of the dress code. The paragraph begins with the existential construction *There has been no change,* rather than *The rules committee has not changed,* or *I have not changed.* The second sentence also employs a pseudo-parallel structure. The verbs *are unchanged* and *are acceptable* are in coordinate clauses that appear parallel, but if we supply the agent for the passive, the sentence reads, *I have not changed the specifications, and only garments that tailors sew according to these specifications are acceptable to me.* The two clauses are not grammatically parallel, but if readers take them as parallel, the makers of the rules become just as invisible in the newsletter as they are in the university memo. And like the university memo, the paragraph ends with commands coded as declaratives: *All students will wear brown footwear. All boys will wear socks.* The use of the modal *will* is ambiguous because it can be construed both as a command and as a prediction of a future state—that the headmaster's declaration will become the new order.

Agents reappear in the third paragraph when students become the grammatical subjects of the first and second sentences, but this construction, like the university memo, defines the problem as the fault of the students. The writer codes actions as states of being. He does not say, *Some students have been wearing clothing that I don't like,* but instead, *A very few students have been in the breach of these regulations.* By transforming actions into states of being, the writer mystifies cause-and-effect relationships.

The issue is no longer students going without socks but one of heresy until students *return to the orthodox.* It is as if the dress code were handed down by God, and the students are blasphemers for not following it to the letter. At no point is there any hint that the rules might be debated, that students might be more comfortable not wearing socks in a city sixty miles from the equator.

The headmaster reemerges in the last sentence of the paragraph when he announces that he will be the strong-armed enforcer if students do not conform. He could have written, *Students will be sent home if their uniforms are not correct,* but he chose to emphasize his role as the guardian of standards. This tactic is part of the appeal to parents. He is saying, in effect, "If you don't clothe your children in the correct uniform, then you force me to send them home." After talking with parents of other children at the school, I sense that the headmaster is talking tough because he doesn't have complete authority in this situation. Because United World College is supported to a large extent by student tuition, the headmaster cannot punish minor offenses severely without losing his customers.[8]

The fourth paragraph offers a justification for the dress code, beginning: *This school stands for something.* Something is the vaguest noun possible in this sentence. In other literature, United World College claims to promote international understanding and world peace by bringing together students from over fifty nations. The second sentence reads: *The uniform is a symbol of our commitment and esprit de corps.* Again the ellipsis is significant. Commitment to what? International understanding? World peace? If so, then how does the wearing of socks help to achieve these goals? The second member of the compound— *esprit de corps*—is more revealing, since it is a term for the morale of a disciplined military unit rather than a diverse group of young people from many nations.

Linguistic theory that attempts to relate language to social practice can offer ways to begin discussing the unstated cultural assumptions of texts, but linguistic analyses such as the ones I have offered of the university memo and the headmaster's newsletter are incomplete unless they take into account the specific historical circumstances in which these texts were produced and read. How institutional settings change the meanings of statements was recognized by J. L. Austin, who discussed a class of utterances called *performative utterances* that cannot be strictly true or false but instead are either felicitous or infelicitous. If someone says, "I pronounce you husband and wife," that utterance can be felicitous only when spoken by a specific person with specific institutional authority in a specific ceremony. The institution sets the conditions for the ceremony to take place by delegating authority to the minister or other person conducting the ceremony. Austin, however, did not attempt to explain the relations between institutions and acts of language, but rather analyzed such conditions as properties of language.

Pierre Bourdieu presents a different view when he calls the institutional distribution of power *symbolic capital*. The relation of language and power within institutions is part of Bourdieu's larger theory of practice set out in his *Outline of a Theory of Practice*.[9] Bourdieu extends the concept of a marketplace to analyze the distribution of cultural and symbolic capital as well as economic capital. Just as in economic markets, those who have extensive cultural capital attempt to hold and enlarge that capital, forcing newcomers to struggle for a share. Those who hold the dominant positions in a culture and most of its capital wish the status quo to be projected as "natural" according to prevailing systems of classification (164).

Bourdieu calls the experience of one's own social world as natural and undisputed the condition of *doxa*. He observes that "the stabler the objective structures and the more fully they reproduce themselves in the agents' dispositions, the greater the extent of the field of doxa, of that which is taken for granted" (165–66). Classifications become self-evident because the culture adheres to this self-evidence. Not only is the arbitrariness of these classifications accepted, but moreover the possibility that the classifications are arbitrary is not even considered. Consequently, doxa is the unquestioning acceptance of the legitimacy of the established order. When those lacking capital begin to oppose the legitimacy of the established order through subversion and heresy, a situation of *heterodoxy* is created. Those who wish to maintain power must then substitute *orthodoxy* for doxa. Orthodoxy is an imperfect substitute for doxa because it can never successfully restore the innocent acceptance of doxa. Instead it must acknowledge the competing possibility and reject it as unacceptable.

The contrast between the statements of dress code from the university and the headmaster of United World College is in part the difference between doxa and orthodoxy. The writer of the university memo can mystify authority because authority is not being challenged. The sheaf of memos I received when I began employment was a kind of institutional memory. The memo on dress was in the same folder as the map of the campus and other informative documents because it contained traditional knowledge – knowledge for which ordinariness represents an important dimension of political power. The headmaster, on the other hand, deals with extraordinary knowledge because the very raising of the topic of dress in a newsletter to parents focuses attention on the arbitrariness of the dress code. He must appeal for orthodoxy when students are actively subverting the dress code, and his accusing of blasphemy those students who violate the dress code is a predictable move in Bourdieu's scheme.

Anyone who has attended a school that requires uniforms knows from experience that dress codes are always scenes of guerrilla warfare. Through subtle ways of wearing clothing – a shirttail out, a hem too short, shoes of a slightly different hue – opposition is expressed and status gained among peers. The headmaster's defense of the dress code is also a defense of the legitimacy of institutional authority. To analyze the memo and the newsletter in depth, one would have to go even beyond Bourdieu's scheme to take into account their Singaporean context, to recognize that the university has adapted a British model within the political system of Singapore, while United World College promulgates British values for the children of an expatriate business community. We do see in both texts that relations of power are sustained by controlling the subject positions that readers are invited to occupy.

"Reading" Ideology

The partial analyses of the memo and the newsletter, just given, demonstrate some of the strengths of a critical linguistics approach. While the texts appear to be different in rhetorical stance, my analyses chart a consistent rhetorical calibration in both texts. At the beginning both appear to be informative, but they are informative only to the extent that they tell readers the rules. Both texts are examples of the discourse of bureaucracy. Critical linguists argue that by moving toward abstraction, removing participants, coding actions as objects, and obscuring logical relationships, bureaucratic discourse reproduces the power of institutions.

While such analyses reveal the workings of power, they also imply a condition of *doublespeak*, that a language of the real lies behind the language of the false. The contrast between what is real and what is false follows from a concept of ideology that can be traced to the earliest use of the term by the French *philosophe*, Destutt Tracy, during the French Revolution. Tracy hoped to introduce a "science of ideas" that would remove the false ideas of religion and bourgeois culture from the minds of the public. Napoleon for a time supported the *philosophes* but later turned against them, accusing them of being concerned only with ideas and thus giving the term *ideology* a negative connotation (Donald and Hall ix). Marx and Engels in *The German Ideology* reinterpreted this concept of ideology when they argued that ideas do not determine social relations but rather they derive from social relations. Marx's and Engels's materialist interpretation separates their definition of ideology from other efforts to "unmask" ideology. The "base-and-superstructure" version of ideology in its "vulgar Marxist" form has the economic base determining directly or indirectly the ideological superstructure.[10] The most famous metaphor for this notion of ideology comes when Marx and Engels compare the mechanism of ideology to a *camera oscura* that produces an upside-down image of the world when workers accept the ruling class's version of the world (14).

In the twentieth century, the "base-and-superstructure" model of ideology has come under heavy criticism, even from Marxist theorists. One of the most influential Marxist theorists on this issue has been Antonio Gramsci, who grants relative autonomy to the superstructure. Gramsci includes in the notion of ideology what he calls "practical political consciousness," fragmented, contradictory, and incomplete sets of ideas that people use to get on in the world. He directs his attention to those ideologies that are broadly held and apparently spontaneous—ideologies he refers to as "organic." Many other twentieth-century theorists have offered a more neutral version of ideology, using the term as a synonym for "systems of belief" or systems of thought" (for example, Clifford Geertz's frequently read essay, "Ideology as a Cultural System"). This "systems-of-thought" notion of ideology is found also in *Language and Control* where Hodge, Kress, and Jones define ideologies as "sets of ideas involved in the ordering of experience, making sense of the world" (81).

The "systems-of-thought" notion of ideology is implicit in Halliday's social semiotic view of language, but the Hallidayan view gives language a very active role in coding experience and in mediating social meanings.[11] This notion of ideology presents two major kinds of difficulty for the project of critical linguistics. First, it does not contain a theory for social critique. Second, it does not presume a determinism between language and thought. Halliday is careful to place language as one of several higher-order semiotic codes, and he makes it clear that it is not adequate to stop at language if one wishes to investigate larger cultural issues. The first difficulty is relatively easy to address. Critical linguists directed their attention toward asymmetries in relations of power that could be related to language. The second difficulty, however, is not so readily overcome, and early work in critical linguistics tended to take the deterministic view that dominant groups manipulate language to maintain their power over subordinated groups.

The lack of elaboration on how ideologies are implicated in social relations left an imbalance of attention on linguistic form. According to Fowler
and Kress, among the most rewarding methods of examining a text is to consider the effects of *transformations*, in particular, nominalizations and passiviza-
tions. They offer the following example:

> In the middle of a report of the wreck of the oil supertanker *Amoco Cadiz* which
> happened towards the end of March 1978—the wrecked ship was in the process
> of breaking up, and oil spilling, at the time the newspaper went to press—the
> *Observer* gives the information "French moves to slap drastic restrictions on super-
> tanker movements have been dropped after British intervention." The nominal-
> izations "moves" and "intervention" have the effect of obscuring the times at
> which these actions took place, and the newspaper's attitude to them. (200)

While Fowler and Kress warn that there is no critical routine through which
a text can be run, they claim that certain kinds of linguistic analysis such as
the unpacking of transformations frequently prove to be "revealing" (198). The
implication of these analyses is that the less transformed or more congruent
version in Halliday's terms is closer to reality. In another book, *Language as
Ideology* (1979), Kress and Hodge attempt to appropriate Chomsky's generative grammar for analyzing ideology in language, introducing an odd blend
of mentalism and materialism. They claim explicitly that "the typical function
of transformations is distortion and mystification, through the characteristic
disjunction between surface form and implicit meanings" (35).

The problem with this assumption might be illustrated with another set
of examples. Below are sections from two articles that concern the issue of
abortion. The first article, "Abortion, Ethics, and the Law," by Claudia Wallis,
is from the July 6, 1987, issue of *Time* magazine. Although *Time* does include
editorials by guest columnists that take particular stands on controversial issues, this article comes from the news sections and is a presumably objective
report on the legal status of abortions. The second article, "New Questions—
Same Old Debate" by John Cavanaugh-O'Keefe," appeared in the April 25, 1987,
issue of *America*, a magazine published by the Roman Catholic church. The
article is labeled *Op Ed*, an abbreviation for "Opinion Editorial," indicating that
the author will take a stance on an issue. Because the article is published in
America, the author also makes certain assumptions about his readers. He takes
for granted that they are opposed to abortion, and he also assumes that
they are familiar with recent battles over doctrine within the Roman Catholic
church.

Here are two sections from the articles that I would like to contrast:

[from *Time*]
The juxtaposition of these two images [hospital staff members attempting in
one instance to save a premature baby while in another aborting a fetus a few

weeks younger] has long preoccupied people on both sides of the abortion debate. If medicine can save the life of an immature fetus, how can society allow the termination of an advanced pregnancy? When does the constitutional obligation to protect a potential citizen begin? How are the fetus's interests weighted against the mother's right to liberty and privacy? (Wallis 82)

[from *America*]

I asked students all over the Berkeley campus: "If I could tell you where an innocent person was scheduled to be killed, would you do anything about it?" Most said "Yes." When I explained that I was talking about Planned Parenthood in Oakland, most disagreed that unborn babies are "persons" and refused to act. Fair enough, though distressing. But what about those millions of people who profess to believe that unborn children are members of the human family? What is their response? Their answer too is "No." Is it possible to justify that refusal? How?

During the 1960's, police in all major cities learned to arrest protesters and demonstrators with whom they agreed. How often we heard the sleepy response, "Just doing my job." Fair enough. But today, "rescue teams" enter abortion clinics, block access to the suction machines and refuse to leave. We insist that our actions are not "protests" but are, in fact, rescue missions. When police officers prepare to haul us out, we state that our simple presence inside the operating rooms is the sole remaining protection for children, and that removing us is cooperating in abortion. All is ready for execution. We point at the suction machines, at the abortionists and at the waiting room where mothers are seated nervously, and we ask to be left in peace.

It seems clear to the rescue teams that arresting and removing them is cooperation in abortion. If the police refuse to arrest, nobody dies. If they make arrests, children die. Their actions are necessary, though not sufficient, to kill those children at that location with that machine. (Cavanaugh-O'Keefe 335)

The language in the article from *America* by Cavanaugh-O'Keefe is less transformed than that of the article from *Time* by Wallis, but I doubt that the East Anglian group of critical linguists would call the Cavanaugh-O'Keefe article less ideological than the Wallis article.

Cavanaugh-O'Keefe says it is regrettable that some people do not classify a fetus as a person, but he is not concerned with convincing them that abortion is morally wrong. Instead, he addresses those Catholics who agree with him that abortion is wrong. He sets out a hypothetical example where police who believe that abortion is morally wrong are asked to arrest protesters at an abortion clinic. Then he poses the moral dilemma directly: "If the police refuse to arrest, nobody dies. If they make arrests, children die." Most of his sentences are congruent. Participants are for the most part represented in the text or readily inferred.

The Wallis article, on the other hand, is heavily laden with nominalizations.

The phrase "termination of an advanced pregnancy" has hidden participants. Someone terminates and something is terminated. And pregnancy itself is not an object but a process with participants. Other nominalizations are more difficult to analyze such as "constitutional obligation." Someone is obligated to do something according to the Constitution or by power of the Constitution. These relationships are extremely complex since what exactly "constitutional obligation" means in a particular instance has been debated inside and outside courtrooms for two centuries. The inclusion of sentences that are grammatically metaphorical invokes the reader's acceptance of the present situation where abortions are legal under certain circumstances.

Cavanaugh-O'Keefe wishes to overturn the present situation. He recognizes that the struggle over a woman's right to an abortion is a struggle over meanings. What Wallis calls an "immature fetus," Cavanaugh-O'Keefe calls an "innocent person," "unborn babies," "unborn children," "children," and a "member of the human family." But on the issue of a "mother's right to liberty and privacy" raised in the *Time* article, Cavanaugh-O'Keefe is silent. The only mention of women is an image of "mothers" seated nervously in the waiting room of an abortion clinic.

The abortion debate is one example that if language is the medium of social action, then language constitutes what is real as well as what is false. There is no "objective" language in the abortion debate. There is no neutral way of referring to an unborn, developing human being. Calling it/him/her a "fetus" or a "baby" activates a particular set of assumptions and beliefs.

The analysis of these examples raises some of the limitations of the East Anglian proposals for critical linguistics. In spite of these limitations, the East Anglian group involved linguistics directly in confronting relations of domination—the critical dimension in Marx and Engels's analysis of ideology. At the same time, they brought to the study of ideology a means of showing how linguistic structures mediate ideology and how ideology can be analyzed in expressions heard and read in daily life. Where critical linguists quickly ran into trouble was in privileging linguistic form. They neglected that different readers interpret and use texts differently, that resistant readings are possible, and that texts themselves contain many contradictions and silences.[12]

Now Hodge and Kress admit they underconceptualized social relations in their earlier work. In the preface to *Social Semiotics* (1988), Hodge and Kress write:

> In *Language as Ideology* we had recognized and assumed the importance of the social dimension, but even so we had accepted texts and the structure of language as the normal starting point for analysis. We now see social structures and processes, messages and meanings as the proper standpoint from which to attempt the analysis of meaning systems. (vii)

To emphasize the separation of their current work from their earlier work, Hodge and Kress now avoid using the term *critical linguistics* to describe their current project. In *Social Semiotics* they do not give up on their goal of analyzing how "dominant groups attempt to represent the world in forms that reflect their own interests" (3), but they maintain that the revival of semiotics is the best hope for providing an analytic practice of how meaning is constituted.

The Linguistics of Clarity

In North America certain Hallidayan concepts used in critical linguistic analyses have become familiar in composition scholarship, primarily through the work of Joseph Williams. In 1979 Williams published an important essay, "On Defining Complexity," which questions the desirability of increasing the complexity of student's written syntax—the central assumption of sentence-combining pedagogy. Williams argues that this goal is benighted, citing as evidence writing programs for professionals on the job that attempt to encourage simpler styles or "to undo what sentence combiners want to do" (598). Williams was not the first to question whether we should encourage students to write more complex sentences. A decade earlier Francis Christensen attacked sentence combining for promoting the wrong kind of growth—growth that he asserted would lead to "the lumpy, soggy, pedestrian prose that we justly deride as jargon or gobbledegook" ("Problem" 575).[13]

What distinguishes Williams not only from other critics of sentence combining but also from other reformers of adult prose such as Rudolph Flesch is Williams's move toward defining complexity in terms other than polysyllabic words and T-unit or sentence length. In "On Defining Complexity," Williams extrapolates from Fillmore's concept of case grammar, where, similar to Halliday's notion of transitivity, a semantic representation is theorized to underlie grammatical structure. Williams draws on psycholinguistic research to make the claim that the clearest style is the one that is most easily processed.

The research that Williams cites suggests that sentences are more quickly comprehended if the grammatical structure coincides with the semantic structure, with semantic agents occupying grammatical subject positions and with the actions they perform coded as verbs. In Halliday's terms, discussed earlier in this chapter, Williams argues that congruent clauses are more easily processed than ones that are grammatically metaphorical. In his textbook, *Style: Ten Lessons in Clarity and Grace,* Williams calls a style with congruent main clauses the "agent-action style" (31). He advances the agent-action style as the first principle of achieving clear prose. He states this claim as a two-part maxim: "In the subjects of your sentences, name your cast of characters. In the verbs of your sentences, name the crucial actions in which you involve those characters" (9). The first example revision in the book demonstrates this principle:

1. Our lack of pertinent data prevented determination of committee action effectiveness in the targeting of funds to those areas in greatest assistance need. [Revised:]
2. Because we lacked pertinent data, we could not determine whether the committee had targeted funds to areas that needed assistance most. (8)

Williams uses these two sentences as touchstones of bad and good prose. He describes sentence 1 as "turgid, indirect, unclear, impersonal, wordy, prolix, obscure, inflated, pompous," and sentence 2 as "clear, direct, concise, flowing, readable" (8).

In the first chapter of *Style,* Williams marches out a familiar list of suspects when he mentions writing that is unnecessarily complex: "When we find this kind of writing in government, we call it *bureaucratese;* when we find it in contracts and judicial pronouncements, we call it *legalese;* when we find it in scholarly articles and books that inflate simple ideas into gassy abstractions, we call it *academese*" (2). He then repeats some familiar charges against institutional language. To explain why these inflated styles have developed, Williams says, "We use complicated language not only to dress up simple ideas but to hide the absence of any ideas. Impenetrable prose will impress those who confuse difficulty with substance" (4). But Williams goes beyond the usual personal, aesthetic, and economic arguments for clear writing when he impugns institutional language for maintaining unequal relations of power: "We use difficult and therefore intimidating language to protect what we have from those who want a share of it: the power, prestige, and privilege that go with being part of the ruling class" (4). This last sentence sounds as though it could have been written not only by a critical linguist but a traditional Marxist. But, as I will discuss below, the style Williams advocates can just as easily be employed to maintain class divisions.

High moral ground for the agent-action style is also claimed by Richard Lanham, whose *Revising Prose* and *Revising Business Prose* have become popular trade books as well as college textbooks. Like Williams, Lanham announces himself as a crusader against bad writing. He lumps traditional targets of stylistic reformers into a single foe, which he refers to as "The Official Style." Lanham claims all dialects of The Official Style suffer from the same imbalance: a "dominance of nouns and an atrophy of verbs, the triumph of stasis over action" (*Revising Prose* viii). His recipe for revision, which he calls the "paramedic method," provides, in his words, "emergency therapy" to "America's literacy crisis" (viii). His basic principle of style is similar to Williams's. He tells readers to "ask 'Who is kicking who?'" and then to "put this 'kicking' action in a simple (not compound) active verb'" (6).

Also like Williams, Lanham advances the clear style as a moral as well as a pedagogic issue. He accuses The Official Style of deadening our sense of ourselves: "The moral ingredient in writing, then, works first not on the morality of the message but on the nature of the sender, on the complexity of the self. 'Why bother?' To invigorate and enrich your selfhood, to increase, in the most literal sense, your self consciousness" (106). Lanham promises that improving your verbal style will not only make your prose more lively but also extend the benefits to your person: "You will become more alive" (115).

M.A.K. Halliday also writes extensively on agency in *Spoken and Written Language* (1985). He presents sets of examples similar to those of Williams and Lanham:

3. Investment in a rail facility implies a long-term commitment.
4. If you invest in a rail facility, this implies that you are going to be committed for a long term. (61)

Unlike Williams and Lanham, however, Halliday does not claim that sentence 4 is better than sentence 3. Instead, he offers these examples as typical of the difference between written and spoken language. Halliday sees a characteristic difference between written and spoken language in the way each achieves complexity. Written language, according to Halliday, is lexically dense in comparison to spoken language. Spoken language, on the other hand, is typically more intricate in its syntax in presenting similar spans of ideas. Halliday illustrates this point with the concept of *lexical density*. Lexical density is the ratio of lexical items (often referred to as *content* words) to the number of clauses. He offers a hypothetical comparison between a sentence in a written text (sentence 5 below) and a spoken equivalent (sentence 6). Double bars mark clause boundaries, and brackets identify the embedded clause in (6):

5. The use of this method of control unquestionably leads to safer and faster trains running in the most adverse weather conditions.||
6. You can control trains in this way || and if you do that || you can be quite sure || that they'll be able to run more safely and more quickly |than they would otherwise| || no matter how bad the weather gets.|| (79)

The written version (sentence 5) contains twelve lexical items in one clause. Thus its ratio of lexical density would be twelve. The spoken version has ten lexical items according to Halliday's count (which omits *do*) and five clauses (not counting the embedded one). Dividing ten lexical items by five clauses gives a lexical density ratio of two in the spoken version. This brief example illustrates Halliday's claim that "written language is corpuscular and gains power by its density, whereas spoken language is wavelike and gains power by its intricacy" ("Language and the Order of Nature" 148). He is well aware that much written language resembles spoken language by this definition, and that some speakers can talk in "written" language. What Halliday views as important is that the development of written language brought a complementary process of interpreting experience.

Written language depends heavily on nominalizations to achieve its density and its intertextuality. Halliday goes much further in unpacking nominalizations than do Williams or Lanham, and his comparisons show why they are a necessary element in language. Halliday is aware that nominalizations are often overused, but he observes that "it is important, if one is critical of such tendencies, to understand how the patterns in question are functional in the language" (75). He performs a similar analysis on the function of prepositional phrases in written language. Contrary to Lanham, who places prepositional phrases on his paramedic hit list, Halliday shows how they are often unavoidable, as in sentence 7 below:

7. In the Newtonian system, bodies under the action of no forces move in straight lines with uniform velocity.

All lexical items with the exception of *bodies* and *move* in sentence 7 are located in prepositional phrases. Halliday argues that it would be very hard to write the sentence without prepositional phrases and nominalizations; indeed, he maintains that many concepts in science and technology could not be expressed without nominalizations. Nominal structures are the necessary building blocks for constructing new claims on the basis of what is known and accepted. Furthermore, Halliday notes that nominalizations are vital for the thematic structure in English. In English sentences we expect the beginnings of sentences to give us a point of departure, what is called the *theme* in linguistic literature. *In the Newtonian system* functions as the theme in sentence 7, referring to some phenomenon that the reader is presumed to be aware of. Halliday describes the theme as "a peg on which the message is to hang" (73). These pegs are frequently nominalizations and prepositional phrases.

Halliday's discussion of transitivity likewise extends beyond Williams's and Lanham's prescriptive advice. In *Style: Ten Lessons in Clarity and Grace*, Williams too acknowledges that nominalizations can at times be useful, and he includes in later chapters the relationships of "old" and "new" information (the "theme/ rheme" distinction) and of topics and comments.[14] These additional principles, however, are mapped onto the first. The yardstick for measuring good writing remains the degree of adherence to an agent-action style, which Williams's own prose emphatically demonstrates. In his textbook, Williams's insistence on supplying agents for his sentences forces him to use frequently the editorial *we*. Instead of writing *Verbs should agree with their subjects,* Williams adds the agent: *"We expect verbs to agree with their subjects"* (202). Sentences of this kind are abundant in *Style*: "Given what we've learned about problems of topic and stress, we can see the problem . . ." (108); "Sometimes we awkwardly split an adjective . . ." (138); "We can maintain a smoother, unbroken rhythm . . ." (139). Williams's exercises for students encourage them to use the same strategy. For an exercise that asks students to revise poorly written examples, Williams offers in the answer section in the back of his book the revision (sentence 9) for the bad example of sentence 8:

8. These technical directives are written in a style of maximum simplicity as a result of an attempt at more effective communication with employees of little education who have been hired with guidelines that have been imposed. (32) [Revised:]
9. We have written these technical directives as simply as possible because we are attempting to communicate more effectively with relatively uneducated employees whom we have hired in accordance with guidelines imposed on us by the federal government. (223)

Notice that the changes in sentence 9 come as a result of inserting *we* into the text: *We have written . . . because we are attempting . . . whom we have hired.* Attempt is changed to *are attempting,* but other nominalizations (*technical directives, employees of little education, guidelines*) are not similarly unpacked. If we had Halliday's equivalent in spoken language, it would likely be much longer and much more grammatically intricate than the four clauses of the revised sentence. Williams's revision is not a categorical shift from a written to a spoken style nor from a "nominal" to a "verbal" style. Rather it is a shift in perspective from an impersonal *These directives are written* to a more personal *We have written these directives.* But the personal *we* is complex. The *we* who wrote the directives may or may not be the same *we* who has done the hiring in accordance with federally imposed guidelines.

Use of the corporate *we* is one of the tactics stressed in popular books on corporate management during the 1980s such as Terrence Deal's and Allen Kennedy's *Corporate Cultures.* Deal and Kennedy declare that a distinguishing trait of successful corporations is, in their words, "a strong corporate culture." In a "strong" culture, employees identify with the corporation and its values. As a result, employees know how "to behave most of the time" (15). Because "they feel better about what they do, . . . they are more likely to work harder" (16). Frequent use of *we* in the texts of a corporation is one of many strategies for encouraging employees' identification with the corporation.

Interestingly, however, the use of *we* in Williams's revision (sentence 9) is not the corporate *we* in the sense of referring to everyone who works for a company. In the revision *we* excludes those employees who were hired as the result of "guidelines imposed on us by the federal government." In this case *we* apparently contrasts the existing staff from those who get hired as a result of equal opportunity programs. From a single example, I do not want to claim that Williams's textbook is covertly racist, but it does suggest that Williams's stated goal of sharing the "power, prestige, and privilege that go with being part of the ruling class" is unlikely to be achieved simply through writing in an agent-action style. Just as was the case in my earlier analysis of articles from the abortion debate, an agent-action style is not less ideological than a highly nominal style.

Even if the agent-action style is not the ultimate solution to the lack of access and accountability of institutions to the people whom they are supposedly serving, the popularity of Williams's *Style: Ten Lessons in Clarity and Grace* and Lanham's *Revising Prose* outside the academy is an indication that many people share the frustrations of being forced to interpret prose they find difficult to read. These frustrations brought a trend to reform legal language that is addressed to the public, a trend that has led to the passage of "plain-language" laws in many states. In "Plain-Language Laws: Giving the Consumer an Even Break," Michael Ferry and Richard Teitelman begin with these assertions:

> "Consumer" contracts are not written for consumers. Their terms are completely skewed in favor of institutions which offer them on a "take-it-or-leave-it" basis. Their extreme bias is masked by impenetrable language. They work most harshly on the poor who have the least power and therefore suffer the worst terms. (522)

The spirit of Ferry and Teitelman's critique is admirable, but the solution of passing plain-language laws to address a multitude of problems associated with legal language is now seen as inadequate. Another attorney, David Cohen, attacks the assumption that consumers are homogeneous, arguing that plain-language contracts and other legal documents may be of most help to those who already are most informed. Being able to read the lease is not much comfort for those who can't pay the rent.

The Contest for Meaning

The critical linguistics movement was an important attempt to transcend disciplinary boundaries, and while its shortcomings were soon pointed out, it brought to abstract discussions of ideology specific examples of how ideologies are reproduced and transmitted; it brought to linguistic analysis consid-erations of reception as well as production; and it succeeded in taking the political analysis of language far beyond the Orwellian critique of lexical items such as *pacification*. More important to current projects in writing research, it problematized linguistic analysis by challenging the division between language and society and by demonstrating that texts are sites of social conflict. But the critical linguistics movement also demonstrates the limitations of linguis-tic theory in general for dealing with issues of conflict. While critical linguists attacked the refusal of sociolinguists to discuss the political implications of "communities" such as speakers of American Black English, critical linguists did not skeptically analyze the notion of community itself. Instead, they analyzed language communities into groups of the dominating and the dominated—a division that Mary Louise Pratt finds characteristic of utopian projects, one that would subsume various lines of difference within one difference. The limi-tations of critical linguistics also demonstrate the difficulties of mapping the social onto structural links or grids and analyzing positions on those grids. Critical linguistics attempted to identify subjectivity with grammatical agency, but later its key figures heavily qualified this association. Subject positions are occupied with different degrees of investment; there is no way of being certain, for example, that the headmaster who wrote the dress code news-letter is not parodying the discourse of educational authority while at the same time deploying it.

The tools of linguistic analysis can be useful in analyzing how subject posi-tions are constructed in particular discourses. The notion of subjectivity it-self, however, is far too complex to be "read off" from texts. It is a more com-plex notion than that of "roles" because it is a conglomeration of temporary positions rather than a coherent identity; it allows for the interaction of a per-son's participation in other discourses and experiences in the world with the positions in particular discourses; and it resists deterministic explanations because a subject always exceeds a momentary subject position. In the next chapter I will examine how analyses of subjectivity might be used in analyz-ing the subject positions privileged in writing classrooms.

4   Ideologies of the Self
in Writing Evaluation

ALONG WITH CHALLENGING the authority and naturalness of representation, postmodern theory has taken as its other main targets the unity of human consciousness and the primacy of human reason. Postmodern theory questions the existence of a rational, coherent self and the ability of the self to have privileged insight into its own processes. Postmodern theory denies that the self has universal and transcendent qualities but instead renders our knowledge of self as always contingent and always partial. Critiques of the subject and reason in postmodern theory are often aimed at the "Cartesian subject," or the "transcendental subject," or the "bourgeois subject." While these conceptions of the subject are often held to represent the "modern" view of the subject, differing conceptions of the subject have led to major arguments within modernism, beginning with the romantics' rejection of rationalism.

Karl Marx's attack on bourgeois individualism and Sigmund Freud's theory of the unconscious are but two of the most prominent reinterpretations of the rational subject of the Enlightenment. An important twentieth-century American tradition also argues for socially constructed selves in the work of theorists such as George Herbert Mead and Kenneth Burke. Furthermore, since the 1930s, long before the structuralist anthropology of Lévi-Strauss, the self had been discussed in anthropology as a peculiarly Western notion.[1] Conceptions of subjectivity and individual consciousness have thus hardly been unproblematic over the last two centuries. Postmodern theorists are not the first to question the notion that the contemplative individual is at the center of the world, as Terry Eagleton says, "striving to gain touch with experience, truth, reality, history or tradition" (*Literary Theory* 196).

Postmodern theorists, however, have gone beyond earlier critiques in several respects. They have shown how no theory can claim to stand outside of a particular social formation and thus any critique must be self-reflexive. In overturning notions of the self and individual consciousness, postmodern theorists stress the multiplicity, temporariness, and discursive boundedness of subject positions. Postmodern theorists have also argued that because subjectivities are located within discourses, they are deeply involved in relations of power and institutional authority. During the 1970s and 1980s many scholars began to use postmodern theory to investigate how the discursive practices of particular disciplines are implicated in maintaining larger relations of power. These investigations eventually reached to how pedagogy presents stable subject positions that would seem to overcome the contradictory nature of subjectivity.

One of the most important of these extensions of postmodern theory for English studies is Catherine Belsey's *Critical Practice* (1980). Belsey describes two metaphors for language that have been dominant during the nineteenth and twentieth centuries: one the empiricist metaphor of language as the transparent window on reality, the other the expressivist metaphor of language as the vehicle for projecting the thoughts and emotions of the individual. She shows how these seemingly contradictory metaphors both assume that language originates within the minds of individuals. Belsey calls the merger of the two metaphors "expressive realism." While different versions of expressive realism may privilege the individual psyche over perceived reality or vice versa, all versions share the assumptions that language exists outside of history and is innocent of politics.

In the classroom, expressive realism resolves some of the major tensions within modernism by fusing realism and romanticism. Realism assumes that language can transmit directly what is signified in external reality. With the romantics came the belief that emotions could be transmitted directly as well; hence literature and art became both mimetic and expressive. The task of the author, poet, or artist was seen as twofold: the artist must represent reality accurately and convey to the viewer the heightened emotions that the artist has experienced. This theory treats the experience of reading as unproblematic. The universal "truths" contained in great art and literature are available to anyone with adequate facilities to discern them. That readers may be from different cultures, different classes, and of different genders does not matter because reading is perceived as the one-way flow from one autonomous mind to another, and the text is a self-contained object for passive consumption. While the implications of expressive realism for the reading of literature were widely studied in the 1980s, the consequences for the teaching of writing have only begun to be investigated.

Evaluation Treated as Process

One of the effects of the process movement has been to occlude the criteria used to evaluate writing. While most teachers of writing still assign grades to papers at some point in the course of instruction, the emphasis has shifted from summative to formative evaluation, or, in the language of process advocates, from a teacher's role as judge to one of coach. Nancy Sommers and others have been influential in convincing writing teachers that evaluative comments on students' texts should serve as aids in revising rather than as justifications of particular grades. The recent literature on writing evaluation, however, tends to restrict the process of evaluation to the *means* of evaluation, largely teachers' and peers' responses to student writing. This literature tends to assume that a broad consensus exists about what constitutes good writing and that teachers can recognize good writing when they see it.

Absent from most current discussions of evaluation is an older notion of process reflected in the etymology of the term. The Latin roots of *evaluation* are *ex* + *valere*—to be "out of" or to "emerge from" value. Each judgment of value is made from some notion of value, usually a notion that is widely shared within a culture. College writing research in the disciplinary period which began, roughly, in the mid-1960s has not told us much about exactly what it is that teachers value in student writing. Researchers who have used statistical methodologies to address this question have thrown little light on the issue. The only consistent finding has been that the length of essays is associated with judgments of quality.[2] Textbooks, by and large, are of little help because they speak of good writing in general terms such as those Michael Adelstein and Jean Pival use to define good writing: "clear," "concise," "effective," "interesting," and projecting "the authentic voice of the writer" (6). And guidelines published by English departments—at least at places where I've taught—are even less specific. An "A" paper is one that "displays unusual competence"; hence, an "A" paper is an "A" paper.

The classroom successes of process pedagogy have drawn attention away from how judgments of writing quality reflect larger cultural assumptions about the purposes of literacy education. Such was not the case throughout much of the history of writing instruction in America. Literacy instruction was closely associated with larger cultural goals, and writing teachers were as much or more interested in *whom* they want their students to be as in *what* they want their students to write. From the early national period through most of the nineteenth century, literacy instruction promoted Protestant and nationalistic values (Heath, "Toward an Ethnohistory"; Spring). By the turn of the century, justifications for the teaching of literacy as well as the materials themselves had become more secular in character (Applebee, *Tradition*). In the early decades of the twentieth century, assumptions from expressive realism were implicit in advanced literacy instruction. Unlike the situation today, writing teachers and administrators in the early twentieth century were well aware of these assumptions and articulated them when examinations were under review.[3]

In this chapter I contrast a report reviewing a 1929 test in English that was used for making college admissions decisions with a recent collection of "best" student essays, *What Makes Writing Good*, by William E. Coles, Jr., and James Vopat. This collection is especially valuable for this inquiry because it includes commentary from the teachers who nominated the student examples. Even if assumptions about the subjectivities that student writers should occupy are not as singular or as well understood as expressive realism, I argue that shared assumptions about subjectives—the selves we want our students to be—still shape judgments of writing quality. I conclude by examining the relation of these subjectivities to institutions.

High and Solitary Minds

In the period between the two world wars, several approaches to the teaching of writing competed in the United States—a few of them quite innovative—but as Berlin notes in *Rhetoric and Reality*, an Arnoldian view of English studies dominated during this period. At Eastern colleges in particular, writing courses were based on reading and responding to great works of literature. The student subject was elevated by the experiences of reading great literature and was expected to draw moral lessons from those experiences.

A broad explication of these assumptions can be found in *Examining the Examination in English*, a 1931 report of an external review of the College Entrance Examination Board's 1929 English examination. The report was written by a nine-member Commission on English, whose chairman was Charles Swain Thomas of Harvard. The other eight members were professors and teachers from Yale, Cornell, Vassar, Wheaton College, Chicago Normal College, Phillips Academy, the Boston Girl's Latin School, and the superintendent of the Brookline, Massachusetts, public schools. The commission began with the same objection I raised earlier about the tautologies that persist in guidelines for writing evaluation. In the general statement given to the readers of the examination, the writer of an examination book given a score of 50 ("failure") is described as "a Candidate who falls just short of showing the minimum ability, together with a faulty technique indicating that he would be a 'bad risk'" (47). The writer of a book marked 85 ("very good") is described as showing "good all round ability that falls just short of excellence (90 group)" (46).

The commission found these definitions vague, and they read ninety-two examination books written in June 1929 to determine why particular marks were given. They focused on the three-hour-long Comprehensive Examination that included three parts. Part I tested for knowledge of literature; part II quoted a poem or prose passage and asked students to interpret it; part

III asked students to write a composition on a topic selected from a list of fifteen that included "Why are popular magazines popular?"' "What makes a good letter?"; "A family reunion"; "All education is essentially self education"; "Art in our industrial age"; "The beach at low tide"; and "Billboard versus landscape."[4] The 1929 questions for part I offered students two options in each of two subsections. Below is the entire question and responses of two young men to question 2 in the first subsection:

Part I

(*Seventy to eighty minutes*)
Write upon either 1 or 2. (About 200 words.)

1. It has been said that literature helps readers better to understand life. Express your opinion of this statement, using specific illustrations from at least four works that you have read.

2. A critic has said that a reader may have these attitudes toward his reading:
   (a) He may be interested primarily in incidents.
   (b) He may share in the emotions and thoughts of the characters in critical moments.

   Illustrate these statements, using specific illustrations from your reading of four works, representing at least two different kinds of literature.

Write upon either 3 or 4. (About 200 words.) Do not refer to any works used in 1 or 2.

3. Poets sometimes reveal to us (a) aspects of beauty in the world of nature which we have not previously observed; (b) insight into emotional experience.

   Give specific illustrations of the truth of these two statements from four poems that you have read.

4. Explain what you have learned about the personalities of two authors as these writers have revealed themselves in their works.

*   *   *

Student One:
Part I

2. The truth of the statements that a reader may be interested primarily in incidents and that he may share the emotions and thoughts of the characters in critical moments may be illustrated thus.

   In reading Quentin Durward I was interested in his actions in one case, that is, when he was fighting the Boar of the Ardennes and nearly had him at his mercy he heard the shouts of Trudchen, the daughter of Pavillon who had aided him. The prize for the head of the Boar was the hand of Isabel, Countess of Croye; nearly all the soldiers in the affray were after the head of the Boar. But Quentin, on hearing the cries of Trudchen, who was being seized by several French soldiers, hesitated but an instant and then left the Boar and went to the rescue of the girl.

In the Nervous Wreck, the Wreck, who is a chemist from Pittsburgh, is supposed to be in bad health, as he claims himself, his "nerves are shot." In reality he is in very good health. He undertakes the job of bringing the rancher's daughter, that is, the daughter of the rancher with whom he is staying, to the railroad in his "flivver." On the way they are lost and finally they land in the bottom of a creek. It is interesting to watch the "nervous wreck" pull the Ford out of the creek with a block and tackle in spite of the girl's belief that it cannot be done.

In the story "The Day the World Ended" by Sax Rohmer, the master mind of Anubis is the most brilliant man on earth. He is years, perhaps even centuries ahead of the times.

One of the characters, Brian Woodville, a reporter in following up the note of John Lonergan tries to penetrate Felsenweir. He has passed two of the death zones and turns around when he sees a figure in black armor, a supernatural figure, advancing toward him. He blazes away at the figure with his revolver without harming it. When he turns to run he is followed by a man resembling a skeleton. Finally the man is catching him and he makes one desperate effort as he is grasped by the shoulders in the claws of the pursuer. Immediately consciousness leaves him.

In "Beau Geste" we become interested in the attitude of Digby at the death of Beau or Michael. As children they had played at being Norsemen and Beau had always said that he wished to die the way the Norsemen died. Digby, on discovering the death of Beau in Fort Zinderneuf places the dead corporal, whom Michael had killed and who at the same time had killed Michael, at Beau's feet, placing Beau on a bed. He sets fire to the bed and says that Beau has had a real Viking's death, even to having a dog at his feet.

Student Two:
Part I

2. From Browning's dynamic poems we may choose many which illustrate interest in incident. In "Bringing the Good News," a poem of progressive action, my interest lies in the accomplishment, the fulfillment of great deed, the carrying, past every obstacle, of the news from Ghent. Browning was ever attracted by people who did what they did to the best of their ability. Were he murderer, philosopher, athlete, or traitor, if he did his work well, he was a hero to Browning. This attitude led to the action and incident of his poems.

In the "Incident of the French Camp" I find myself moved not only by interest in the act of the heroic lad who brought tidings from the enemy's camp, but by the thoughts of the boy and the emotion of his general. The drama of the scene is vital and illustrates the truth that the reader is interested in incident.

On the other hand, the poignancy and breathtaking sympathy I feel upon reading of the exploit illustrates the fact that one shares in the emotions and thoughts of the characters.

Another proof of this point I find in "Macbeth." In the sleep-walking scene, who has not felt the gripping ice fear, the utter despondency, the futility which haunted Lady Macbeth's subconscious mind?

In "Hamlet" I have felt the emotion of Horatio when asked by his dearest and most trusted friend to swear upon the cross. How wretched must have been his heart, his very soul, when Hamlet would not take his word alone!

Again, in "Hamlet," I have shared the burning frenzy of hot-headed Laertes, bent upon avenging Polonius.

For me, in almost every work, my interest lies in the emotion which the characters create in me.

These students were writing quickly. They had only thirty-five to forty minutes for each subsection of part I. The essay in the first book shows signs of the pace. In the paragraph on the "Nervous Wreck," the writer forgets a key detail and awkwardly circles back to keep from scratching out a sentence: But he does manage to do what the assignment calls for, discussing incidents and characters' emotions in four separate works. The writer of the second book handles the question with more ease. He begins by praising Browning in resonant phrases: "the accomplishment, the fulfillment of the great deed, the carrying, past every obstacle, of the news from Ghent." While the writer demonstrates familiarity with Browning and Shakespeare, by the end this essay too breaks down. The last example where the writer claims to have "shared the burning frenzy of hot-headed Laertes" must have caused even a few of the commission members to wince.

Like the original readers and the Commission on English who reviewed their scores, I would rank the second essay better in overall quality than the first. The second essay exhibits more of the conventions of academic discourse than the first. The examples are better developed and more closely related to the thesis. But the Commission on English did not see the difference as merely one of degree. The writer of the first book received a mark of 50, rejecting the writer as a "bad risk," while the writer of the second book received an 85, placing him in the top 5 percent as a near excellent prospect.

The commission interpreted the difference between the two books. For the first book they write:

> This paper fails because the candidate has shown no real acquaintance with standard literature. He refers to *Quentin Durward* with a slight reference and mentions two poems of Wordsworth [in part III]. He shows that his chief interest, however, is in stories which are trivial and sensational. . . . Whatever the study of literature has done for him, there is no evidence here that it has formed his taste or has given him even slight reflective power. (60)

By contrast, the commission's response to the second book matches the writer's enthusiastic prose:

> One notices immediately in this book an unusual range, vitality, and originality of vocabulary. . . . There is present here the beginnings of unmistakable literary and intellectual power of a mature kind. (81)

The commission assumes that the writer of the first book has in fact read the "right" works of literature. The problem is that the great works have not had the right effect; if they had, the writer wouldn't waste his time on popular literature like "Nervous Wreck." No doubt the commission viewed the first book as a sign of a broader "withdrawal of adequate consideration of the classics," a tendency the commission called "dangerous" (207).

The correct attitude is detailed in a sample essay written for part III in response to the topic "Why are popular magazines popular?"—an essay in a book which was described as possessing "striking originality of thought, with unusual power of analysis and presentation." The student writer claims,

> The question is very easy to answer. Since nine-tenths of the people of America have never really visited their minds at all, not daring to, I suppose, after planting there such poor, puny plants, the popular magazine is popular. However when we have answered our first question in this facile manner, we are merely confronted with another, for we find that there must be some quite definite thing to fill that large abyss where the forests of imagination should have grown. (85)

Later in the essay the "large abyss" becomes "those limitless fields of the mind [that] go all unexplored, and the deep pools of thought [that] are stagnate." According to the commission on English, these flights of metaphor are exactly what the examination is supposed to encourage, that pupils should have the opportunity "to exercise and reveal their powers" (196). The commission's examples echo Ruskin's discussion of the effects of great art in *Modern Painters*, a description that Belsey finds the epitome of expressive realism. Ruskin held that the representational aspects of art are available to everyone, but the expressive aspects are available only to those with "high and solitary minds."

The commission uses similar language in describing the goal of teaching writing, which "is not the mere composition of some indefinite entity known as 'a theme.' [The student] must understand that true originality will be the result of discriminating and vigorous perception and thought" (185). The commission continues,

> He should learn . . . that verbal expression is one of the best means he has of developing his power to think, to perceive, and even to feel, with clarity and sensitiveness. It is of supreme importance, moreover, that a student should learn to disregard the attitude of those in his class, who, confining themselves to the range of the mediocre in choice of theme, vocabulary, and sentence patterns, tend at times to ridicule a pupil who ventures to speak and write as ably as he knows how on topics that demand an intellectual and emotional reach safely above the area of the commonplace. (186)

The phrase "safely above" suggests that a great deal more is involved than a few purple passages about the classics in examination books.

In a study of the relationship of aesthetic taste to social class, Pierre Bourdieu observes that "nothing more rigorously distinguishes the different classes than the disposition objectively demanded by the legitimate consumption of legitimate works, the aptitude for taking a specifically aesthetic point of view on objects already constituted aesthetically—and therefore put forward for the admiration of those who have learned to recognize the signs of the admirable" (*Distinction* 40). The preservation of an asymmetry of literary taste among different social classes suited the purposes of the College Entrance Examination Board, whose member institutions educated the children of the elite. Apparently no one told the writer of the first book that the safe route on the Comprehensive Examination was to cite *Hamlet* as an example and not worry about getting too carried away. As a result he was not admitted to a prestigious college. The wrath provoked by his discussion of "Nervous Wreck" illustrates another of Bourdieu's points—that "tastes are perhaps first and foremost distastes" (53).

The commission, however, saw the sorting of the "intellectually weak" from those with the "power of reflection about what they have read" as just one function of the examination (51). The commission was well aware that college entrance examinations determine high school curricula and that encouraging the development of "special powers" promoted competition among students. It confidently pronounced, "It has been indisputably proved in many universities that what are known as 'honors' courses prove to be attractive to the better class of pupils. . . . As the spirit of competition stimulates striving to win a school or college letter, so it stimulates a student to work for honors" (203). The emphasis on "the spirit of competition" is what makes the commission's notion of self a particularly American version, one that is still with us today.

Authentic Voices

The assumptions underlying the evaluation of the writing of college students today would seem to be much more complex than they were in 1931. In a nation where over half of those who graduate from high school go on to college, distinctions made among students according to their responses to canonical literature have become much less relevant; indeed, the teaching of canonical literature as the primary subject matter for writing courses has diminished considerably since World War II, leaving no single model of writing instruction to replace it. Given the resulting multiplicity of approaches to the teaching of writing, the relationships between assumptions about "good" writing and the privileging of particular selves among our students would seem more difficult to analyze than ever. But if we should not expect to locate a well-articulated set of assumptions such as Ruskin's and Arnold's statements on expressive realism, neither should we pretend that current assumptions cannot be identified.[5]

For a description of the selves that writing teachers now privilege in "good" writing, William Coles and James Vopat's *What Makes Writing Good* is an extremely valuable source of data. Coles and Vopat describe the idea for the book as coming in a conversation following Coles's presentation at the 1981 Wyoming Conference on Freshman and Sophomore English. After Coles had discussed what he considered the best student paper he had ever received, Coles and Vopat speculated on what sorts of writing other teachers might select. They asked forty-eight teachers to contribute one example of student writing that "in some way demonstrates excellence," along with the writing assignment and a commentary explaining how the example is distinguished.

It is hard to imagine a broader range of contributors, extending from distinguished theorists (such as Wayne Booth, James Britton, Edward Corbett), to empirical researchers (for example, Linda Flower, Andrea Lunsford), to technical writing teachers (Paul Anderson, Carolyn Miller), to linguists (James Sledd, Joseph Williams), to practicing writers (Donald Murray, Roger Sale). Diverse viewpoints on the profession are represented (David Bleich, Frank D'Angelo, Walker Gibson, William Irmscher, Richard Ohmann, Ira Shor, Donald Stewart, Richard Young). But the range of contributors is not matched by a similar range of student writing. By my count, at least thirty of the examples in the collection are personal experience essays—twenty of them autobiographical narratives—and several of the remaining eighteen include writing about the writer. Only four examples are in the genres of professional writing (two letters and two reports). Four examples briefly discuss works of literature, but there is no literary analysis paper of the kind described in rhetoric texts. Only two essays present sustained analyses of other texts. One of them is an essay nominated by James Vopat on Studs Terkel's *Working*, and the other, nominated by Joseph Williams, contrasts the first two speeches in Thucydides' *History of the Peloponnesian War*. Not one essay resembles the frequently assigned "research paper."

I have no simple explanation for the strong preference for autobiographical essays.[6] Perhaps it is because, as Michael Holzman suggests in commenting on the narrative he nominated, our students "have some highly unusual stories to tell" (156). But the commentaries on the autobiographical narratives suggest something more is involved than their engaging quality. Several teachers mention that while the particular example they discuss is flawed (spelling and mechanical errors are reproduced), the student achieves excellence because he or she is either "honest" (James Britton, Roger Garrison, Larry Levy, Erika Lindemann), writes in an "authentic voice" (Harvey Daniels, Leo Rockas), or possesses "integrity" (Walker Gibson). For example, Erika Lindemann says, "Good writing is most effective when we tell the truth about who we are and what we think. What makes Norma's [the student writer's] paper, 'At the Beach,' so powerful is that she is honest about her feelings toward her parents" (161). Norma Bennett's paper is a narrative of a summer vacation spent with her two divorced parents who now go to different resorts. Her mothers wears her PTL ("Praise the Lord") jacket (in the days before Jim and Tammy Bakker's fall) and spends much of the day either sleeping or sobbing. Her potbellied father also spends much of the day sleeping—passed out drunk on the beach with a twenty-five-year-old woman in a white string bikini while Norma babysits for the woman's young child. I have a great deal of sympathy for students like Norma Bennett, who must cope with difficult family situations as well as the pressures of college, but why is writing about potentially embarrassing and painful aspects of one's life considered more honest than, say, the efforts of Joseph Williams's student, Greg Shaefer, who tries to figure out what Thucydides was up to in writing about the Peloponnesian War?

James Britton and his colleague, Steve Seaton, make comments similar to Lindemann's about a narrative by Maggie Turner, who relates her parents' reactions to her boyfriends. Britton and Seaton comment: "In our view, a principal virtue of Maggie's writing is in its *honesty*; one reads it with a continuing sense of the writer's struggle to say what she means and mean what she says" (79). This honesty, according to Britton and Seaton, reflects on the teaching: "For her to write with such honesty on the topic of family relationships betokens an unusual trust in the reader she has in mind, her teacher. Such a relationship of trust must be the outcome of successful teaching of this class over a period of time—something that must be *earned*, can't be *demanded*" (79). I don't understand why, as Britton and Seaton suggest, receiving such papers from students is a benchmark of successful writing instruction. I have read narratives written for large-scale writing assessments that deal with intense personal events such as the experience of being raped, yet the writer had no knowledge of who would read the paper or what would become of it.

The comments of other teachers in the Coles and Vopat anthology imply that autobiographical writing is more "truthful" than nonautobiographical writing. Larry Levy says, "I wanted students to develop a response beyond stereotype and mass culture to their own questions" (125). Stephen Tchudi says, "I hope to engage students in writing from their own experience. I also want to push my freshmen away from writing the standard 'five paragraph' freshman theme, with its canned openings, wooden organizational structures, obligatory endings" (175). Roger Garrison declares, "Good writing is inevitably honest writing. Every writer, beginner or not, needs what Hemingway called 'a built-in crap detector.' All of us, like it or not, are daily immersed in tides of phony, posturing, pretentious, tired, imprecise, slovenly language, which both suffocate and corrupt the mind" (273). I don't doubt these teachers' claims that assigning autobiographical narratives often produces a freshness of insight that students might not achieve with typical transactional forms of student writing such as the standard research paper. As Harvey Daniels wryly observes, autobiographical papers can be "a welcome burst of enjoyment amid the often dreary and endless process of evaluating student work" (260).

In several of the commentaries on the autobiographical narratives, however, is an assumption that individuals possess an identifiable "true" self and that the true self can be expressed in discourse. This same assumption even carries into the student essays. Peggy Bloxam, James Vopat's student who writes about degradation in Studs Terkel's *Working*, summarizes the stories the workers tell about their jobs: "These people all feel degraded, and no wonder. They are lowering their moral and intellectual standards to meet the demands of a job. In a sense, they are denying their true selves and imposing over it a false self" (351). Bloxam then cleverly equates writing about degradation to the workers' degradation: "I sit and stare at a piece of paper when I could be writing a paper for a different class. These are degrading circumstances because they are limiting the real potential of the worker. Here, too, a false self possessing characteristics totally divorced from those of the real self has taken over" (351). Bloxam's distinction sounds like, and perhaps even draws on, the traditional Marxist concept of ideology as "false consciousness," a distorting lens imposed on the working class concealing their true selves. Bloxam sees the self as an essence waiting to be freed rather than an essence waiting to be discovered through writing. The question which remains for both traditional Marxists and "authentic voice" proponents is how do we distinguish the true self?

One of the autobiographical narratives in *What Makes Writing Good* offers a splendid case in point because the teacher, Rebecca Blevins Faery, speaks of the student's essay as a way "to lay claim to the self she is in the process of becoming" (334). Below is the essay that the student, Lindsay Lankford, wrote:

On Writing Letters

My post office box is empty today, as it is almost every day. To peer inside is always an afterthought, seldom rewarded. Once a month, though, I'm assured of mail. C & P Telephone Company loves me, and sends me nice long bills, each call marked in minutes and money owed. These bills, and the stubs in my checkbook from their payment, are all that remain of past communications. The telephone, however, is fast and easy to use. Letters can take days, sometimes weeks to reach their destination. Furthermore, writing letters involves a great deal of time and effort; yet letters have some very real advantages.

I spent a year in Paris and quickly discovered that transatlantic phone calls were not within my budget. So I was left with that most archaic mode of communication, the letter. And I loved it. Every Sunday morning was devoted to my weekly letter home, a letter which often took all morning. I'd go through the whole week in memory, and re-live it. I'd go to the *tabac*, and remember how pleased I was when the little man with his dirty black apron complimented my slowly improving French. Or I'd be in the Jeu de Paume, and feel again the excitement I felt when I finally learned to love Cezanne. I'd recall how bitterly and miserably cold I was last Thursday, and how really good the coffee tasted in that cafe near Sacre Coeur. I'd remember walking out of Notre Dame at seven p.m., after an hour of warm and rich Vivaldi, and finding Paris dusted with snow, glinting and sparkling in the streetlights. Or summer nights in the Latin Quarter, drinking *vin ordinaire* in outdoor cafes, talking too much about Life and Art and the Future, subjects that are always and can only be discussed after too much wine.

My Sunday letters were the times when I put these vignettes together, and made my memories concrete and coherent. Mama has kept these letters for me, in a manila folder in the top drawer of her Louis XV desk. And whenever I want them, whenever I want to remember, they are there for me. For although I addressed them to Mama and Daddy, they were always written essentially to myself. Mama and Daddy saw Europe through my eyes, with my perceptions and impressions. My letters were unselfconscious and utterly honest, for the time and space lag between the letters made intimacy easier. My parents learned more about me from a year of letters than they had in nineteen years of personal interaction.

I loved their letters to me, too. They were never filled with earth-shattering news, but they revealed a lot. Actually, most people's lives are dull; it's the way they perceive their lives that is interesting. My sister Allison lives in the Negev Desert, in a tiny trailer. Her world consists of her husband, their two small children, and very little else. Her letters were always wrinkled, smeared with something sticky, covered in crayons and written over extended periods of time. They were a mess: descriptions of the gingerbread village Allison had made for the Christmas party, their plans for moving back to the States, Lauren's latest word, and details of Elizabeth's third birthday party. Allison's letters were disjointed, but ebullient. Living on an army base in the Israeli desert would seem a barren existence, yet Allison's letters describe a busy and happy, if somewhat chaotic, life.

I saw Mama's world through her letters. With her eyes and her words, I saw the spring I was missing in Birmingham, how bright the azaleas were, how she'd never seen so many dogwoods in bloom. I realized how acute her perceptions are, how she notices the little details. She wrote of the garden, of the ever-growing, never-ending crop of green beans. Of the squirrel without a tail, how well he had adapted. From her letters, I knew how empty the house felt when Daddy was away on business, and then how cozy it was when he returned and they made great pots of seafood gumbo together. Mama's sphere is small: her house, her friends and her husband. Yet her letters taught me that her deep awareness of her world gave it its richness.

Daddy didn't write much, but his few letters were remarkable for what they revealed. Daddy is sixty-two and still passionate about learning. Daddy, who had one year of French in college and that forty years ago, wrote to me in French. My mental image of Daddy in his office, surrounded by French diction- ary and grammar book, is very precious. I treasure the idea of Daddy as the student, instead of the one who knows all. And what Daddy can't say in English, he can write in French: *Je t'aime* ended every letter.

My post office box is empty today, and very likely to remain so tomorrow. For we've all slipped back into old patterns, old ways of communicating. Some- times, we still find time to send little notes, notes written in haste and without much pleasure. These new letters are little more than abbreviations of the de- tails we once vividly described. I think we all miss our old letters, although we neither discuss nor write them anymore. The barriers are back up. We're careful again, wary of the reckless revelations we once shared. The physical distances between us are less now; cautiously, we distance ourselves in spirit.

I've still got those old letters. They are priceless to me. For writing deals harshly with the banal, the superficial. The things we say to each other can sel- dom survive on paper. The things we dare to write are those we really mean. (330–32)

Lankford shows an awareness of the essay as a form, beginning with phone bills and check stubs as images of writing in our culture, juxtaposing scenes of intercontinental letter writing, then deftly returning to the empty post office box at the end. She wrote the essay in an advanced expository writing class, a course where Faery says, "I am most attracted by the idea of exposition as an act that, at best, *exposes* or *reveals* the truth about something" (332). The truth Faery finds in Lankford's essay is "a harsh one, because she passes an unmerciful judgment on our era, which has dispensed with the practice of writing as a way of developing a picture of the world and of forming connec- tions and relationships which make people feel at home in it and not alone" (335).

I too am touched by this essay. I enjoy getting long letters from overseas, and I would like to imagine my children writing long letters to me someday. I don't doubt Lankford's sincerity about the disappointment of going to the mailbox after a year of receiving letters from family and friends on other con- tinents. At the same time, I'm struck by how similar student and teacher sound. Lankford plays teacher/critic when she describes her sister's letters as "disjointed but ebullient," praises her mother's inclusion of "little details," and lauds her father's efforts at brushing up his French. I'm also struck by how closely the description of Paris matches the one I formed from images in films and novels before I visited the multicultural city. From Vivaldi at Notre Dame to the value of writing, the truths "exposed" and "revealed" in the essay are a series of recognitions for a college English teacher. What else did she see in Paris?

Let me put it a different way. Could Lankford have written a similar essay if she had visited a place unfamiliar to us? Within a mile of my house in Austin, Texas, immigrant Mexican families have lived temporarily in storm sewers. What if Lankford had gone to live with them? Could she have written in the same way about her elation when they complimented her slowly improving Spanish? Would the warmth of their fire have felt as good as the warmth of coffee in the cafe near the Sacré Coeur? Would her mother have written to her about the blooming dogwoods and the squirrel without a tail? Would her father have closed by saying *Te quiero* instead of *Je t'aime*? Most of all, would Lankford have discovered the value of letter writing as a means of calling attention to the plight of the immigrants and getting help for them?

I'm not advocating that students adopt 1930s Soviet-style social realism as their model. The point is that Lankford's skill is demonstrated in assembling a series of subject positions. By bringing the essay effectively to closure at the end, she creates the illusion of a unified and knowing self that overviews the world around it. The epigrammatic conclusion reaffirms that she is the source of her language, that as she puts it, "The things we dare to write are those we really mean." Lankford agrees with "authentic voice" proponents that language transparently reveals what is going on in our consciousness. Because the self Lankford constructs is sensible and knowing, we trust her perceptions of reality—the characterizations of her father as the executive who continues to study, her mother as the homemaker who misses her father when he is away, and her sister as the busy mother of two small children. We "recognize" these people because they occupy familiar positions in middle-class nuclear families. It is the very ease of these recognitions—their natural and common-sense quality—that troubles many feminist scholars. Lankford's mother and sister may well be happy in, as Lankford puts it, their small spheres. For many other women, however, there's something quietly and frighteningly oppressive in Lankford's sentence, "Her world consists of her husband, their two small children, and very little else." Many of these women have sought to expand their own small spheres only to be confronted with patriarchal discourses that define a woman's chief concerns in relation to men and her family. By claiming universal meaning for acts of finding the self through displacing the Other, the values ascribed to personal narratives, as Bizzell and Herzberg note in their review of *What Makes Writing Good*, often "serve a profoundly conservative political agenda" (247).

Not all the student writers attempt to smooth over the contradictions inherent in the concept of a self. Coles's own "best" essay—the one he offered at the Wyoming Conference and the one that inspired the volume—is also an autobiographical narrative, written in response to the question, "What is the proper metaphor with which to define a university so far as you are concerned?" Unlike most of the other autobiographical narratives in the Coles and Vopat collection, it does not present a unified subject position nor does it finally decide on a single metaphor for the university. The student writer, George Humphrey, weaves together several conflicting discourses and images that college students experience without attempting to resolve the conflicts in the essay that follows:

> Next to this desk at which I write is a couch where my wife is sleeping. She is nineteen. So am I. The couch is old, with large stuffed pillows and a rounded stuffed back. It is covered with a dirty red, rough material. The wooden legs are curved and scratched. The couch reminds me of one my grandmother used to have, except hers had small lace doilies on the arms. Ours does not.
>
> Out of the window above the couch I can see the back of the Medical School, a corner of the old Dental School, and the University power plant. The windows of the power plant have a blue-green tint to them, and it looks as though the machinery behind them is under water. The buildings do not look much like Ivory Towers. From here, now, they look like a factory.
>
> A factory. I remember when my parents came to visit us a few weeks ago my father, who is an engineer, was very interested in the power plant. He said the next time he came he would like to go over and "check it out."
>
> "I'll just tell them my son is a student here and I'd like to see what kind of a set up you've got for him."
>
> My mother, on the other hand, was more interested in the garden in front of the Museum of Art. She also likes the couch.
>
> "Well," we said, "it's comfortable anyway."
>
> The Rapid Transit runs past the window of our apartment; so, as I look out at the power plant, I can see the lighted cars running by. Every ten minutes.
>
> When I look out the window over my desk I see two pear trees and a small garden. There is no trace of the University, and, in ten minutes between trains, our apartment could be in the country, instead of University Circle. But the Rapid goes by, and my attention is drawn past my wife and the couch to the University in the other window.
>
> Last year I lived in the dorms. I remember looking out the window of my room on the sixth floor of Clarke Tower. I could see the dorm parking lot and a few houses on the other side. Nothing from there looked much like a university: it looked like a regular city block.
>
> I used to have conversations about D. H. Lawrence with a friend in the ele-

vator. It started one day when I noticed a copy of *The Rainbow* under his arm, and he noticed a copy under mine. The conversations did not last long—just long enough for the elevator to get from the 6th floor to the lobby, but now the only time I see my friend is in a class we have together. We say hello, but that is about all we say.

My wife has started to read Lawrence, though, and I talk with her about him.

Sometimes in our apartment we're conscious of the Rapid going by; sometimes we're not. (324–25)

Whatever George Humphrey does in this essay, he doesn't, as Faery says of Lankford, lay claim to the self he is becoming. It is quite different from most of the other personal narratives, and Coles's response is different as well. Just as there is a strong sense of historical specificity in Humphrey's essay—even where he thinks he is varies almost by the minute—Coles likewise avoids claiming to have found the silent self lurking behind the essay. Although Coles avoids explicit theorizing about language and subjectivity, his reading of Humphrey's essay takes a postmodern turn:

World folds into world and back again as perspective melts into perspective ("Sometimes in our apartment we're conscious of the Rapid going by; sometimes we're not.") Life at a university is life on a Möbius strip, where all opposites meet even as they are held from joining. The proper metaphor for a university then, this writer suggests, is whatever meaning a university student can make at any given moment of the many kinds of self-consciousness a university is designed to promote.

I think.

Because I'm not sure that the university as a unique kind of no-place, as a language-learning center, for example, is as explicitly and firmly at the heart of things in this paper as I'd like to imagine it is. (327)

Coles apparently comes to his historically contingent and unstable reading of George Humphrey's paper by way of psychoanalytic theory. If one grants the possibility of an unconscious mind, then sincerity becomes a partial and bracketed concept. How can one possibly express one's *full* self, including the unconscious part? And what if one is sincerely expressing one's conscious self but unconsciously repressing something that remains unexpressed? Is the writer sincere or insincere?

A defender of Coles, Joseph Harris, says the problem with defining good writing as honest writing "is that it reduces writing to a simple test of integrity. Either your guts are out there on the page or they're not. It's easy to see, then, why so many students are baffled or intimidated when we ask them to write about what they really know. For what do they really know?" ("Plural Text" 161). To ask students to write authentically about the self assumes that a unified consciousness can be laid out on the page. That the self is constructed in socially and historically specific discursive practices is denied. It is no won-der, then, that the selves many students try to appropriate in their writing are voices of moral authority, and when they exhaust their resources of analy-sis, they revert to moral lesson—adopting, as Bartholomae has noted, a pa-rental voice making clichéd pronouncements where we expect ideas to be extended ("Inventing").

If Harris is right in claiming that Coles has been widely misunderstood within the profession, perhaps it is because recognizing the sources of con-tradictory and incompatible discourses in student writing runs squarely against both the expressivist and rationalist traditions of teaching writing that deny the role of language in constructing selves. Those who encourage "authentic voices" in student writing often speak of giving students "ownership" of a text or "empowering" students. The former conflates the capitalist notion of prop-erty rights (as when my creative writing colleagues down the hall talk about selling the movie rights to their books) with autobiographical writing. The lat-ter notion sounds like something all teachers would support (for who among us would "disempower" students?), but it avoids the question of how exactly teachers are to give students power. Is it self-expression or is it in earning power? The freedom students are given in some classes to choose and adapt autobiographical assignments hides the fact that these same students will be judged by the teachers' unstated assumptions about subjectivity and that every act of writing they perform occurs within complex relations of power.

These definitions have changed significantly since 1931 when *Examining the Examination in English* was published, but certain assumptions have lingered. While we no longer hold that the experience of reading literature will directly lead students to a position of heightened awareness, judging from many of the essays in *What Makes Writing Good*, teachers of college writing teachers are still very much concerned with the self. I am not suggesting that a single no-tion of self is shared by those who speak of an "authentic voice," but the as-sumptions can be traced historically. Modern American notions of the indi-vidual self derive in part from nineteenth-century liberalism and utilitarianism, which in turn drew on Thomas Hobbes's theory of the atomic, self-interested self. The blend of economics and psychology in these notions of self remains evident in writing pedagogy. As I note in the introduction, two notions of the individual are often conflated—the self-aware Cartesian subject possessing a unified consciousness and the "freely" choosing competitive individual of capi-talism. The ease with which writing textbooks tout the economic advantages of writing indicates the extent to which the Hobbsian concept of self-interest endures.

Nevertheless, economic explanations do not account fully for the repro-duction of notions of individualism in writing instruction. Marcel Mauss's his-torical study of the idea of self, first published in 1938, gives some indication of the depth and scope of the concept. Mauss found that the concept of self arose in medieval Christianity but that the self as a discrete philosophical category developed in the seventeenth and eighteenth centuries culminating in the work of Kant and Fichte, where every action is the act of individual consciousness. Mauss recognized that Western notions of self make other notions opaque or invisible. What has been added since 1938 to Mauss's theory of the social construction of the self are theories of how notions of the self are interpellated in subject positions in particular discourses. For example, the often quoted beginning of Foucault's "The Discourse on Language" alludes to how institutions persuade reluctant writers and speakers to believe that there is a place and voice for everyone in official discourses.

The self in student autobiographies, then, is not one that emerges like a butterfly from a chrysalis, as Faery implies when she names the subject position in Lankford's essay as "the self she is becoming," but one that is discursively produced and discursively bounded. The student selves we encounter in *What Makes Writing Good* are predominantly selves that achieve rationality and unity by characterizing former selves as objects for analysis—hence the emphasis on writing about past experience rather than confronting the contradictions of present experience as does Coles's student George Humphrey.

The teachers' commentaries on the narratives of past experience imply that success in teaching depends on making a student aware of the desired subject position she will occupy. Wayne Booth's student, Michael Fitzgerald, says of himself: "I know that I have a long way to go, but I want to get there" (292), and Booth ends his comment with the sentence: "He is on his way" (297). But where is he going? It is this notion of the student writer as a developing rational consciousness that makes most talk of empowerment so confused. This essentialist concept of power is not necessarily endemic to writing about the self. The many varieties of autobiographical writing have provided sites for resistance to dominant discourses, and several of the student narratives in the Coles and Vopat anthology are significant explorations of some of the subjectivities offered in our culture and some of the contradictions among those subjectivities. But what is very little explored in the teachers' commentaries on the narratives is the institutional setting of student writing about the self and how that setting is implicated in the production of "honest" and "truthful" writing.

Technologies of Confession

The institutional setting has a great deal to do with why the adjectives "honest" and "truthful" are reserved for personal narratives that are potentially embarrassing and even damaging to the writer. The presentation of autobiographical writing in popular rhetoric textbooks such as *The St. Martin's Guide to Writing* (discussed in chapter 5) bears many of the characteristics of the institutional confession. The authors of *The St. Martin's Guide* tell student writers to "remember that writing about significant remembered events requires a certain honesty and self-reflection" (Axelrod 50). In *The History of Sexuality*, volume 1, Foucault writes, "Since the Middle Ages at least, Western societies have established the confession as one of the main rituals we rely on for the production of truth" (58). He goes on to observe,

> We have since become a singularly confessing society. The confession has spread its effects far and wide. It plays a part in justice, medicine, education, family relationships, and love relations, in the most ordinary affairs of everyday life, and in the most solemn rites; one confesses one's crimes, one's sins, one's thoughts and desires, one's illnesses and troubles; one goes about telling, with the greatest precision, whatever is most difficult to tell. One confesses in public and in private, to one's parents, one's educators, one's doctor, to those one loves; one admits to oneself, in pleasure and in pain, things it would be impossible to tell to anyone else, the things people write books about. One confesses— or is forced to confess. (59)

Foucault would agree with the teachers who claim that students writing personal narratives are involved in the production of "truth," but he also argues "that its production is thoroughly imbued with relations of power" (60). Foucault points out that confessions are not merely "a ritual of discourse in which the speaking subject is also the subject of the statement, [but] it is also a ritual that unfolds within a power relationship, for one does not confess without the presence (or virtual presence) of a partner who is not simply the interlocutor but the authority who requires the confession, prescribes and appreciates it, and intervenes" (63). The literature on responding to student writing says a great deal about teachers as interlocutors of personal narratives, about how teachers might encourage students to say more about themselves, but the literature says very little about teachers as representatives of institutional authority in this process. James Britton and Steve Seaton end their commentary on Maggie Turner's narrative with the following sentence: "Her own life has indeed become observable, and the observation gains something—a gain in self-understanding" (79). But such claims leave much unstated. Why should teachers of writing want students to make their lives "observable" and what benefits result from "a gain in self-understanding?"

Foucault argues that power presumes a relationship between one who dominates and one whom is dominated and that "'the other' (the one over whom power is exercised) be thoroughly recognized and maintained to the very end as a person who acts" ("The Subject and Power" 220). Perhaps Seaton's and Britton's claim that "honest" writing about personal experience is indicative of successful teaching and "unusual trust" is far more valid than I acknowledged earlier, but it can also be interpreted as an institutional exercise of power. When a teacher obtains a revealing personal disclosure, a different relation of power is constructed between teacher and student than typically is constructed in transactional forms of writing.

Those teachers of writing who define good writing as truth-telling assume that truth comes from within and can be conveyed transparently through language. The teacher as receiver of truth takes the position of bearer of authority who can certify truth—as do several of the commentaries in the Coles and Vopat anthology that speak of good writing as "that kind of writing that elicits in the reader a universal human response" (86). The authority to determine which truths are universal places the teacher in a position of privilege because the teacher is outside of the petty interests of history but within the boundaries of universal truth. Such an assignment of authority through a teacher's claim to recognize truth is characteristic of Foucault's description of the modern exercise of power. Foucault writes that power is most effective when it is least visible: "Power is tolerable only on condition that it mask a substantial part of itself. Its success is proportional to its ability to hide its own mechanisms" (*History of Sexuality* 86). If the goal of teachers of writing who speak of "empowerment" is to create more equitable relations of power in our classrooms and in our institutions, then they might begin asking what relations of power come into play when they give a writing assignment that encourages students to make revealing personal disclosures.

In the next chapter I extend this Foucauldian critique to examine how subjects are created through everyday practices of teaching writing.

5

Coherent Contradictions: The Conflicting Rhetoric of Writing Textbooks

IN 1976 RICHARD Ohmann published *English in America*, a political analysis of English studies that stands out from its time like one of the sandstone monoliths that tower over Monument Valley. Ohmann devotes a good chunk of the book to the teaching of writing. In one chapter Ohmann surveys fourteen rhetoric textbooks intended for first-year English, a course he refers to as "English 101," finding that these textbooks teach writing in ways that reproduce the status quo. He says the books "divorce writing from society, need, and conflict" and "break [writing] down into a series of routines" (160). The closest these books come to offering students opportunities for political engagement is in their chapters on argument, but here too argument is taken out of social life. The books present argument as if inequalities of power between writers and readers are insignificant and there is no history of conflict into which writers must insert themselves. Ohmann quotes one of the books that urges students to lead a potentially hostile reader through the same processes of thought that the writer went through. Ohmann then adds, "Imagine Cesar Chavez leading the brothers Gallo through the 'processes of thought' by which he arrived at his position" (156).

While Ohmann's critique remains potentially stinging, many of its claims are now taken for granted. Few would dispute his assertion that a strong relationship exists between the economic system and the educational system. This relationship is assumed by those who blame the educational system for what they describe as a national failure to keep up with the economies of Japan and West Germany, and it is underscored by university administrators who promote university-corporate ties. Ohmann admits that the crux comes with explaining the specifics of the relationship. Any broad generalizations about connections between college writing programs and the national economy would seem to be immediately undercut by the diversity of writing programs even across similar kinds of institutions.

Ohmann limits the scope by analyzing textbooks. By considering only text-books, Ohmann lacks data on how the books are used by teachers, and thus he has little to say about classroom practices in teaching writing. But if text-books are not reliable sources of data for how writing is actually taught, they do reflect teachers' and program directors' decisions about how writing should be represented to students. That the choice of a textbook is also considered significant within the field is evident when teachers answer with the name of a textbook when asked how they teach writing. While writing textbooks have diversified in the decade and a half since *English in America* appeared, one can still find many of the characteristics that Ohmann identifies in a class of rheto-rics called "mainstream" rhetorics that sell tens of thousands of copies an-nually. Indeed, one of the books that Ohmann discusses, James McCrimmon's *Writing with a Purpose*, is still being used today in its ninth edition.

This chapter explores why Ohmann's critique seemingly had so little effect either on textbook publishing or on scholarship concerning textbooks, even though the brilliance of his critique was widely appreciated and the book con-tinues to enjoy the status of an underground classic. The direction I take here is not to attempt to refute Ohmann's claim that textbooks are related in com-plex ways to political and economic structures but rather to suggest that they are also embedded in a long history of institutional practices and discourses that, as Foucault has demonstrated, are themselves mechanisms of power working quietly across social hierarchies and traditional political categories. Ironically, a major source of contradictions in writing pedagogy results from the dogmatic teaching of a truncated conception of coherence, which sup-ports bureaucratic rationality where reason is restricted to narrow channels of expertise and questions of ethics are suppressed. Even the champion of Enlightenment rationality, Jürgen Habermas, critiques "instrumental rational-ity" that supports bureaucracies by providing their justification and control-ling mechanisms, and he argues instead for a "communicative rationality" that would integrate the discourses of the arts, science, and morality.

I argue that the preservation of a truncated rational subject in writing pedagogy is not only a matter of relations between the educational system and the economic system but also involved in the disciplinary regime of com-position studies. Although much has changed in composition teaching since 1950, many of the minute practices that construct a rational subject have re-mained in place to the extent that some of the harshest critics of first-year composition accuse it of becoming "a last bastion of defense of traditional humanism against radical postmodern critical theory" (Zavarzadeh and Mor-ton 13). I intend to show in this chapter that suppressing contradictions to achieve coherence involves more than training students for a future in cor-porate America or shaping students as rational subjects. I contend that the practice of making contradictions coherent has a great deal to do with the power a writing teacher exercises in the classroom.

Coherent Contradictions

Mainstream rhetoric texts typically include sections on clarity and coherence that offer similar advice. In "Use Definite, Specific Concrete Language," an essay published in 1979, Ohmann criticizes such advice for limiting students' opportunities for reflecting on experience. He observes that maxims of clarity push the student writer "toward the language that most nearly reproduces immediate experience and away from the language that might be used to understand it, transform it, and relate it to everything else" (396). Although Ohmann does not discuss the ideological consequences of the mechanical kind of coherence described in rhetoric textbooks, such advice from his viewpoint would be another way of minimizing conflict. For example, in The Practical Stylist, Sheridan Baker coaches students, "The *topic sentence* is the key. It assures that subsequent sentences will fall into line" (48). One issue that Ohmann doesn't raise in English in America is why textbooks that urge students to write coherently are themselves so often incoherent.

An interesting case in point is Baker's Practical Stylist, a book second only to Writing with a Purpose in longevity among current rhetorics and a book that remained much the same throughout its first six editions. The major change from the first edition (1962) to the sixth (1985) has been the expansion of the beginning of the book. Baker starts the first edition with a page-and-a-half section titled "The Stylistic Approach," and the first sentence reads: "Style in writing is something like style in a car, a woman, or a Greek temple—a kind of linear mastery of materials that stands out from the landscape and compels a second look" (1). The dissonant juxtaposition of coordinate terms in a simile that renders cars, women's bodies, and Greek temples equivalent objects of consumption is an earmark of Baker's own style. In the introductory chapter of the sixth edition, Baker praises the virtues of writing:

> In writing, you clarify your own thoughts, and strengthen your conviction. Indeed you probably grasp your thoughts for the first time. Writing is a way of thinking. Writing actually creates thought, and generates your ability to think: you discover thoughts that you hardly knew you had, and come to know what you know. (2–3)

In just four sentences Baker presents three different relations of language and thought—language embodies [preexisting] thinking; language is thinking; [preexisting] language generates thinking. These relations underlie some of the major debates in Western philosophy over the last three centuries, yet they are passed to students as if they are simple, unitary truths, falling in line from the topic sentence, just as cars, women's bodies, and Greek temples are objects for the extended gaze of the male spectator.

Later in the chapter he tells students to write with their own voices. Your writing, he counsels, "should be alive with a human personality—yours—which is probably the most persuasive rhetorical force on earth. Good writing should have a voice, and the voice should be unmistakably your own" (6). But on the very next page Baker admonishes students to suppress that voice: "*Generalize your opinions and emotions. Change* 'I cried' to 'The scene is very moving.' The grammatical shift represents a whole change of viewpoint, a shift from self to subject. You become the informed adult, showing the reader around firmly, politely, and persuasively" (7). According to Baker, you should be yourself as a writer only if you become a "reasonable adult" (7), the petty tyrant who can give orders politely but firmly, the effective middle manager in a bureaucratic hierarchy. Baker's contradictory declarations about writing meanwhile are overwhelmed by the clashing of opposing discourses. The first two paragraphs of the book are at the same time monotonal in intonation and wildly cacophonous in meaning:

WRITE FOR YOUR SHARE

Writing is one of the most important things we do. It helps us to catch our ideas, realize our thoughts, and stand out as fluent persuasive people both on paper and on our feet in front of the meeting or the boss. Reading and writing have already enlarged your education and your speech. Even television, in its news and advertising, and in most of its shows, pours into our thoughts the words and habits that literacy—and written scripts—has built into our speech and thinking.

This language we share is Standard English—sometimes called "edited Standard American English," unfortunately making it seem like some unnatural necessity for the business we would rather not do. But it is our living language, in speech as well as print. Actually, even our most local and private dialects partake of its forms and vocabulary, our "inner speech," as several psychologists and linguists have recently called it. . . . Writing simply straightens out and clarifies our intuitive editing, and in turn makes the editing itself more fluent. Writing perfects thought and speech. Indeed, over the millions of years from our first emotive screams and gurgles of pleasure to the bright dawn of literacy, writing—thinking in full dress—seems to be where speech has been going all the time. (1–2)

Forget for the moment the mixed metaphors of thought in these two paragraphs—that our ideas are floating phantasms that writing can "catch," containers into which content can be poured, crooked lines that can be straightened, and bodies that can be dressed. Overlook also the incredible distortion of linguistic and psycholinguistic research in the second paragraph where speech is regarded as a poor imitation of written English—screams and gurgles before the advent of literacy—not to mention the biases of race, class, ethnicity, and nationality implicit in his statement, "This language we share is Standard English." Look instead at the different vocabularies from which Baker draws. The passage moves from style as "dress for success" that impresses the boss to the sonorous language of intellectual development, then to the power of television, next to a jingoistic claim for standard English as an organic language, then to the popular phrase "inner speech" appropriated from a Marxist psycholinguist, then to vague conjecture about written editing as somehow clarifying "inner speech," and finally to the grand narrative of human consciousness where the light comes on with the arrival of literacy. What is going on here?

One possible explanation is that Baker is a benighted writer, but that explanation is too easy. Since this book is now in its *seventh* edition, many people obviously think otherwise. Moreover, similar discontinuities exist in textbooks written by the most highly regarded scholars in the field. For example, in the concluding chapter to *Revising Business Prose*, Richard Lanham gives two main reasons for using his "paramedic method" for revising prose—reasons of "efficiency" and "ego" (82).

Lanham argues for "efficiency" in terms of money-saving brevity. The "ego" reason is presented as the "sincere" writer who manages to create a style that "can represent his unique selfhood" (87). Lanham says that when the two reasons are put together, "we discover a paradoxical convergence, |and| more often than not the two kinds of justification support one another" (89). Lanham's "paramedic method" that cuts the "lard factor" of excess words is in harmony with trend in business to cut costs to the minimum in order to register the highest profits possible each quarter. Cutting costs, however, often means firing many workers and cutting wages and benefits of those who remain. I doubt that using the "paramedic method" to revise sentence 1 into sentence 2 in order to represent the writer's unique selfhood would be of much comfort to the recipients of this memo:

1. Spiraling costs and the need to maintain the continued profitability of this division require a termination of employer's contributions toward hourly employees' health insurance.
2. To save money we will no longer pay for your health insurance.

If life in business really were as potentially harmonious as Lanham suggests, then the massive displacements of people caused by corporate mergers during the last decade would not have occurred. "Bottom-line" efficiency as practiced in business continually conflicts with the human feelings that Lanham advocates.

Another explanation of the contradictions in textbooks is offered by Stephen North in *The Making of Knowledge in Composition* (1987), a book that reassesses the contributions of practitioners to the field of composition. North argues that the knowledge of practitioners has been dismissed by the triumphant researchers and scholars in the disciplinary period of composition, what North refers to as "Composition with the capital C." North sees the structure of practitioners' knowledge as fundamentally different from the knowledges of the research and scholarly communities in composition studies. Researchers and scholars define their own projects in relation to other lines of inquiry and forms of knowledge, and thus the relations of knowledges are often ones of *exclusion*. The relations of knowledge within the practitioner community, on the other hand, are ones of *inclusion*. North describes the knowledge of practitioners as *lore*, a knowledge characterized by contradiction because it is driven by the pragmatic logic of "what works." Because there is no accountability for why something works in a classroom, nothing is ever discarded from lore. North describes current assumptions about teaching writing with the metaphor of a "House of Lore," a sprawling collection of rooms built from a variety of materials without a blueprint or regard for the coherence of the overall structure (27).

The contents of current rhetorics illustrate North's metaphor. For example, the instructor's preface in the first edition of Rise Axelrod's and Charles Cooper's *The St. Martin's Guide to Writing* (1985) claims that one of its innovations is the particularization of invention. Chapters 2 through 10 are organized around writing assignments that contain specific guides to invention. The instructor's preface indicates that the authors see these specific guides as superior to general invention heuristics. Nevertheless, the general heuristics—clustering, listing, outlining, cubing, Burke's pentad, looping, drafting, and journals—are all tossed into a chapter in the "Research" unit in the back of the book. In the second edition the general heuristics remain, although now in a unit called "Writing Strategies" in the middle of the book.

The overlay of several sets of invention heuristics is a vivid example of the eclecticism of lore. As attractive as North's House of Lore metaphor might be, however, there is much that it fails to explain. If nothing is ever discarded from lore, then little of it can be employed at any particular time. Why some rooms in the House of Lore are crowded while others sit vacant for years or how the surrounding neighborhood affects the House of Lore are unimportant for those guided by lore. These issues are omitted because the question of "what works" is assumed to be transparent; teachers know what works when they see it. But as we have seen in the examples of "good" student writing in chapter 4, judgments of what works in writing are thoroughly cultural and change over relatively short historical spans.

Where the metaphor of the fixed structure of a House of Lore is misleading is in its suggestion that certain practices "persist" in the teaching of writing. If practices are considered only in terms of how they are labeled, then they can be traced through the history of teaching writing. But if such practices are considered *in relation* to the larger curriculum, they do not seem so stable. "Free writing," for example, may appear to share a continuous set of assumptions from Peter Elbow's *Writing without Teachers* to *The St. Martin's Guide to Writing*, but in relation to other practices described in the respective books, free writing has a quite different meaning in the overall curriculum that each book sets out. The House of Lore metaphor does not explain how practices are continually being reconstituted and reworked and how those reworkings produce contradictions. The contradictions in rhetoric textbooks must be analyzed in terms of the relations of textbooks to their audiences of teachers and students, which in turn requires examining the institutional and social settings in which they are written and used. These kinds of unbounded questions quickly become very complex.

Linguistic Analysis of Ideology in Textbooks

One approach to relating the discourse of textbooks to larger social, economic, and political structures is through the analysis of ideologies inherent in the language of textbooks. One such approach to the "micro" analysis of ideology inherent in language is "critical linguistics," which is the subject of much of chapter 3. Critical linguistics would associate the contradictions in American composition textbooks with those in capitalism, where a subject is supposedly free to choose in the marketplace but is also subjected to the laws of the marketplace and therefore obedient to authority. In the third chapter I discuss the tradition of systemic-functional linguistics that underlies critical linguistics, and now I want to turn briefly to the Marxist background of critical linguistics.

In Britain there has been a rich tradition of Marxist cultural criticism in the twentieth century exemplified by the work of Raymond Williams, but the catalyst for much of the British movement in the 1970s and 1980s to examine specific cultural practices in terms of the social workings of ideology was the theory of the French Marxist Louis Althusser. Althusser today is so far out of critical fashion even in Marxist circles that he serves as little more than a straw man if he is mentioned at all. Joseph McCarney remarked recently in *New Left Review* that Althusser's reputation is "near to total eclipse" (115).[1]

Althusser nonetheless succeeded in redefining ideology as sets of cultural practices, rather than as systems of ideas, by applying to a definition of ideology the concept of the decentered subject from structuralism combined with the psychoanalytic work of Jacques Lacan. Althusser brought the definition of ideology close to Lévi-Strauss's definition of culture, but from his Marxist perspective Althusser emphasized that dominant ideologies appear as "natural" and as "common sense." Ideologies constrain the potentially limitless possibilities of meaning in a chain of signifiers by providing apparently coherent positions in the face of the contradictory flux of society. People occupy these positions in a process Althusser calls "interpellation," drawing on Lacan's concept of the "imaginary." Just as a child "imagines" the self to be the unified whole reflected in the mirror, people imagine themselves to be free when they "choose" to occupy a particular subject position such as employee, wife, or proselyte. Althusser argues the contrary position—that individuals do not exist outside of the discourses of ideology but rather are the effects of discourses through a Lacanian process of structuring the ego in imaginary coherence.

The key move in Althusser's analysis of ideology is the imaginary placement of the individual at the center in control of her or his own destiny. The discourses of ideology "interpellate" human beings by offering them an array of subject positions in which people recognize themselves and assume themselves to be the authors of those positions. The term *subject* thus contains a pun. People are *subjected* to dominant ideologies, but because they recognize themselves in the subject positions that discourses provide, they believe they are *subjects* of their own actions. Their recognitions, according to Althusser, are misrecognitions because they fail to see that the subject positions they occupy are not their own constructions but are historically produced. The imaginary quality of the identification with a subject position gives ideology the appearance of common sense and makes ideology such a potent force in shaping people's lives. Critical linguists incorporated Althusser's redefinition of ideology within a central claim of systemic-functional linguistics that particular discourses encode particular sets of social relations. Much more important to the critical linguistics project, however, was indirect influence of Althusser that led to the movement in British literary studies and cultural studies to consider texts as sites of ideological struggles over meaning (see Easthope).

To demonstrate a critical linguistics analysis of the contradictions in composition textbooks, I will consider a pair of writing tasks that are common in professionally oriented college writing courses: a résumé and a letter of application for a job. Nearly all business writing textbooks include these assignments. Marla Treece's *Communication for Business and the Professions* (1986) is typical of current textbooks written for such courses. The first chapter emphasizes writing with readers in mind by taking the "you-attitude," a frequent codification of this principle in business writing pedagogy. The "you-attitude" is defined as "looking at a situation from the viewpoint of the reader or listener" (21).

Communication for Business and the Professions devotes separate chapters to résumés and application letters. The chapter on résumés asks students ready to apply for a job to first analyze their qualifications:

> When you plan a sales campaign, one of your first steps is to make a product analysis. You look at the product, test it, and compare it with competing brands. You then decide on your central theme, or the most important selling feature, also called the central selling point.
>
> As you plan a job-seeking campaign, you make the same analysis about your-self. You analyze the "product," compare it with competing ones, and note how the product fits the market for which you are preparing your application. (241)

Later when the chapter turns specifically to writing the résumé, the author urges students:

> *Present your qualifications from the standpoint of how the employer will benefit from hiring you.* To do so, emphasize your experiences that seem the most advantageous to the successful handling of the job. This orientation in a résumé is another applica-tion of the you-attitude. (250)

The chapter concludes with several examples of résumés that suggest how students might present themselves. The first sample résumé begins:

REBECCA S. ROSENBERG

1472 Tutwiler Avenue   513-000-0000

Cincinnati, Ohio 45208

Objective

To obtain a position in Sales Training/Development in a business setting, prefer-ably with Electronic Data Systems Corporation, and use ability to help others in-crease sales effectiveness through personal relationships

Work Experience

October, 1980–Present. Sales Representative, Checks, Inc., 417 Constitution Square, Cincinnati, Ohio 45230

Responsible for establishing and increasing sales through direct personal contact at approximately 200 banks in northern Kentucky.

Conducted and aided cross-selling and security training programs for bank personnel in more than 30 banks. Now writing training programs for all branches of Checks, Inc.

Following the chapter on writing résumés is a chapter on writing application letters. It also advises students to "use the you-attitude in that you stress benefits for the reader" (267). Students are told to state their work experience in terms that "relate to the work for which [they] are applying" (267). Students are also told not to use the words *I, me,* and *my* to excess and to "avoid beginning several sentences with I" (267). The "you-attitude" is represented in *Communication for Business and the Professions* as conveying traditional rhetorical advice about audience and purpose.

From a critical linguistics perspective, however, we get a very different view of what the student is being urged to do. First, the language used in résumés is unusual. Agents are consistently deleted in résumé descriptions: "Maintained power control packages"; "Performed and supervised technical training of personnel"; "Completed the following Management Training Programs." The awkwardness of these phrases indicates a highly stylized genre. The writer of the Rebecca S. Rosenberg résumé states that she has an "ability to help others increase sales effectiveness through personal relationships," which might be more commonly phrased as: "Because I have sold services [the assumed product of Checks, Inc.] to people face-to-face, I have been able to show other workers how to do it as well." But in the résumé specific social actions are coded as abstract nouns such as "sales effectiveness" and "personal relationships," and a series of actions she has performed during work is coded as an "ability." Elsewhere in the chapter Treece suggests how most mundane kinds of work can be dressed up as valuable qualities. A job as a checker in a grocery store gives one "abilities" in "working harmoniously with other employees" and "courteously serving the customers."

Treece presents the shift from a verbal style with agents represented in the text to an abstract nominal style with agents absent as following the "you-attitude," the principle of writing with a reader in mind. But what reader can the writer have in mind? In most cases, writers of résumés have little sense of who will read their applications nor do they know what "subtext" a particular job announcement might contain—the unarticulated part of a job description. If in most instances the writer cannot write for a specific reader, then how does the writer decide that it is better to write "Maintained power control packages" rather than "I fixed electric motors on my last job"?

Language similar to the résumé phrases often appears in job advertisements. The same process of transforming specific experience into abstract qualities is involved in writing a job description for such ads. Fixing an electric motor when it breaks down becomes "Maintain power control packages" in the ad copy. Neither the writer of the ad nor the writer of the résumé can truly assume the you-attitude since neither is likely to know the other. Instead, résumés and job advertisements are examples of the "it-attitude." Both the résumé writer and the ad writer locate themselves within the discourse of the institution. No one says "maintain power control packages" except those who write the institution's official discourse and those who seek to identify with the institution in order to gain employment.

When students ask for help in writing application letters, they often struggle much more than the task seems to require. Their problem, I think, is the one that Treece identifies. To be a successful job hunter, Treece writes, you must analyze yourself as a "product" and "note how the product fits the market for which you are preparing your application." Consider the beginning paragraph from a letter signed by "Walter W. Williams":

> A comprehensive educational program in accounting at the University of Ha-
> waii, leading to a Bachelor of Science in Accounting degree, is an important
> qualification for beginning work in your firm. In addition, I offer competence,
> dedication, and ambition. (276)

Williams completely effaces himself in the first sentence, referring to himself as a degree in accounting. In the next sentence he adds features to the product: "competence," "dedication," and "ambition." To what these features refer is not recoverable. Williams mentions no previous experience working as an accountant, so what is he "competent" to do? Likewise, to what or whom is he "dedicated"? And what is he "ambitious" to gain or achieve? The writer chose these features because they are valued in capitalist discourse. They indicate that Williams will be both suitably aggressive and, at the same time, a "team player."

Suppressing self-reference in a letter of application, therefore, is not a matter of stylistic preference, nor is genre-specific advice ideologically innocent. Williams is subsumed by rather than the shaper of his language. In Althusser's terms, he has voluntarily assented to his subjectivity within the dominant ideology and thus has reaffirmed relations of power. By presenting himself as a commodity rather than as a person, he has not only made an initial gesture of subservience like a dog presenting its neck, but also signaled his willingness to continue to be subservient.

Foucault's Critique of Marxism

As suggestive as both traditional Marxist and critical linguistics analyses might be, they tend to become reductive by tracing all action eventually back to the relation of labor and capital. Even with allowances for the relative auton-omy of culture or "superstructure," the privileging of a single source of causa-tion eventually renders most teachers as dupes of false consciousness because they think they are acting in their own and in their students' interests when in reality they are serving the interests of the ruling class. The key assumption of Marxist theory—that a theorist can posit a center to a social formation and work outward from that center—has come under many attacks from postmodern theorists, who would deny the totalizing impulse to discover a center or an origin and who would argue instead for a plurality of radical critiques.

One of the most important of these theorists is Foucault, who rejects the central assumption of Marxist analyses that specific power relations can be deduced from the mode of production. Instead, he argues that practices and technologies of power *precede* the relations of production rather than the other way around, as traditional Marxism would have it. In *Discipline and Punish*, Foucault demonstrates that the techniques of domination in the organization of the workshop were necessary preconditions for the rise of capitalist relations of production. Foucault looks to a kind of lore for understanding power, but Foucault's lore takes shape in minute and local practices rather than in a guiding knowledge, or a House of Lore.

Foucault, like Althusser, offers an incisive critique of the liberal humanist conception of the subject as self-present, rational consciousness. Like Althusser, he notes that "there are two meanings of the word *subject*: subject to someone else by control and dependence, and tied to his own identity by a conscience or self-knowledge. Both meanings suggest a form of power which subjugates and makes subject to" ("The Subject" 212) Unlike Althusser, Foucault denies that subjectivities "are merely the consequences of other economic and social processes: forces of production, class struggle, and ideological structures which determine the form of subjectivity" ("The Subject" 213). Instead, the subject is an active site in the reproduction of discourses and social practices.

Foucault's doublet of power/knowledge is explored in *Discipline and Punish*, which, in tracing the rise of the modern prison also considers how subjectivity is constituted in discourses and practices. Foucault does not offer a single explanation for abandonment of torture as a chief means of punishment and the development of prisons as the successor to torture, but rather sees prisons as part of complex social formations and more generalized practices of disciplining individuals. These disciplinary practices would appear to be relatively minor procedures in comparison to the rituals of state power such as public torture. Their effect comes, however, in establishing ongoing economies of power rather than the sporadic exercise of power in rituals like torture. Foucault writes: "Discipline 'makes' individuals; it is the specific technique of a power that regards individuals both as objects and as instruments of its exercise" (170).

The success of disciplinary power, Foucault continues, is in its use of relatively simple instruments: observation, normalizing judgment, and their combination in the examination. One of the most effective devices of power is the examination, a "tiny operational schema" as Foucault refers to it, which has become a commonplace method of extracting knowledge in situations of teaching, hiring, applying, and curing. The examination according to Foucault "translated the economy of visibility into the exercise of power" (187). It was also a means of constituting individuals within the discourses of institutions. Individuals are transcribed onto a grid of features established in the examination, then categorized and transmitted to a central body. These procedures make every individual into a "case," one that can be compared, measured, and judged in relation to others.

Foucault's notion of power rejects a central assumption of liberal humanism: that power is located in the structure of legal authority and in resistance to that authority. Instead, power is involved in all practices; power is *productive*. Thus the result of the technologies of observation, surveillance, and record keeping is not principally the repression of the individual but the making of individuals, the literal molding of "docile bodies."[2] Foucault finds in the accumulation of files in institutions the birth of the social sciences, and here is where his pun on the notion of a *discipline* becomes most illuminating. Academic disciplines grew out of disciplines of social practices rather than directing the establishment of those practices. Furthermore, the social sciences have not broken away from minute practice but remain closely in support of certain kinds of exercise of power such as the case study. What Foucault calls the "political technology of the body" required the parallel development of a knowledge. He writes:

> We should admit rather that power produces knowledge (and not simply by encouraging it because it serves power or by applying it because it is useful); that power and knowledge directly imply one another; that there is no power relation without the correlative constitution of a field of knowledge, nor any knowledge that does not presuppose and constitute at the same time power relations. (27)

The merger of practice and discourse theorized by Foucault emphasizes the importance of language in regulating and justifying practice. The reformist discourse of criminology brought new modes of control that were less brutal than torture but more coercive because prisoners were subjected to constant scrutiny. Foucault describes in *Discipline and Punish* the introduction of Bentham's panopticon, an architectural configuration that allowed the continuous surveillance of prisoners by a single warder. The panopticon was advanced as a reform but, as is clear from Foucault's account, substituted one form of domination for another by allowing the continuous visibility of prisoners and the recording of their actions in dossiers. This technology of power was made possible and supported by a new discourse of criminology that legitimated practice.

The analysis in *Discipline and Punish* suggests that the entire society is involved in a massive apparatus of power that "normalizes" individuals. Individuals are not so much "repressed" as they are "shaped" by the technologies of power. The exercise of power, therefore, is just as much involved in the construction of the "rational" subject as it is in disciplining prisoners. By demonstrating through his genealogical method how rational subjects are historically constituted through discourses and practices, Foucault also removes the vantage point of the theorist who aspires to stand above the social formation in order to erect overarching explanations such as those of Marxism. Instead, Foucault claims he is interested in writing "the history of the present" by examining how the practices of modern institutions came to be implemented and justified (*Discipline* 35).

Purposeful Writing

Foucault continued his critique of power in his next book, the first volume of *The History of Sexuality*, which also rejects the idea that power descends from the ruling classes and is imposed repressively.[3] Instead, Foucault argues that "power comes from below; that is, there is no binary and all-encompassing opposition between rulers and ruled at the root of power relations" (94). Foucault then continues,

> Let us not look for the headquarters that presides over |power's| rationality; neither the caste which governs, nor the groups which control the state apparatus, nor those who make the important economic decisions direct the entire network of power that functions in a society (and makes it function): the rationality of power is characterized by tactics that are often quite explicit at the restricted level where they are inscribed (the local cynicism of power), tactics which, becoming connected to one another, attracting and propagating one another, but finding their base of support and their condition elsewhere, end by forming comprehensive systems: the logic is perfectly clear, the aims decipherable, and yet it is often the case that no one is there to have invented them, and few who can be said to have formulated them. (95)

Thus, for Foucault power is decentered, dispersed, discursive, and multiple in nature, and to theorize a center of power such as Marxism's mode of production, Weber's bureaucracies, and feminism's patriarchy becomes a misleading and fruitless endeavor. Foucault's microphysics of power directs our attention away from profound and deep meanings and toward surface practices.

A Foucauldian analysis gives us a very different kind of explanation of the contradictions in writing textbooks—an explanation that cannot be validated by a metanarrative such as a Marxist account of the relationships of the practices of schooling to modes of economic production. Rather we would have to proceed directly to an analysis of the practices of writing as they are set out in textbooks. In an essay written in 1982, two years before his death, Foucault discusses the power relations involved in the constitution of subjects:

> Perhaps the equivocal nature of the term *conduct* is one of the best aids for coming to terms with the specificity of power relations. For to "conduct" is at the same time to "lead" others (according to mechanisms of coercion which are, to varying degrees, strict) and a way of behaving within a more or less open field of possibilities. The exercise of power consists in guiding the possibility of conduct and putting in order the possible outcome. Basically power is less a confrontation between two adversaries or the linking of one to the other than a question of government. ("The Subject" 220–21)

Foucault's suggestions direct us toward analyzing how textbooks "conduct" students through acts of writing and at the same time set out a possible field of "conduct" for a student writer that has implications beyond the classroom.

For this investigation one textbook stands out as extraordinarily important because it has been in print continuously since 1950 and has been revised in its nine editions to reflect changes in the profession. That book is James McCrimmon's *Writing with a Purpose*, a book that Robert Connors described in 1981 as emblematic of current-traditional rhetoric in its first seven editions. With the infusion of writing as process in later editions by coauthors Joseph Trimmer and Nancy Sommers in 1984 (eighth edition) and with Trimmer as the principal author in 1988 (ninth edition), *Writing with a Purpose* has continued to be resilient, still controlling a large share of the market for rhetoric texts in first-year college writing courses. Connors makes an important point in claiming that to follow "the changes and mutations in successive editions of a popular text like McCrimmon's is to gain a clearer picture of where composition teaching has been . . . and of where it may be going" ("Current-Traditional Rhetoric" 209).

The several editions of *Writing with a Purpose* do give a valuable record of the pedagogical trajectory of composition studies. While the macrostructure of *Writing with a Purpose* remains much the same over all nine editions (two of the four parts—the handbook and special assignment sections—are in all long editions), continuous rewriting has occurred within that structure. In his analysis of the first seven editions, Connors observes a dynamic flux within *Writing with a Purpose*, but a flux that tends to return to stasis. With the seventh edition, Connors concludes that after various efforts in the earlier editions to include new developments in the field, the book "could not complete the effort, and relapsed into traditional treatments of almost everything" (215). One could extend Connors's critique to the ninth edition (1988), which includes a heavily revised part 1 on "The Writing Process," but follows in part 2 with chapter titles familiar to McCrimmon users since 1950: "Common Methods of Development" ("Patterns of Development" in 1950), "Argument," "Paragraphs: Units of Development," "Sentences: Patterns of Expression," "Diction: The Choice of Words," and "Tone and Style." Part 3, "Special Assignments" has chapters on the essay examination, the critical essay, and the research paper that have been in all editions—as has a handbook section on grammar and mechanics at the end (which began as part 2 in the 1950 edition).

The long-lived success of *Writing with a Purpose* in the fickle market for rhetoric textbooks is remarkable. What perhaps explains more than anything else its extraordinary longevity is its common-sense, no frills, "let's get down to business" approach. At the beginning of the first edition (1950), there are no appeals to the value of writing ability in subsequent college courses or in future careers. McCrimmon assumes that students know why introductory composition is required. He starts with the bare assertion, "All *effective writing is controlled by the writer's purpose*," which he briefly elaborates:

> The writer, therefore, must always begin with a clear sense of purpose. This means that before he starts to write he must give careful attention to two related questions: "What *precisely* do I want to do?" and "How can I best do it?" Answering these questions properly is the first step toward writing well. (3)

The assertion that writing begins with the writer's purpose was not revolutionary. In a history of invention in current-traditional rhetoric, Sharon Crowley observes in *The Methodical Memory* that identifying one's aim had been a starting point for invention since Campbell's *Philosophy of Rhetoric* was published in 1776 (95). McCrimmon followed the deep rut of a long traveled path.

McCrimmon's innovation was refurbishing current-traditional rhetoric to suit the prosperity of postwar America. To explain the concept of writing with a purpose, he offers an analogy with golf:

> Imagine an expert golfer on the point of attempting a twenty-foot putt on a rolling green. What is his purpose? To say that he wants to sink his putt is to describe his purpose in terms too general to be helpful. For him, the most important decision is *how* the shot should be played. There he studies the contour of the green, observes the grain and texture of the grass, and plans the course which he wants his ball to follow. Only when he has thought out his problem in this way can he be said to know what he wants to do. His precise purpose, then, is to stroke the ball in such a way that it will follow the contour of the green in

a *predetermined* path to the cup. In much the same manner a writer must try to understand what is involved in making his writing do what he wants it to do. This means, first, that he must know precisely what his purpose is and, second, that he must be aware of how particular decisions about choice of material, organization, development, style, diction, and grammar will help or hinder that purpose. (3–4)

If I can move McCrimmon's analogy off the green and out to the fairway, choosing a pattern of development is like choosing the club best for the shot and making errors in diction, usage, grammar, and mechanics is like landing in a sand trap on the way to the green. The sand traps have been large and numerous in all nine editions. Of the twenty-seven chapters in the 1950 edition, seven are on grammar and mechanics, another six are on diction, and a glossary of usage is at the end of the book. The handbook section and the glossary of usage are still present in the ninth edition (beginning in the sixth edition in 1976, a shorter edition without a handbook was also published).

But to make the critique that *Writing with a Purpose* recycles again and again the lessons of current-traditional rhetoric only confirms the proven formula of textbook publishers: in order to succeed, mix a little that is new with much that is old. After all, one can hardly expect the publisher to change radically the content of its best-selling book. Similarly, it seems hardly surprising to point out that throughout much of its history, *Writing with a Purpose* is addressed to the young men of the bourgeoisie, with women included almost as an afterthought. Writing topics directed toward women students in the 1950 edition include: "Being a good hostess"; "How to give a party"; "Be your own interior decorator"; "The importance of the right neighborhood"; "Keeping up with the movie stars"; "Marriage or career?"; "How important are social graces?" and "What do people find to talk about on a date?"[4]

Instead, I would like to focus on the aspects of *Writing with a Purpose* that have significantly changed, rather than what has remained much the same, because these changes represent what has been proclaimed as a paradigm shift in the teaching of writing. Connors reviews how process notions enter *Writing with a Purpose* in the third edition of 1963, when McCrimmon introduced the tripartite division of planning, writing, and revising.

McCrimmon was ahead of the textbook field in presenting the soon to be familiar three-stage model of composing and even ahead of the research community where Rohman and Wlecke are often credited with popularizing the stage model in a report published in 1964. But McCrimmon did not go far beyond the three-stage model in incorporating process concepts, and Connors finds in the fifth, sixth, and seventh editions a retreat toward traditionalism. Connors surmises that during the 1970s the publisher, Houghton Mifflin, became content with the place of *Writing with a Purpose* as the foremost traditional textbook and gave it a facelift in a "classic," conservative format in the seventh edition.

Apparently this strategy was not completely successful, because in the eight edition the book moved strongly in the direction of process with co-authors Joseph Trimmer and Nancy Sommers. In a foreword to the eighth edition, McCrimmon himself criticizes the earlier editions of *Writing with a Purpose*:

> Earlier editions tended to view the writing process as a linear progression—first prewriting, then writing, then rewriting—and in some editions each of these stages became a major unit of the book. However convenient this division may have been as a pedagogical device, it was certainly an oversimplification of how writers go about the process of writing. The Eighth Edition corrects this over-simplification by the concept of thinking-in-writing. . . . |Writers| do not think *and* write; they think *as* they write. (xiii)

Trimmer and Sommers in the preface describe their intent to "retain and rein-force |the| traditional features of the text," but also to "introduce and incor-porate the best of contemporary theory and practice in the teaching of writ-ing" (xiv). They describe a new part 1, "The Writing Process," as "completely new" and covering "all aspects of composing from planning through revising" (xiv). While these claims are perhaps hyperbolic, the eighth edition of *Writing with a Purpose* represents a major shift, one that is unprecedented in its history.[5]

Whereas all earlier editions begin with the student writer facing the task at hand, the eighth edition starts with a discussion of fear of writing ("Most people experience at least a mild case of nervousness—and sometimes abso-lute alarm—when they begin a writing assignment" |5|). It includes a long quota-tion from A *Moveable Feast* in which Hemingway describes how he would begin a new piece of writing. From this quotation the authors extrapolate three max-ims: (1) "*Experienced writers have faith in their writing habits*," to which the authors add that experienced writers "believe that those writing habits that have worked before—a special environment, a disciplined schedule, and familiar tools—will work again"; (2) "*Experienced writers understand the stages in the writing process*"; and (3) "*Experienced writers rely on the basic elements in any writing situation to guide them as they work*" (6–7).

In the exercise at the end of this section, students are asked to perform a self-examination of their writing habits. The questions guide students to discuss if their writing habits resemble other work habits, what kind of physi-cal environment they require to write, and what writing tools they prefer using. The remainder of the chapter offers three sections on topics familiar from earlier editions: "Selecting Your Subject," "Analyzing Your Audience," and "Deter-mining Your Purpose." In the eighth edition, however, these sections are de-veloped beyond the brief maxims of previous editions. Rather than telling students that "the choice of the real subject then establishes the focus of the paper" (seventh edition 11), the eighth edition gives a list of five questions with subordinate questions attached that interrogate the textbook user about her choice of subject. The first of these questions is typical of the others:

1. *What do I know about my subject?*
Do I know about my subject in some depth, or do I need to learn more about it? What are the sources of my knowledge—direct experience, observation, reading? How does my knowledge give me a special or unusual perspective on my subject? (17)

Similar sets of questions are offered in the other two sections that ask about potential readers and the writer's motives for writing.

This extensive elaboration of elements of an abstracted process of writing continues in the second, third, and fourth chapters on "Planning," "Drafting," and "Revising," respectively. These chapters are the most noteworthy difference between the seventh and eighth editions. The second chapter in the seventh edition, titled "Getting and Using Information," divides the process of information gathering into "Selecting Information from Experience" and "Observing the Subject." The chapter advises students: "You will often be your own best source of information" (26). But it gives no specific advice concerning how this source is to be tapped beyond a suggestion to scan your memory. Likewise, the advice on observing is offered in expository form without specific procedures to follow. The second chapter in the eighth edition, on the other hand, includes an array of tactics for accessing what writers know already. The section on "Using Memory in Writing" describes four strategies—code words, brainstorming, freewriting, and keeping a journal—and it offers examples of each strategy. For "Using Observation in Writing" the eighth edition also sets out four strategies—lookout spots, scouting, mapping, and speculating—each explained in step-by-step fashion.

The change from the seventh to the eighth editions might be characterized as a change of emphasis from the "what" to the "how" of writing in the early chapters. If we continue Connors's analysis of the first seven editions of *Writing with a Purpose* as reflecting the trajectory of the teaching of college writing, the major shift from the seventh to the eighth edition speaks to the dominance of process pedagogy in the 1980s. Without a major infusion of the lessons of process, the sales of the book likely would have dwindled such a point that it would not have been kept in print. Even Connors, who aimed in his sympathetic reading of *Writing with a Purpose* to balance the dominant attention to process pedagogy at the expense of older methods, wrote that he had come to see current-traditional rhetoric "as an ailing friend" (220). Although Connors wished to value practitioners' knowledge, including the work of textbook writers, he too assailed McCrimmon for ignoring the research of his time. Indeed, it is hard not to lapse into this narrative of process as progress, that the coming of writing as a process represented a significant advance over current-traditional writing pedagogy. Few college teachers of writing today would advocate returning to the predominantly grammar, mechanics, usage, and patterns-of-development curriculum of the 1950s.

Disciplinary Modes of Control

Yet if we can suspend briefly this narrative of process as progress and consider instead Foucault's doublet of practice and theory, then a different relation between practice and theory might be articulated from the usual claim for theory driving practice. Suspending the narrative of process as progress also gives space to explore Foucault's claim, quoted above, that "the exercise of power consists in guiding the possibility of conduct and putting in order the possible outcome." In *The History of Sexuality*, volume 1, Foucault maintains that to consider power only as repressive neglects many of the polymorphous techniques of power. Foucault insists that power is decentered. It is not a thing "that is acquired, seized, or shared, something that one holds on to or allows to slip away; power is exercised from innumerable points, in the interplay of nonegalitarian and mobile relations" (94).

While textbooks embody but a few of the many relations of power in a writing classroom, they do contain descriptions of idealized practices and codifications of power relations in specific discourses. Rhetoric textbooks such as *Writing with a Purpose* both conduct students and offer them a conduct to follow. Many of the critics of the current-traditional writing curriculum have faulted the conduct it offers, a conduct that is set out in terms of language and form. Those who have characterized current-traditional rhetoric point to the dominating influence of the modes, the division of discourse into words, sentences, and paragraphs, and an overriding emphasis on style and usage (R. Young 31). This conduct has a largely punitive orientation, as even the headings in the first edition of *Writing with a Purpose* suggest: for example, the subheadings in the "Clarity" section include "Confused Sentence Structure," "Faulty Pronoun Reference," "Misleading Word Order," and "Confusing Omissions."

But McCrimmon was also well aware that conduct is productive and that his lessons on language helped to confirm the status of a college graduate as a member of the bourgeoisie. In the first edition he defines nonstandard English as "the language of the farm, the factory, the mine, the lumber camp, the railroad, and, in general, of those occupations which do not require what we call 'higher education.'" In contrast, standard English is defined as the speech habits of those who enjoy a favored economic and social status in our society, and since this class may be roughly described as the educated class, we may say that standard English is the way that educated people speak and write. It is, therefore, the kind of English written and spoken by business executives, lawyers, doctors, ministers, teachers, writers, editors, artists, engineers, and other professional people, and, of course, *by their wives*. (229, emphasis added)

The assumption in the last sentence that the domain of the professions is exclusively male is consistent with the gendered writing assignments alluded to earlier. There is nothing troubling for McCrimmon about the social divisions marked by·language; it is as if class differences are as natural as the seasons. He starts the chapter on "Levels of Usage" with the assertion: "Everyone knows that the way people speak reflects the social and economic background from which they have come" (228). McCrimmon does not shirk the task of maintaining the fences. He admonishes students (and their teachers), "The admission that nonstandard English is satisfactory for the purposes for which it is used does not mean that standard English has no priority in the concerns of a college English class, or that nonstandard usage is defensible in college writing; . . . *nonstandard English has no place in college writing*" (230). While McCrimmon is a liberal in deferring to usage rather than holding out for an absolute standard of correctness, at the same time he grants full authority to the middle class for setting the rules.

But to focus on McCrimmon's faith in language as a means of separating the middle class from those below eases toward the deception Foucault warns against—the understanding of power as repressive and flowing downward from the top of the social hierarchy. The central argument of the two great works of Foucault's genealogical period, *Discipline and Punish* and *The History of Sexuality*, volume 1, is that power does not operate by repressing individuals but by constituting them through regimes of practices supported by specialized knowledges. McCrimmon himself takes a similar view. Of conventions of language he writes, "It may be necessary—for most freshman it usually is—to revise one's work to fit the conventions, but, like learning the mechanics of a golf stroke, that should be a preliminary discipline. It should not be ignored, but the ideal should be to make it automatic" (first edition 287). Thus performing the exercises in *Writing with a Purpose* is like going to the driving range with an expert instructor looking over your shoulder. But good habits can guarantee success only if everything can be made habitual, and one finds in all editions of *Writing with a Purpose*, as well as in other best-selling rhetoric textbooks intended for the first-year composition market, an aspiration for completeness. For major types of writing situation in college, part 4 of the first edition, "Special Assignments," gives structural templates and procedures to follow. For instance, the chapter on essay examinations gives a list of steps to follow with attached explanations: "Come Prepared"; "Come Relaxed"; "Before Beginning to Answer Any Part of the Examination, Read the Whole of It, Paying Special Attention to Directions"; "If You Are Given a Choice of Questions, Make Your Choice Carefully but Quickly, and Then Stick to It"; and so on (532–33). Just as for the golf stroke, following the step-by-step equivalents in writing of keeping the head steady, the elbow in, and the weight balanced will bring success.

The orderly steps in the first edition are not so very different from the steps for various invention heuristics that Trimmer and Sommers added in the eighth edition. The first through seventh editions start the process of writing with the anticipation of quickly honing a thesis statement. The eighth edition allows for a much longer period of discovery and supplies activities that will enhance discovery. But the conception of the student writer has not changed across editions over forty years. The subjectivity the student writer is invited to occupy is similar to the subjectivity the eighth edition posits for the ideal imagined reader: "an attentive, sensible, reasonably informed person who will give you an objective reading so long as you do not waste his or her time" (19–20).

This notion of the student writer as a rational, coherent, and unitary individual follows from the first sentence in the first edition, "All *effective writing is controlled by the writer's purpose.*" It is not an exaggeration to say that this sentence set the direction for college writing instruction in the second half of the twentieth century. While the discipline of composition studies as reflected in textbooks has made the conception of purpose more complex, it has remained an unproblematic concept in all but a few books published during the last few years.[6] The point has been made over and over again that in most writing situations the process of writing is a great deal more dynamic than the stages of prewriting, writing, and rewriting imply, yet the complexity of this dynamism is restricted to the direct operations of writing. Writing may be a messy process, but the writer is still very much in control. Writing problems may be difficult, but they are resolvable if the writer uses the right strategies.

The difficulty for students that a comprehensive rhetoric textbook such as the eighth edition presents is knowing *which* of the many strategies it presents to use on a particular occasion, especially when such strategies are not addressed to particular writing tasks or even recommended to be used in linear fashion. The way the authors of the eighth edition resolve this difficulty is to present actual or hypothetical examples of student writers who apply the advice of the book to produce essays. In chapter 1, which contains advice about "selecting your subject," "analyzing your audience," and "determining your purpose," the fast food of McDonald's is used as an example of subject matter for student papers:

> Perhaps your experience cooking or serving hamburgers last summer suggests that McDonald's might make an interesting subject. Although you know a great deal about this subject, you may find it difficult to focus your knowledge until you identify your audience. After some deliberation, you decide that you have at least three possible audiences: (1) those who love McDonald's—junk-food addicts who relish every item on the menu; (2) those who hate McDonald's— health-food addicts who despise every odor emanating from the Golden Arches; and (3) those who are indifferent to McDonald's—a group whose members have never tasted a Big Mac or have eaten one only on occasion. (20)

The authors then discuss how writing for each of these three potential audiences would shape the paper that results: "As you think about the health-food addicts, you might recall the pep talks you received from your supervisor at McDonald's about the 'all-natural' content of the food" (21). From this relatively simple heuristic of classifying potential readers, the authors generate several possibilities for a paper on McDonald's food. The example thesis that results from the heuristic is predictable: "McDonald's food inspires extreme responses of loyalty or loathing from those who eat or think about eating it" (27). This thesis locates readers according to their responses to McDonald's advertising; you either have positive associations with the images of family and a mythic traditional America or you reject these images, much as Americans did with the image of Ronald Reagan. The nutritional content of McDonald's food is hardly at issue. You either feel good eating at McDonald's or you don't. Consequently, I would expect many of the papers written from such a thesis to be filled with the language of McDonald's advertising, quoted either approvingly or sarcastically. What isn't discussed is what other kinds of papers might result from the experiences of students who have worked in the fast-food industry. The one major advantage these students have in writing on this topic is not even acknowledged with a question as simple as: "What do you know about the fast-food industry that most people don't know?"[7]

The difficulty of bringing the massive amount of material in *Writing with a Purpose* to bear on a particular task is also illustrated in the only example of a paper written in multiple drafts, a case study that appears in chapter 4 on "Revising." This case study includes four drafts based on a student's high school class trip to Washington, D.C. The first draft is a narration of the preparation for the trip, the bus ride to Washington, and what the students saw when they got there. In the "Revision Agenda" following the draft, the writer criticizes his effort. He says he has too many subjects and needs to focus on one of them. In the second draft he writes about the experience of standing in line to visit Washington Monument, talking to other tourists, squirting the girls in his group with a "greenie-meanie" squirt gun, and finally getting to the top. He criticizes this draft in the Revision Agenda for getting sidetracked when he starts talking about personal experience. He vows to make the next draft "more objective."

The third draft resembles a guidebook version of Washington Monument, with details such as how long it took to build, how much it cost, interruptions during construction, and the date of the dedication. This draft is criticized for being too dry. The fourth version includes unusual facts about the Washington Monument ("In 1966, 76-year-old Edna Rousseau made 307 round trip climbs on the 898 steps.") This time the writer says in the Revision Agenda, "I see mainly strengths" (145). What the writer apparently didn't see, however, was the chapter on "Writing the Research Paper" in whatever rhetoric textbook he was using. There is no documentation offered for where his unusual facts came from. Aside from the issue of plagiarism, the writer turns away from any possibility of reflecting on the experience of his trip. He might have asked why school groups make pilgrimages to Washington. He could have probed why his most vivid memories are those of standing in line two hours for a thirteen-second elevator ride. He could have written about how such experiences are collectively interpreted. But he does not reflect on the experience because his revision strategy of being "more objective" means repeating what others have said and written about Washington Monument.

Some of the writing assignments in *Writing with a Purpose* do suggest ways of using the strategies in the book. One in the chapter on "Planning" asks students to "investigate a center of activity in your community—a grocery store, a gas station, a bank" (ninth edition 27). The assignment asks students to free-write to determine their attitude toward the place, then to map the activity that goes on in the place, then to interview the people who work there, and finally to read a variety of material on some problem facing this place. This assignment is potentially a very rich one. It involves students in several different kinds of writing activities that could occupy most of a semester-long writing course. It requires students to confront some of the difficulties of reporting research, such as how to represent the participation of the researcher. Yet the strategies for dealing with these issues are not to be found. What students are given, then, is not a set of strategies that can be followed for every writing situation, nor even strategies that can be directly brought to bear on the writing assignments offered in the book. Instead, they are supplied with confidence in their own rationality, a confidence made visible by translating rationality into a set of prescribed behaviors.

Certainly, confidence is important for student writers, and belief that a set of procedures will be productive is one basis of confidence. Too often, however, writing textbooks close off possibilities for student writers rather than opening them. In an insightful essay, Kurt Spellmeyer uses Foucault's discussion in "The Discourse on Language" of the competing tension between *inclination* and *institution* in discourse to illustrate the dilemma of the student writer. Spellmeyer describes students as caught between the advisors of *inclination*, who would present discourse as "the paradise of self-expression," and the advisors of *institution*, who would characterize discourse as a fixed routine (717). Both are traps, according to Spellmeyer, because, as David Bartholomae discusses in "Inventing the University," *inclination* pretends that acts of discourse are acts of charity when they are often ones of aggression, while *institution* pretends that authority is gained by remaining within the boundaries of a discourse when in fact authority is often gained by expanding or transgressing those boundaries. Instead of attempting to stamp out contractions only to have them reappear in other forms, students might insert themselves into the discontinuities of a discourse. Spellmeyer argues that the many discontinuities, ruptures, and contradictions in the discourses of the academy provide students with spaces where they might insert their own discursive histories and experiences. Textbook writers could also learn much from pursuing the implications of their own contradictions.

Molding Docile Bodies

Foucault maintains that under modern disciplinary regimes of power—the regimes of schools, factories, hospitals, asylums, and prisons—those who are the least powerful become the most individualized because the least powerful are treated as "cases." This form of individuality turns the subject into the object of normalizing judgments. In the analysis above we saw in successive editions of *Writing with a Purpose* a gradual replacement of the "hard-line" approach to errors with an increasingly detailed set of prescribed behaviors for composing. A better example for investigating disciplinary technologies in writing pedagogy might be *The Saint Martin's Guide to Writing*, a book that is claimed by its authors, Rise Axelrod and Charles Cooper, to "take the best that has been thought and said in the field of rhetoric and composition and turn it to practical use" (v).[8]

Sales figures for textbooks are closely kept secrets, but there is no doubt among competing publishers that the first edition (1985) and the second edition (1988) of the *The Saint Martin's Guide* have been at or near the top in sales of rhetoric textbooks for first-year college composition courses. Unlike the process-oriented revisions of *Writing with a Purpose* in the eighth and ninth editions, which must have been constrained by the enduring loyalty of many teachers to the traditional concept of the first seven editions, the *The Saint Martin's Guide* was designed from the keel up as a book embodying process pedagogy. The authors are well qualified to deliver on their stated aim "to teach [students] to manage the writing process," and judging by the popularity of the book, college writing teachers and administrators have found their efforts a success.

"Manage" is a key concept in *The St. Martin's Guide*. In the introduction, Axelrod and Cooper announce that "greatness as a writer may be a dream that only a few of us will pursue, but we can all learn to write well enough to handle any writing situation we encounter in college or on the job" (3). The authors offer several reasons for learning to manage writing: to think better, to learn better, to communicate better, and finally and most important, to earn better:

> Your first job may not require you to write, but later advancement often depends on skill in writing letters, memos, reports, and proposals. The United States is now an "information" society, one in which the ability to organize and synthesize information and to write intelligently and effectively is even more important than it was in the past. The ability to write will continue to be a decisive factor in the careers of larger and larger numbers of people every year. (3)

Axelrod and Cooper follow their own advice by appealing to the values of their target audience. They are out to sell a product, and that product is the writing process. They promise control through effective management:

> You can learn about your own writing process and develop new skills to make the process easier to control. You can accept the fact that writing requires planning and rewriting, and give yourself the time you need to draft and revise your essays. You can expand your repertoire of writing strategies and learn what is expected of the particular kinds of writing you need to do. This book will help you to manage your writing process better. (6)

In spite of the disclaimer that they take a "descriptive, rather than prescriptive, point of view" on style and usage, Axelrod and Cooper's management style is rigidly prescriptive.[9] *The St. Martin's Guide* tells students:

> If you draft by hand, have plenty of paper and pencils or pens within reach. Be generous in supplying yourself with tools. Have a big stack of paper. Have a dozen sharpened pencils, an eraser, and a good pencil sharpener close by. (8–9)

And when it comes to format, there is one way prescribed: "Write on only one side of the page. Leave wide margins. Write on every other line or triple-space your typing" (9).

The management of the writing process is set out in part 1, "Writing Activities," where each of nine chapters poses a writing assignment, supplies example readings, and offers a "Guide to Writing" that the authors claim "will lead students through the entire process, from invention through revision and self-evaluation" (vi). The first of these chapters on "Remembering Events" is a critical one because it not only provides the model "Guide to Writing" on which the guides in the other chapters are based, but also goes a long way toward defining the subjectivity that the authors wish student writers to occupy.

The assignment for this chapter asks students to write a personal narrative: "Write an essay about a significant event in your life. Choose an event that will be engaging for readers and that will, at the same time, tell them something about you. Tell your story dramatically and vividly, giving a clear indication of its autobiographical significance" (49). Axelrod and Cooper write that "the goal of autobiography is to present yourself, to recall an event that will disclose something significant about your life. . . . You may tell it seriously or humorously. But you must tell it honestly" (19). Good essays on this topic, they repeat several times in the chapter, require significant "personal disclosure." Four of the five example narratives included in this chapter are specifically praised for their personal disclosure (three by professional writers: Russell Baker, Linda Ellerbee, and John Edgar Wideman, and one by a student, Jean Brandt). This appeal for personal disclosure seemingly threatens the rational subjectivity of a "process manager" that the book aims to produce. Among the list of possible events for the writing assignment is "any incident charged with strong emotions such as love, fear, anger, delight, jealousy, embarrassment, guilt, frustration, hurt, pride, happiness, joy" (49). Reporting such emotionally charged incidents would seem to run counter to the stance of cool rationality that *The St. Martin's Guide* privileges.

But what makes *The St. Martin's Guide* extremely effective in its own terms is that it can leave room for emotional excess because it has the means of quickly reining in those excesses. The appeal for personal disclosure is accompanied with a requirement for "emotional distance." In commenting on Russell Baker's narrative of an incident during his military flight training, Axelrod and Cooper write:

> Baker risks personal disclosure. He reveals how inept and inexperienced he was, letting us see him fail and exposing himself to ridicule. He appears to take neither his failure nor his success seriously, however. He has both in perspective. Perspective comes with emotional distance, which itself often comes with time. (35)

In summing up all the readings, the authors observe, "In addition to disclosing their remembered feelings, writers convey the event's autobiographical significance" (47). This significance is where universal experiences of humanity arise from personal experience: "In reading about the lives of others, we see something of our own lives mirrored back at us" (48).

The Guide to Writing leads students through a process to achieve the perspective that will allow them to convey the autobiographical significance in what they have written. They are asked to write about their present perspective for ten minutes and then sum up in two or three sentences the importance of the event in their lives. The last two sets of questions designed for peer reviews ask:

> 8. Now that you have analyzed the draft closely, reconsider the autobiographical significance. Does it seem perceptive? Were you surprised by any of it? Can you see any way to make the disclosure more meaningful?
> 9. Consider how the essay caused you to reflect on your own life. Was it important to you personally? If so, how? If not, how might it be made more so? (57)

If the student is told that the draft lacks autobiographical significance by peers or the teacher, then additional revision guidelines tell how to find autobiographical significance: "If you want to establish greater emotional distance, consider whether you should change your tone or add commentary. Try analyzing or evaluating the experience. Put it into a larger perspective. Look at it as if it were someone else's experience. What insight could you offer?" (58).

The student example in this chapter is "Calling Home" by Jean Brandt, a first-year college student, who writes about an experience when she was thirteen of shoplifting a 75-cent Snoopy button, getting caught, being arrested and locked up, and being forced to call her parents from jail. Axelrod and Cooper fault the Brandt essay for lacking emotional distance. They criticize her for not including her present perspective, not explaining why she stole the Snoopy button, and not telling what she learned from the experience. Axelrod and Cooper speculate, "Perhaps the reason her writing lacks insight is that Brandt still does not have sufficient emotional distance to understand the experience" (44). Although Axelrod and Cooper admit that not every autobiography should end with a moral lesson, they never mention that the significance of the experience might be contradictory nor do they discuss how she might have reflected without moralizing.

A much more difficult essay for the concept of emotional distance is "The Argument" by John Edgar Wideman, a selection from his book *Brothers and Keepers*. Axelrod and Cooper mention in introducing the selection that Wideman has "little emotional distance from his experience even after twenty years" (31). Wideman narrates an incident during his first year at the University of Pennsylvania in 1959–1960, when he was one of ten black students in a class of 1,700. Wideman was visiting one of the five other black freshmen in his dormitory room. A white student who was also in the room began challenging Wideman's preference for contemporary rhythm and blues, claiming that the authentic blues is old-time, country blues, reeling off names like Leadbelly and Big Bill Broonzy. Wideman wanted to hit him but didn't, and instead, he writes, "[I] let anger and shame and humiliation fill me to overflowing so the hate is still there, today, over twenty years later" (33). The selection ends with this paragraph:

> Why did that smartass white son of a bitch have so much power over me? Why could he confuse me, turn me inside out, make me doubt myself? Waving just a tiny fragment of truth, he could back me into a corner. Who was I? What was I? Did I really fear the truth about myself that much? Four hundred years of oppression, of lies had empowered him to use the music of my people as a weapon against me. Twenty years ago I hadn't begun to comprehend the larger forces, the ironies, the obscenities that permitted such a reversal to occur. All I had sensed was his power, the raw, crude force mocking me, diminishing me. I should have smacked him. I should have affirmed another piece of the truth he knew about me, the nigger violence. (33–34)

Axelrod and Cooper deserve praise for including a selection that forces students to confront the troubling issues of the colonization of a dominated culture, campus racism, and the discomfort black students often feel on predominantly white campuses. Yet in commenting on this essay, Axelrod and Cooper write about the last paragraph: "These questions lead us beyond Wideman's personal story, helping us to generalize from his particular experience. Indeed, autobiography should not only provide insight into one person's life but also teach us about human experience in general" (35).

What is the universal lesson to be drawn from Wideman's questions? What lesson about "human experience in general" can come from the experience of a handful of young black men and women going to school with upper-middle class whites in the late 1950s? How many white students are educated on campuses where there are only nine other white students in a class of 1,700 and then are told that the authentic white music they should be listening to is Scottish ballads? Translating Wideman's rage into a lesson on human experience in general becomes a way of avoiding his particular experience and of not seeing the pervasive racism he encountered. Allowing the students to respond, "Yes, I've been angry too, and that's a universal emotion" permits them not to examine why Wideman's anger is so debilitating, why it made him distrust his black friend whom he needed, and why he still carries that anger after many years have passed. If there is a universal lesson to be drawn from the treatment of Wideman's narrative in *The St. Martin's Guide*, perhaps it is how easily the experiences of those who are different from us can be appropriated.

Coherence and Liberal Humanism

By moving students to think of their own most emotionally charged experiences in terms of emotional distance and autobiographical significance, Axelrod and Cooper diminish the political significance of those experiences. A first draft of Jean Brandt's "Calling Home," reproduced in the "A Writer at Work" section at the end of the chapter on "Remembering Events," raises issues of justice (she is handcuffed to a table while she calls her mother) and of the function of police. The goal of finding autobiographical significance, however, leads her away from discussing political issues in the final draft. What is achieved by constructing this subjectivity becomes more evident in the later chapters in part 1 on topics such as "Reporting Information," "Proposing Solutions," "Making Evaluations," and "Speculating about Causes."

In the second edition of *The St. Martin's Guide* a chapter on argumentation, "Taking a Position," was added to replace an autobiographical chapter on "Remembering Places." The readings in the "Taking a Position" chapter concern pornography, abortion, animal rights, and journalistic and political ethics— all controversial topics and ones that would appear to contradict Richard Ohmann's assertion that composition textbooks minimize social conflict. But while *The St. Martin's Guide* encourages students to write about controversial issues, the concept of "emotional distance" moderates strong responses to these issues.

The choice of selections and the commentary on the selections, as well as the Guide to Writing, direct students that to gain credibility, they must write in "a reasonable tone." Kristin A. Goss, the writer who takes a stand against the placement of an ad in a campus newspaper that recruits women to pose nude, is criticized for using "feminist buzzwords" such as *exploitation, sexism,* and *sex object* (201). On the other hand, Axelrod and Cooper praise Albert Rosenfeld, the writer of an essay against animal rights, who uses the discourse of scientific progress ("It would be tragic indeed—when medical science is on the verge of learning so much more that is essential to our health and welfare— if already regulation-burdened and budget-crunched researchers were further hampered" |191|). The commentary that follows Rosenfeld's essay begins:

> Writers of position papers attempt to establish their credibility by the way that they present their argument, in particular by the tone they adopt. Rosenfeld tries to present the issue neutrally, giving the impression that he is objective. This *appearance* of objectivity is basic to this argumentative strategy: to make his readers think he is uninvolved and, therefore, more likely to be right. (192–93, emphasis added)

At no point in this commentary or in the commentaries on other essays is there a discussion of whose interests are at stake in a particular conflict, and seldom is there discussion of how the language the writers use is related to those interests—for example, "Medical science is on the verge of learning so much more that is essential to our health and welfare."[10] Instead, the lesson of this essay, as for other essays, is: "As a writer of position papers, you too should also try to establish your credibility with readers" (193).

Presumably the one topic that is least amenable to a "reasonable tone" is abortion, but Axelrod and Cooper find a writer who argues both sides. Rachel Richardson Smith takes a very unusual position on this issue: "I find myself in the awkward position of being both anti-abortion and pro-choice" (186). Axelrod and Cooper praise the writer for "establishing a bond of shared feelings and values between herself and her audience" and at the same time presenting "herself as an independent thinker by criticizing both camps" (188). In the Guide for Writing, students are urged to look for common ground and to respect the views of their opponents, even in cases such as the debate over abortion where the opposing views are hardly reconcilable.[11]

This assumption that some bedrock of common human values underlies any dispute works against understanding conflicts of interests as a source of political resistance, but Axelrod and Cooper are not concerned with finding the bedrock version of liberal humanism for the resolution of all conflict. What is important is not the discovery of an underlying rationality but the presentation of the self as reasonable, authoritative, and objective. Textual coherence is privileged because it reduces conflict to a matter of textual tensions. Even the most irresolvable tensions—those of pro-life versus pro-choice proponents —can be resolved by harmonious balance and a reasonable tone of voice. Thus the fundamental lesson on argumentation in *The St. Martin's Guide* is that an ounce of image is worth a pound of substance.

The coherent textual unity that reflects liberal consensus, however, is possible only as long as the *author*-ity of the author as a rational, knowing subject is maintained. The critical question in what is described as an era of postmodernity is whether the rational subject continues to exist outside the classroom as an important social construct, especially since so much communication is electronically mediated. Mark Poster argues that electronically mediated communication disrupts the interpretative basis of the rational subject. He claims, "To the extent that the mode of information constitutes a variety of multiple, dispersed, decentered, unstable subjects which contest the culture of identity, a new political terrain may be mapped" (138). In the next chapter I explore the implications of Poster's claim for the teaching of writing.

6

The Achieved Utopia of the Networked Classroom

DON DELILLO'S 1985 novel, *White Noise*, begins with a line of shining station wagons arriving at a college campus for the start of fall semester, depositing their contents of bicycles, stereos, radios, personal computers, cartons of records and tapes, refrigerators, hair dryers, sports equipment, and shopping bags full of junk food. The narrator of the novel, Jack Gladney, notes the satisfaction in the faces of the parents at "seeing images of themselves in every direction"–the women "crisp and alert, in diet trim, knowing people's names," the men "accomplished in parenthood, something about them suggesting massive insurance coverage" (3). But Gladney's response to this fall ritual is not so much of distanced amusement as it is of emptiness. Gladney is professor and founder of Hitler studies, a unit housed in a building with the popular culture department ("known officially as American environments" [9]), where Gladney's colleague, Murray Siskind, envies his success and aspires to raise Elvis to comparable status.

White Noise is about a technologically transformed America with "white noise" as its soundtrack–the continuous deluge of words, pictures, numbers, facts, graphics, and statistics, punctuated by clips of disasters, "floods, earthquakes, mudslides, erupting volcanoes," that leave viewers eager for more, "for something bigger, grander, more sweeping" (64). In the culture of the simulacrum where image has superseded reality, Hitler has become simply another figure from popular culture, a man in a military uniform who drew large crowds. The pace of change in this society is unrelenting, leaving even college students behind like discarded styles. Murray Siskind tells his students,

> "Kids are a true universal. But you're well beyond that, already beginning to drift, to feel estranged from the products you consume. Who are they designed for? What is your place in the marketing scheme? Once you're out of school, it is only a matter of time before you experience the vast loneliness and dissatisfaction of consumers who have lost their group identity." (50)

163

DeLillo depicts a society where consumption is not only the center of life but where objects and signs have merged, where one's identity is constituted by objects, where machines speak in a "language of waves and radiation" in a world beyond ours, where holographic scanners that infallibly decode the data from each item in the supermarket checkout line are the interface between the dead and the living. The "primal force" in this society is television: "Sealed-off, timeless, self-contained, self-referring." Murray Siskind enthusiastically proclaims, "It's like a myth being born right there in our living room, like something we know in a dreamlike and preconscious way. . . . The medium practically overflows with sacred formulas if we can remember how to respond innocently." The jingles for Murray are the religious chants and mantras of today: "*Coke is it, Coke is it, Coke is it*" (51).

The world of *White Noise* is one that others have characterized as postmodern. In *America*, Jean Baudrillard describes the United States as the center of what he calls "hyperreality," a condition where images, signs, and codes no longer represent reality but in effect constitute reality, becoming "more real than real." In hyperreal America simulations become the substance not only of fashion, food, cosmetics, furniture, and architecture, but also of economics, politics, and other domains of the social. Baudrillard writes,

> everything is destined to reappear as simulation. Landscapes as photography, women as the sexual scenario, thoughts as writing, terrorism as fashion and the media, events as television. Things seem only to exist by virtue of this strange destiny. You wonder whether the world itself isn't just here to serve as advertising copy in some other world. (*America* 32)

The characters in *White Noise* travel within this vision of America. Early in the novel Jack takes Murray to see "THE MOST PHOTOGRAPHED BARN IN AMERICA," to which Murray responds in Walker Percy–like fashion: "No one sees the barn. . . . Once you've seen the signs about the barn, it becomes impossible to see the barn" (12). Later when a toxic cloud escapes from a ruptured tank car, the forced evacuation of the town where Gladney lives is used as a substitute for a scheduled practice evacuation. When Gladney asks an official how the evacuation is going, the man replies: "There's a probability excess. Plus which we don't have our victims laid out where we'd want them if this was an actual simulation. In other words we're forced to take our victims as we find them" (139).

The inability to distinguish simulations from reality takes on the dimensions of metaphysical critique by the end of the book. Wounded in a bungled attempt to murder his wife's ex-lover, Gladney wanders into a Catholic hospital in a derelict neighborhood and begins quizzing the nun who is treating him about her belief in heaven. She answers him sharply, "Do you think we are stupid?" (317). She then lectures him that a nun's life is to pretend to believe so that others would believe that someone still believes. "Hell," she tells him, "is when no one believes" (319).

Some commentators on recent literature and culture assert that DeLillo in *White Noise* and in other novels presents the depthlessness of postmodernity through the experience of life as spectacle with nothing real but the orgy of promiscuous images and runaway technology, an era of radical superficiality where commodities form a language of signification and where we are so saturated by simulations that meaning has evaporated. One of the questions I pose in this chapter is that if we have indeed entered the era of postmodernity, then why has there been so little change evident in the classroom conditions for teaching college writing? I am not discounting changes brought by the process movement, the spread of collaborative learning, and other trends, nor am I pretending that these developments are not related to changes in the larger society. But these developments are from a teacher's perspective.

I introduce in chapters 4 and 5 Foucault's analysis of disciplinary technologies to show how the practices of composition teaching, whether called current-traditional or process-oriented, are involved in the production of rational subjects and are an exercise of disciplinary power. The question I raise in this chapter is what might happen if we were to disrupt standard classroom practice and introduce new forms of written discourse? Would it be more difficult to preserve the rational, autonomous subject? We can now ask this "what if" question because different groups of writing researchers have brought new forms of writing to the classroom through the use of electronic written discussions on networked computers and the use of nonsequential writing known as *hypertext*.

The possibility that changing technologies for writing might reveal changes in our students is almost as radical a suggestion as the possibility of a major cultural transformation in our own lifetime. In literary studies, composition studies, and rhetoric, as John Slatin has observed, scholars for the most part have been indifferent to technology. Extended arguments over the impact of technologies on writing have been displaced to the effect of literacy on classical Greece. Because the involvement of technology in writing has been occluded, until very recently discussions of the impacts of using computers for writing have tended to be limited to the familiar topics of research on composing—for example, do computers encourage more revisions?

It has only been with the advent of hypertext, which exists only on a computer, and programs that allow written discussions, enabling all students in a class to "talk" at the same time, that previously unimagined impacts of computers for writing have come to be appreciated. These technologies suggest a very different role for computers in a writing classroom. Rather than extending existing typewriter and printing press technologies, computer technologies for writing have created new possibilities for writing and for the teaching of writing. An even more challenging thesis can be raised from discussions of postmodernity. Instead of a scenario of technological determinism where computers are changing radically how we think and how we teach writing, perhaps radical changes in our thinking are embodied in the software for hypertext and electronic written discussions and in the ways writing might be taught using hypertext and electronic written discussions.

In spite of the many grandiose predictions concerning the effects of computers on the future of education, computers have come quietly to the teaching of writing. Many students acquired or gained access to personal computers during the 1980s, and they discovered what nearly everyone else who uses computers for writing has discovered—that computers make the physical act of writing a great deal easier because they eliminate retranscribing when a text is changed, they allow various manipulations of texts such as cutting and pasting from one text to another, and they are capable of producing printed texts of high quality. But if technical advances made possible by computers were found highly desirable, they were not thought of as revolutionary, in part because they seem to fit hand in glove with the process movement. Because of the ease of producing and changing texts, word processing programs encourage students to relax while writing, and they facilitate writing pedagogy that requires successive revisions. These kinds of activities, however, do not radically alter the nature of a writing class, which is one reason why scholarship on computers and writing has remained, in the words of the editors of *Computers and Composition*, "on the margin of English studies" (Hawisher and Selfe). As one colleague put it, "I never sang hallelujahs about my Smith-Corona; why should I get excited about my IBM PC?"

Another reason scholarship on computers and writing has remained on the margins is that when teachers at various levels have used computers for instruction, all too often they have been employed as "electronic workbooks," serving up a drills-and-skills curriculum in prepackaged modules. For those who advocate curricula-by-objectives, the belief that students learn best if they are given bite-sized chunks of knowledge one at a time, the computer replaces the weak link in the delivery system: the teacher. In the view of the architects of curricula-by-objectives, computers are "teacher proof" because they deliver exactly the same lesson as long as the electricity is on and students are in front of the screen. Such uses of computers have perpetuated earlier stereotypes of computers in education as reductive, antihumanistic, and tools for domination.

But computer technologies used for teaching writing have now diversified to the degree that broad generalizations are no longer possible. These technologies now make it possible for a writing class to communicate electronically on networks, and using networked computers to teach writing can change the nature of a writing class. One of the authors of the software for networked writing classrooms, Trent Batson, sees networked computers as creating "entirely new pedagogical dynamics" (32). While these technologies do not bring about a technological determinism, claims such as Batson's are not exaggerated.[1] By allowing everyone to "talk" at once, the use of networked computers for teaching writing represents for some teachers the realization of the "student-centered" classroom. The utopian dream of an equitable sharing of classroom authority, at least during the duration of a class discussion, has been achieved.

In this chapter I describe my experiences with the achieved utopia of the student-centered classroom made possible by networked computers. I discuss classes from two different semesters of a lower-division elective writing course that I teach regularly at the University of Texas using networked computers. The first writing class I taught using networked computers in spring 1988 led me to draw conclusions similar to those of other computer-writing teachers and researchers, who have advanced, as Hawisher and Selfe observe, "a reformist vision of computer-supported classrooms—one in which students are active, engaged, central, and one in which technology is helping teachers address racism, sexism, inequitable access to education and other disturbing social/political problems now operative in our educational system" (8).

As I have continued to use networked computers over several semesters for different undergraduate and graduate courses, however, I have come to bracket my conclusions about the first class. Subsequent experiences have problematized the concept of a student-centered classroom and have suggested that discussions of postmodernity have some bearing on our present circumstances for teaching writing. Perhaps Jean Baudrillard's epigram for *America*, taken from a car mirror, is appropriate for this chapter as well: "Caution: Objects in this mirror may be closer than they appear!"

Electronic Written Discussions

Networked computers are now used to allow students to communicate with each other in two ways. The first approach is to use some version of electronic mail. Electronic mail makes communication possible outside of scheduled class times and across great distances, allowing students at remote locations to participate in a class discussion. This approach does not require computers for every student nor does it require that computers even be located in the writing classroom. The second approach is far more computer-intensive. It requires that each student in a class have access to a computer configured in a network so that class discussions can be conducted in writing during class time. Two conferencing software programs have been written and extensively tested for such classes: *Realtime Writer*, which is part of the ENFI software developed at Gallaudet University, and *InterChange*, developed at the University of Texas by members of the Daedalus Group.[2] These programs have spread quickly across campuses in large part because students are enthusiastic about using them.[3]

The English Department at Texas has offered both literature and writing classes taught either exclusively or in part in the computer classroom of the department's Computer Research Laboratory. At the time these classes were taught, the classroom was equipped with twenty-four online IBM personal computers linked in a token ring network, which makes possible both approaches to networked communication as well as allowing students to use computers for more usual activities of composing and revising.[4] *InterChange* has drawn the most attention because of the copiousness and intensity of discussions. Students see an ongoing list of messages sent by everyone in the class, scrolling upward on their screens as they are posted. When students decide to contribute to the discussion, the software permits them to introduce with one key stroke a "message" window on which they can compose. Another key stroke allows them to "send" that message, which then appears at end of the list of messages on the screens of all the students in the class. The result is a hybrid form of discourse, something between oral and written, where the conventions of turn-taking and topical coherence are altered. Another difference from oral discussion is that students can move back and forth in the emerging transcript to check what was "said" earlier. Students as well as teachers can obtain a printed copy of the transcript at the end of class, which gives everyone an opportunity to reread and interpret the entire discussion.

The Thinking and Writing Class: Spring 1988

Thinking and Writing is an elective writing course at Texas that has a lower-division number, but typically enrolls sophomores, juniors, and seniors, many of whom are fulfilling a university "substantial writing component" course requirement. Different sections of the course have different content, and the emphasis in my classes has been to engage students in the practices of academic writing using popular culture as a general subject matter. In spring 1988 we met three days out of four in the computer classroom, holding an informal class in a nearby lounge every fourth day to keep in mind the faces that went with the names that flashed across the screen. We used InterChange half the time we were in the computer classroom. On other days students worked on group assignments, conducted peer reviews using electronic mail, and composed draft essays for the course. The class from which the following transcript is taken occurred midway through the semester and was connected to an assignment that asked students to write a microethnography. For this class, students read as an example of an ethnography *The Cocktail Waitress* by James Spradley and Brenda Mann. Earlier they had read and discussed Clifford Geertz's "Deep Play: Notes on the Balinese Cockfight" and chapters from Spradley's *Participant Observation*, a guide for writers of ethnographies.

The transcript represents what appeared on the students' screens. Attending the class were twenty-one (seventeen women and four men) of the twenty-two students enrolled in the course (the absent student was a woman). The unusually high number of women in the course, as far as I was able to determine, was one of those accidents of chance that occur in large state universities. (There were also a disproportionate number of majors in education. Apparently an adviser in education, where women majors greatly outnumber men, had suggested that students take my class.) I also invited a visitor to attend this particular class: JoAnn Campbell, who at that time was a graduate student teaching the same course using the same texts in a conventional classroom. When we had used InterChange before, we had used the standard option, which lists each message under the name which the student uses to log in. For this class we tried for the first and only time a pseudonym option available in the program. The first 87 messages of a 191-message transcript are reproduced below. This segment was produced in about twenty minutes.

The first message refers to a paragraph on page 23 of *The Cocktail Waitress*. Here is the relevant section:

Holly

At times, some of the girls sensed it vaguely. But for Holly, the mixture of feelings was always there, sometimes clear and intense, other times beneath the surface. Working at Brady's made her feel more like a woman and less like a woman than anything she had ever experienced. And these conflicting emotions were often simultaneous, causing her to both question and accept the identity of "Brady Girl."

Brady's Bar was a man's world and being part of it brought an excitement all its own. You dressed for the men, served drinks to the men, laughed at jokes told by men, got tips and compliments from men, ran errands for men. Men called you sweetie and honey and sexy. Men asked you out, and men made passes. . . . And as you left after work, Mark or another bartender would give you a loving pat—and tell you how much you were appreciated. It was a good feeling to be needed.

Before they entered the program, each student selected a pseudonym. My messages and JoAnn Campbell's messages appear under our names.[5] One student, Greg Harvey, also elected to use his name rather than a pseudonym. The message numbers were added later for the purpose of this discussion, but the errors remain uncorrected. By this point in the semester, most students valued speed over correctness.

March 24, 1988

1. *Lester Faigley*:
   I'd like you to take a look at a paragraph on p. 23 in the middle. It starts out "Brady's Bar was a man's world . . ." Who do you think wrote this paragraph? James Spradley or Brenda Mann?

2. *JoAnn*:
   I'm concerned about the relationship among the waitresses. Spradley writes that there's only a thin veneer of solidarity. And of course the antagonism between them and the female customers is really evident. So how do women join together and work for change?

3. *President Reagen*:
   Well, I guess you're all wondering why I called you here today! Well, I'm not real sure either so we'll have to see how it goes.

4. *Art*:
   This paragraph was definitely from a woman's point of view. I think that the paragraph has a lot of truths in it though.

5. *A. Hitler*:
   Brenda Mann must have said this, unless James Spradley likes getting called sweetie and honey by men.

6. *Lester Faigley*:
   Yeah, JoAnn, I just read an article about how female bartenders in Britain don't like to serve female customers. Why is this? Is it just because women don't tip well, as is mentioned on p. 142? Or is there more to it?

7. *Karen*:
   I think James Spradley probably wrote this paragraph. I can't see that a woman could possibly have written about "feeling needed" in that way.

8. *t.c.*:
   Probably, Brenda wrote the paragraph because only the cocktail waitress herself knows how much the men are a part of her world.

9. *JoAnn*:
   I would guess Spradley wrote it, just because he's talking about the excitement, and I would think Mann (ironic sort of name isn't it?) wouldn't have written the last line in the paragraph: it was a good feeling to be needed. What about the sentence saying she felt more like a woman and less like one? Are men doing the defining here?

10. *angel*:
    I don't think Brenda Mann wrote the paragraph. I don't think that the waitresses

felt that the bartenders gave them "loving pats". Also I think that the paragraph might have been a little more negative and a little less about the role of men.

11. *Mickey:*

    Truthfully, it is hard to tell. I can see points for either side.

12. *jimmy:*

    Brenda Mann probably wrote the paragraph because it seems like it's from a woman's point of view.

13. *Kenny g:*

    Most women usually need a common interest to get things started. In the outside world they come together by common desire for equal wages, credit in the job market, and all other issues that affect all women. I became involved in a ERA argument. I am not even a avid supporter. But, I joined the fight w/ another girl because we were both being attacked.

14. *xerxes:*

    I agree Karen. The statement about "feeling needed" bothered me, too. I mean feeling needed is one thing, but feeling used is quite another.

15. *jane doe:*

    I think that Spradley wrote this with a bit of a sarcastic tone.

16. *LSP:*

    I think Brenda Mann wrote it, or at least said it in an interview.

17. *Rae:*

    Brenda Mann probably wrote this paragraph because there is constant reference to "you" which makes it seem in this context from a woman.

18. *Gordon Sumner:*

    I think it was written by Spradley, he makes it sound like the waitresses'liked being treated in this manner.

19. *Lester Faigley:*

    I really don't know who wrote it. This is the third time I read COCKTAIL WAITRESS, and I started thinking more this time about how it was written. I had assumed that Brenda Mann probably wrote this part since she knew these women, but that last line is something else.

20. *President Reagen:*

    Well, I think that Brenda Mann would have written this paragraph because it seems to be from a womans point of view. I think that some women who work as cocktail waitresses like the way that all of the customers make them feel needed in a sense. I think this paragraph is simply stating how some waitresses like to be appreciated, as does everyone.

21. *George Strait:*

    I think Brenda wrote the paragraph because it describes what men do to waitresses in bars. I doubt these men were doing this to other men.

22. *JoAnn:*

    Does anybody blame the waitresses for their condition? Why didn't they protest more? Seems to me some things just wouldn't be said today, but I may be optimistic or naive. Has the accepted kind of discourse changed significantly in fifteen years?

23. *Karen:*
    JoAnn, I think that a man is defining this. Maybe it's just me but I can't see a women placing herself in such a subordinate and demeaning way. Just the way he describes about the things they do makes it sound like they absolutely live for the male approval. Yuck!

24. *Mickey:*
    Good point Rae. But then I can also see a male saying something about bring-ing "an excitement all its own." Then again only a women would know that she has been called sweetie, honey, and sexy. But yet, the loving pat part seems to come from a man because a women would not look at it this way.

25. *Lester Faigley:*
    We talked about how much things had changed in the last class, and several people said not that much.

26. *t.c.:*
    It really depends on your state of mind. Some women would not find this type of behavior offensive. I think that some women really do feel needed in this type of situation.

27. *Kenny g.:*
    I believe that Spradley wrote it because it offers stereotyp|ical| feelings about how a woman would feel being harassed. I think most women would react stronger than the author portrayed.

28. *Art:*
    I think that it probably could have been written by either. The point of view that they are expressing is fairly common in a way. I think in a sarcastic way the author is saying that girls like to be thought of as attractive and needed, but the tone here expresses that in a bar scene it is an exaggeration of what happens in real life.

29. *A. Hitler:*
    I agree with Ron Reagan—even though the "loving" pats and nicknames "sweetie and honey" are very sexist, it is attention nevertheless.

30. *jane doe:*
    In reference to the sentence about feeling more like a woman and less like a woman is a very strong sentence. It relays two different ideas about working in a bar. When you feel like a woman it's probably because of all the attention you get, but at the same time all this attention may seem confusing. The woman may begin to feel like an object.

31. *LSP:*
    Maybe these women like the way the men treat them. There are people out there who have to find other ways of being needed. It does sound as if women are putting themselves in demeaning positions, but maybe it's true. I don't know.

32. *Megan:*
    I blame the waitresses at least in part for their condition because they were far too passive if they didn't like the way they were treated. I guess perhaps they didn't protest more because they didn't want to lose their jobs, but I don't think that very many women today would work under those conditions.

33. *President Reagan:*

    Well, Karen, I think that I will have to disagree on the statement that you made about women dressing to please the male population. I don't believe the waitresses dress the way they do to please men, but to simply get better tips by looking good.

34. *JoAnn:*

    The notion of the object seems important, and I think is a real part of the antagonism between waitress and female customer. If these women are treated this way because they are women, and not because they are Holly and Sharon, then it's real threatening when other women enter the domain. After all, you can be exchanged just like, that.

35. *Lester Faigley:*

    I like the point you make, jane doe, that women become like objects. Spradley and Mann talk about this briefly on page 10.

36. *angel:*

    I think things have changed. Certainly no one or not many people react to someone being a cocktail waitress in the same manner that the women in this piece said that their friends and relatives reacted.

37. *JoAnn:*

    Hey, Pres. Reagan, who is giving the tips?

38. *Gordon Sumner:*

    Things have changed. Women don't like being called "girls" anymore. Just as you wouldn't call a man "boy". Of course it still happens. You still get jerks in bars that want more than a drink and end up making complete asses of themselves.

39. *Karen:*

    I was just referring to the paragraph. Whoever wrote it is the one who said that they dressed for the men.

40. *A. Hitler:*

    I think the women, divided for some reason, were afraid to protest their conditions individually for fear of being fired.

41. *fred:*

    I think the waitress is partially at blame in her situation. She could protest this environment if the waitresses banded together. It seems that the waitresses acted this way to define their femininity, just as the men wanted to show their masculinity. The women work at the bar because they cannot express their feminity in their situations such as school and other jobs.

42. *jimmy:*

    I agree with what t.c. said about some women actually enjoying this kind of male behavior. There are probably some women who are cocktail waitresses as well as hundreds of other jobs that have never gotten so much attention in their life. These women may be fewer, but who really knows? I see it as running along the same lines as this situation: a girl jogging gets whistled at four times. She feels complemented and flattered. The same thing happens to another girl and she is repulsed and embarrassed.

43. *Kenny g:*
    Megan, you need to go to a convention sometime. Watch how alot of the men grope their waitresses after a few drinks. Women are not much better.

44. *Mickey Mouse:*
    I agree with Megan on it being their fault. If they could change their attitude and were not afraid to stray from the norm, I think they could get a little more respect.

45. *LSP:*
    I agree with Old Pres. I think the waitresses probably make themselves to look good to get better tips. That's different from dressing up to impress your boy-friend or girlfriend.

46. *xerxes:*
    I think the waitresses dress the way they do because the person in charge gives them certain dress codes. Also, if they complain too much to the men they serve they are in danger of losing their tips and possibly their jobs.

47. *Art:*
    The waitress is not just putting up with a situation, she is working to make money. I don't think the bar scene is much different now than it used to be. People just don't always see the things that happen to a cocktail waitress when she is working.

48. *t.c.:*
    Megan, the waitress has to put up with a lot. If she protested each time that she was called "sweetie" or "honey", she would quickly lose money and maybe her job. Sometimes, the waitress doesn't like her treatment, but she seldom complains if she is a good waitress.

49. *President Reagan:*
    Well, as the real President Reagan would say, I am not able to answer that question at this time.

50. *fred:*
    Why do men achieve male solidarity in the bar, while the waitresses remain divided?

51. *JoAnn:*
    Mickey Mouse, you say they could change their attitude and get more respect, but how is that done? If this is the norm, if this is the way we see women respond on tv, in movies and books, where do we get a new norm? how do we adopt a new attitude when the power is in the hands of men?

52. *Gordon Sumner:*
    You have to remember that it is a job requirement to dress in a certain fash-ion, and an occupational hazard to be bothered by drunken men. They can always quit if they don't want to put up with it.

53. *Lester Faigley:*
    Good point, fred.

54. *kenny g:*
    xerxes has a good point. IF the waitress says anything to her customer or

her boss she/he runs the risk of loosing money. The reason most people are in this line of work is for the money.

55. *George Strait*:

Mr. President, do you not know the answer or are you just covering up?

56. *Mickey*:

I agree Pres. I'm sure the waitresses do dress for the men because that is where they get their tips. Part of the responsibility of being a "good" waitress is that you have to put up with these snide remarks. Maybe if women were the patrons then the male waiters would have to put up with them.

57. *Mickey Mouse*:

Waitresses are not the only ones who have to put up with being called things such as "sweetie" and "honey." I work in an office where the women secretaries are called these sorts of names by the older (and higher status) men. They have to put up with it also, because if they don't they will get on these people's bad side real fast.

58. *Lester Faigley*:

Mickey, you get at what Spradley and Mann call the asymmetrical relationship. Men can get away with referring to women's bodies as "two fried eggs thrown against the wall," but women can't come back at the men.

59. *Gordon Sumner*:

Good point JoAnn, things can't change overnight.

60. *Rae*:

Maybe the cocktail waitress could change her behavior, dress etc . . . and maybe she couldn't. It is almost impossible for us to determine this unless we were actually there or have had sufficient experience in this area. A comment was made somewhere in this ethnography that the waitresses had to learn to take the bartenders and men's jokes and comments or it would be very difficult for them. I don't think this meant they would be fired, but it would just make their job a little easier. This is true today. Everyone at some time or another has to put up with something that they would rather not, but most of the time it is easier to cope with if you go along with it rather than fight it. Perhaps this is what the cocktail waitresses were doing.

61. *xerxes*:

JoAnn, yes! The role of women in this society is laid out on t.v. in magazines—everywhere, and the role that is prescribed is not a good one. But, if enough women realize that to look like a fashion model and to please men is not where it's at eventually some radical changes will happen.

62. *Karen*:

Women see themselves as objects (some women anyway) and then society keeps assuring them that this is true. Advertisments are the worst. Commercials either portray women as housewives with rollers in their hair and screaming kids or as glamour type fashion models that very few people could actually look like with the products they try to sell.

63. *Dolly Wolly*:

I think that some waitresses feel flattered by these type of compliments while others feel insulted. It all depends on your self concept of yourself in relationship to others. Some women are afraid to give a guy a dirty look when they don't like something he said because they don't want to appear cold and unfriendly.

64. *jimmy:*
There is no easy answer to how women should become more equal to men, it is going to happen gradually. Change doesn't happen overnight.

65. *angel:*
Gordon, it's easy to say "just quit" but it's not easy to do when you need the money.

66. *LSP:*
I think that if the women don't want to put up with the men they should find another line of work or wait tables in a different setting. I know alot of women don't like the way the men treat them, but what about the men who get tormented by a bunch of drunk women and strip joints. They could be dancing and taking their clothes off just for the money too, yet you never hear much about them complaining about the harassment because they are getting tips put into their G-strings.

67. *JoAnn:*
Gordon, I'm a little troubled by your comment, for I don't think my point was that things can't change overnight, although that seems often to be the case. But why is it just up to the women to risk their employment and earning power to get change? When will men join them and work toward this?

68. *Kenny g:*
What about a group of girls who go to a bar and sit their eyeing every guy who walks in. Isn't this the same treatment. Men do it. But, I think that it doesn't stand out as much because it is normal to see them do it. this same group of girls, is likely to get some unfavorable propositions from the male patrons because of their aggressive behavior.

69. *Mickey:*
Basically, I think it is just who ever is at the bottom end of the totem pole has to put up with everyone else. It just so happens that the waitresses are below the customers and the waitresses are female while the customers are male. Can anyone come up with an example of where women are above men on the totem pole?

70. *t.c.:*
Fred, actually the cocktail waitresses band together. When a certain customer walks in that has been a problem in the past, all the waitresses sypathize with the one whose section he ends up in. There is some solidarity among the waitresses themselves.

71. *Greg Harvey:*
I think as far as calling women's bodies names and patting their butts, that it seems to be the way we have been educated in our society to act and ERA or not that social conditioning will take a long time to change.

72. *Gordon Sumner:*

JoAnn, what man do you know that will help in giving away some of his power?

73. *President Reagen:*

Well, I myself being a waiter, the type of waiter who serves in banquets and parties where alcohol is served alot, I can turn this point around to show my view. When I said the waitresses dress as they do for more money, I think all of us can see how that is true. But as far as the remarks go, I have recieved a few remarks myself from women at parties who had a few too many drinks. So I don't feel that only women are the only ones who feel this way some times.

74. *xerxes:*

LSP, there will always be small instances where reverse discrimination occurs, but really can we justify everything by saying it happens to a few men as well?

75. *Art:*

I think a lot of waitresses band together because they can all relate to the same types of experiences. tc is right, they do sympathize with each other and help each other out in a bad situation.

76. *Karen:*

Good point, xerxes!

77. *Lester Faigley:*

Yes, pres, but isn't it a lot more institutionalized for men to grab women and make remarks about their bodies? Isn't is always a little surprising when it happens the other way around?

78. *Karen:*

The waitresses may band together but there is still that division between the waitresses and the female customer.

79. *JoAnn:*

Gordon, good question, and so power is the issue. What we need is a structure that doesn't make power so appealing, that brings responsibility with it, that mandates the sharing of it.

80. *LSP:*

There are more than a few places. Pres. Reagan said that he gets remarks from women who have had a few drinks and he's a waiter that works banquets and stuff like that. I'm not saying that male discrimination is more prevalent than female discrimination, but it does exist and you don't hear about it as much. What about the things male nurses go through, or male secretaries. It's out there.

81. *jane doe:*

It is very doubtful that a man will put aside his pride or shall I call it a "macho ego" to help women gain any power because men like where they have women: right under the palm of thier hand.

82. *Lester Faigley:*

Yeah, Karen, take a look at p. 81. A waitress says, "I hate every one of them [the women]."

83. *Art:*

The point being that when men make comments about women, and grab at them it is almost accepted by most people as normal, but when a woman makes comments to a man she is considered loose.

84. A. *Hitler*:
Correct, Lester. It is socially accepted for a man to grab a woman's butt or make a remark towards her, but if the roles are reversed people think the woman is drunk or crazy or a whore.

85. *President Reagen*:
Yes I guess it is a little surprising, and nice I might add! But I just wanted everyone to realize that women are not so morally above men that they are not capable of doing the same thing!!!!!

86. *t.c.*:
Dr. Faigley, the difference in men behaving like jerks and women doing it is that men can get away with it and are even encouraged by their friends. However, when women behave this way, they are brazen and too forward and often labled as sluts.

87. *Mickey*:
Wait a minute Hitler! Who said it was socially acceptable to grab a woman's butt? It may be socially acceptable for men but it's not for women.

This pseudonymous networked discussion was not markedly different from other occasions when students sent messages using their own names. I had heard reports coming from the campuses where ENFI software was being used that students often used profanity and wandered off the topic in electronic discussions, but no discourse of this sort had occurred in this course.[6] I was also aware of the "flaming" phenomenon on electronic bulletin boards, where writers often express anger in hyperbolic and vituperative fashion. I thought if I would see profanity and flaming, it would come when we used pseudonyms, but it did not happen in this class.

While this transcript may appear fragmented, especially if you have not seen transcripts of electronic written discussions before, there are identifiable lines of coherence that run through it. It begins with two bids for topics by Lester and JoAnn, and most of messages 4 through 20 come in response to Lester's question about the paragraph from *The Cocktail Waitress* in message 1. JoAnn's focus in message 9 on a sentence from the same paragraph ("she felt more like a woman and less like one") also draws comments in the early going, especially from Karen (23) and jane doe (30). JoAnn's questions in 22 direct the discussion more specifically to the waitresses' responsibility for their working conditions ("Does anybody blame the waitresses for their condition? Why didn't they protest more? . . . Has the accepted kind of discourse changed significantly in fifteen years?"). These questions initiate a series of responses beginning with Lester (25), t.c. (26), LSP (31), Megan (32), angel (36), Gordon Sumner (38), A. Hitler (40), and fred (41). Megan's complaint in 32 that the waitresses "were far too passive" leads to another series beginning

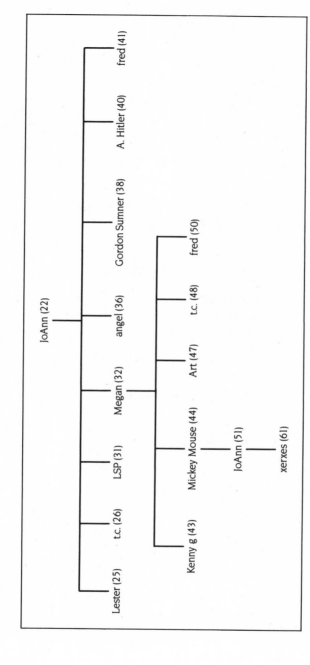

Comments in Response to JoAnn's Message 22

with Kenny g (43), Mickey Mouse (44), Art (47), t.c. (48), and fred (50). Mickey Mouse's agreement with Megan in 44 is questioned by JoAnn in 51, who then is supported by xerxes in 61, which in turn leads to additional responses. (See figure 3.)

While students can move back and forth in the transcript while messages are being added, most stay at the end, reading messages as they are sent and then jumping in with a contribution when a particular message provokes a response. Messages that initiate several responses I will refer to as "hot" messages. JoAnn's message 22 is a "hot" message since it initiates seven or eight direct responses which then foster other sets of responses.

The Reconfiguration of Discursive Relations in the Networked Classroom

Several studies of classroom discourse in the United States, Britain, France, and Australia have described a three-part sequence of initiation, reply, and evaluation.[7] In this sequence a teacher initiates a topic (What is the capital of Canada?"), a student replies ("Ottawa"), and the teacher evaluates the reply ("That's correct"). Unlike ordinary conversation, where when one speaker concludes a turn, another speaker can take over, classroom discourse is usually tightly controlled. The teacher begins by choosing the topic, then selects which student will speak, and concludes the sequence by taking back the floor when the student finishes. These steps typically are bounded by verbal and nonverbal markers. For example, teachers often slow the cadence of their speech and lower their voices in evaluations, then speak more rapidly and given nonverbal cues when they introduce a new topic (Mehan, *Learning Lessons*).

The *InterChange* session begins like usual classroom discourse with the teacher asking a question of the class. But unlike a usual classroom teacher, Lester cannot recognize one student to answer his question. Because most of the class responds quickly to his question, there is no opportunity for Lester to make a conventional evaluation statement. When Lester replies to his students in 19, he does not evaluate the students' responses, nor does he supply the answer, nor does he introduce a new topic. By this time he has lost control of the floor. JoAnn's "hot" message 22 initiates a string of responses, but she too loses control quickly. While the students respond to JoAnn in messages 31, 32, 36, 38, 40, 41, and 42, JoAnn and Lester have jumped ahead to comment on jane doe's message 30, which examines social definitions of women.

Lester's and JoAnn's advantage in faster reading and writing becomes a disadvantage when they run ahead of the class. The next hot messages are Megan's message 32 and President Reagen's [sic] message 33, which together initiate most of the messages from 43 through 56. JoAnn gets drawn away into a conversation with Gordon Sumner beginning in 59, effectively taking her out of a topic-initiator role. Lester has hardly been a force in the discussion since message 1, in part because of his continual direct references to the text (which the others do only indirectly). By the end of this section we see a reversal of roles, with the teacher replying and students making evaluative comments. Lester's response in 77 to President Reagen is in turn evaluated by A. Hitler in 84 ("Correct, Lester"). In terms of discourse structure, Lester has become a student in his own class. The paradox is that the class discussion has gone much farther and much faster than it could have with Lester standing at the front.

As in other classes that have used electronic written discussions, not only is the discourse structure radically different from what goes on in a typical classroom, but so too is the level of participation. Even though I had no way of knowing who participated and who didn't, fifteen students joined in by message 21 and five others by the end of the transcript.[8] Students were well aware that their participation made the class distinctive.

Michael Allen, a student in the class, commented at the end of the semester: "In my freshman English class, two or three people dominated class discussions every class meeting. But that was not the case in this class. Everyone was allowed an equal chance to participate and ask questions to anyone in the room. . . . Without the interaction of the students, this class would not have gone anywhere." Furthermore, in an oral discussion that took place later in the course, several of the women agreed that they never would have talked so much if the class had depended exclusively on oral discussion. One woman remarked to me outside of class that she had never said anything in a classroom since the tenth grade.

Cynthia Selfe ("Technology") and Jerome Bump also report greatly increased participation of women in classes using electronic written discussions. This participation runs counter to frequent accusations of sexism in computer software and in stereotypes associated with computers (see, for example, Marcus). The experience of teaching this class convinced me that even if patriarchal social structures do not vanish when students use InterChange (note that several of the women chose male pseudonyms), some of the socially defined limits assigned to gender are mitigated. When we talked about InterChange in our oral discussions, students said that it provided a degree of anonymity, even when names were attached to the responses. A student in the class, Michelle Davis, commented about our written discussions late in the course:

> Clearly, the main advantage of using InterChange discussions is that it allows you to be both anonymous and public at the same time. By this I mean that your opinions and comments come across the screen for everyone to read and interpret. However, you are not put on the spot by having everyone look at you when you speak. Furthermore, you have no idea when the people are reading your comments or if they are reading them at all. All comments were treated with the same respect and courtesy. All comments were based on their own merits. The students' comments were just as important as the professor's. However, this would not have been the case had the professor's comments been highlighted.

Davis's observations are supported by the conclusions of other studies that compare oral conferences with written electronic conferences. Psychologists Sara Kiesler, Jane Siegel, and Timothy McGuire find that communication is more equitable and less inhibited when such factors as appearance, paralinguistic behavior, and the gaze of others are removed in written electronic conferences. In a study of computer-conferencing in a corporate setting, Shoshana Zuboff also reports benefits to those who feel disadvantaged in face-to-face meetings: "People who regarded themselves as physically unattractive reported feeling more lively and confident when they expressed themselves in a computer conference. Others with soft voices or small of stature felt they no longer had to struggle to be taken seriously in a meeting" (370–71).

Women are not the only marginalized group whose members see advantages in written electronic discussions over conventional oral discussions. A student from Sri Lanka in a graduate course noted that his foreign accent was absent on InterChange, giving him greater license to speak. Another remark came from the only Hispanic student in the Thinking and Writing class who later told me he had used the pseudonym "President Reagen." He wrote of his experience in the class: "Something that the InterChange did do that is sometimes not done in conversation is that it made everyone equal. One comment had no more impact than another because the computer has only one color and the same print."

Resisting Closure

Besides the evident disruptions of discourse conventions that lead to a sharing of classroom authority, a more subtle kind of disruption occurs in networked discussions, one that might be described in terms of the contour of the discussion. In oral class discussions, the remarks that stand out are those that neatly state positions and seem to tie up segments of knowledge. In Inter-Change transcripts, however, there are no such peaks followed by nods of agreement. The movement of discourse in *InterChange* is more wavelike, with topics ebbing and flowing intermingled with many crosscurrents. Not only do the many voices act out Bakhtin's principle of multiaccentual nature of the sign, but the movement recalls the opposition he described between the monologic centripetal forces of unity, authority, and truth and the dialogic centrifugal forces of multiplicity, equality, and uncertainty.

The responses of the student who chose the pseudonym President Reagen are important for charting this movement. I suspect that most of the class guessed Reagen's identity because of this student's characteristic humor in networked discussions. He was older than most of the other students, the only Hispanic, the only business major, and more politically and socially conservative than most, if not all, of the others. Even though I frequently disagreed with his views, I admired his rhetorical skills in fast exchanges and his willingness to debate when the odds were against him. Seventeen of the other twenty students in the room were women, several of whom had expressed feminist sympathies if not feminist positions in previous discussions, and his two teachers tipped their hand in this direction early in the session.

After announcing himself in 3 (the only student to do so), in 20 President Reagen treats Lester's question as unproblematic: "Some waitresses like to be appreciated, as does everyone." His next comment in 33 challenges Karen, who in 23 claims that the waitresses live for male approval. Reagen says, "I don't believe the waitresses dress the way they do to please men, but to simply get better tips by looking good." JoAnn comes back quickly in 37, "Hey, Pres. Reagan, who is giving the tips?" but Reagen succeeds in getting Karen to qualify her comment in 39, "I was just referring to the paragraph," and in drawing support from LSP in 45.

Reagen then begins to display his rhetorical shrewdness. In 49 he deflects JoAnn's question with humor: "Well, as the real President Reagan would say, I am not able to answer that question at this time." He then waits for an opportunity. He picks up on the discussion of sexist remarks initiated by t.c. in 48 ("If |a waitress| protested each time that she was called 'sweetie' or 'honey,' she would quickly lose money and maybe her job") and continued by Mickey Mouse in 57 ("Waitresses are not the only ones who have to put up with being called things such as 'sweetie' and 'honey'"). In 73 Reagen reiterates his denial of a patriarchally organized society by arguing that people are just people. He begins by establishing his credibility: "I myself being a waiter, the type of waiter who serves in banquets and parties where alcohol is served alot, I can turn this point around to show my view."

Reagen then claims the consensus of the class for his earlier point even though only one other student supported him: "When I said the waitresses dress as they do for more money, I think all of us can see how that is true."

Then he disposes of sexist remarks in similar fashion on the basis of his having received lewd remarks from drunken women: "So I don't feel that only women are the only ones who feel this way some times." Reagen tries to restructure the debate in universal moral terms. By arguing that women can make sexist remarks, he reduces sexist remarks to a trivial issue of universal morality and not a manifestation of patriarchy. Reagen's claims for unvarying human nature, however are quickly challenged when other students point out that sexual harassment is socially sanctioned; t.c. writes that the difference between men harassing women and women harassing men is "that men can get away with it" (86), thus locating meaning within the social forces active at the moment of interpretation rather than in universals.

Another example of how dichotomies are deconstructed comes in response to JoAnn's question, "Why didn't [the waitresses] protest more?" After the class goes back and forth, Rae enters a long response at 60: "Maybe the cocktail waitress could change her behavior, dress etc . . . and maybe she couldn't. It is almost impossible for us to determine this unless we were actually there." The idea of resistance itself turns out not to be a simple concept but one that is historically situated. I noticed in this class and in other classes that student's initial reaction to this lack of closure often takes the form of trying to get in the last word, even if it means staying after class. But classes do not come to a definitive end because each comment always raises the potential for another response. By sharing experiences of interpretation over a semester, most students come to acknowledge that the terms in which we understand experience are not fixed but vary according to our personal histories and are always open to new possibilities for creating meaning.

Discourse of Postmodernity?

I remember the first time I saw a transcript of an electronic written discussion. Paul Taylor, the principal author of the InterChange software, brought one to a graduate course I was teaching in fall 1987. Seemingly out of the blue, a text was laid before us that answered the implicit question raised by the postmodern theory we had been reading: What would a nonliterary text look like that is inherently multiaccentual and defies the conventions of clarity, unity, and coherence? I do not claim priority for this recognition because postmodern theory with its deconstructions of the points of the rhetorical triangle—writer, subject, and audience—has been frequently used for discussing electronic texts as postmodern forms of discourse.[9]

Lyotard even uses metaphors of electronic communications technology when describing the nature of the social bond in The Postmodern Condition. He locates a "self" at "'nodal points' of specific communications circuits, . . . one is always located at a post through which various kinds of messages pass" (10). When a speaker makes an utterance, Lyotard argues that a "displacement" occurs that necessarily provokes countermoves, and thus for Lyotard a theory of communications is a theory of agonistics or "language games." Lyotard sees the grand narratives of the Enlightenment as having illegitimately monopolized the discourse of philosophy, and he would replace these narratives with a plurality of voices.

Just as in Lyotard's postmodern condition of knowledge, the teacher's role as guarantor of authority—providing the "metanarrative" that gives coherence—is disrupted when a class makes extensive use of electronic written discussions. Electronic discussions both invite participation and seriously limit a teacher's ability to control the direction they take. Just as the authority of the teacher is decentered, the authority of the text is also decentered in electronic written discussions, demonstrating Lyotard's claim that truth is local and contingent. Students are often shocked to find that other students arrive at different interpretations from theirs, even from readings of seemingly transparent, commonplace texts. Thus they are forced to confront different ways of constituting meaning from experience and to negotiate those meanings with other students.

These characteristics of postmodernism would appear to favor the trend toward social constructionism in the teaching of college writing, but to discuss only those aspects of postmodern theory that support current interests in the teaching of writing is another example of appropriating theory selectively. *InterChange* makes possible a utopian vision of class discussion where everyone with minimal keyboard skills can participate and where the links of knowledge construction are more likely to run from student to student rather than from teacher to student. This equality of participation, however, does not necessarily lead to "community building" as some teachers have theorized, following Kenneth Bruffee's model of collaborative learning, where conversation leads to cooperation (see, for example, Schriner and Rice). Indeed, Lyotard theorizes just the opposite, that conversation is inherently agonistic and to speak is to fight. As I continued teaching in the computer classroom, my enthusiasm for electronic written discussions began to be accompanied with uneasiness, and gradually I realized that my uneasiness was closely related to what Lyotard describes as the postmodern condition.

The Thinking and Writing Class: Fall 1989

By fall 1989 I had brought students' concern with difference closer to the center of my Thinking and Writing course. The discussion reproduced below was a small group discussion that took place during the fourth week of class. For this particular class students were asked to discuss two readings: the prologue from *Jane Fonda's Workout Book* and two short chapters on cultural attitudes toward women's bodies from Rosalind Coward's *Female Desires*. My purpose for assigning these readings was to prepare students for their second major writing assignment that asked them to analyze media images. There were three discussion groups of six students each, and I moved among them electronically, asking an occasional question. Since I am going to raise issues of difference, I should note that Samuel McCray is African-American, Richie Kwan is Chinese-American, and Delores Garza is Mexican-American.

September 28, 1989

1. *Samuel McCray:*
   JANE FONDA HIT THE NAIL RIGHT ON THE HEAD!
2. *Scott Barnes:*
   About what did Jane hit right on the head?
3. *Samuel McCray:*
   SHE WAS RIGHT ABOUT HOW OUR CULTURE DEFINES BEAUTY. ESPECIALLY WHEN SHE USED THE EXAMPLE OF THE VIATIMESE AD TO MAKE GIRLS EYES ROUNDER.
4. *Richie Kwan:*
   explain samuel
5. *Scott Barnes:*
   I think Jane's assessment is interesting. She does do her best to dispel all the 'diet for beauty' ideals of the seventees. However, I think she falls right into the role that Coward talks about, that willpower can make you beautiful.
6. *Delores Garza:*
   Samuel, Do you mean what she is saying about women. That they let others influence what they think about themselves. (If that made any sense)
7. *Delores Garza:*
   Do you guys think that these ideas still apply today. What do you guys consider attractive in women?
8. *Samuel McCray:*
   DELORES—YES IN A SENSE THEY DO. THERE ARE EXCEPTIONS.
9. *Scott Barnes:*
   I doubt anyone would argue over that point Samuel. What else could define beauty but culture, one might ask.
10. *Robin Jackson:*
    Jane is emphasizing that in today's society women are faced with the responsibility (so to speak) of looking the absolutely the very best she can. The problem is in that statement—looking the very best she can. Not all women have it in their genes to be 5'8", 115 lbs., and have an hour glass figure that men find so attractive. A lot of women today feel they have to look like a model to be considered attractive to men. I call BULL____ on that! Feedback?
11. *Delores Garza:*
    Robin, How did you feel about this article? If you were overweight and un-

attractive, would you consider artificial means to become what others wanted you to become?

12. *Richie Kwan:*

    jane fonda is a stupid, capitalizing bimbo who does not really care about help-ing others look their best. she is just as guilty as aiding to the diet craze by creating another craze. Who's to say that's any better.

13. *Delores Garza:*

    Samuel, What are the exceptions you are talking about?

14. *Samuel McCray:*

    DELORES - CHECK ANY SORITY AND YOU CAN SEE THE ANSWER TO THAT. DON'T GET ME WRONG, I LIKE A FINE BODY JUST LIKE THE NEXT GUY, BUT I LOOK FOR A INDIVIDUAL PERSONALITY.

15. *David Small:*

    We feel better when we're healthy. That's no revelation. But health, Fonda and Coward hit the nail on the head, doesn't come from crash diets or violent workouts. Health is moderation isn't it? Moderation in work, play, food, rest, the whole bit.

16. *Richie Kwan:*

    Samuel you can honestly say that looks have nothing to do with your dating habits. i think your wrong. any guy will back me wired up to a lie detector.

17. *Scott Barnes:*

    I agree Robin, why should a women have to look like some cheap model to be beautiful? We all know that beauty is only skin deep, but sometimes I think men are driven by anatomy other than their brains. Maybe I just have bad luck, but most of the truly beautiful women I have met end up having some irritating character flaw that makes us incompatible. I try to look at a women for who she is, not for what she looks like, but, sometimes you just can't help admiring a woman for her looks alone.

18. *Samuel McCray:*

    DELORES - EXCEPTIONS ARE PEOPLE THAT KNOW WHO THEY ARE AND WHAT THEY LIKE AND WON'T LET PEER PRESSURE DECIDE FOR THEM.

19. *Delores Garza:*

    I agree with you Richie. Exercising is good for your body, but overdoing can do more harm than good. Jane Fonda did stress that a good workout every day will make you healthy, but what does she define as a good workout? Does she mean that a workout is not considered good until the person passes out or drops dead.

20. *Robyn Hamilton:*

    I am going to pay you guys a big credit and say that women have brought this obsession upon themselves. I don't know of many men that have divorced their wives because they maybe gained 10 lbs. over the past 20 years, or have not retained that "girlish glow" for that many years. This whole subject has to do with aging. Lets face it—people are scared to death of getting old and becoming "unattractive". What a shame. If society didn't place such an em-phasis on physical beauty, these problems wouldn't exist.

21. *Scott Barnes*:
    Samuel - Is you CapsLock key on? Press it once to turn it off (the key is below the right shift key).
22. *Robin Jackson*:
    Samuel - I hate to tell you but not all sorority girls have thin thighs and tight tummies.
23. *David Small*:
    When girls go out, do they dress up for men or for women?
24. *Richie Kwan*:
    why is it that when men get a little older and fatter, it is thought of as getting character? and for women it is just getting old and fat. I, as a man take some fault to that claim, but mostly it is the attitudes and instabilities of the women?
25. *Scott Barnes*:
    Unfortunately, I think society places emphasis on other transitory qualities than just beauty. Fame and fortune often influence peoples views. As for women bringing this on to themselves, I disagree. I think it may stem back to the 'Women should be SEEN and not heard' mentality. If a woman can only be seen, she should at least be seen as beautiful.
26. *Samuel McCray*:
    Thanks Scott, to Richie - Yes I've went out with some girls for the soul perpose of there looks. But as I matured these girls started to look the same, empty.
27. *Douglas Little*:
    Men I think dress up for women, but girls spend those extra hours before a date putting on makeup and fixing the runs in their hose even when you tell them that you don't care, that they look great and you just want to go because you're already late.
28. *Delores Garza*:
    I know they say that a person should not judge a book by it's cover, but I think it would be impossible to say that you don't notice the outward appearance of a person first. I mean you don't walk down the street and say "Hey that guy a has a great personality". It is more likely you would say, "That guy is fine"
29. *Robin Jackson*:
    There is absolutely nothing wrong with admiring women for their looks, it is a natural process of sexual arousal (Samuel - I learned that in psychology). However, it is a little ridiculous to keep yourself from asking a girl out if she's a little "plain" as far as looks go.
30. *Scott Barnes*:
    I know what you mean David, 'Who is she trying to impress', you think. The answer, unfortunately, is often herself.
31. *Samuel McCray*:
    David- women compete with each other everyday, thats why they spend those extra years getting ready for a date.
32. *Richie Kwan*:
    don't any of you guys take a look at a gorgious looking girl and assume she

must be dumb as a rock, and when we see a very ugly girl, we assume that she has a good personality.

33. *Samuel McCray*:
    Richie - NO
34. *Richie Kwan*:
    liar

This small group discussion follows a different trajectory from the pseudonymous discussion of *The Cocktail Waitress* in the spring 1988 class. Unlike the *Cocktail Waitress* discussion, students do not expand on points of potential agreement and instead move toward disagreement. Samuel makes a strong claim in messages 1 and 3 that culture defines beauty, and in response to Delores's questions in 6 and 13, Samuel supports his claim in 14 by noting the similarity in appearance of women in sororities, though he distances himself from the patriarchal implications of his claim by insisting that he looks for an "individual personality." Richie, who has dismissed Jane Fonda in 12 as a "stupid, capitalizing bimbo," challenges Samuel directly in 16 for denying the influence of appearance, implying that Samuel is a liar ("any guy will back me wired up to a lie detector"). Three topics are introduced that have the potential to develop into extended discussions: David's remarks on the relationship of exercise, health, and beauty in 15, Robin's point about our culture's fear of aging in 20, and Richie's and Scott's comments on the responsibility of men for patriarchal definitions of beauty in 24 and 25. But when Richie ask the men directly if they automatically assume a beautiful women is "dumb as a rock" in 32, Samuel quickly replies "no" in 33, and Richie retorts by calling him a "liar" in 34.

The aggressive tone of this small group discussion surfaced in other electronic and oral discussions we had in the course. Part of the increase in hostility as compared to my spring 1988 Thinking and Writing class may have been owing to a reversal of the gender ratio. Instead of 17 women and 4 men, there were 13 men and 7 women in the fall 1989 class.[10] The class was also more racially and ethnically diverse: there were five Hispanics, one Chinese-American, and one African-American. The economic backgrounds of the students were varied, and four of the most vocal men were members of fraternities, one of whom wore T-shirts bearing antifeminist slogans.[11]

Throughout the course students explored these differences in relation to the readings, and at times the discussions became heated. In one discussion, for example, when several students began writing about racism and social hierarchy in fraternities and sororities, one of the fraternity members replied, "The cream rises to the top." The tension in the concluding remarks between Samuel and Richie demonstrates that electronic discussions are just as likely to move toward dissensus as consensus, toward name-calling rather than agreement.

Marshall Kremers says that such hostility in electronic discussions comes from the "shock of being granted total freedom of expression, a privilege we can hardly blame them for being unable to handle since we never gave it to them in the regular classroom." Kremers writes that in his classes that use the ENFI software, "before students understand that the network belongs to them . . . there seems to be a kind of mutiny going on. They write a lot of garbage, some of it obscene" ("Sharing Authority" 35). He quotes an excerpt from transcripts where students refuse to consider the assigned subject matter and type chitchat and nonsense syllables to each other.

I would not describe my students, however, as being unable to handle authority. They stayed on the topic for remainder of the hour, producing another forty-eight messages, and they moved on from the disagreement over male desires. What the students did not always do was maintain bourgeois standards of politeness in classroom discussions. These violations of politeness conventions often occurred when students raised issues of difference in their terms. I would argue that electronic written discussions create dissensus because they give voice to diversity. In a conventional oral discussion I doubt that the two women would have spoken as freely as they wrote in this exchange, especially early in the semester and especially considering that Delores Garza's home culture is one that makes it difficult for women to speak in public.[12]

But, at the same time, electronic written discussions have made problematic what I felt were my most secure assumptions about teaching. Implications of postmodern theory for the networked classroom do not stop with giving voice to difference, decentering the authority of the teacher, or with demonstrating the social construction of knowledge. We are in what Lyotard calls a "legitimation crisis," where there is no external authority to which we can appeal nor any way we can establish enduring values. If Lyotard were only talking about the latest trend among the Parisian philosophical elite, I wouldn't be disturbed, but many of our students take similar views. Richie Kwan sums it up when he accuses Jane Fonda of substituting one craze for another. He asks, "Who's to say that's any better?" Truth in the postmodern condition becomes a matter of consumer choice. In postmodernity the only logic we have to fall back on is the "logic" of the marketplace, which is why Fredric Jameson calls postmodernism the logic of late capitalism. Electronic written discussions are governed by the logic of consumer choice. Topics are introduced and consumed according to what students like at that moment and what they don't like.

This logic of consumption has transformed the basic economic notion of "need," because the values given to commodities are controlled less by the relation of commodities to primary needs than according to how commodities function within cultural systems of signs. The disintegration of the boundary between "real" and "false" needs is the basis for Jean Baudrillard's vision of postmodernity in *Simulations*, where consumption becomes a language used by individuals and groups to describe themselves. The distance between object and sign collapses as the image overrides the content. Was Ronald Reagan really the president or just a smiling B-movie actor all along? Was there really an invasion of Grenada on October 25, 1983, justifying the distribution of over 8,000 medals for heroism, or was it just a media event produced for TV to distract us from the killing of 241 of the Marines in Lebanon two days before? In his recent work, Baudrillard claims that these kinds of questions are no longer relevant. Things are interpreted as "real" only if they can be experienced electronically, which is perhaps why people now drive to the Grand Canyon to see an IMAX movie of the Grand Canyon on a seven-story screen.

While many college English teachers are fascinated about the new possibilities that networked computers bring to the classroom, many others are frightened by the possibilities, and they should be, because much more is at stake than relinquishing some of the teacher's traditional authority. Many see classroom acts of writing, especially writing about the self, as part of a much longer process of intellectual self-realization. Writing about the self is given great importance because it encourages reflection about self-development. This legacy of modernism is challenged by writing on computer networks in general (here I'm speaking of asynchronous as well as synchronous discussions).

Networked writing displaces the modernist conception of writing as hard work aimed at producing an enduring object. Acts of networked writing are most often quickly produced, quickly consumed, and quickly discarded. Electronic mail systems are designed to require that some action be taken on messages received, which usually is scanning and deleting them. Even more unsettling for traditional writing teachers is the vivid demonstration of the decentering of the subject in electronic discussions. When students in networked classrooms comment on previous electronic discussions, they frequently remark that they can remember what was said but not who said what.[13] It is also difficult for teachers to maintain a notion of students discovering their authentic selves through writing when student writers try on and exchange identities in electronic discussions, even from one message to the next.

The decentering of the subject in electronic texts is taken to an even more radical extreme when students use pseudonyms in discussions. Researchers have made claims that the use of pseudonyms in electronic discussions leads to even greater participation and self-disclosure (Cooper and Selfe; Spitzer). My initial experience with using pseudonyms in the spring 1988 class led me to draw similar conclusions. In the remainder of the transcript after the excerpt I quoted above, students discussed instances of sexual harassment that they had experienced and the contexts in which these incidents had taken place. Several of the students commented afterward that they felt something important to them had happened in that class, that they had connected what they were reading with their lives outside the classroom. I remember feeling quite proud that the discussion had taken place, although I also realized that I had little to do with its outcome beyond choosing the readings.

I have continued to use pseudonyms once a semester, and nothing quite so remarkable has happened since. Most often the pseudonymous discussions resemble the regular networked discussions; in fact, in smaller classes particular writers come to be identified by the character of their messages, and pseudonyms prove to be very thin disguises. In my fall 1989 class I debated whether to use pseudonyms. By the beginning of November the students had completed three essays, each of which had been composed in multiple drafts with peer reviews. The students were able writers, and they had done well working in groups in the directed activities that made up most of the class such as short analyses, summaries of readings, and peer reviews of essays. When I assigned group tasks such as summaries, either in face-to-face groups or on the computers, all the groups were able to cooperate to produce competent work. Several of the students, however, did not conceal their dislike for each other.

I did not expect the students to resolve their differences in a discussion using pseudonyms, but as Marshall Kremers puts it, I decided to "ride the beast" to see where it would take us. I held the only pseudonymous discussion of the term on November 2, 1989, a little over a month after the small-group discussion quoted above. My initial message in this discussion (sent under my own name) posed a question about the assigned readings for the day, which were a student paper analyzing roles offered to women in *Women's Day* magazine and a short article from *Ladies' Home Journal* titled "How to Keep Your Man Monogamous" (Penney), an article typical of the grocery store variety of women's magazines that assigns women the responsibility of maintaining a marriage.

At the beginning of class I presented students with a quote from Arlie Russell Hochschild's *The Managed Heart*, which argues that because women lack the same access to power, authority, and status that men enjoy, they must use feeling as a resource and become what she calls "emotional managers." I asked if the *Ladies' Home Journal* article supported or contradicted Hochschild's claim. I will pick up the transcript early in the discussion after one round of messages had been sent giving short responses to my question. The students in this class were very fluent technically, and as you read, imagine these messages scrolling upward on the screen one after another in rapid succession:

November 2, 1989

1. *Adam Heart*:
   What should we say?
2. *yeah boy*:
   what's up butthead?
3. *arm pit*:
   isn't this so fun. let's not talk about the reading!!!
4. *INDIANA JONES*:
   Monogamy is a thing of the past.
5. *Laverne*:
   What does the article support, yeah boy?
6. *Cherri Champagne*:
   Monogamy sucks.
7. *Biff*:
   Like, its the same, dude.
8. *joe*:
   butthead?
9. *GARFIELD*:
   Yes, I think it does support it.
10. *Mighty Mouse*:
    Cherri Champagne, How about STD's?
11. *yeah boy*:
    someone reply to the article.
12. *King Kong Bundy*:
    Ich weiss es nichts.
13. *joe*:
    monogamy is not a thing of the past i mean how can you sleep with a zillion different people with all the creepy crawlies out there?
14. *Cherri Champagne*:
    What are STD's
15. *Laverne*:
    O.k. LJH article supports Hoschchild or whatever her name is.
16. *butthead*:
    Joe - It's easy!
17. *arm pit*:
    joe use a rubber
18. *GARFIELD*:
    Indiana, what do you man that monogamy is in the past?
19. *yeah boy*:
    you tell him butthead.
20. *Laverne*:
    STD's are sexually transmitted diseases, Cherri dingbat!
21. *Gary*:
    Why does monogamy suck?
22. *INDIANA JONES*:
    KKB - Wir machen kein fremdspachen, bitte.

23. *joe:*
stds - - sexually transmitted diseases some of them never ever go away
24. *Adam Heart:*
Who agrees with the article's views that males and females have distinctly different emotional makeups? And what about the statement that women carry all the burden in a seriously emotional relationship.
25. *Cherri Champagne:*
Pick a partner who has come to believe in fidelity through trial and error.
26. *BIKER:*
I think the article supports it. I forgot who wrote it earlier, but the article does ask the woman to put here needs aside and focus on making the man happy. I personally feel that it has to go two ways.
27. *Mr. Spock:*
I think Penny's article is a little weird. I think it presents ideas and solutions that are inherently obvious. A major part of her article is telling women to listen to their mates. If you have to tell someone that, they aren't truly your mate in the first place.
28. *joe:*
butthead - do you own stock in a condom manufacturer?
29. *Mighty Mouse:*
I think both articles said the same thing. The article from LHJ supports the fact that women are the ones concerned with emotion. I mean the article says women are supposed to make the first move. I personally think that is a bunch of b.s.
31. *yeah boy:*
cherri - if you pick your partner like that you need to see a doctor
32. *Madonna:*
Yeah for monogamy!!! With the fear of AIDS and other sexually transmitted diseases, I don't think monogamy is a thing of the past.
33. *Alf:*
The article is talking about monogamy in marriage. I think everyone wants your husband or wife to be monogamous don't you?
34. *King Kong Bundy:*
Indy, fur wie lange haben sie (oder du) Deutsch gemacht?
35. *Mighty Mouse:*
STD's are sexually transmitted diseases!!!
36. *yeah boy:*
the name Madonna and a statement like that just doesn't mesh
37. *Cherri Champagne:*
Fuck marriage. What about healthy, happy sexual relationships?
38. *mr. pumpkin:*
What about monogamy Im all for it. Although the girls that I encounter aren't the same way.
39. *GARFIELD:*
Adam Heart, I agree that males and females have distinctly different emo-

tional makeups. I also believe that women carry all the burden in a seriously emotional relationship.

40. *Mighty Mouse*:

    Butthead, I hope you are not saying that it is easy to sleep with a zillion people?!!!

41. *Gary*:

    Women carry all the burden in a seriously emotional relationship? Words from a FEMALE chavinist pig!!

42. *Laverne*:

    I think it goes two ways, too. I would hate to be the one always taking notes on my mate and paying so much attention and never being worried about myself or getting any attention.

43. *yeah boy*:

    Hey Cherrie - can we meet?

44. *El Vira*:

    No wonder society is so screwed up today. Too many people have attitudes like the Biffs, Cherris, and Yeah Boys. You guys are so messed up. You know what happens if there is no monogamy in the world? People run around having sex with every Dick, Tom, and Harry and then there are a bunch of mixed up children with no examples to follow, no family unit and no morals. We might as well have a nuclear war!

45. *INDIANA JONES*:

    KKB - Funf Jahren, zwei im Hochschule und drei an der Uni.

46. *Laverne*:

    Allright, Cherri! Are you saying who needs marriage to have sex?

47. *yeah boy*:

    El Vira and Cherri need to meet and duke it out

48. *Madonna*:

    Maybe I am changing my ways! I like a change - I change my hair color often, don't I?

49. *arm pit*:

    The WOMEN'S DAY article clearly shows how women are trapped in a realm of emotion where they must use emotion to keep order. Whereas the man can cause the problems. The article is making women seem like it is their duty to give into the needs of the man, while the man only decides whether this behavior will make him decide to not sleep around.

50. *yeah boy*:

    Madonna, you sure do. quite often

51. *rah*:

    El Vira - you're getting a little dramatic aren't you? Anyway, we all know that monogamy isn't for wimps or machos who feel that they have to prove themselves all the time.

52. *Cherri Champagne*:

    No Laverne. I'm saying that you should not marry someone in order to have sex.

53. *Mighty Mouse*:
El Vira, I totally agree with you.

54. *Alf*:
yeah El Vira!!!

55. *butthead*:
M. M. - It's pretty easy - a little wine, dancing, some attention, it doesn't take much. You just have to feed on their emotions.

56. *King Kong Bundy*:
Indy, Gut! Ich denke, dass wir mit die andere Leuten sprechen sollon.

57. *yeah boy*:
Butthead, you're so macho, what a maniac.

58. *Mighty Mouse*:
Indiana Jones, will you please write in English!!!

59. *Cherri Champagne*:
Guys are bad lays.

60. *INDIANA JONES*:
HELP - I'VE LOST TRACK OF THE CONVERSATION!

61. *yeah boy*:
cherri, so are girls better in your opinion?

62. *Laverne*:
Cherri, what Guys? Certainly not all guys.

63. *Cherri Champagne*:
Girls know what men want. Men don't know what women want.

64. *Biff*:
El vira, whats wrong with my attitude?

65. *yeah boy*:
indiana, that's because you've been speaking another language

66. *joe*:
cherri - I don't think all guys are bad lays, just the ones that roll over and sleep after 3.5 minutes of grunting

67. *butthead*:
Cherri - obviously you haven't met yeah boy!

68. *King Kong Bundy*:
Hey, what's wrong with everyone doing their own thing, monogamy or just being a stallion. I mean there will always be enough "family units" in our world.

69. *INDIANA JONES*:
CHERRIE - I GUESS LESBIANS ARE

I remember vividly watching this transcript as it was composed. The messages seemed like they were coming from outer space; that beyond the giggly, junior-high-school-bus level of the discussion of sexuality, it had a ghostly quality, an image of the dance of death on the graves of the old narratives of moral order. One way of interpreting this transcript is that it was a collective act of opposition. Given that the teacher was "away" even though he was sitting in their presence, there was no need to do what the teacher had asked. As "arm pit" exclaims in 3, "isn't this so fun. let's not talk about the reading!!!" My initial response was to take it personally. I had anticipated that the students might take a shot or two at me because I had argued vigorously in earlier discussions, and a few students were unhappy with their grades at the midterm evaluation. But instead they wrote me out of the conversation. I had not planned to remain silent during the discussion, but I had no opportunity to enter it.

Looking back on this class, however, I am not sure that calling it an instance of opposition reflects students' perceptions of the discussion. The choice of pseudonyms like "arm pit" and "butthead" at the beginning of the discussion suggests to me now that a few of the students entered with the intention to fight. The character that soon takes over the discussion, however, is Cherri Champagne. INDIANA JONES and Cherri denounce monogamy in 4 and 6, but it is Cherri's comments in 25 ("Pick a partner who has come to believe in fidelity through trial and error") and 37 ("Fuck marriage. What about healthy, happy sexual relationships?") that effectively divert the sporadic discussion of the sex roles in the *Ladies' Home Journal* article. When I read Cherri's first two or three messages, I suspected that one of the men in the class might have taken this pseudonym, but as the discussion went on, I changed my guess about Cherri's identity to one of the women in the class who may have decided it was payback time for some of the fraternity men's previous insults.

These insults were typical of butthead's comment in 55 ("It's pretty easy [to sleep with women] - a little wine, dancing, some attention, it doesn't take much. You just have to feed on their emotions"), a comment which yeah boy quickly endorses in 57 ("Butthead, you're so macho, what a maniac"). Cherri turns the insults back on the men by first taking over the discussion with her rejection of monogamy and then announcing, "Guys are bad lays" (59). Others in the class, presumably the men, respond with homophobic accusations to which Cherri retorts, "Girls know what men want. Men don't know what women want" (63). The men fall headlong into the trap that Cherri sets for them.

My reading of Cherri, of course, is but one reading, heavily dependent on my constructions of gender politics and intentions. In electronic discussions there is always an excess of meaning that defies the effort to dig out an underlying meaning. Because the fall 1989 discussion with pseudonyms made me more uncomfortable than any other class I've experienced in the networked classroom, I would like to label it as my "worst" class using pseudonyms as opposed to my "best" class using pseudonyms in spring 1988. But I cannot defend these labels because in both classes students claimed and used classroom space for their own purposes.

Where I would argue that the discussion in the spring 1988 class surpassed that of the fall 1989 class was in how students collectively perceived the re-spective discussions. For several of the women in the spring 1988 class, the electronic discussions problematized their silence in oral discussions. If they could speak so freely in electronic discussions, then why, they asked, was it so difficult to speak in conventional classes? The men in the class, including the teacher, were also confronted with the issue of the silencing of women and were forced to think consciously about who was not speaking.

The character of the oral discussions changed in the spring 1988 class as the semester progressed with more students participating and setting topics. I asked students to comment about the class at the end of the course, and several women noted that they they were more aware of the politics of talking in class and that they should not be content to sit silently. This awareness also led students to consider other classroom relations. A student in another networked discussion wrote: "When I first came to this class, it seemed ab-normal to participate all the time. Now it seems abnormal to sit still and listen to a lecture for an hour and a half."

When at the end of the term in fall 1989 I asked the students to write informally about their experience in computer-assisted Thinking and Writing, they were generally positive about *InterChange*, the critical viewpoints of the materials we read, and the multiple draft sequence of composing essays with intervening peer and instructor reviews. For example, one student wrote, "[The class interaction] helped us to analyze and think on our own, which is some-thing that hasn't been required of me very much at this university." But there were relatively few statements claiming a collective sense of the experience as compared to the spring 1988 class. One of the men in the fall 1989 class remarked about the pseudonymous *InterChange* session:

> The day we used false names was beneficial because it allow[ed us] to say things and not feel embarrassed. I personally said things that were rude and disgusting, not to be gross but to show how some people really feel and to show how people overreact. Some things I said were complete nonsense but the girls jumped all over me. It show[ed] how sensitive they are towards them-selves. Most of the guys could take the criticism and laugh it off, but the girls let it affect them.

I doubt this student's claim to know the gender identity of those using pseudonyms and his gender stereotyping. But the contradiction in his defense of being "rude and disgusting" both to "show how some people really feel and to show how people overreact" reflects an all too frequent distancing of responsibility for racist, sexist, and homophobic slurs on campuses today. Dur-ing the 1989–1990 academic year, the University of Texas had a series of na-tionally publicized incidents of racial harassment, incidents that have become commonplace across the nation. In one of these incidents fraternity members distributed a T-shirt with the celebrated athlete Michael Jordan portrayed as Sambo dunking a basketball. The fraternity members claimed not to understand why anyone would be offended by this image.

The hostility in the fall 1989 pseudonymous discussion is a phenomenon like the outburst of anti-Semitism in Eastern Europe following the overthrow of communist governments that comes as an unwanted companion of radical freedom. The tenor reminds me of the British tabloid press, which is populist and antiestablishment, but full of jingoism, sexism, racism, and homophobia. It is what Jean Baudrillard says we should expect in a postmodern world: "The world is not dialectical—it is sworn to extremes, not to equilibrium, sworn to radical antagonism, not to reconciliation or synthesis" (*Fatal Strategies* 7). Baudrillard sees our primary drive today is for intensity, "for escalation, for an increase in power, for ecstasy" (7). He defines *ecstasy* as "the quality proper to any body that spins until all sense is lost, and then shines forth in its pure and empty form" (9), and he says that "anti-pedagogy is the ecstatic—that is, pure and empty—form of pedagogy" (10). Baudrillard might well see the fall 1989 discussion with pseudonyms as an example of the "ecstasy of communication," the pure, empty form of antipedagogy where there is not so much an abandonment of old values, as El Vira charges in outrage, but rather "a headlong flight forward from the hemorrhage of objective causality" (13).

Electronic written discussions raise some very complex issues for teachers who use this technology. At times this technology seemingly produces the "regime of phrases'" theorized by Lyotard in *The Differend*, which creates the space that allows mute voices to speak and gives opportunities for resistance to the dominant discourses of the majority. Electronic discussions would seem to confirm Lyotard's assertion that agonistics is the inevitable condition of contemporary life and that the best we can do is to allow everyone to speak. At other times, however, *InterChange* discussions move toward consensus and, contrary to Lyotard's claim that consensus is always repressive, demonstrate why consensus is at times politically desirable.

Thus I do not see easy conclusions about the politics of pedagogy arising from electronic discussions but instead a need to theorize at greater depth and to take into account the richness of the classroom context. If teachers are to find ways for students to discover the historical depth absent from postmodern culture, then teachers must help them not only to critically examine and deconstruct the narratives of modernity but also to reconstruct and rewrite those narratives. While electronic discourse explodes the belief in a stable unified self, it offers a means of exploring how identity is multiply constructed and how agency resides in the power of connecting with others and building alliances. In the next chapter I will consider Fredric Jameson's and Jean Baudrillard's descriptions of postmodernism as a historical condition and how student writing reflects and disputes these descriptions.

7

Student Writers at the End of History?

IN THE PREVIOUS chapter I described how new electronic technologies have brought about new modes of writing and new modes of classroom interaction. These technologies have destabilized traditional hierarchies between teacher and students and among students themselves, and they have dislocated traditional subjectivities of classroom writers, inviting them to take on multiple identities. The dispersed subjectivities in classroom discussions using networked computers may be related to larger changes involved in the increasing use of electronically mediated language in our culture.

Computerized written communication is but one form of an array of electronic communication technologies that include television, radio, film, telephones, FAX machines, videotapes, audiotapes, and other kinds of electronically transmitted data. Much speculation concerning the effects of these technologies on writing has blamed the electronic media, especially television, for an alleged decline in literacy, following Newton N. Minow's famous 1961 description of television as a "vast wasteland."[1] The more hostile critics accuse the electronic media of destroying values and linear thinking. Allan Bloom, for example, denounces Walkman headphones and MTV for turning the lives of the young "into a nonstop, commercially prepackaged masturbational fantasy" (75).

The milder critics argue that much of the time now spent watching television and listening to rock music was formerly devoted to reading—and thus, whatever the content of television and rock, good or bad, the importance of literacy has declined. All of these claims, however, remain quite controversial. The issues in debates over literacy have been often heavily burdened with political agendas, and in this context too often discussions of the effects of electronic communications technologies have offered utopian and dystopian visions without acknowledging the complexity of the present situation.

In this chapter I reflect more broadly on the impact of electronic technologies on writing. I begin with the theory advanced by Walter J. Ong that students live in a condition of secondary orality and that deficiencies in their writing can be traced to this condition. Then I move to the more radical theories of postmodernity of Fredric Jameson and Jean Baudrillard, which have large implications for the kinds of discourse students might produce. I end by examining Jameson's and Baudrillard's theories in relation to student writing. Their theories question whether students are any longer capable of critiquing the social formations they occupy. Jameson says we live in an age that has forgotten how to think historically. Baudrillard would regard those who speak of fostering political agency among student writers as pursuing a nonexistent dream, claiming that the historical consciousness for such agency has imploded in hyperreality, where the signs of the real have become what is taken as real.

Ong's Secondary Orality

A few theorists have considered the impact of electronic technologies on writing in a larger historical perspective. The most prominent of these theorists for scholarship in rhetoric and composition has been Walter J. Ong, who extrapolates from Eric Havelock's scholarship on the effects of literacy in ancient Greece. In *Preface to Plato* (1963) and later in *Origins of Western Literacy* (1976), Havelock argues that the Greek invention of the alphabet allowed memory to be externalized, releasing the ancient Greeks from the burden of memorization and offering them new opportunities for analytic thought. By enabling the Greeks to compare texts and locate inconsistencies, literacy overturned the authority of the oral tradition and brought about new forms of cognition.

Ong finds in Havelock's analysis of Greek civilization a movement from a typically oral kind of thinking that is situated and participatory to a typically literate kind of thinking where detached, linear reasoning prevails. Ong has expanded on how literacy restructures processes of thought in books including *The Presence of the Word* (1967), *Interfaces of the Word* (1977), and *Orality and Literacy* (1982). His most influential text for English studies, however, has been a short, frequently reprinted essay, "Literacy and Orality in Our Times" (1978), which sets out the implications of his theory of literacy for contemporary students. In this essay Ong theorizes that those in "primary oral cultures" cannot realize the fuller human potential and the higher level of consciousness itself made possible by literacy because literacy is not merely necessary for gaining access to knowledge but is a prerequisite for the cognitive operations required in a technologically advanced culture.

Ong cites as evidence the work of his former student Thomas J. Farrell, who like many others finds that "students make assertions which are totally unsupported by reasons, or they make a series of statements which lack connections" (3). Ong and Farrell believe that unsupported assertions and unconnected statements are dominant discursive forms in oral cultures. Furthermore, they see oral consciousness as spreading rather than retracting because both agree that we are in an age of "secondary orality" produced by the ubiquity of recorded music, radio, and television. Ong characterizes the inhabitants of black urban ghettos as living in a primary oral culture and other young people who experience a high level of orality through exposure to electronic media as living in a culture of "secondary orality."

In an attempt to extend Ong's argument about the effects of orality on thought, Farrell uses the notion of a cognitive divide between orality and literacy to explain why African-American children score lower than white children on standardized tests. In "IQ and Standard English" published in *College Composition and Communication* in 1983, Farrell points to the absence of the copula "BE" in certain forms of Black English Vernacular (BEV). Farrell associates the absence of BE with coordinate constructions or parataxis, which Ong believes is a trait of the oral mind. Farrell alleges that the absence of BE derives from the "primary oral culture" of the ghetto, and he then suggests that because "black Americans are essentially an oral people much like their African ancestors" (473), they should be given specific training in the grammar of standard English in order to help them cope with the demands of literacy.

Farrell's generalizations about race and language ran into immediate and angry opposition.[2] Farrell assumes that African-Americans are culturally deficient and that the chief barrier to economic security for poor African-Americans is their language. He also neglects existing scholarship on the logical structure of Black English Vernacular by Labov and others. In spite of the rejection of Farrell's theory about causes and consequences of alleged "linguistic deficiency" among speakers of BEV, the inspiration for Farrell's work—Ong's theory of a divide between the kinds of reasoning possible in oral and literate cultures—remains in high repute, even though Beth Daniell has demonstrated that Ong's theory contains the same weaknesses and ethnocentrism as Farrell's. While few in composition studies openly agree with Farrell's charges of logical deficiency among speakers of BEV, the association of parataxis with orality and hypotaxis with literacy that underlies Farrell's theory are passed along as fact with little or no supporting evidence.

If researchers seek to investigate the parataxis-versus-hypotaxis hypothesis in student writing, perhaps a better source of data would be students who are proficient in the conventions of written English and who make relatively few errors. The persistence of comma splices among such writers might be taken as evidence of paratactic thinking. For example, I noted the following example in a college student's microethnography on the clothing retailer, Banana Republic:

> When trying on clothing the customer enters a small dressing room right off the main floor. The only cover is a small cloth in a dark brown and gold leopard skin pattern that doesn't reach to the floor, the customer is given a dangerously exposed feeling.

This example came from a very competent essay, one that combined careful observation with interpretative insight and one that had been reviewed by the student and two of her classmates. Yet I was stopped by the second sentence when I read it, and I wondered why no one, writer or peer reviewer, had felt the absence of a "Because" at the beginning of the sentence. If we apply Farrell's argument to this example, the second sentence is a case of a paratactic construction appearing where an hypotactic relationship is logically implied.

But even if one could amass numerous examples of this kind and prove their anomaly through statistical analysis, the argument that such "errors" are somehow associated with a culture of "secondary orality" would remain very speculative. Comma splices can be found in edited journalist prose, and they may reflect a relaxing of formal conventions that has been under way throughout this century. Furthermore, the characterization of oral language as more paratactic and written language as more hypotactic may be little more than another folk belief about language that runs contrary to actual practice. M.A.K. Halliday has shown that oral language is typically more grammatically complex than written language.[3]

Perhaps researchers like Farrell are looking in the wrong places for evidence of the impact of electronic communications technologies. To attempt to throw light on major shifts in consciousness by examining their manifestation in errors in student writing is suspect from the outset because it ignores a multitude of mediating cultural influences, not the least of which is schooling. There are also good reasons to reject Ong's association of electronically transmitted communication with his notion of oral culture. While much of television is "oral" in the sense that actors are speaking lines, newscasters are reading scripts, and singers are reciting jingles, there is also a significant "written" component in captions and in various forms of graphics, which have in turn influenced newspaper layouts. Even rap music, which certainly grows out of an oral tradition, contains many literate references.[4]

Ong's broad category of "orality" also neglects fundamental differences between electronic broadcast media and oral language. The oral face-to-face situation that Ong describes is inherently dialogic. Speakers can be elliptical because hearers have the opportunity to question them or to signal their lack of understanding or disagreement. Electronic media, on the other hand, are inherently monologic. Some radio programs invite listeners to call in, and some viewers of television have limited opportunities to respond to programming by telephone or through cable systems, but by and large the flow of radio and television is one-directional. Oral face-to-face situations also depend on the physical presence of speakers, on their appearance, gestures, and tone of voice. While images of physical presence are conveyed through television, other electronic media efface physical presence.

"Secondary orality" is an unsatisfactory way of conceiving of the effects of an array of electronic communications technologies. Electronic technologies have the paradoxical effects of both helping to bring about commonality and at the same time social division. While we may be more aware of what is happening on the other side of the planet than we were a few years ago, we are often less aware of what is happening on our own block. Rapidly changing electronic technologies are also located among other social changes; they influence and are influenced by these changes, and they are embedded within larger cultural changes.

Jameson's and Baudrillard's Visions of Postmodernity

A number of theories of postmodernity, both popular and scholarly, explore how electronic technologies are involved in larger cultural changes. Two of the most ambitious theories are those of Fredric Jameson, who reinterprets Marxist theory in the context of postmodernity, and Jean Baudrillard, who is decidedly anti-Marxist. Jameson's analysis of the disintegration of bourgeois subjectivity in literary texts presented in *The Political Unconscious* (1981) is extended to contemporary culture in his influential 1984 essay, "Postmodernism, or The Cultural Logic of Late Capitalism," and in a 1991 book with the same title, discussed in the introduction. To review the main argument, Jameson theorizes that we have entered a new stage of "late" capitalism that he calls "multinational capitalism"—a "purer" form of capitalism that has increasingly penetrated and homogenized geographical, cultural, and psychic spaces. Postmodernism, therefore, is not the new cultural dominant as such, but rather a reflex of a new stage of capitalism.

Jameson has mixed feelings about postmodern culture. On one hand, he claims that postmodern culture represents the democratization of nineteenth- and early twentieth-century bourgeois culture, and thus a completion of modernization—a movement so powerful and encompassing that "old fashioned forms of socialism or communism are just no match" (Hall and Jameson 31).[5]

On the other, Jameson repeats the Frankfurt School's nostalgia for modernism by arguing that postmodern thought lacks the possibility of critical distance from social, economic, and political formations that modernity claimed for the autonomy of art, the isolated genius, and even the entrepreneur.

Jameson believes that a critique of domination is very difficult to mount because consumer society has masked conflicts in advanced industrial societies by redefining needs as consumer commodities and thus leaving no space for self-determination outside the established order.[6] Jameson says that because

> the corporate is now at one with culture, . . . [a] politics that wanted to take on the corporate would, therefore, have to take on postmodernism itself and its corporate culture. That's a very complicated thing to do and it's something which often strikes people as puritanical or oversimplified because you then seem to be repudiating all of the postmodern as a form of decadence and ruling-class culture, when it's much more ambivalent. (Hall and Jameson 31)

Jameson's critique of postmodernity develops from his claim of the postmodern absence of *depth*, a word he acknowledges using in several senses. In an interview in which he reflects on his definition, Jameson says that the vanishing of visual depth in the arts has been accompanied by disappearance of interpretative depth; thus, "historicity and historical depth, which used to be called historical consciousness or the sense of the past, are abolished" (Stephanson, "Regarding Postmodernism" 4). He connects this transformation to our emotional reaction to the world. Where the predominant psychological affect of modernism was the sense of loss expressed in high art in works such as Eliot's "The Waste Land," the postmodern affect is one of varying emotional intensities and, according to Jameson, is best expressed in schizophrenic or drug language. Because discontinuity has become the predominant relationship, we expect "that it is natural to shift from one thing to another."[7] The frequent breaks become the meaning itself, diminishing the content.

Jameson admits there is deep paradox in the concept of postmodern as periodization. He writes,

> [There is a] seeming contradiction between the attempt to unify a field and to posit the hidden identities that course through it and the logic of the very impulses of this field, which postmodernist theory itself openly characterizes as a logic of difference or differentiation. If what is historically unique about the postmodern is thus acknowledged as sheer heteronymy and the emergence of random and unrelated subsystems of all kinds, then, or so the argument runs, there has to be something perverse about the effort to grasp it as a unified system in the first place: the effort is, to say the least, strikingly inconsistent with the spirit of postmodernism itself. ("Afterword" 372–73)

Jameson counters the charge of contradiction by arguing that those who accuse him of being misguided in proposing a unified theory of differentiation confuse levels of abstraction and that a theory does not have to be like the phenomena it describes. He claims that he is only describing the totalization of late capitalism, with its increasing penetration into cultural and psychic spaces. Totalizing theory, he specifies, "often means little more than the making of connections between various phenomena" ("Afterword" 376); it does not have a *telos* of its own, it does not necessarily lead to totalitarianism. His argument thus rests on two claims: that relationships in contemporary culture are systemic and not random and that these relationships can be theorized.

If we grant for the moment Jameson's totalizing description of postmodernity as an underlying cultural logic in advanced capitalist societies, we are still left with the question of why there has not been a large-scale crisis of postmodernity in composition studies. Jameson allows that the culture of the West simultaneously occupies different worlds. In terms of production we still find many elements of Fordism and pre-Fordism remaining in emergent post-Fordism.[8] Perhaps a more specific answer, however, is that the lingering modernism in composition studies has a great deal to do with its location in the academy. Jean Baudrillard, who sees the United States as the model for the rest of the world in the future, wryly notes that the people least able to understand America are its intellectuals, who are "shut away on their campuses, dramatically cut off from the fabulous concrete mythology developing all around them" (*America* 23).[9]

Like much of Baudrillard's writing, this generalization is a caricature, for those who are dedicated to theoretical analysis of culture in America represent only a tiny minority of academics. Yet to criticize Baudrillard's generalizations as being overdrawn is a too easy dismissal of his work; he is more poet than social scientist. His description of the United States as the only interesting place on the planet, where immediacy is king, where people live for sensation, exhilaration, and acceleration, expresses how media images merge with our desires and the desires of our students. To denounce Baudrillard for failing to see poor people in America misses the point. Baudrillard's travelogue is America's image of itself—the America of beer commercials where a swimming pool and a woman in a swimsuit appear from a suitcase opened in the middle of a desert. He implicitly answers the charge that he doesn't see poor people with the reply that Americans don't see them either because they are not a part of the electronic media's construction of America.[10]

Baudrillard is the Oscar Wilde figure among Parisian intellectuals of the late 1970s and 1980s, and he takes special delight in deflating the theories of his competitors. He is an anathema to the Left because of his thorough rejection of Marxism and the mode of production as the organizing principle of society. Neither is he a comfort to traditional conservatives with his rejection of the culture, philosophy, politics, and morality of modernity. Indeed, he places politics on the same plane as sports, as merely another form of entertainment. Because Baudrillard is hostile to French feminism, perpetuates racial stereotypes, valorizes science and machines, sees California as utopia, theorizes politics as a play of signs, and is generally oblivious to human suffering, he is an easy figure to dismiss and at times even seems to aim to present himself as a straw man by inviting academic critics to expend their wrath against his own insubstantial image, labeling one of his texts "Forget Baudrillard."

But in spite of Baudrillard's objectionable attitudes and his insistence on a decisive historical break from modernity to postmodernity rather than a complex and uneven transition, even his most severe critic, Douglas Kellner, who spends an entire book railing against Baudrillard, credits him with being an incisive observer of trends. Like Jameson's version of postmodernity, Baudrillard's initial theoretical and empirical investigations of postmodernity in the late 1960s were influenced by Frankfurt School critiques of consumer society, especially Marcuse's *One-Dimensional Man* (1964). In *Le système des objets* (1968) and *La société de consommation* (1970), Baudrillard explores the commodification of culture in capitalist societies, specifically how the desiring individual is surrounded by a proliferation of objects and how the organization of these objects becomes a system of signs that overrides traditional meanings. Acts of consuming become ways of speaking and participating in a culture whose structure is based on the desire for and consumption of new objects. Baudrillard concludes that because consumption has become the symbolic as well as the economic basis for Western culture and has given rise to a global system of signs, the possibility for revolution arising from the working class has ended.

Shortly Baudrillard dismissed Marxism entirely by discrediting the classical Marxist theories of need and use value. In *The Mirror of Production*, published originally in 1973, Baudrillard charges that Marxism, like liberal political economy, is far too conservative in assuming that human activity is rational in its intent and that value results directly from utility and thus is related directly to needs. In regarding labor power as an absolute, Baudrillard argues that Marxists are complicit with capitalists who make the apology that they are only giving people what they want; Marxists simply show the other side of the equations. Baudrillard writes:

> Marxism assists the cunning of capital. It convinces men that they are alienated by the sale of their labor power, thus censoring the much more radical hypothesis that they might be alienated as labor power, as the "inalienable" power of creating value by their labor. (31)

Baudrillard deconstructs needs and use values by demonstrating that they no longer refer to an objective reality but to their own logic; they are involved principally in the reproduction of the code that sustains them. If commodities as signifiers are detached from referents such as use value, then the contradictions involved in production claimed by Marx cease to exist and capitalism becomes an incessantly growing system of signs, a symbolic overflow resulting from an excess of human energy and desire that he later describes in *Fatal Strategies* with metaphors of obesity and cancer.

By the mid-1970s Baudrillard advanced a radical social theory of the impact of "knowledge" industries, electronic media, computers, and other technologies on contemporary society that has become recognized as one of the principal theories of postmodernity. His work in this period draws from the work of both poststructuralists and situationalists, especially Guy Debord's *The Society of Spectacle*, which describes contemporary life as based on an immense accumulation of spectacles. Two of Baudrillard's studies from this period were translated and published together in English as *Simulations*, which claims that the difference between reality and representation has disappeared, leaving us in a condition of what he calls "hyperreality":

> It is no longer a question of imitation, nor of reduplication, nor even of parody. It is rather a question of substituting signs of the real for the real itself, that is, an operation to deter every real process by its operational double, a metastable, programmatic, perfect descriptive machine which provides all the signs of the real and short-circuits the vicissitudes. Never again will the real have to be produced—this is the vital function of the model in a system of death, or rather of anticipated resurrection which no longer leaves any chance even in the event of death. A hyperreal henceforth sheltered from the imaginary, and from any distinction between the real and the imaginary, leaving room only for the orbital recurrence of models and the simulated generation of difference. (4)

Baudrillard traces a succession of phases of the image from representing reality, to distorting reality, to masking the absence of reality, to finally "bearing no relation to any reality whatever" (11). The last phase is what he calls the "pure simulacrum," which is crucial to Baudrillard's notion of hyperreality because it presumes a primacy of the model. In *Fatal Strategies* he observes: "Just as the model is truer than true (being the quintessence of the significant features of a situation), and thus procures a vertiginous sensation of truth, fashion has the fabulous character of the more beautiful than beautiful: fascinating. The seduction it exerts is independent of all value judgment" (8).

Baudrillard uses Disneyland as "a perfect model for all the entangled orders of simulation"—ostensibly a celebration of illusion and fantasy, ideologically a "panegyric to American values," but even more important, a simulation "presented as imaginary in order to make us believe that the rest is real, when in fact all of Los Angeles and the America surrounding it are no longer real, but of the order of the hyperreal and of simulation. It is no longer a question of false representation of reality (ideology), but of concealing the fact that the real is no longer real."[11]

The collapse of meaning in hyperreality dissolves the social, which has always been precariously at odds with the individual in America. Individuals are "seduced" into participation in various electronic communication networks, and they become "terminals" in these networks. In *America* Baudrillard asks, "Just look at the child sitting in front of his computer at school; do you think he has been made interactive, opened up to the world? Child and machine have merely been joined together in an integrated circuit" (36). He compares the cult of the body in America, where the body is "not a source of pleasure, but . . . an object of frantic concern," with America's "other obsession: that of being 'into,' hooked into your own brain. What people are contemplating on their word-processor screens is the operation of their own brains" (35). Baudrillard would see research in the cognitive operations of writing as part of a larger American fascination with what he calls the "the *spectacle* of the brain and its workings" (36). Computers are the intellectuals' equivalent of a Walkman, a joining of human and machine in an endless feedback loop. He denies that our fascination to be hooked up to ourselves is narcissism but rather "an effect of frantic self-referentiality" (37).

These brief quotes give a sense of Baudrillard's cartoonlike treatment of the contemporary United States. He says the reason America is so misunderstood is that no one has asked what a successful revolution looks like. For Baudrillard, America is a successful revolution, a realized paradise. By this logic he says that America can have no pity for the poor: "If utopia has already been achieved, then unhappiness does not exist, the poor are no longer credible" (*America* 111). In Baudrillard's view, this image of America as utopia was the key to Reagan's success and why his administration pronounced a "Last Judgment" of damnation for the poor:

> Reagan has never had the faintest inkling of the poor and their existence, nor the slightest contact with them. He knows only the self-evidence of wealth . . . . The have-nots will be condemned to oblivion, to abandonment, to disappearance pure and simple. This is "must exit" logic: "poor people must exit." The ultima-

tum issued in the name of wealth and efficiency wipes them off the map. And rightly so, since they show such bad taste as to deviate from the general consensus. (111)

Poor people are stuck in the Must Exit lane of the freeway, and when they are off the freeway, they are doomed to die miserable deaths on the streets—a style of death Americans used to associate with India and the most desperate nations of the world but which now is quotidian in major American cities. The poor did not exist under Reagan for the same reason the poor do not exist for many college students today—most surprisingly, even for some of those students who grew up poor—because being poor is not part of postmodern America.

Most students quite understandably want to be rich because commodities are the primary signifiers in postmodern America. To be poor means effectively not to exist. Baudrillard, however, is not disturbed by this indifference but rather sees it as an indication that a profound change has taken place—a change that has created a "Fourth World, the world to where you can say, 'Right, utopia has arrived. If you aren't part of it, get lost!'"—the world where the disenfranchised are "thrown out to go off and die their second-class deaths" (112). He views the decline of the West with a distanced amusement. In an interview published in 1984, Baudrillard commented:

> Postmodernity is neither optimistic nor pessimistic. It is a game with the vestiges of what has been destroyed. This is why we are "post"—history has stopped, one is in a kind of post-history which is without meaning. One would not be able to find any meaning in it. So, we must move in it, as though it were a kind of circular gravity. We can no longer be said to progress. . . . But it is not at all unfortunate. I have the impression with postmodernism that there is an attempt to rediscover a certain pleasure in the irony of things, in the game of things. (quoted in Kellner 117)

Since we are at the end of history, or, as Baudrillard later qualified this statement, at the end of being able to talk about history, there is nothing left to do but "play with the pieces" of the deconstructed universe.

Postmodern Theory and Student Texts

Dismissals of Jameson's and Baudrillard's versions of postmodernity follow predictable lines. Critics attack Jameson's version for the contradictions inherent in the linking of Marxism and postmodernity. In a 1990 interview with Jameson, Stuart Hall confronts him with the discontinuity of his subtle analysis of the logic of postmodernity combined with his faith in the modernist logic of Marxism:

> The analysis that you offer, both of what's happening in the West, in late-capitalism as you define it, and of the contradictory developments in eastern Europe, is very challenging, putting together many puzzling elements in a new way. You respond to the postmodern in a very flexible, complex way. Yet underneath that is an absolutely unquestioned faith in the logic of classical marxism. How do you keep these two things simultaneously? (31)

Jameson replies that it is "a question obviously hard to answer on the basis of individual belief or conviction because it could just be an aberrant personal religion of some sort." His response moves toward classical Marxist thinking in historical stages. He says, "I'm convinced that this new postmodern global form of capitalism will now have a new class logic about it, but it has not yet completely emerged because labour has not yet reconstituted itself on a global scale." Jameson holds out for maintaining a Marxist view of emancipation through the eventual socialization of labor at a time when for many others the faith in the revolutionary potential of the proletariat has become little more than a lost hope.

Baudrillard's version of postmodernity is even more objectionable for many theorists of various persuasions. Even though he is identified in France with the political Right, his celebration of the collapse of meaning would hardly comfort conservatives like Allan Bloom, who begins *The Closing of the American Mind* with the lament that "almost every student entering the university believes, or says he believes, that truth is relative" (25).

Nor would anyone committed to political activism be satisfied with Baudrillard's position that both the political Right and Left cling to obsolete beliefs of modernity in an era of postmodernity that is beyond traditional politics. At a time when widespread misery has become part of the daily landscape even in affluent centers of the West, few committed to activism will find his nihilistic answer—"to play with the pieces" of what's left—acceptable. Kellner ends his book on Baudrillard by calling him a "court jester" and claiming that "he has fantasized himself into a repetitive metaphysical orbit with no apparent exit, and that, unless a dramatic reversal appears, his work will become ever more bizarre, trivial, reactionary and pataphysical" (217). In Baudrillard's defense, it should be said that he sees the role of the intellectual as a negative one because intellectuals are always on the margins of society. Moreover, to dismiss Baudrillard as irresponsible is almost like complaining that he doesn't wash windows either; he no longer believes that politics as traditionally understood has anything more to do with everyday life than any of the rest of the multitude of images we encounter daily.

If Jameson and Baudrillard represent two different positions on postmodernity, then a third position represented by Kellner is that postmodernity does not exist–or at least not yet. Kellner argues that even if we may be in a transitional age, many aspects of the old order remain including "capital, the Right, and a conservative academy" (215). Kellner admits that Left has suffered under many illusions such as belief in the revolutionary proletariat and the certainty of socialism, but he maintains that the critical social theory of the Left remains the best alternative.

Jameson's position is more ambivalent. He would locate us in period of postmodernity but would describe postmodernity in terms of a transition from state/monopoly capitalism to multinational corporate capitalism. Baudrillard assumes that there has been a decisive break between modernity and postmodernity that has caused the death of the social and, consequently, denies any possibility of collective political practice. Baudrillard finds Marxist theory based on the mode of production no longer useful in a world where signs and simulations are the primary determinants of the social order.

The question I would like to return to now is whether any of these versions of postmodernity lead to insights concerning the writing of college students. In chapter 2 I discuss proposals for making cultural studies a main concern of writing curricula in a broader effort to reintroduce public discourse into undergraduate education. Both Jameson's and Baudrillard's analyses of postmodernity make this effort problematic. Jameson's critique of postmodernity raises an issue similar to Habermas's insistence on the potential for rational discourse discussed in chapter 1. Jameson holds out for the possibility of rational critique. He suggests that the conditions for public discourse are now extremely complex because capitalism has evaporated national boundaries but public discourse is still possible.

Yet, at the same time, Jameson is fascinated by postmodernity, and his intricate prose with its pastiche of discourses draws energy from what he criticizes. Because Jameson's writing is complicit with postmodernity, it raises doubts as to whether there is any detached or noncontradictory discourse for offering critiques of contemporary culture. Baudrillard's answer to this question of the possibility of critique is not only "no," but to even ask the question for him represents little more than a nostalgia in which academics are prone to wallow. But in spite of the unrelenting cynicism of his position, I find Baudrillard valuable particularly in one respect: students often sound very much like him.

Baudrillard claims that "quotidian reality in its entirety . . . incorporates the simulatory dimension of hyperrealism" (*Simulations* 147). If Baudrillard's claim is valid, then the key assumption of a cultural studies pedagogy–that students can usefully investigate how mass culture is produced, circulated, and consumed—is called into question. Baudrillard's critique is far more extreme than merely arguing that students are situated within their culture and that any conclusions they reach will be circumscribed by that culture. Baudrillard rejects the idea that we can somehow get outside the flow of codes, simulations, and images to discover any space for social critique. Instead, the process is just the opposite: as society is increasingly saturated with ever expanding quantities of information, objects, and services, the space for the autonomous subject with a capacity for critical thought collapses. In *Fatal Strategies*, Baudrillard writes with sly pleasure about what he calls the revenge of the object:

> We have always lived off the splendor of the subject and the poverty of the object. It is the subject that makes history, it's the subject that totalizes the world. . . . Who has ever sensed the foreboding of the particular and sovereign potency of the object? In our philosophy of desire, the subject retains absolute privilege, since it is the subject that desires. But everything is inverted if one passes on to the thought of seduction. There, it's no longer the subject which desires, it's the object which seduces. Everything comes from the object and everything returns to it, just as everything started with seduction, not with desire. (111)

Baudrillard claims the object is supreme because it does not live off the illusion of its own desire; it gets along quite well without it. The fatal strategy comes when the fascination with the object overpowers the subject. He continues: "Desire does not exist; the only desire is to be the destiny of the other, to become for him the event that exceeds all subjectivity, that checks, in its fatal advent, all possible subjectivity, that absolves the subject of its ends, its presence, and of all responsibility to itself and to the world, in a passion that is—finally, definitively—objective" (114).

To explore how Baudrillard's argument pertains to student writing, I would like to look at a student's text from a lower-division elective writing course. This particular example came from the Thinking and Writing course which I describe in chapter 6, though a different class from the two from which I quote transcripts. For the first assignment in this course, I asked students to write on the topic, "What Style Means to Me." I selected this topic because in *All Consuming Images*, a book we read in the course, Stuart Ewen discusses students' responses to this topic. Ewen describes the results of this assignment as "astonishing," and he characterizes the papers as among the best he had ever received because they were so diverse, reflecting the varied backgrounds of students who attend Hunter College. With a more homogeneous population of students at the University of Texas than Ewen's students from

New York City, I too found the results astonishing, but not in the same ways that Ewen did. Below is a paper written by a student about the visit of her younger sister to the Texas campus:

Round-up weekend at UT was a mere two weeks off and I was extremely excited that my sister, a popular high school senior in Dallas, had just called to tell me of her decision to visit the campus that weekend. She was in a state of vacillation trying to decide which college would be right for her—UT or one on the West Coast. Her impression and UT's impression of her would shape her ultimate decision.

Since I wanted her to eventually enroll at UT, I saw her visit as my opportunity to show her the campus and be received enthusiastically by all my friends, especially those in the popular fraternities. I appraised all the available frat men I knew of the date of her arrival and then waited patiently until the Big Day arrived.

At last, Round-up weekend began. Kimberly, my sister, arrived as she promised, and I was positively aghast at what I saw! I then knew that my work was really cut out for me. Time was short, so I went right to work. First of all, the boyfriend who arrived with her and intended to escort her throughout the weekend had to go. Pale, wimpy and thin, he was a true High School Harry, and he was a definite threat to the image she had to portray in order to accompany me at the fraternity party that night. Like me, she would need a strong, muscular and tanned jock to date and ensure her success at the University of Texas.

Once the escort arrangement was understood, we could proceed to equally urgent matters—the hair!! A touchy subject, I was hoping she would notice my long, straight hair, the trademark of the popular sorority girls. Permed and poufed, Kim's hair balked while I carefully braided it and hoped for the best.

Finally satisfied with the looks of her hair, I caught a glimpse of Kim putting on her new tie-dyed outfit. How would I ever convince her that my cut-off jean shorts and Ralph Lauren Polo shirt was an infinitely superior choice, considering the wisdom gained during my three-year residency at UT? Over her protests that I looked like a "bag lady lurking in the streets," she hesitantly changed into the outfit I chose for her and left the back shirt tail untucked, as that was the way to wear it. I could sense her confidence and reassurance growing when two of my friends came over and complimented her. From then on it was easy sailing. Sure now that she would not look like a nerd, she easily relinquished the geeky, pushed-down socks that were popular in high school in exchange for my matching pair of Polo socks. Although I was nervous about her debut into the college scene wearing her Keds tennis shoes, she did not fit into my size six brown flats, so we left for the party.

Our next session on "acceptable campus behavior" had to be quick, as the walk to the frat house was short. I advised her to carry a drink in her hand at all times, smile like crazy and to ditch her date subtly, should Mr. Right happen along. As I anticipated, her blind date turned out to be a dork who kept muttering, "it doesn't matter if I act stupid; I'll never see these people again anyway."

I steered her rapidly to my boyfriend's fraternity big brother, a real hunk, who took her over immediately. I was relieved to see what a great time she appeared to be having and congratulated myself for a job well done. Her metamorphosis was complete.

This narrative is so fluent in its brand-name consciousness that I suspected the student might have written it as a parody of the assignment. Her later papers, however, convinced me that this narrative was indeed her interpretation of sisterhood is powerful. I don't want to suggest that this extreme consciousness of fashion is something new. Awareness of style dates at least as far back as the surviving images of people in ancient Egypt. What is perhaps new is the completeness with which a style is occupied—the metamorphosis that the writer speaks of in the last sentence. Baudrillard argues that "what we all want as objects (and we are objects as much as subjects . . .) is not to be hallucinated and exalted as a subject . . . , but rather to be taken profoundly as object" (124). Baudrillard would find in the last line the proof of his argument because metamorphosis is a central metaphor in his argument, the metamorphosis of subject to object.

Here is a student writing about what the economic collapse of Texas in the mid-1980s meant to him:

I slowly became aware of our financial troubles when my parents began to argue. The tension in the house even caused me and my sister to become ill tempered. The family arguments stemmed from the underlying pressure created by the lack of money, and the freedom that accompanies it. It felt like we were being boxed in. Slowly but surely, we began to lose our freedoms as well as our possessions. The first thing to go was my Dad's gorgeous blue Eldorado that he had worked so hard to get. The car not only symbolized our success but also our freedom. I remember my first thought when the car was not in the driveway. I naively thought that Dad might have wrecked it.
   "Dad, what happened to your car?"
   "Oh, I gave it back to the bank."

This student also writes of a metamorphosis of subject to object, where the value of agency, "freedom," becomes translated into a gorgeous blue Eldorado. This metamorphosis is a common one in America, one expressed in the GMC "Mr. Goodwrench" jingle: "It's not just your car, it's your freedom." Baudrillard describes the loss of objects as the loss of the self in *America*: "Disenfranchising. You lose your rights one by one, first your job, then your car. And when your driver's license goes, so does your identity" (112).

Propelling this metamorphosis of subject to object is a cynical energy that Baudrillard calls an "evil genie" because it undermines all narratives of human progress and the rational systems of morality and science. Baudrillard writes:

> Competition is stronger than any morality, and competition is immoral. Fashion
> is more powerful than any esthetic, and fashion is immoral. Glory, our ancestors
> would have said, is more powerful than merit, and glory is immoral. The de-
> bauchery of signs, in every domain, is much more powerful than reality, and
> the debauchery of signs is immoral. Gambling, whose rules are immemorial,
> is more powerful than work, and gambling is immoral. Seduction, in all its forms,
> is more powerful than love or interest, and seduction is immoral. (*Fatal Strategies*
> 73)

Baudrillard argues that the motives of supposedly rational society are not
progress or the increasè of collective happiness or the improvement of quality of life. These characteristics, he says, interest no one except those who
design opinion polls. Baudrillard contends that what fascinates everyone and
thus what drives our society is the debauchery of signs. For the spectacle
of anything, "we are ready to pay any price, much more than for the 'real'
quality of our life" (*Fatal Strategies* 74). The student who transformed her sister
understands this cynical energy even better than Baudrillard because she writes
without the ironic detachment of Baudrillard. Her sense of self is set out exclusively in how she believes she is perceived by others. While Baudrillard
maintains the dualism of morality and immorality, the student needs no such
dualism. The "pale, wimpy and thin" high school boyfriend "was a definite threat
to the image [her sister] had to portray." Ditching him was not a matter of
morality or immorality, he simply "had to go." He didn't match the image; therefore, he was in the Must Exit lane. He had to get off the expressway.

By abandoning all pretense of responsibility and celebrating the "fatal
strategies" of postmodernity, Baudrillard is able to give a vision of postmodernity that is far more disturbing than those who would maintain a critical
stance toward images and commodities in order to hold out for the possibility of collective social responsibility. The profound cynicism that Baudrillard
describes surrounds us. Baudrillard finds it in "West Coast music, therapies,
sexual 'perversions,' the skyscrapers of the East, leaders, gadgets, artistic
movements, all parade by in successive waves in the same ceaseless rhythm.
And our own cultural unconsciousness, deeply nourished on culture and meaning, can howl in dismay at the sign of this spectacle; the fact remains that
it is there, in the immoral promiscuity of forms, all races, in the violent spectacle of change" (*Fatal Strategies* 74–75). Barbara Ehrenreich finds it in the
frenetic busyness of the upwardly mobile middle class, where the loss of in-
trinsically meaningful work has to be compensated for by strenuous consumption, which in turn has to be compensated for by strenuous exercise (240).
Cornel West finds it not only in "a vast and growing black underclass, an underclass that embodies a kind of *walking nihilism* of pervasive drug addiction,
pervasive alcoholism, pervasive homicide, and an exponential rise in suicide,"

but also in a black middle class, "highly anxiety ridden, insecure, willing to be co-opted and incorporated into the powers that be" (Stephanson, "Interview" 276). And, unfortunately, this profound cynicism is present in many students.

Writing Local Narratives

Baudrillard's claim that we live in a culture of the simulacra where we are at so many removes from "real life" that all we see are faint afterimages allows him to make provocative analyses of contemporary media. Indeed, the distinction between news and entertainment in the media is almost gone; gossip about stars crowds out hard news on the front page and the *USA Today* devoted as much coverage to its ratings of ads aired during the 1990 Super Bowl as to the details of the game itself.[12] But at the same time, the media do not constitute all of life. The aspect of postmodernity that Baudrillard misses is the extreme heterogeneity of discourses circulating today. Because people in technologically advanced nations encounter more competing discourses than ever before, the construction of meaning is now extraordinarily complex and problematic. This complexity, however, does not necessarily lead to the collapse of meaning; just the opposite might be argued. Stuart Hall writes that "there is all the difference in the world between the assertion that there is no one, final, absolute meaning—no ultimate signified, only the endlessly sliding chain of signification, and, on the other, the assertion that meaning does not exist" ("On Postmodernism" 49). Postmodernity, then, becomes not so much an epoch but a recognition that "you are going to have to operate your analysis of meaning without the solace of closure" (49). Although this recognition "puts one in the universe of the infinite plurality of codes," Hall argues that "it does not destroy the process of encoding, which always entails the imposition of an arbitrary 'closure'" (49).

This lack of closure and the heterogeneity of discourses in contemporary culture may even be a cause for optimism. In aftermath of the overthrow of what Lyotard refers to as "magisterial" discourses—discourses that claim the status of a body of truth—a proliferation of suppressed discourses arises, as we have seen an enormous literary and artistic productivity recently from men and women of a multitude of racial and ethnic groups and from different sexual orientations. Lyotard finds it paradoxical that idea of emancipation which has guided the grand narratives of the nineteenth and twentieth centuries— the Marxist narrative of emancipation of the worker through the awareness of labor as a class and the capitalist narrative of emancipation of the poor from the "trickle down" of wealth from development—has so often had just the opposite result. The root difficulty in these grand narratives lies in their claim to universality and their pretense to speak for everyone at some point in the future. The use of *we* in these discourses reproduces the primary tension between a diverse and contingent present and the promise of a unified future. The *we* assumes the right of *I* to speak for the *you* and the *they*. Lyotard interrogates the *we* that asks the question, "Shall we continue to think and act on the basis of the Idea of a history of humanity?" ("Universal History" 316). If the answer to the question is no—and Lyotard says it "has to be no"— "then the status of the *we* which asks the question must also be reviewed."

Responses to the loss of the modern *we* can take many forms ranging from mourning to terror, from despair over the loss of God to Auschwitz. Lyotard, however, avoids the entropy of Baudrillard and the prescriptivism of an Allan Bloom or a Nicolae Ceausescu. As an alternative, he examines how a child learns a culture. The names of that culture are not given as "rigid designators" but occur in narratives in different kinds of discursive genres. Lyotard says that the advantage of a narrative is that it can combine different genres and authorizes a local *we* that delineates a sense of self. In telling their own stories, marginalized groups can gain local legitimacy and can oppose majority discourses.

Lyotard's analysis of postmodern knowledge as arising from the multiplicity of discourses in contemporary culture, and the conflicts among those discourses, has important implications for the teaching of college writing. Postmodern epistemology denies the metanarratives of modernity and upholds the construction of local knowledges agreed upon by participants in that knowledge. Lyotard's theory of postmodern knowledge not only grants space for agency but also insists that subjects are like nodes in networks of discourses that combat the entropy of the overall system by constantly innovating. He writes,"No one is ever entirely powerless over the messages that traverse and position him at the post of sender, addressee, or referent" (*Postmodern Condition* 15).

Asking students to write narratives about the culture in which they participate is one way of allowing them to explore agency and to locate themselves within their culture. Teachers of college writing traditionally have assigned personal narratives, which for some students, particularly older students, can be a means of analyzing the discourses that have shaped them and confronting the discourses they have struggled against. Too often, however, such narratives are presented as quests for the"authentic self" (see chapter 4), and as Adrienne Rich observes, finding the authentic self often means displacing the Other and even colonizing the Other's experience ("Notes").

There are other ways of using narratives to explore the politics of location. Microethnographies are one kind of writing activity that can involve students in how mass culture is produced, circulated, and consumed, and how people actually *use* mass culture.[13] Microethnographies also raise other questions about what it means to conduct research and what are the limitations of observation and reporting. Below is the first half of a microethnography of the *Rocky Horror Picture Show*, one of the more remarkable popular culture "texts" of recent years because it became an occasion for marginalized groups of young people to act out their resistance to mainstream culture.

"The Horror! The Horror! "
Kyle Tyson

It is just before midnight.

The theatre is dimly lit as people drift in and out. Regulars, some in costume or with bags, claim the front row. Some talk/gossip amongst themselves in cliques while others walk in and out of the theatre frantically.

"Where the fuck is Robert?"

"I haven't see him yet, guy."

"Shit!"

"Isn't he doing Frank tonight?"

"Yeah."

"He's always late. Deal with it."

More regulars wander in, drop their bags in the front seats, and go to the lobby to chain-smoke until the movie starts. Some of the performers are in costume while others get made up and change in the restrooms or down front in the theatre.

As midnight grows nearer, most of the regulars are inside the theatre. One walks down screaming "Attitude check!"

"FUCK YOU!" the regulars, and a few audience members, yell back.

"Horniness check!"

"FUCK ME!"

"Ego check!"

"FUCK IT!"

Give me an 'R'!"

"R!"

"Give me an 'O'!"

"O!"

"Give me a 'C'!"

"C!"

"Give me a 'K'!"

"K!"

"Give me a 'Y'!"

"Y!"

"What's that spell?!"

"UH!"

Next is B-R-A-D. *"ASSHOLE!"*

J-A-N-E-T? *"Slut!"* they respond, with faint echoes of *"Bitch, whore."*

"Welcome to *The Rocky Horror Picture Show* in Austin. The longest continuous running *Rocky Horror* show . . ."

"*IN THE WORLD!*" Slight applause.

"A few announcements before we begin, from the management."

Boos and hisses.

"If you are caught smoking—"

"*OR TOKING!*"

"—or consuming alcoholic beverages you will be . . ."

"*THROWN OUT WITHOUT A REFUND!*" A "*So don't get caught*" addition.

"Also, if you brought rice or waterguns we'd appreciate you not using them. The rice gets into our fishnets and it's a real bitch when our mascara runs."

The lead caller and another regular mumble to each other. "Oh! And due to the fire code, no open flames are permitted inside the theatre."

"Does this mean Robert can't do the show?" another regular jokes.

"Also, if you aren't aware of it already, there will be profanity—"

"*FUCK YOU!*"

"—and people performing the movie in front of the screen, so this is the time to get a refund if this is not what you're here to see."

The main caller looks toward the back of the theatre and then asks for the time. He shrugs.

"Give me an 'S'!"

"*'S!*'"

"Give me an 'M'!"

"*'M!*'"

"Thanks!" Slight laughter.

"*V-D.*"

"No thanks."

"Give me a 'Q'!"

"*'Q!*'"

"Give me another 'Q'!"

"*ANOTHER 'Q!*'"

"Give me one more 'Q'!"

"*ONE MORE 'Q!*'"

"Give me one last 'Q'!"

"*ONE LAST 'Q!*'"

"What's that spell?"

"*FORK YOU!*'"

The main caller nods to someone at the back of the theatre and they begin to chant: "*LIPS! LIPS! LIPS!*"

The lights darken and an AMC Midnight Express short begins, with the regulars shouting responses. The Twentieth-Century Fox logo appears and the show is underway. "*A LONG, LONG TIME AGO IN A GALAXY FAR, FAR AWAY, GOD SAID, LET THERE BE LIPS.*" Red lips appear against the black screen. "*AND THERE WERE LIPS. AND THEY WERE GOOD. HIT IT, LIPS!*" The lips start singing.

The Rocky Horror Picture Show, a weekend/midnight/cult/audience participation film, has been running in Austin for over eleven years. It started at the Riverside Twin and now plays at the Northcross 6 Theatres. *Rocky Horror* is unusual as a movie. It is a rock'n'roll musical about a bisexual transvestite scientist named Frank'N'Furter (in the Dr. Frankenstein mold . . . sort of), his creation—Rocky Horror, and Brad and Janet—two all-American kids who seek to use the castle telephone on a stormy night because of a flat tire. *Rocky Horror* is even stranger as an event, where regulars, or "groupies," go every Friday and Saturday night to act out the film and scream responses back to the screen. It is *the* audience participation film.

To an outsider, *Rocky Horror* might seem fun, trivial, nonsensical, pointless, or, even, offensive, but to those who go weekly, perhaps seeing the film hundreds of times, it is a subculture with a reality all its own. *Rocky Horror* in Austin has an offbeat following with its own rules, morals, and idiosyncrasies. Most of them are outsiders in one way or another. Some are high school drop-outs. Some are college students. Some are gay. Some are science fiction enthusiasts. Some are Christians. Some are into drama. Some are New Wavers. The list continues.

There are many divisions and classifications within the *Rocky Horror* crowd. All are distinct, and yet, most of its members fit into many of the prominent group classifications.

HOMOSEXUALS

(Homosexual, as used here, refers to gay males. Although technically it refers to gay members of either sex, the common social label, today, refers to males.)

Due to its bi-sexual themes, *Rocky Horror* has always appealed to members of the gay community. This is true across the country. In 1985, roughly half or more of the males involved in *Rocky Horror* were gay.

Zachary, a homosexual who no longer goes to the show except on rare occasions, played the parts of Brad and Frank at different times during his involvement with *Rocky Horror*. He was part of the show when it played at the Riverside Twin and left in the fall after the group moved to Northcross (after the Riverside discontinued it) in the spring of '85.

Zachary left when many of the other regulars of the time were leaving (most of them veterans of the Riverside days). This departure caused a drastic decline in the homosexual population around *Rocky Horror*. Currently, there are very few gay males who attend the film regularly as line callers or performers.

Despite the potential implications of the homosexual decline, it is important to not that it is not due to a morality shift (during '85 bi-sexuality was the "in" thing) but, instead, due to cycles the show goes through periodically, where various groups shift in influence and significance.

LESBIANS

While the number of gay males has declined around *Rocky Horror*, part of '86 and much of '87 has seen a dramatic increase in the number of gay females. Much of this is probably due to the relative safety and appeal lesbianism has in an age of teen pregnancy and AIDS-scares. In many ways lesbianism is now an "in" thing just as bi-sexuality was in '85. Regardless of the cause, many females in high school and early college years are turning to, or experimenting with, lesbianism.

Donna is one of the high school students who is gay. She likes some of Rita Mae Brown's novels and is an honor student at her high school. She is not a cast member but attends the show frequently. She finds women more attractive, and yet is sought after by various males at various times, most of who probably think she is just a close friend of her girlfriend.

Both gay sections are filled with intelligent, frequently academically successful people, who also fit into many of the other prominent sections.

SCIENCE FICTION ENTHUSIASTS

Rocky Horror has always attracted comic book buffs and science fiction lovers. It is partially due to the fact that *Rocky Horror* was created in partial homage to some of the classic science fiction/horror films of the 1930s, '40s, and '50s. More influential, however, is the fact that it has an appeal to outsiders and introverts as a place to "let it out" and express one's self nontraditionally and more anonymously in a dark movie theatre.

Since the latter part of '86, this section increased drastically as well. *Dungeons and Dragons*, a role-playing fantasy game, is now very popular around *Rocky Horror* because of this segment's influence, with Sundays designated as "game days" for many.

Many in this group are underachievers working in dead-end jobs and using *Rocky Horror* and *Dungeons and Dragons* as their major socialization and escapism from reality. However, many attempt to utilize this escape element to regroup and try another avenue of work or school. It seems that as the average age of the *Rocky Horror* regulars increases (going from high school/barely post-high school ages of 16–19 to early to late college ages of 18–22), the need to escape/regroup seems so common that *Rocky Horror* alone is not enough.

Glenn, an average high school student who graduated in '83, is an avid science fiction reader. He loves *Dungeons and Dragons*, *Car Wars*, and other games (including quite a few video games). He was an introvert and credits *Rocky Horror* with opening him up to people. "It gave me confidence," he notes. Despite its helpfulness, he grew tired of the "bullshit" and left in the fall of '86, but, like so many others, did not stay away. He used to play Brad, but does not wish to perform at all any more. He goes to see friends and scream. He has tried courses at Austin Community College but never managed to organize himself well enough to devote adequate time to perform in school as well as he would like. Still, he plans to keep trying until he can organize his situation, amidst family and interpersonal relationships and conflicts.

In the remainder of this essay, Tyson discusses other groups associated with *Rocky Horror*, and he ends by locating himself in relation to the film as event, focusing on his response to the suicide of one of the regular audience performers.

Asking students to write microethnographies requires them to perform many of the activities required by traditional writing assignments. They must observe and record carefully. They must analyze their data, making decisions about what is important and unimportant. They must classify their data into categories. And if they are successful, they must be able to draw generalizations from their data. But even more valuable is the opportunity for students to explore their own locations within their culture.

Kyle Tyson effectively answers both Jean Baudrillard's claim that images have become the dominant signifying system to the extent that critical discourse is no longer possible and Allan Bloom's claim that students have lost the capacity for critical thought because they no longer believe in the master truths of Western culture. He also refutes orthodox Marxists who would see popular films as contributing to ideological hegemony. Tyson succeeds in showing how temporarily occupied subjectivities quite literally can be taken on as roles and acted. He does not stop, however, with analyzing the fictive character of those subjectivities but shows how they can be used as a means of opposing dominant discourses. *Rocky Horror* is a location where customs and rules are violated as indicated by the disclaimer spoken at the beginning of the film. ("There will be profanity," to which the audience replies, "Fuck you.") Tyson's analysis of *Rocky Horror* as Bakhtinian carnival demonstrates that meanings of texts produced for mass consumption can be appropriated and subverted.

I will conclude with one more short example which came from a special summer section of first-semester composition for scholarship African-American and Mexican-American students. This course is part of a minority retention program, and I teach this class regularly in a computer-equipped classroom. In summer 1991 one of the issues students chose to write about was censorship, and not surprisingly, the several of the students who wrote on censorship focused on rap music. The students were quick to point out that the profane antifeminist language that led to the banning of an album by 2 Live Crew was tolerated in comedians such as Andrew Dice Clay and Eddie Murphy. But they also placed the censorship of rap in a historical context. They noted that rap has been popular among African-Americans since the 1970s, but it was only when rap began to attract a "crossover" audience of young white people that efforts to censor rap began.

Discussions of rap, however, led to a split within the class when women rappers such as Queen Latifah, Roxanne Shanté, M. C. Lyte, Salt-N-Pepa, and B.W.P. (Bytches with Problems) were introduced into oral and online discussions. The African-American men accused the women rappers of jumping on the bandwagon and denied their status as true rap artists, which provoked angry exchanges with the African-American women in the class.

Four of the African-American women changed their paper topic in order to defend women rappers. Andrea Johnson took the opportunity to teach the rest of the class a lesson in African-American history. Here is the first paragraph of her essay:

> "Ladies First," Queen Latifah's theme song, gives the reference for all female rappers demanding respect. Women rappers who are not acknowledged has become one of the unspoken controversies in rap. While women are fighting for their respect, rap groups like 2 Live Crew are acquiring unwanted publicity for their rap music. The industry must have forgotten, or never known that in 1850 "pattin juba" was the similar act of rapping performed by black females. In doing this whoever was performing the act would stamp her feet, beat her chest, and start rhyming, sometimes throwing insults at her surrounding friends. The only difference is that they are not getting today the amount of attention that they received during that time when people would crowd around the performer and praise her. It is hard for a woman to become acknowledged in any industry but especially in rap. When women rappers emerged on the scene, they were just a novelty, now they are professionals looking for respect.

Johnson is well aware of the importance of understanding history to be able to speak. Her argument reminds me of bell hooks's observation that the major barrier African-American women confront is not being silenced but being listened to: "Certainly for black women, our struggle has not been to emerge from silence into speech but to change the nature and direction of our speech, to make a speech that compels listeners, one that is heard" (6). I teach many students like Andrea Johnson who, in spite of their years of saturation with electronic media, lack neither the ability to think critically nor to think historically. What they too often have lacked is a chance to be heard.

The brief excerpts from Kyle Tyson's and Andrea Johnson's essays suggest that some students at least are more aware of how agency can be constructed from multiple subject positions than are many theorists. Nevertheless, the difficulties such students face in being heard in a complex, diverse society are not trivial. In the last chapter I turn to how subjectivity and discursive relations might be reconceived to reflect the complexity and diversity of our society.

8

The Ethical Subject

I HAVE ARGUED throughout this book that many of the conflicts within composition studies concern larger cultural conflicts over the question of the subject. While only recently the question of the subject has been foregrounded within composition studies, it nevertheless underlies longstanding debates within the discipline. I describe in chapter 2 how the privileging of "truth-telling" and writing about the self in the early stages of the process movement in the 1960s and early 1970s occurred against a backdrop of numerous calls for social groups and individuals to look within themselves for their own identities. Nor is it coincidental that alternatives to the Western logocentric tradition in writing classes were explored (for example, Hayakawa's uncharacteristic suggestion of modeling the practice of surrealist poets for composition students) and experiments in antipedagogy were tried (for instance, Lutz's freshman English as a "happening") during this period.

In retrospect, the process movement was aligned with certain trends that have since been described as postmodern, especially in its conception of the text and the relationship between writers and readers. Process theory views the text as open-ended, as potentially always changeable instead of as a static object. Similarly, the widespread practices of peer reviews and multiple drafts have tended to make classroom readers active participants in the production of texts, reducing the distance between writers and readers. But just as in the larger culture where the counterculture art, music, and dress of the 1960s were soon coopted and commodified, the radical beginnings of the process movement were also domesticated. A primary means of that domestication, as I discuss in chapters 4 and 5, is the preservation of the belief that the student writer is a rational, autonomous individual. This belief is maintained by a fiction of textual coherence. The student writer's skill in representing his or her life experience as complete and noncontradictory is taken as confirmation that the rational subjectivity of the author is identical with the autonomous individual.

225

Even though this conflation of the author as rational subject and the autonomous individual remains widespread in writing research and pedagogy, it has not gone without challenge. I outline in chapter 1 how the notion of a discourse community was used to contest dominant individualistic views of composing in the 1980s and how the student writer was redefined as a social subject. Kenneth Bruffee's career as a composition scholar is emblematic of this trend. In 1971 Bruffee attacked Peter Elbow's antiauthoritarian pedagogy as encouraging "rampant individualism" instead of offering an alternative vision of classroom authority, and in "The Way Out" (1972) Bruffee advocated a method of "collaborative learning" that builds a writing course around a series of peer critiques.

By the early 1980s, Bruffee began to connect collaborative learning with Richard Rorty's neopragmatism and social constructionist philosophy, which anticipated a direction that many composition teachers and scholars would take ("Liberal Education"). From Rorty, Bruffee adopts the metaphor for writing as "conversation," emphasizing the communal nature of discourse and a view of knowledge as socially negotiated. In his 1984 essay, "Collaborative Learning and the 'Conversation of Mankind,'" Bruffee links collaborative learning to the mission of liberal education in teaching students the discourse of professional communities. Bruffee's goal of incorporating students into professional communities by showing them that knowledge is consensual, however, soon was called into question.

Greg Myers accuses Bruffee of focusing exclusively on the students' assumed common goal of joining professional communities and ignoring the social differences that divide them ("Reality"). Consensus, according to Myers, is not monolithic but develops from conflict. Myers points out that the open admissions policy at CUNY that led Bruffee to experiment with collaborative learning was not the result of a Kuhnian paradigm shift in composition studies but of political conflicts in New York City during the 1960s (168).

Myers's questioning of Bruffee's unproblematic use of community and consensus was followed by other critiques of the use of notions of community in composition studies. In the first chapter I discuss several of these critiques that fault the uncritical use of community for suppressing the conflicts that exist within any social group. These critiques also suggest that the appeal to community is a means of relocating the wholeness of the self-aware subject within a coherent social group. A holistic and closed notion of community encourages a simplified view of a discursive field, where the influences of the contradictory and multiple discourses that one encounters in everyday life are minimal. The subject becomes a participant within a language game on a contained field of play.

Postmodern theory, on the other hand, would situate the subject among many competing discourses that precede the subject. The notion of "participation" itself becomes problematic in its implication that the subject can control its location and moves within a discourse. By divorcing the subject from prevailing notions of the individual, either the freely choosing individual of capitalism or the interpellated individual of Althusserian Marxism, postmodern theory understands subjectivity as heterogeneous and constantly in flux. The present frustration of those who have followed the course of theory I have just sketched—those who have used notions of community as a critique of the autonomous individual, but then have had these notions of community unravel into complex sets of power relations—is where to locate agency in a postmodern subjectivity.

The instability of the subject in postmodern theory is one aspect of the "impasse" of postmodern theory, which I discuss in the introduction. The subject, like judgments of value and validations, has no grounding outside contingent discourses. Many recent books and collections address the dilemma of the postmodern subject (such as P. Smith's *Discerning the Subject*; Susan Miller's *Rescuing the Subject*). This interest in the subject has brought a new initiative for exploring the relations between rhetoric and ethics.

One of the reasons that the Sophists have become focus of scholarship in the history of rhetoric is their interest in ethics.[1] In this chapter I discuss Lyotard's proposal for relocating the political within ethics and the implications of that proposal for literate acts. But before I take up that proposal, I would like to consider again the impact of electronic technologies on subjectivity by placing current computer technologies in the perspective of a series of electronic communications technologies beginning in the nineteenth century. The dispersal of the subject in electronic communications technologies suggests that we need new ways of talking about subjectivity and raises the issue of what metaphor of the subject might be most useful for articulating a postmodern ethics.

Subjectivity and New Technologies for Writing

The ubiquity of electronic technologies involved in writing and the evident changes in the nature and uses of writing produced by those technologies has made the absence of consideration of the medium of writing impossible to continue. No doubt we are also more aware of the electronic technologies because they are presented as transforming agents in claims that we have entered an era of postmodernity. But if we examine the history of electronic technologies and uses of literacy, we may find reasons to qualify the decisive break that is claimed for postmodernity. While electronic technologies are usually associated with the present era of television and computers, they have now existed for nearly a century and a half, beginning with the first message sent by telegraph in 1844.

The telegraph made possible the creation of national financial markets and led to later developments such as standard time zones and news photography. Carolyn Marvin has analyzed how electronic technologies caused an almost immediate renegotiation of social space. For example, asymmetries of dress and manner that marked social class became invisible when people communicated by telephone, leading to fears in the last decade of the nineteenth century that the social barriers maintained previously through distance might crumble when telephone use became widespread. In a longer perspective, the effects of electronic technologies might be viewed as continuous rather than discontinuous. Nevertheless, these effects have accelerated in the last half of the twentieth century. The penetration of electronic technologies into what had previously been considered private space has rapidly increased since mid-century, and now computer technologies are more and more becoming the medium for literate activities.

Although there has been no shortage of "futurists" who have predicted massive social changes accompanying the advent of the Information Age, scholarly discussion on the effects of writing technologies on literacy has remained cautious and muted. This reticence might be expected, since both rhetorical theory and literary theory have tended to discount the effect of medium. The introduction of electronic forms of writing that can only exist only in computer environments such as hypertext, electronic discussion groups, and large databases have forced a reconsideration of the nature of writing.

Because a printed book is a physical artifact, a reader typically approaches a printed book with the expectation that it will present itself as a unified whole with a consistent persona of an authoritative author. An electronic text such as a database or hypertext allows the reader to participate in the construction of the text and thus creates a very different relation between author and reader. Jay David Bolter explains this difference in *Writing Space: The Computer, Hypertext, and the History of Writing* (1991):

> Printing . . . tended to magnify the distance between the author and the reader, as the author became a monumental figure, the reader only a visitor in the author's cathedral. Electronic writing emphasizes the impermanence and changeability of text, and it tends to reduce the distance between author and reader by turning the reader into an author. (3)

Electronic texts allow a reader to create alternative structures, which are possible but not encouraged by the linear structure of a printed book. Because an electronic text facilitates many different readings and thus changes each time it is read, it lacks the authority of a unified persona. Instead, the persona in an electronic text necessarily appears to be fragmented and partial in perspective. The unity constructed in the reading of an electronic text comes from the reader's links between parts of the text. If, for example, an expert reader of a database seeks information concerning a specific question, the experience of reading may seem logical and unified. If, on the other hand, a novice reader dips into a text of electronic fiction, the experience of reading may seem extremely fragmented to the point of being nonsensical.

The conception of writing advanced in composition textbooks is one very much tied to the printed book. The successful writer is presented as one who leads the reader through a text with the devices of thesis statements, paragraphs organized around main ideas, and explicit transitions that trace a linear path through a text. By achieving the appearance of unity through these devices, writers are told that they can gain the credential of authority. Electronic texts dispute this promise of authority. What is valued in an electronic is not the illusion of completeness and closure, but the expanse that an author of an electronic text can create.

One of the first attempts to consider the impact of electronic technologies on communication in terms of postmodern theory is Mark Poster's *Mode of Information* (1990). Poster makes the configuration of communication in any society analogous to Marx's mode of production in being worthy of study and analyzable as an autonomous level of experience. He theorizes that changes in the "wrapping" of language affect how meaning is constructed; thus the shift from oral and print "wrapped" language to electronically "wrapped" language reconfigures a subject's relation to the world. He delineates three stages of symbolic exchange: an oral stage where "the self is constituted as a position of enunciation through its embeddedness in a totality of face-to-face relations"; a print stage where "the self is constructed as an agent centered in rational/imaginary autonomy"; and an electronic stage where "the self is decentered, dispersed, and multiplied in continuous instability" (6). Poster denies that these stages are sequential but instead views them as coterminous, with elements of each existing in the others.

Poster focuses on how electronically mediated language brings about a dispersal of subjectivity. The absence of the immediate context and the imaginary authorship of print creates a condition of self-referentiality, where one has to remake oneself continually while writing without being aware of how one is being constructed by others. Electronic technologies for writing do not support the illusion that the author is present on the page, speaking directly to us. Instead, writing appears as signs on the screen coming from seemingly nowhere, sometimes linked tenuously to a name and sometimes not, with a piece of discourse from the remote past looking no different from what was composed on the terminal beside you only moments before. As one of my students put it, electronic class discussions "aren't really anonymous, but they feel anonymous."

Poster suggests a technical determinism for this phenomenon, but I would offer a more qualified explanation that electronic technologies provide the *occasion* for displaying new forms of subjectivity as well as a causal force. Most of acts of reading in our culture—reading signs, reading labels, reading instructions, reading forms, reading most of what's in a newspaper—also "feel anonymous," and rarely are author's names attached to such quotidian texts. Like most of the food we eat, the products we consume, and the services we use each day, these ordinary texts have passed through the hands of many strangers before we encounter them.

I would argue that the changes are as much due to a recognition among those who have access to electronic technologies beyond the broadcast media that nearly everyone in advanced technological societies lives in a multiplicity of complex urban networks. Similarly, electronic class discussions demonstrate to students that, in large universities at least, classrooms are urban spaces bringing together a range of differences even when students are relatively homogeneous in race and class. It is not so much that the authority of the instructor is dispersed but that the illusion that students form a coherent group is shattered when what would seem to be facile points of interpretation produce divergent responses. The security of the classroom as a community or the security of groups within that classroom is violated when intragroup differences quickly arise. The multiplicity of subjectivity is not necessarily a thing to fear because in classrooms it fosters discursive richness and creativity. But it does require theorizing and, if teaching practices are to be involved, new metaphors for the subject.

The Metropolitan Subject

The subject has been the locus of numerous cultural debates since World War II. Fears of fascism and communism remained after the war, and debates over the subject were staged in the modernist terms of individual struggling against the constraints and conforming pressures of society. Throughout the 1950s conformity was represented as a threat to American society in books like Hoffer's *The True Believer*, Wilson's *The Man in the Gray Flannel Suit*, and Whyte's *The Organization Man*. But after the disruptions of the 1960s and early 1970s, intellectuals such as Daniel Bell began to express an opposite fear—that American individualism had gone out of control, destroying social needs through excessive hedonism. Bell advocated a return to the Protestant ethic as a balance to the hedonistic calls of the free market. Many other social and political theorists criticized capitalist society for promoting self-interest over social vision. These theorists appealed to ideals of community as an alternative to atomistic individualism.

In *Justice and the Politics of Difference*, Iris Young charts a response to individualism from political theorists that parallels the critique of the autonomous individual writer in composition studies. Young notes that political theorists writing in the 1980s such as Michael Sandel and Benjamin Barber criticize liberalism's concept of justice for presupposing the self as an antecedent unity prior to its desires. The self in liberalism is assumed to exist in its separate, private space, motivated only by its desires. The subsequent model of society, therefore, is based on relations of competitiveness. Sandel and Barber argue instead for a concept of the self that is constituted in its relations with others. In a social conception of the self, the primary social relation becomes not competitiveness among individuals in fulfilling private desires but actions and beliefs that affirm what individuals hold in common. Young agrees with Sandel's and Barber's charge that liberalism views society as little more than the field on which individuals compete, and she shares their goal of offering an alternative to liberal individualism. Young, however, questions whether the ideal of community is an adequate alternative. The critiques of Sandel and Barber present a dichotomy between individual and community, one that Young says "would lead us to think that liberal individualism and communitarianism exhaust the possibilities for conceiving social relations" (226).

Young argues that the ideal of community is persuasive for many people because it implies that you can understand others as they understand themselves and that others will understand you as you understand yourself. Postmodern theory challenges this belief. Young also claims the ideal of community is politically problematic because it tends to suppress differences among its members and exclude those who are labeled as different. As it is popularly conceived, *community* provides little or no understanding of the politics of existing societies but rather is the expression of a desire to transcend a present state of alienation. Thus like the concept of the autonomous subject that denies differences among people by positing an underlying rational unity for every individual, the concept of community performs an analogous denial by presenting the fusion of its members as the ideal.

The ideal of community privileges face-to-face relations as the primary form of social interaction. While Young does not deny the value and enjoyment of living and working in small groups, she contends to advance such small groups as the ideal social organization is hopelessly utopian. She finds the metaphor of community inadequate to represent contemporary life in technologically advanced nations. Her point is well taken. Even in isolated rural communities, which would seem to best embody the notion of a small group of people organized by face-to-face relations, the metaphor of community is misleading. Satellite technologies permit many rural dwellers to have nearly the same access to broadcast media as do the inhabitants of major cities. Those who own satellite dishes in rural areas often receive more channels than a typical urban cable system. A national newspaper, *USA Today*, is now distributed in most rural communities. National retail chains now build stores in small towns and mail-order retailers make available nationally advertised products. Nearly everyone in the United States has access to a telephone. While many people in rural communities remain poor, even in economically impoverished communities residents are far more cosmopolitan in their attitudes than in earlier decades. Many have been forced to move to new regions in search of employment.

In an intensely urbanized society, holding up community as an ideal can be a way of avoiding politics. Calls for community are antiurban and look with nostalgia to a less complex past. They ignore how communities are to interact even if extensive decentralization might be achieved. At a time when in our daily lives we wear clothing, eat food, and buy products made in many different countries, and when economic and environmental issues are increasingly global, relations among communities will necessarily be configured in vast complex networks. At worst, community can be used as a justification of race, ethnic, and class prejudice. The myth of community lies behind acts of violence and exclusion against those who are considered outsiders in certain neighborhoods.

What is needed to replace the individual/community dichotomy, Young maintains, is a politics of difference, and she looks to postmodern theory because it conceives of the subject as a play of differences that cannot be reduced to a whole. Young describes a politics of difference as an "openness to unassimilated otherness," and in order to practice a politics of difference, there must be discourses and spaces where differences are preserved and appreciated. Young advocates using city life as an alternative to both liberal individualism and the ideal of community. In cities people are more open to the possibilities of interacting with strangers and often find stimulation in such interactions. Young does not pretend that today's problems of city life do not exist, but she also maintains that present cities give "hints of what differentiation without exclusion might be. . . . In the good city one crosses from one distinct neighborhood to another without knowing precisely where one ended and the other began" (239). Social justice in the city requires a politics of difference, a politics that "lays down institutional and ideological means for recognizing and affirming diverse social groups by giving political representation to these groups, and celebrating their distinctive characteristics and cultures" (240).

Lyotard and the Question of Justice

Young's call for an urban subjectivity open to unassimilated otherness is one of numerous appeals in postmodern theory for openness to heterogeneity. Such openness is the justification for Lyotard's rejection of "grand narratives" in *The Postmodern Condition*. *The Postmodern Condition*, however, has caused a great deal of confusion over Lyotard's conception of a just society. In many respects it is unrepresentative of Lyotard's provocative examinations of heterogeneity. *The Postmodern Condition* was written on commission from the Conseil des Universitiés of the government of Québec as "a report on knowledges in the most highly developed societies" (xxv), and it led Lyotard to speculate broadly on the influences of technology on contemporary knowledge and the state of science.

These sociological pronouncements in *The Postmodern Condition* have drawn much criticism, especially the concluding utopian suggestion that the public be given free access to computer data banks (67). This proposal appears to Lyotard's critics as representing a liberal pluralism that is oblivious to existing political relations. For example, Seyla Benhabib asks: "Can IBM or any other multinational corporation democratize its trade secrets and technical information? Is the military likely to democratize its trade secrets and technical information?" (122). In a caustic review, Terry Eagleton calls Lyotard's work on postmodernism "the politics of an ageing hippie" ("Awakening").

Lyotard is also accused of contradicting himself in *The Postmodern Condition* when he opposes grand narratives with "little narratives." He would seem to be privileging one discursive form over another, in direct contradiction to his call for the heterogeneity of language games. His advocacy of dissensus and paralogy instead of consensus would, as Geoffrey Bennington points out, produce a grand narrative of dispersion (116). Lyotard even acknowledges the contradictoriness of his position in *Just Gaming*, a book that consists of a series of dialogues between Lyotard and Jean-Loup Thébaud. After arguing for the "justice of multiplicity," Lyotard admits that it is upheld by a universal principle of the incommensurability and singularity of language games. Thébaud, taking the last turn in the book, tells Lyotard: "Here you are talking like the great prescriber himself" (100). The book ends with a parenthetical "laughter."

Lyotard apparently was sensitive to the criticism *The Postmodern Condition* received. In the preface to *The Differend*, published in French in 1984, five years after *The Postmodern Condition*, Lyotard rejects what he describes as the current "weariness" of theory with "new this, new that, post-this, post-that" and says that "the time has come to philosophize" (xiii). The problem that Lyotard poses in *The Differend* is the question of how justice is to be determined when each party in a conflict does not agree on the relevant rule of justice. In such cases, Lyotard says a *differend* results as opposed to a *litigation*, where the parties agree on the relevant rule of justice. In chapter 3 I analyze an example of a differend in the conflict between pro-choice and pro-life forces over abortion rights. There is no universal, objective discourse that these sides recognize, and thus there is no real debate over abortion. The pro-choice side claims the primacy of a woman's right to control her body; the pro-life side claims the primacy of the life of the human embryo. As soon as the terms *baby* or *fetus* are introduced in such discussions, the differend of the other is silenced.

In *The Differend* Lyotard raises what might be the most difficult example for someone accused of advocating relativism and solipsism—the Holocaust—in particular, the death camp Auschwitz. Lyotard confronts the revisionist historian Robert Faurisson's claim that he can find no credible witness who can testify to the existence of gas chambers to illustrate the double bind of victims of the Holocaust. According to Faurisson, the only credible witness is one who actually saw people die in the gas chamber. But the only people who had this experience of the gas chamber are dead and cannot testify that the gas chamber existed. Because of a lack of credible witnesses, Faurisson claims that the Holocaust cannot be proven. The basis of Faurisson's denial of the Final Solution comes from an illegitimate extension of what Lyotard describes as the cognitive genre that ostensively establishes reality. By following literally the rules of a positivist historian, Faurisson is able to deny that the Final Solution existed. The limitations of the positivist historian in the face of Auschwitz for Lyotard come to represent both the limitations of understanding reality and the limitations of genre. The differend is located not just in the conflict between Faurisson's claim and the suffering of the victims, but in the erasure of the terror of the Holocaust in the cognitive genre. Speaking of Auschwitz as a cognitive event renders it no different from other events that kill many people such as earthquakes.

To illustrate the differend, Lyotard distinguishes between a plaintiff who has incurred damages, and has the means to prove those damages, and a victim who lacks these means. The "perfect crime," according to Lyotard, is not to kill all the witnesses but to obtain the silence of witnesses and render their testimony inconsistent or insane: "If there is nobody to adduce the proof, nobody to admit it, and/or if the argument which upholds it is judged to be absurd, then the plaintiff is dismissed, the wrong he or she complains of cannot be attested. He or she becomes a victim. If he or she persists in invoking this wrong as if it existed, the others . . . will easily be able to make him or her pass for mad" (8).

The process of turning the plaintiff into a victim by silencing a differend was demonstrated in the U.S. Senate hearings concerning charges of sexual harassment against Supreme Court nominee Clarence Thomas in 1991. The plaintiff, Anita Hill, was unable to prove her charges of damages before a male tribunal, and she was dismissed as "fantasizing" the charges against Thomas. The refusal of the Senate Judiciary Committee to acknowledge that the wrong of sexual harassment might be different from other kinds of wrongs and that Hill's reluctance to make a formal complaint at the time the harassment occurred might be considered a usual rather than unusual response to sexual harassment was a silencing of a differend. Given the rules of evidence that obtained for this hearing, Hill was unable to convince those who had come out in favor of Thomas's appointment that a wrong had occurred. Lyotard writes that the differend is "the case where the plaintiff is divested of the means to argue and becomes for that reason a victim" (9). In one sentence he describes the fate of Anita Hill before the Senate Judiciary Committee.

The differend arises from the incommensurability of what Lyotard calls "language games" in *Just Gaming* and *The Postmodern Condition* and "regimes of phrases" in *The Differend*.[2] Totalitarianism proceeds from the assumption that one regime of phrases can serve as a metalanguage. The source of totalitarianism is not an aberration of a just order but rather lies in the assertion that a description of an ideal state can serve as the basis of justice. In *Just Gaming* Lyotard critiques the assumption that the "just" follows from the "true." The translation of *Au Juste* as *Just Gaming* is unfortunate because it can be understood as "mere" gaming, when in fact, the language games Lyotard describes are quite serious. The broad question he addresses is the one I quote from Patricia Bizzell in the introduction: how do we create "a positive program legitimated by an authority that is nevertheless nonfoundational?" Lyotard argues that the first step is to disallow any notion of justice based on truth. The claim to know what justice is in advance of the case in point leads to terror. "The question of justice for a society," he maintains in *Just Gaming*, "cannot be resolved in terms of models. This is very important because I think that we are always tempted, whenever the question of justice arises, to go back to a model for a possible constitution, to be drawn up by a possible constitutional convention" (25). A second kind of terror is the embodiment of justice in majority rule. "Majority," he says, "does not mean large number, it means great fear" (99).

He advocates instead that justice be worked out on a case-by-case basis. The obligation of the judge is to the pursuit of justice and not to an ideal justice. Lyotard writes that the thinker he is closest to is Aristotle, "insofar as he recognizes—and he does so explicitly in the *Rhetoric*, as well as in the *Nicomachean Ethics*, that a judge worthy of the name has no true model to guide his judgments, and that the true nature of the judge is to pronounce judgments . . . without criteria. This is, after all, what Aristotle calls prudence" (26). Instead of starting with preestablished criteria and then applying those criteria to a particular case, Lyotard holds out for an indeterminate notion of justice that acknowledges the singularity of the particular event. Thus Lyotard's notion of justice is one compatible with the Sophistic doctrine of *kairos*.

Ethics and Postmodern Pedagogy

The Differend can be read as an argument for locating ethics within a postmodern pedagogy. Lyotard would not have us look to external discourses of the "true" but to the discursive practices of the classroom. *The Differend* sets out a particular approach to reading that Lyotard playfully summarizes in the preface "Reading Dossier." Lyotard writes that "in the next century there will be no more books. It takes too long to read, when success comes from gaining time" (xv). He says his summary will allow the reader "to 'talk about the book' without having read it" (xiv). For those who undertake the book, Lyotard requires only the condition "that he or she agrees not to be done with 'language' and not to 'gain time'" (xiv).

Lyotard's condition in this summary anticipates the actual practice of reading *The Differend*, where assumptions that might lead to prejudgments are consistently challenged. *The Differend* is organized by numbered paragraphs and extensively cross-referenced. In many cases the cross-referencing is circular, and the final sentence directs the reader to begin the book again. The result is that no reading of *The Differend* can ever be completed. The book is arranged to prevent the illusion that any one linkage is the only or best linkage.

Lyotard raises the issue of linkage even within a sentence. His basic unit of discourse is the phrase, which for him is the irreducible event of discourse ("*There is no phrase* is a phrase" 65). Whether the phrase is in any sense "true" is irrelevant. The phrase merely occurs, or as Lyotard says of the phrase, "It happens." Phrases call forth other phrases, and the linkage between these phrases is open. Lyotard describes rules for linking phrases as genres. "Genres of discourse," according to Lyotard, "determine stakes, they submit phrases from different regimens to a single finality: the question, the example, the argument, the narration, the exclamation are in forensic rhetoric the heterogeneous means of persuading" (29). The difficulty, however, is knowing which genre to employ. Because genres are incommensurable, that is, phrases cannot be subjected to a single law, many genres of linkage are possible but one is selected. Thus any linkage can give rise to a differend. Here is one of Lyotard's explanations in *The Differend*:

> A phrase comes along. What will be its fate, to what end will it be subordinated, within what genre of discourse will it take its place? No phrase is the first. This does not only mean that others precede it, but also that the modes of linking

implied in the preceding phrases—possible modes of linking therefore—are ready to take the phrase into account and to inscribe it in the pursuit of certain stakes, to actualize themselves by means of it. In this sense, a phrase that comes along is put into play within a conflict between genres of discourse. This conflict is a differend. (136)

Lyotard questions the authority of any genre to suppress differends. His critique of "grand narratives" such as Marxism is made emphatically in *The Postmodern Condition*, but in the final section of *The Differend* he is equally critical of the reduction of everything to "exchange value" in capitalism. By placing an exchange value on time, one makes time the equivalent of money. Lyotard refers to this reduction as the hegemony of the economic genre.

Throughout his later work he disputes the aspiration of philosophy to provide a metalanguage for other disciplines. He says, "An intellectual is someone who helps forget differends by advocating a given genre . . . for the sake of political hegemony" (142). The role of intellectuals for Lyotard should be just the opposite: "One's responsibility before thought consists, on the contrary, in detecting differends and in finding the (impossible) idiom for phrasing them" (142). Lyotard relocates ethics in the material practices of reading and writing.[3] In a traditional view of the relationship between rhetoric and ethics, ethical values preexist rhetoric. Rhetoric in the traditional view becomes the means to persuade people to be ethical.[4] In a postmodern theory of rhetoric, there is no legitimate preexisting discourse of values for rhetoric to convey. Ethics becomes a matter of recognizing the responsibility of linking phrases. In the choice of a genre there is an obligation in the sense that "you ought to link like this to get that" (116). Thus in the choice of genre there is an ethical decision. It is not an arbitrary decision. It is not a matter of anything goes, of simple relativism, or in the parlance of composition studies, "writer-based prose." Lyotard insists on the obligation of making a responsible decision. There is, however, no external discourse to validate this choice.

Lyotard's refusal of the authority of one genre over others has parallels in composition studies. James Britton and his colleagues based their critique of the teaching of writing in British schools on the privileging of "transactional" writing for the purpose of verifying that students have learned certain facts from previous lessons. Britton urged the introduction of expressive writing into the secondary curriculum. Art Young later applied Britton's critique to writing in American universities, advocating that students write poems, plays, and stories in writing-across-the-curriculum classes. These proposals, however, are not the same as Lyotard's politics of the differend. Even though Lyotard favors narratives in *The Postmodern Condition*, in the *The Differend* he does not argue for displacing one genre by another but rather recognizing the incommensurability among genres. It is not a question of balancing genres, but one of refusing to accept the denial of conflict within the limits of a single genre.

Lyotard would not have writers look to an external theory of ethics but would encourage them to consider the implications of their linkages. I would like to consider again an example, which I discuss earlier in the book, to show how an ethics is located in the practices of composing. In chapter 3 I analyze an exercise in Joseph Williams's *Style: Ten Lessons in Clarity and Grace* in which Williams places the agent "we" in the revised sentence:

> These technical directives are written in a style of maximum simplicity as a result of an attempt at more effective communication with employees of little education who have been hired with guidelines that have been imposed. (32)
> [*Revised:*]
> We have written these technical directives as simply as possible because we are attempting to communicate more effectively with relatively uneducated employees whom we have hired in accordance with guidelines imposed on us by the federal government. (223)

Williams maintains that the second sentence is more "readable" because it supplies an agent, *we. We* is often used in appeals to the ideal of community. It presumes a commonality and neglects differences among those it aspires to include. But at the same time, as Iris Young points out, it creates boundaries that would exclude those considered as the Other. In this case *we* does not refer to all those who work for a particular company, but it divides the company between those who have been hired at the will of the employer and those that the company has been forced to hire. The community invoked by the *we* has exclusionary implications. Lyotard argues in *Peregrinations* that every use of *we* carries an obligation to interrogate the basis of that commonality and who that *we* should be or should become (35).

Even this short example suggests the work Lyotard has left undone. Seyla Benhabib accuses Lyotard of naiveté in assuming that marginalized groups can participate in democratic pluralism when they lack access to organizational and informational resources. Benhabib notes, "At present, these groups include increasing numbers of women, minorities, foreigners, unemployed youth, and the elderly" (123). Perhaps this criticism is the most telling of Lyotard. Lyotard does not offer a way of theorizing inequality nor does he suggest how subjects are to be located. In earlier chapters of this book, I discuss several theorists identified with cultural studies and feminism and Foucault's later work on genealogical practice that all insist that acts of discourse must be considered as historically situated and that discourse and practice cannot be separated. In the previous chapter I argue, using examples from student essays, that many students share this awareness of how historical positioning shapes the production and participation in cultural activities.

The student examples suggest that ways of theorizing subjectivity are needed that neither hold out for liberal humanism, collapse subjectivity into vague notions of community, nor reject the idea of the subject altogether. Iris Young's urban subject gives a means of thinking through the complexity of the momentarily situated subject. The primary contribution of *The Differend* to Young's notion of the urban subject is in conceiving at a microlevel how urban subjects encounter boundaries in both crossing social divisions and in the personal experience of negotiating among many competing discourses. Because Lyotard works at the microlevel, he brings a specificity too often lacking in theoretical discussions and provides a heightened awareness of differences.

Even if Lyotard in the end still does not offer more than a call for justice, *The Differend* remains important for composition theory because it points to a missing ethics throughout the activities of composing, for all are involved in linkage. To detect differends requires a momentary delay of those linkages and a questioning of their ethical implications. The advice of rhetoric following from Aristotle is to select and to limit, to discover the best available means of persuasion. I do not see Lyotard as attempting to overturn this tradition, but I do see him contesting the tyranny of coherence by investigating the politics of articulation.

Lyotard, like Aristotle, finds ethical commitment in rhetorical acts. But at the same time, he recognizes that communicating in the world of the late twentieth century is not the same as in the Athenian polis. His ethics takes account of the metropolitan subject living in an increasingly complex and complicated world. Schools are part of that increasingly complex and complicated world. Mike Rose's description of UCLA as "the wild intersection of cultures, spectacular diversity, compressed by a thousand social forces" can be extended to the student body of the urban classroom (*Lives* 3). Bringing ethics into rhetoric is not a matter of collapsing spectacular diversity into universal truth. Neither is ethics only a matter of a radical questioning of what aspires to be regarded as truth. Lyotard insists that ethics is also the obligation of rhetoric. It is accepting the responsibility for judgment. It is a pausing to reflect on the limits of understanding. It is respect for diversity and unassimilated otherness. It is finding the spaces to listen.

Notes
Sources
Index

Notes

Introduction

1. A more general problem is how to define modernism. On this issue Boyne and Rattansi write: "It is important to restrict the term *modernism* to refer to the set of artistic, musical, literary, more generally aesthetic movements that emerged in Europe in 1880s, flourished before and after the First World War and became institutionalised in the academies and art galleries of post–Second World War Europe and America. A brief and selective list of eminent figures usually regarded as distinctly modernist begins to give an indication of the nature of the modernist project: Matisse, Picasso, and Kandinsky in painting, Stravinsky, Debussy, and Schoenberg in music, Henry James, Joyce, and Kafka in literature, poets such as Eliot, Pound, Rilke, and Mallarmé, and dramatists such as Strindberg and Pirandello. Of course, at this point the heterogeneity of modernism also becomes apparent, both across languages and aesthetic projects" (6).

2. For discussions of the theoretical problems in constructing values within contingent discourses, see Haraway, the essays in *Life after Postmodernism* (ed. Fekete), and Barbara Herrnstein Smith's *Contingencies of Value*.

3. In contrast, Peter Bürger's influential *Theory of the Avant-Garde* places the beginning of aesthetic postmodernism with the avant-garde movements of dada and surrealism.

4. See Cooke; Harvey, chaps. 7–11; and the essays from the "New Times" project (Hall and Jacques).

5. The term *Fordism* was first used by Antonio Gramsci in "Americanism and Fordism," published in *Selections from the Prison Notebooks*.

6. In a 1982 stratified survey of the writing of 200 college-educated people according to type of employer and type of occupation, Faigley and Miller found that everyone in an occupation that requires a college education writes on the job. Furthermore, in professional and technical occupations that employ over half of those who graduate from college, people write for 29 percent of total work time. More recently, Ede and Lunsford surveyed nearly 700 members of seven professional organizations. Respondents reported that they spent 44 percent of work time in some "writing-related activity," and 98 percent ranked writing as important or very important to their jobs

(*Singular Texts* 60). For a discussion of other surveys of writing in the workplace, see Anderson.

7. Crowley estimates that half of today's college writing students still are taught by a current-traditional approach (*Methodical* 139).

8. Vitanza finds a great reluctance among composition theorists to acknowledge the radical questioning and deferral of a course of action in postmodern theory. He places nearly everyone in composition, ranging from Berlin to Flower, in the same leaky boat of modernism.

9. The 1985 conference focused on Lyotard and the visual arts, and the proceedings volume includes criticism of Lyotard's position and Lyotard's responses (Appignanesi).

Chapter 1. In the Turbulence of Theory

1. Toril Moi describes the first French feminist groups organizing as a direct result of women's participation in the May revolution, where according to Moi they "had fought alongside the men on the barricades only to find that they were still expected to furnish their male comrades with sexual, secretarial and culinary services as well" (95).

2. Foucault claims his project represents "neither a theory or a methodology" ("The Subject and Power" 208). Lyotard uses the term *postmodern* while at the same time distancing himself from it as "a mood, or better a state of mind" ("Rules and Paradoxes" 209).

3. In 1967 Derrida published three books, *Of Grammatology, Speech and Phenomena*, and *Writing and Difference*, that marked the onset of poststructuralism. De Man introduced Derrida to many literary scholars in the United States in *Allegories of Reading* and *Blindness and Insight*.

4. For a summary of the treatment of MacCabe in the British press, see Easthope 133–34.

5. For representative overviews of postmodern theory, see Best and Kellner, *Postmodern Theory*; Harvey, *The Condition of Postmodernity*; Hutcheon, *The Politics of Postmodernism*; Huyssen, *After the Great Divide*. Dismissals of postmodern theory are abundant from viewpoints of both the political Left and Right (e.g., Callinicos, *Against Postmodernism*; Bloom, *The Closing of the American Mind*). In France, the backlash against Foucault and other postmodern theorists is led by Luc Ferry and Alain Renaut, who would trace the questioning of the subject to the influence of Heidegger, whose antihumanism they argue is also right-wing and authoritarian. This assignment of linear influence from Heidegger both taints the major French thinkers of the 1960s and 1970s with Heidegger's allegiance to the Nazi party, and it sidesteps such issues as Foucault's denial in his genealogical period, contra Heidegger, that there are no deep truths to be found.

6. Composition studies has but barely finished erecting the structure of the discipline. Overviews of the discipline that claim any scholarly continuity and coherence

date only to the mid 1970s (e.g., Tate; Winterowd, *Contemporary Rhetoric*), comprehensive bibliographies of work in the field only began to appear in the mid 1980s (Lindemann), and it was not until the publication of Bizzell and Herzberg's *The Rhetorical Tradition* in 1990 that an undergraduate or graduate survey course of major historical texts in rhetoric could be organized without considerable difficulties in obtaining key texts. It has yet to enjoy the relatively stable period of a mature discipline.

7. Culler discusses the accusations of traditional critics against deconstruction in the late 1970s. Some of the more caustic attacks on deconstruction in the 1980s came from the Left, notably Eagleton's *Literary Theory: An Introduction* published in 1983, which argues that deconstruction's claim of the epistemological impossibility of knowledge is a false dilemma and that the undecidability of meaning obtains only when texts are stripped of their histories. For Eagleton undecidability is a justification for inaction, a rejoicing in philosophical angst that is politically conservative.

8. Connors ("Composition Studies and Science"), among others, found this claim greatly exaggerated.

9. There are many such instances in research on writing as process where assumptions of a stable self, an innate "writing process," a world directly accessible to observation, and the neutrality of language begin to unravel, but rarely are these frayed threads pulled. For example, Donald Murray writes: "Minute by minute, perhaps second by second—or less at certain stages of the process—the writer may be rehearsing, drafting, and revising, looking back and looking forward, and acting upon what is seen and heard during the backward and forward sensing. The writer is constantly learning from the writing what it intends to say" ("Writing as Process" 7). Murray's last sentence gestures toward a Derridean view of writing, where meaning is continuously deferred as added meanings displace earlier meanings. But Murray could not pursue such implications because he theorized the source of meaning in the mind of the individual writer.

10. In a 1971 article titled "The Problem of Problem Solving," Ann Berthoff denounces problem solving: "The case can easily be made that problem-solving, as conceived by educational psychologists, is the concept of learning our bureaucratized society needs in order to realize the philosophy of education that is most in keeping with its institutional biases. The concept of problem-solving serves the belief that the school's function is to prepare citizens for life in a technological society" (239). See also Nystrand's 1982 critique of Flower and Hayes's model ("Rhetoric's 'Audience'"). Nystrand considers linguistics' concept of a speech community for use in composition studies.

11. For a list of ethnographic studies of writing, see Lauer and Asher, 49–53.

12. See essays in collections edited by Odell and Goswami; Jolliffe (*Advances*); Simons; and Bazerman and Paradis; as well as recent books by Bazerman (*Shaping Written Knowledge*) and Myers (*Writing Biology*).

13. Brodkey (*Academic Writing*) dispels the notion of a single academic community. For a discussion the practical consequences of multiple communities for writing teachers, see Faigley and Hansen.

14. Stewart repeats a fear of groups that was raised in the 1940s and 1950s when

he writes that social constructionism has the potential to lead to "the police state, the group mentality to the point at which it eliminates 'non-social' types such as the Jews in Nazi Germany" (74). See Holt's reply to Stewart's charges ("Towards a Democratic Rhetoric").

15. Along with his colleagues at Pittsburgh, Bartholomae has developed a curriculum that aims at teaching the language of the university to enable students to invent themselves as readers and writers (Bartholomae and Petrosky, *Facts*).

16. Berlin offers a broader overview of examinations of the role of rhetoric in ideology in "Rhetoric Programs after World War II: Ideology, Power, and Conflict."

17. For an overview of recent work, see Flynn, "Composition Studies."

18. See Ede and Lunsford, "Why Write . . . Together" and "Why Write Together: A Research Update" for accounts of how they initially viewed their collaboration.

19. However, Covino's and Susan Miller's ("Is There a Text") articles from 1981 and 1982 respectively that recognize the challenge to authorial intention presented by deconstruction.

20. See also the last three chapters in *The Post-Colonial Critic*, a collection of interviews with Gayatri Chakravorty Spivak. Spivak says: "If you take the theoretical formulation of deconstruction, you have a stalling at the beginning and a stalling at the end (*différance* at the beginning, and *aporia* at the end), so that you can neither *properly* begin nor *properly* end. Most of the people who are interested in deconstruction are interested in these two things. But I'm more interested in what happens in the middle; and I think the later Derrida is too" (136).

21. Hutcheon claims that the self-reflexive and parodic character of postmodern art is an ironic way of stating this recognition (3).

22. In "What is Enlightenment," Foucault argues against the notion that one can either be "for" or "against" the Enlightenment. He reminds us that the Enlightenment is a set of historical events located in European history and not necessarily connected to the survival of liberal humanism in the twentieth century.

23. Foucault has been the major figure in demonstrating how modernist rationality has produced new forms of domination throughout his major work, including the practices and discourses of asylums (*Madness and Civilization*), hospitals (*The Birth of the Clinic*), prisons (*Discipline and Punish*), and the regulation of sexuality (*The History of Sexuality*, vol. 1).

24. Few would argue with Callinicos's statement that "Jürgen Habermas is without any doubt the major philosopher of the contemporary Western left" (92).

25. See Iris Young, *Justice and the Politics of Difference*, chap. 4.

Chapter 2. The Changing Political Landscape of Composition Studies

1. Schilb has made this proposal in "Deconstructing Didion" and "Composition and Poststructuralism."

2. Goldwater's hawkish stance on the then small-scale conflict in Vietnam, especially his proposal to use tactical nuclear weapons, has often been advanced a major

cause of his defeat. But other than his promise to oppose civil rights legislation, which was popular among voters in states in the Deep South, none of his social proposals gained wide appeal.

3. Connors describes how the teaching of college writing was from its beginnings in the late nineteenth century characterized by massive workloads for little monetary reward. He states that by 1900 the teacher of rhetoric had become "increasingly marginalized, overworked, and ill-paid" ("Rhetoric in the Modern University" 55). Connors attributes the rapid diminution of the nineteenth-century rhetoric teacher to two factors: the rise of the research university based on the German model that omitted rhetoric and the shift from oral to written discourse with a resulting increase in the workload of the individual teacher. By 1930, Connors notes, the "underclass" of poorly paid writing teachers was disproportionately composed of women, a trend that has yet to be reversed ("Overwork").

4. "Fordism" and "post-Fordism" are discussed in the introduction.

5. Ehrenreich mentions specifically the following occupations: "schoolteachers, anchorpersons, engineers, professors, government bureaucrats, corporate executives (at least up through the middle levels of management), scientists, advertising people, therapists, financial managers, architects" (12).

6. Ehrenreich 202. In 1988, Mishel and Simon noted that top executives made thirty-one times the average salary of workers, a ratio nearly twice that of West Germany. The same year *Business Week* surveyed 678 chief executive officers whose average compensation in 1987 was 1.8 million dollars, a 48 percent increase over 1986 ("Executive Pay"). Considering that the rate of inflation was 4.4 percent in 1987, top executives more than kept up with the cost of living. In the meantime, production and nonsupervisory workers earned 10 percent less in 1986 than they did in 1973 after wages were adjusted for inflation (Kolby 62).

7. Ehrenreich cites the annual American Council on Education and UCLA survey of college freshmen in which 75.6 percent of students in 1987 listed "being very well off financially" as their primary goal, a percentage that increased for eighteen consecutive years from 39.1 percent in 1970. By 1990 that statistic has dropped to 73.7 percent, and responses to other questions show increasing concern for social issues and the environment, taken by some to indicate a dissatisfaction with the status quo ("Survey of College Freshmen").

8. Rose lists a few of these complaints in *Lives* (5–7). Trimbur ("Literacy") observes that the literacy crisis of the mid 1970s is only the latest in a long series of fears reaching back over a century that literacy education will not distinguish the middle class from those below.

9. Shor discusses the political forces behind the literacy crisis of the 1970s in *Culture Wars*, chap. 3.

10. CLAC, the newsletter for the Conference on Language Attitudes and Composition, was founded in response to pressures for "competency" testing and back-to-basics curricular measures. The first issue was in February 1977, edited by Tim Barnes, Jim Nattinger, Shelley Reece, and Tony Wolk.

11. Jacoby discusses some of the more prominent cases.

12. The American Council of Education reports in *Minorities in Higher Education: Eighth Annual Status Report* that the college participation rate for dependent low-income black high school graduates between eighteen and twenty-four years old declined from 39.8 percent in 1976 to 30.3 percent in 1988; for low-income Hispanics during the same period, the rate fell from 50.4 to 35.3 percent. For middle-income blacks, the participation rate dropped from 52.7 in 1976 to 36.2 percent in 1988; for comparable Hispanics, the rate went down from 53.4 to 46.4 percent.

13. Knoblauch observes that such programs aimed at teaching what Giroux and others call "critical literacy" can be found "only in a few academic enclaves, where it exists more as a facsimile of oppositional culture than as a practice, and in an even smaller number of community-based literacy projects, which are typically concerned with adult learners" ("Literacy" 79).

14. Whether cultural studies as an academic enterprise can maintain its overtly political critique remains to be seen. In a chapter arguing the need for cultural studies, Giroux, Shumway, Smith, and Sosnoski note that American studies was openly political at the outset only to have the political critique muted as it became entrenched as a discipline.

15. Johnson outlines the theoretical background of British cultural studies. See also Hall, "Cultural Studies." For a discussion of trends in American work on mass culture, see Lazere.

16. Marilyn Cooper writes about an experience similar to Sirc's in a first-year, second-quarter research writing class. Cooper says she grew tired of reading papers "consisting of partially digested information on Star Wars or AIDS" ("Unhappy Consciousness" 29). She decided to plan the course in response to a book she knew students would disagree with and yet would have to come to terms with the theory on which the book is based in order to express that disagreement. Cooper chose Herbert Marcuse's *One Dimensional Man*, a book that also talks about the closing of the American mind but from the perspective that critical thought has become increasingly impossible in advanced industrial societies. Cooper refused to interpret this difficult book for the students. She organized the course using collaborative learning so that students would have to work through Marcuse's concepts in peer discussions and background reading, and she had them evaluate his claims in reference to contemporary culture. Predictably, a few students were upset about the course. One student wrote in his journal, "What does it matter whether my needs are true or false as long as I'm happy?" (33). Another complained, "You want us to think" (44). But by the end of the quarter several of the students had come to appreciate other perspectives besides the one they brought to the course. Cooper notes, "Our primary goal in first-year writing classes often seems to be to make our students happy" (57). She admits that to an extent this role is commendable, but it also "causes students to see writing classes as different, marginal, subordinate to the 'real' classes that form the substance of their education" (58).

17. In a report to the Committee on Education and Labor of the U.S. House of Representatives, Malveaux quotes the following 1984 figures for persons over age twenty-five employed in full-time jobs according to level of education. Although the

income levels of black women and white women appear close in the table below, the unemployment rate for black women was 2.25 times higher than for white women from 1980 to 1985.

Education	Black Women	White Women	Black Men	White Men
Elementary school	$10,804	$10,849	$14,109	$17,114
High school	$13,619	$14,733	$16,724	$24,000
College (4+ years)	$21,222	$22,089	$28,244	$34,403

18. Brodkey describes the course and the controversy surrounding it in "Making a Federal Case out of Difference."

19. *The Daily Texan* 13 Sept. 1990:11.

20. In the mid-1980s Accuracy in Academia claimed there were 10,000 Marxist professors in the United States (Lazere).

Chapter 3. The Linguistic Agent as Subject

1. A partial list of these researchers includes Betty Bamberg, Robert de Beaugrande, Deborah Brandt, Linda Brodkey (*Academic Writing*), Gregory Colomb and Joseph Williams, Marilyn Cooper ("Context as Vehicle"), Barbara Couture, George Dillon, Jeanne Fahnestock ("Semantic"), Lester Faigley ("Problem of Topic"), Donald Freeman, George Gopen, John Mellon ("Dominant Nominal"), Louis Milic, Greg Myers (Pragmatics"), Martin Nystrand (*Structure*), Louise Phelps, Victor Raskin and Irwin Weiser, John Schafer, William Vande Kopple, and Stephen Witte. The diversity of this work reflects an spectrum of linguistic inquiry across disciplines and across continents during the 1970s and 1980s. Some notion of the scope of this work can be gathered by thumbing through the four-volume *Handbook of Discourse Analysis* edited by Teun van Dijk, which includes chapters on current issues in sociolinguistics, text linguistics, pragmatics, conversational analysis, and other subfields concerned with language in society.

2. Chomsky repeated this caveat most recently in an interview in April 1990 (Olson and Faigley). However, he did suggest that the principles and parameters approach which he initiated in lectures given at a conference in Pisa, Italy, in 1979, may indeed be the linguistics revolution that others attributed to earlier versions of generative grammar.

3. Newmeyer charts a diminishing of Chomsky's influence, seeing its nadir in 1970 at the high point of generative semantics only to recover dramatically with the introduction of the principles and parameters approach. Another pervasive influence toward formalism in the 1980s has been the association of linguistics and artificial intelligence. The demand for increasingly sophisticated parsers has directed attention toward aspects of language most amenable to formal analysis.

4. At the same time Chomsky was disposing of structuralism in American linguistics, the semiological version of structuralism associated with literary theory and anthropology rose in France led by Roland Barthes (*Elements of Semiology*) and Claude Lévi-Strauss. The resulting confusion helped further to divide linguists from literary scholars, since the former viewed the latter's embrace of structuralism as a backward step.

5. Hodge and Kress later moved to Australia and have continued to collaborate on the critical analysis of communication (see *Social Semiotics*). Fowler remained at East Anglia and returned to his earlier work in literary study. Richardson provides a helpful review of the East Anglian proposals for critical linguistics and objections to those proposals. Fairclough includes critical linguistics in *Language and Power*, his 1989 introduction to "critical language study."

6. Another neo-Whorfian position developed at the same time in radical feminist critiques of language in North America and in Britain. These critiques maintain that the possibility of nonsexist language is an illusion. Adrienne Rich writes that when women "become acutely, disturbingly aware of the language we are using and that is using us, we begin to grasp a material resource that women have never before collectively attempted to repossess" ("Power" 247). The problem women encounter using language is not simply a matter of the more familiar features of sexist language such as the use of male pronouns to refer to people in general. Instead, patriarchy is embedded in the ways language interprets the world. The term *motherhood* typifies patriarchal control of language for Rich and other radical feminists. Dale Spender in *Man Made Language* argues that many women experience neither joy nor fulfillment in motherhood and consequently feel themselves inadequate because "their meanings do not mesh with the accepted ones" (54). That *motherhood* can only be used positively reveals one way language helps to maintain unequal relations of power between men and women. Radical feminists claim that when women use male-controlled language, they either falsify their own experience or fall silent.

7. For an explication of similar tactics in the writing of scientists, see Gragson and Selzer.

8. Notice too the *we* in the embedded clause, *we all have more important things to do*. In the first paragraph *we* refers to staff and students at U.W.C. In this clause *we* refers to staff and parents. By shifting the referents of *we*, the headmaster subtly reinforces the mutuality of parents and school as agents of authority.

9. Thompson discusses other works of Bourdieu that analyze the relation of language and power in *Studies in the Theory of Ideology*, chap. 2.

10. Whether Marx maintained this view throughout his life has been much debated. Several arguments have been made that Marx adopted a less reductionist view in later works. See, for example, Donald and Hall xv–xvi.

11. In this respect Halliday's view of language as social semiotic has parallels with Foucault's analysis of discursive practices in *The Archaeology of Knowledge*.

12. See Kress, "Discourses, Texts, Readers," for self-criticism of the earlier critical linguistics position.

13. What Christensen neglected to say was that the nonrestrictive modifiers loaded

with details that he urged students to use also increased their syntactic maturity, according to Kellogg Hunt's indices. Hunt explained this point to Christensen in a letter that Christensen included as a footnote in "The Problem of Defining a Mature Style," but evidently Christensen failed to understand Hunt's explanation.

14. See Colomb and Williams for discussion of the linguistic traditions on which Williams draws in *Style: Ten Lessons.*

Chapter 4. Ideologies of the Self in Writing Evaluation

1. In 1938 the French anthropologist Marcel Mauss argued that the idea of the individual self is uniquely Western. A great deal of ethnographic evidence has been gathered that supports Mauss's position, and more recently anthropologists have examined the ways in which languages embody notions of the self. One reason why the notion of the self as an autonomous, individual consciousness is plausible in the West is that the grammars of European languages are compatible with notions of individualism. In European languages the fact that "I" or "*yo*" or "*je*" or "*ich*" refers indexically to the speaker of the utterance suggests that the speaker possesses an autonomous consciousness and at the same time is aware of that consciousness. But in certain non-European languages the "I" can in some circumstances refer to others as well as the speaker. Greg Urban has found that in Shokleng, a Brazilian Amerindian language, "I" can point to both the speaker's physical self and an imaginary self that maintains reference with third-person forms. The subjectivity constructed in Shokleng discourse, therefore, can extend beyond the individual body to assume multiple voices, constituting a self that is distinctly cultural.

2. See Diederich for further discussion.

3. See Trachsel for an excellent review of the vast literature on writing assessment that arose along with the growth of college English departments and the use of essay examinations for college admissions in the first decades of the twentieth century.

4. Jolliffe ("Moral Subject") sees such topics as eliciting lessons of moral improvement, which show the influence of Matthew Arnold on university English studies in general.

5. Although the Scholastic Aptitude Test eventually replaced the CEEB's two essay examinations in English (the Restricted and Comprehensive Examinations) for use in college admissions, essay examinations are still used in the Advanced Placement Program. In 1976 Ohmann claimed this examination rewards "docile" and "objective" responses (*English* 56, 57).

6. In a review of *What Makes Writing Good,* Patricia Bizzell and Bruce Herzberg discuss the predominance of personal essays. They find two major problems with what they claim is the advancement of the personal essay as the touchstone of good writing: "First, it is simply not true that all good writing shares the virtues of the personal essay," and second, "Teaching the personal essay as if it embodied universal standards of the good . . . implies that there are universal standards of the good" (245, 246).

Chapter 5. The Conflicting Rhetoric of Writing Textbooks

1. Because Athusser's major works were written while he was engaged in internal struggles within the French Communist party, they all have local subtexts which at times are revealed in the footnotes but make his highly abstract style even less pleasurable to read. Tragically, in 1975 he murdered his wife and lived until his death in 1989 in an institution for the criminally insane. Althusser's influence comes principally from two books, *For Marx* (1965, translated into English in 1969) and *Lenin and Philosophy and other Essays* (1968, translated into English in 1971), and more specifically, from a single chapter in each of the respective volumes, "Marxism and Humanism" and "Ideology and Ideological State Apparatuses."

2. In the early seventeenth century, Foucault notes that soldiers were "found" because they had recognizable qualities. They possessed certain physical characteristics that made them stand out from other men: "a lively, alert manner, an erect head, a taut stomach, broad shoulders, long arms, strong fingers, a small belly, thick thighs, slender legs, and dry feet" (*Discipline and Punish* 135). By the late eighteenth century, the soldier had become a lump of clay out of which a soldier could be constructed: through training the manner of the peasant could be replaced with the air of the soldier.

3. *The History of Sexuality*, vol. 1: *An Introduction* was to be the first of a six-volume series on how sexuality is socially constructed. Foucault, however, became bored with the project (see his comment in an interview with Dreyfus and Rabinow 229) and turned to the development of the self in volume 2 (*The Use of Pleasure*) and volume 3 (*The Care of the Self*). Volume 1 contains one of Foucault's most elaborated statements on power in part 4, "The Deployment of Sexuality." Foucault's concern with power is indicated by the original title, *La Volonté de savoir* ("The Will to Knowledge"), which suggests a Nietzschean conception of power.

4. *Writing with a Purpose* is typical of other textbooks of its time in respect to gender. For example, *Think Before You Write* (Leary), an anthology published in 1951, includes but one essay by a woman among its 48 selections. This essay, "Colleges Don't Make Sense" by Marion Walker Alcaro, argues *against* liberal arts education for women who intend to marry on the grounds that their time would be better spent learning how to manage a house and take care of children. Alcaro writes that her training in art history "came in handy when I went to Florence. . . . But I was lost in a furniture store when I chose the furnishings for my first house. What a conglomeration I picked out for my family to live with!"(26).

5. The ninth edition brought few major changes from the eighth edition. The most noticeable difference of the ninth edition from the eighth is the four-color format and the inclusion of color photographs scattered throughout the text (announced in red letters in the preface as an "Integrated Art Program").

6. One of the first textbooks to contest the notion of reading as locating an author's purpose and writing as an isolated transmission of purpose was Bartholomae and Petrosky's *Ways of Reading* (1987).

7. For examples of what sorts of narratives students might produce, see chap. 1, "McDonald's—We Do It All for You" in Barbara Garson's *The Electronic Sweatshop*.

8. All quotations are from the second edition unless otherwise noted. A third edition was published in 1991. I thank Ann George and Richard Watkinson for their insights concerning *The St. Martin's Guide*.

9. The general guidelines about how, when and where to write are reminiscent of institutional practices of schooling that Foucault discusses in *Discipline and Punish*. Foucault observes disciplinary control demands that the body must be used correctly to make the best possible use of time. He notes that good handwriting "presupposes a gymnastics," and he quotes from an eighteenth-century manual that goes into great detail about where each limb should be placed during writing and at what attitude it should be held (152).

10. Axelrod and Cooper do note that describing dogs and cats as *strays* renders them a public nuisance.

11. In an Althusserian critique of the *St. Martin's Guide*, John Clifford writes, "Like almost all contemporary rhetorics, *St. Martin's* creates the illusion that we can transcend ideology with three well-developed paragraphs of evidence" (44).

Chapter 6. *The Achieved Utopia of the Networked Classroom*

1. Joy Peyton has noted that networked computers bring about a new pedagogical dynamic only if the teacher wants it to occur ("Technological Innovation").

2. Bump describes the workings of these two programs in more detail. *InterChange, Realtime Writer*, and other similar forms of electronic written discussions were being used on over forty campuses in March 1990 according to an informal census taken by Trent Batson (personal communication). Peyton ("Computer Networks") has published a bibliography on studies and discussions of electronic conferencing software.

3. See Bump for a discussion of students' attitudes toward synchronous and asynchronous electronic discussions.

4. These machines have since been replaced with IBM PS/2 Model 70 computers and a second networked classroom equipped with Apple Macintosh IIsi computers was added in 1991.

5. While my classes typically use pseudonyms at least once a semester, I have not used a pseudonym because I do not want students occupied by guessing who I am. The pseudonyms are the ones the students elected to use. I have changed students' actual names here and elsewhere in this chapter.

6. Kremers's initial response to ENFI discussions was one of anger and frustration ("Adam Sherman Hill"), but this reaction later moderated ("Sharing Authority").

7. See Mehan, "The Structure of Classroom Discourse," for a review of this work.

8. The one student not represented came late and sat for most of the class waiting for the old messages to load. With newer equipment and software, these delays have been significantly reduced.

9. Barker and Kemp discuss computer-based conferences as postmodern; several people have written about the poststructuralist or postmodern qualities of hypertext; see, for example, Bolter, Landow.

10. In a study of writing groups in a conventional classroom, Kathleen Murphy

reports that comments in all-male groups tend to be more declarative and prescriptive while comments in all-female groups tend to be more affirming. In mixed groups women tend to serve as the "conversational housekeeper," maintaining the conversational flow.

11. One shirt proclaimed, "Ten reasons why a beer is better than a woman" and listed items such as "Beer always gives good head."

12. In fact, Delores wrote at the end the course that she wished all of our discussions had been on the network. In reference to a particular oral class discussion near the end of the course, Delores wrote, "I had some comments to make, but I hate speaking in class. The last time I tried speaking in an English class, everyone turned around and looked at me. My face turned a deep shade of red, and I almost forgot what I wanted to say. I know my voice was shaking and I just wanted the earth to open up and swallow me."

13. A student in the spring 1988 Thinking and Writing class wrote at the end: "I can remember a lot of what was said throughout this class. However, I cannot tell you who specifically said what." See also Selfe, "Technology"; Spitzer. Students' remarks echo the question, "What difference does it make who is speaking?" with which Foucault ends his influential essay, "What is an Author?"

Chapter 7. Student Writers at the End of History?

1. Minow, the newly appointed chairman of the Federal Communications Commission, told the assembled executives of the National Association of Broadcasters in May 1961, "When television is bad, nothing is worse" (Adams). Minow's efforts to upgrade programming were met with cries of censorship from the television industry, and Minow resigned two years later.

2. See responses to Farrell's article in the December 1984 issue of *College Composition and Communication.*

3. Halliday's work on lexical density versus grammatical complexity is discussed in chapter 3.

4. For example, Ice-T's "Freedom of Speech" on *The Iceberg* tape/CD contains an elaborate defense of the right to free speech.

5. In this same published conversation with Stuart Hall, Jameson says of the collapse of communism in Eastern Europe, "1989 was really the result of the passage of the eastern countries into a whole new world system that has been becoming visible and organized over the last 10 to 15 years" (31).

6. In this claim Jameson reiterates Marcuse's argument in *One Dimensional Man.*

7. Stephanson, "Regarding" 5. Stephanson's question to Jameson that prompted the quoted response implicates television in teaching this new cultural logic: "During the sixties, I was once told that the average camera movement—a change of view, a zoom, a pan—did not go below something like one per 7.5 seconds in an ordinary thirty-second commercial, the reason being that this was considered the optimum of what human perception could handle. Now, it is down to something like 3.5 or less. I have actually timed commercials in which there is about one change every two seconds, fifteen changes in a matter of thirty seconds." Stephanson's figures are even con-

servative. In a frequently broadcast commercial featuring the athlete Bo Jackson during fall 1989 (the "Bo knows" commercial), there were 29 changes in 30 seconds. In the sequel where Bo Jackson pretended to play guitar with Bo Diddley that appeared a few months later, there were 32 changes in 30 seconds.

8. These terms are discussed in the introduction.

9. Poster notes: "There are only two social groups in advanced society who by their daily practice are encouraged to regard texts as having transcendent primacy in human experience: orthodox rabbis and academicians in the humanities and some of the social sciences" (80).

10. Mark Crispin Miller discusses how potentially threatening poor people are effaced in the electronic media in chapters of *Boxed In*, such as an ad for Jamaican tourism where all young males are absent. Jamaica is presented as a country of women and old men, waiting for the "massa's" return.

11. *Simulations* 23, 24, 25. Baudrillard sees Ronald Reagan's presidency as a confirmation that America has entered postmodernity. He notes that Reagan obtained a much broader consensus with his smile than Kennedy could with his intelligence and political acuity. The vacant smile is one of Baudrillard's most suggestive images of America. He writes that the ubiquitous smile in America is "the smile the dead man will wear in the funeral home. . . . The smile of immunity, the smile of advertising: 'This country is good. I am good. We are the best.' It is also Reagan's smile—the culmination of the self-satisfaction of the entire American nation—which is on the way to becoming the sole principle of government. Smile and others will smile back. Smile to show how transparent, how candid you are. Smile if you have nothing to say. Most of all, do not hide the fact that you have nothing to say nor your total indifference to others. Let this emptiness, this profound indifference shine out spontaneously in your smile" (*America* 34).

12. The January 29, 1990, issue of USA *Today* gives a full page to its ratings of the ads and about a half-page to direct game coverage. Feature stories about players, fans, and media coverage also greatly exceed the space given to the game itself.

13. Another approach is to use narratives to chronicle the landscape of popular culture. In connection with Barbara Ehrenreich's *Fear of Falling*, I have asked students to trace some issue from the 1960s to the present as it was represented in the media in order to supplement or contest Ehrenreich's narrative. Students worked in groups on this project, and they selected issues of interest to them. What they found out surprised them. For example, the group that studied the women's movement found that abortion was only one of an array of issues in the 1960s and came increasingly to represent the women's movement following the *Roe* v. *Wade* decision in 1973. The class accomplished the goals of assigning a conventional research paper, such as finding sources, evaluating sources, and incorporating them as support of an argument, but they were also able to work collectively to produce a complex view of the trajectory of social issues during their lifetimes.

Chapter 8. The Ethical Subject

1. See Jarratt, *Rereading the Sophists*.

2. Even in *Just Gaming* Lyotard is careful to point out that the notion of a game

does not imply a conscious player: "They are games that make us into their players" (55).

3. For a discussion of the implications of *The Differend* for literary theory, see Readings.

4. Porter contrasts Richard Weaver and Kenneth Burke. Weaver maintains a traditional view, looking to ethics for stability. Burke, on the other hand, allows that rhetoric and ethics are interdependent.

Sources

Adams, Val. "F.C.C. Head Bids TV Men, Reform 'Vast Wasteland.'" *New York Times* 10 May 1961, late ed.: 1, 91.

Adelstein, Michael E., and Jean G. Pival. *The Writing Commitment.* 4th ed. San Diego: Harcourt, 1988.

Adler, Jerry. "Taking Offense." *Newsweek* 24 Dec. 1990: 48–54.

Adorno, Theodor. *Negative Dialectics.* New York: Continuum, 1973.

Althusser, Louis. "Ideology and Ideological State Apparatuses." *Lenin and Philosophy and other Essays.* Trans. Ben Brewster. London: New Left Books, 1971. 121–73.

———. "Marxism and Humanism." *For Marx.* Trans. Ben Brewster. New York: Pantheon, 1969. 219–47.

American Council of Education. Office of Minority Concerns. *Minorities in Higher Education: Eighth Annual Status Report.* Washington, DC: American Council of Education, 1989.

Anderson, Paul V. "What Survey Research Tells Us about Writing at Work." *Writing in Nonacademic Settings.* Ed. Lee Odell and Dixie Goswami. New York: Guilford, 1985. 3–83.

Annas, Pamela J. "Silences: Feminist Language Research and the Teaching of Writing." *Teaching Writing: Pedagogy, Gender, and Equity.* Ed. Cynthia L. Caywood and Gillian R. Overing. Albany: SUNY P, 1987. 3–17.

Appignanesi, Lisa, ed. *Postmodernism: ICA Documents.* London: Free Association Books, 1989.

Applebee, Arthur N. *Tradition and Reform in the Teaching of English: A History.* Urbana: NCTE, 1974.

Applebee, Arthur N., with Anne Auten and Fran Lehr. *Writing in the Secondary School: English and the Content Areas.* NCTE Research Report No. 21. Urbana: NCTE, 1981.

Applebee, Arthur N., with Judith A. Langer, Russell K. Durst, Kay Butler-Nalin, James D. Marshall, George E. Newell. *Contexts for Learning to Write: Studies of Secondary School Instruction.* Norwood, NJ: Ablex, 1984.

Atkins, C. Douglas, and Michael L. Johnson. "Introduction." *Writing and Reading Differently: Deconstruction and the Teaching of Composition and Literature.* Ed. Atkins and Johnson. Lawrence: UP of Kansas, 1985. 1–14.

Austin, J. L. *How to Do Things with Words*. Cambridge, MA: Harvard UP, 1975.

Axelrod, Rise B., and Charles R. Cooper. *The St. Martin's Guide to Writing*. New York: St. Martin's, 1985. 2nd ed., 1988.

Bakhtin, M. M. "Discourse in the Novel." *The Dialogic Imagination*. Trans. Caryl Emerson and Michael Holquist. Ed. Michael Holquist. Austin: U of Texas P, 1981. 259–404.

Baker, Sheridan. *The Practical Stylist*. New York: Harper, 1962. 6th ed., 1985.

Bamberg, Betty. "What Makes a Text Coherent?" *College Composition and Communication* 34 (1983): 417–29.

Barbato, Joseph. Rev. of *Paradigms Lost*, by John Simon. *Change* 12 (Sept. 1980): 62.

Barber, Benjamin. *Strong Democracy*. Berkeley: U of California P, 1984.

Barker, Thomas T., and Fred O. Kemp. "Network Theory: A Post-modern Pedagogy for the Writing Classroom." *Computers and Society: Teaching Composition in the Twenty-First Century*. Ed. Carolyn Handa. Portsmouth, NH: Boynton/Cook, 1990. 1–27.

Barthes, Roland. *Elements of Semiology*. Trans. Annette Lavers and Colin Smith. New York: Hill and Wang, 1967.

———. *Mythologies*. Trans. Annette Lavers. New York: Hill and Wang, 1967.

Bartholomae, David. "Inventing the University." *When a Writer Can't Write*. Ed. Mike Rose. New York: Guilford, 1985. 134–65.

———. "The Study of Error." *College Composition and Communication*. 31 (1980): 253–69.

Bartholomae, David, and Anthony Petrosky, eds. *Facts, Artifacts and Counterfacts: Theory and Method for a Reading and Writing Course*. Portsmouth, NH: Boynton/Cook, 1986.

———. *Ways of Reading: An Anthology for Writers*. New York: St. Martin's, 1987.

Batson, Trent. "The ENFI Project: A Networked Classroom Approach to Writing Instruction." *Academic Computing* (February 1988): 32–33, 55–56.

Baudrillard, Jean. *America*. Trans. Chris Turner. London: Verso, 1988.

———. *Fatal Strategies*. Trans. Philip Beitchman and W.G.J. Niesluchowski. Ed. Jim Fleming. New York: Semiotext(e), 1990.

———. *The Mirror of Production*. Trans. Mark Poster. St. Louis: Telos, 1975.

———. *Simulations*. Trans. Paul Foss, Paul Patton, and Philip Beitchman. New York: Semiotext(e), 1983.

———. *La société de consommation*. Paris: Gallimard, 1970.

———. *Le système des objets*. Paris: Denoel-Gonthier, 1968.

Bazerman, Charles. "Scientific Writing as a Social Act: A Review of the Literature of the Sociology of Science." *New Essays in Technical Writing and Communication: Research, Theory, and Practice*. Ed. Paul V. Anderson, R. J. Brockmann, and Carolyn R. Miller. Farmingdale, NY: Baywood, 1983. 156–84.

———. *Shaping Written Knowledge*. Madison: U of Wisconsin P, 1988.

Bazerman, Charles, and James Paradis, eds. *Textual Dynamics of the Professions: Historical and Contemporary Studies of Writing in Professional Communities*. Madison: U of Wisconsin P, 1991.

Beaugrande, Robert de. *Toward a Science of Composition*. Norwood, NJ: Ablex, 1985.

Becker, Alton. "A Tagmemic Approach to Paragraph Analysis." *College Composition and Communication* 16 (1965): 237–48.

Bell, Daniel. *The Cultural Contradictions of Capitalism*. New York: Basic Books, 1976.

———. "The Social Framework of the Information Society." *The Microelectronics Revolution*. Ed. Tom Forester. Cambridge, MA: MIT P, 1980. 500–49.

"Bell Names Commission to Study Ways to Raise Excellence." *New York Times* 27 Aug. 1981, late ed.: A28.

Belsey, Catherine. *Critical Practice*. London: Methuen, 1980.

Benhabib, Seyla. "Epistemologies of Postmodernism: A Rejoinder to Jean-François Lyotard." *Feminism/Postmodernism*. Ed. Linda J. Nicholson. New York: Routledge, 1990. 107–30.

Bennington, Geoffrey. *Lyotard: Writing the Event*. Manchester: Manchester UP, 1988.

Berlin, James A. "Composition Studies and Cultural Studies: Collapsing Boundaries." *Interdisciplinarity and Composition*. Ed. Ann Ruggles Gere. New York: MLA, in press.

———. "Response." *College English* 51 (1989): 770–77.

———. "Rhetoric and Ideology in the Writing Class." *College English* 50 (1988): 477–94.

———. *Rhetoric and Reality: Writing Instruction in American Colleges, 1900–1985*. Carbondale: Southern Illinois UP, 1987.

———. "Rhetoric Programs after World War II: Ideology, Power, and Conflict." *Rhetoric and Ideology: Compositions and Criticisms of Power*. Ed. Charles W. Kneupper. Arlington, TX: Rhetoric Society of America, 1989. 6–19.

———. *Writing Instruction in Nineteenth-Century American Colleges*. Carbondale: Southern Illinois UP, 1984.

Bernstein, Richard. "The Rising Hegemony of the Politically Correct." *New York Times* 28 Oct. 1990, natl. ed.: Sec. 4, 1, 4.

Berthoff, Ann E. "The Problem of Problem Solving." *College Composition and Communication* 22 (1971): 237–42.

Bérubé, Michael. "Public Image Limited: Political Correctness and the Media's Big Lie." *Village Voice* 18 June 1991: 31–37.

Best, Stephen, and Douglas Kellner. *Postmodern Theory: Critical Interrogations*. London: Macmillan, 1991.

Bizzell, Patricia. "Beyond Anti-Foundationalism to Rhetorical Authority: Problems Defining 'Cultural Literacy.'" *College English* 52 (1990): 661–75.

———. "Cognition, Convention, and Certainty: What We Need to Know about Writing." *PRE/TEXT* 3 (1982): 213–43.

———. "Forming the Canon in Composition Studies." Conference on College Composition and Communication. Atlanta, March 1987.

Bizzell, Patricia, and Bruce Herzberg. Rev. of *What Makes Writing Good*, edited by William E. Coles, Jr., and James Vopat. *College Composition and Communication* 37 (1986): 244–47.

Bizzell, Patricia, and Bruce Herzberg, eds. *The Rhetorical Tradition: Readings from Classical Times to the Present*. Boston: Bedford, 1990.

Bloom, Allan. *The Closing of the American Mind*. New York: Simon and Schuster, 1987.

Bloomfield, Leonard. *Language*. New York: Henry Holt, 1933.

Bolter, Jay David. *Writing Space: The Computer, Hypertext, and the History of Writing*. Norwood, NJ: Erlbaum, 1991.

Booth, Wayne C. "The Rhetorical Stance." *College Composition and Communication* 14 (1963): 139–45.

Bourdieu, Pierre. *Distinction: A Social Critique of the Judgement of Taste.* Trans. Richard Nice. Cambridge, MA: Harvard UP, 1984.

———. *Outline of a Theory of Practice.* Trans. Richard Nice. Cambridge: Cambridge UP, 1977.

Boyne, Roy, and Ali Rattansi. "The Theory and Politics of Postmodernism: By Way of an Introduction." *Postmodernism and Society.* Ed. Boyne and Rattansi. New York: St. Martin's, 1990. 1–45.

Braddock, Richard. "Letter to Mrs. Martin Luther King." *College Composition and Communication* 19 (1968): 239.

Braddock, Richard, Richard Lloyd-Jones, and Lowell Schoer. *Research in Written Composition.* Champaign: NCTE, 1963.

Brandt, Deborah. "Text and Context: How Writers Come to Mean." *Functional Approaches to Writing: Research Perspectives.* Ed. Barbara Couture. London: Frances Pinter, 1986. 93–107.

Britton, James, Tony Burgess, Nancy Martin, Alex McLeod, and Harold Rosen. *The Development of Writing Abilities (11–18).* London: Macmillan, 1975.

Brodkey, Linda. *Academic Writing as Social Practice.* Philadelphia: Temple UP, 1987.

———. "Making a Federal Case out of Difference: The Politics of Pedagogy, Publicity, and Postponement." *Writing Theory and Critical Theory.* Ed. John Clifford and John Schilb. New York: MLA, in press.

———. "Modernism and the Scene(s) of Writing." *College English* 49 (1987): 396–418.

———. "On the Subjects of Class and Gender in 'The Literacy Letters.'" *College English* 51 (1989): 125–41.

Bruffee, Kenneth A. "Collaborative Learning and the 'Conversation of Mankind.'" *College English* 46 (1984): 635–52.

———. "Collaborative Learning: Some Practical Models." *College English* 34 (1973): 634–43.

———. "Comment on John Trimbur, 'Consensus and Difference in Collaborative Learning.'" *College English* 52 (1990): 692–94.

———. "Liberal Education and the Social Justification of Belief." *Liberal Education* 68 (1982): 95–114.

———. "The Way Out." *College English* 33 (1972): 457–70.

Bump, Jerome. "Radical Changes in Class Discussion Using Networked Computers." *Computers and the Humanities* 24 (1990): 49–65.

Bureau of the Census. *Statistical Abstract of the United States, 1989.* 109th ed. Washington, DC: U.S. Department of Commerce, 1989.

Bürger, Peter. *Theory of the Avant-Garde.* Trans. Michael Shaw. Minneapolis: U of Minnesota P, 1984.

Burke, Kenneth. A *Rhetoric of Motives.* Englewood Cliffs, NJ: Prentice-Hall, 1950.

Callinicos, Alex. *Against Postmodernism: A Marxist Critique.* Cambridge: Polity, 1989.

Cavanaugh-O'Keefe, John. "New Questions—Same Old Debate." *America* 25 Apr. 1987: 334–35.

Caywood, Cynthia L., and Gillian R. Overing, eds. *Teaching Writing: Pedagogy, Gender, and Equity.* Albany: SUNY P, 1987.

Chase, Geoffrey. "Accommodation, Resistance and the Politics of Student Writing." *College Composition and Communication* 39 (1988): 13–22.

Chomsky, Noam. *Aspects of the Theory of Syntax*. Cambridge: MIT P, 1965.

———. *The Generative Enterprise*. Dordrecht: Foris, 1982.

———. Rev. of *Verbal Behavior*, by B. F. Skinner. *Language* 35 (1959): 26–58.

———. *Syntactic Structures*. The Hague: Mouton, 1957.

Christensen, Francis. *The Christensen Rhetoric Program*. New York: Harper, 1968.

———. *Notes Toward a New Rhetoric*. New York: Harper, 1967.

———. "The Problem of Defining a Mature Style." *English Journal* 57 (1968): 572–79.

Cixous, Hélène. "The Laugh of the Medusa." Trans. Keith Cohen and Paula Cohen. *Signs* 1 (1976): 875–93.

Clark, Gregory. *Dialogue, Dialectic, and Conversation: A Social Perspective on the Function of Writing*. Carbondale: Southern Illinois UP, 1990.

Clifford, John. "The Subject in Discourse." *Contending with Words: Composition and Rhetoric in a Postmodern Age*. Ed. Patricia Harkin and John Schilb. New York: MLA, 1991. 38–51.

Clifford, John, and John Schilb. "A Perspective on Eagleton's Revival of Rhetoric." *Rhetoric Review* 6 (1987): 22–31.

Cohen, David S. "Comment on the Plain English Movement." *Canadian Business Law Journal* 6 (1982): 421–46.

Coles, William E., Jr., and James Vopat. *What Makes Writing Good*. Lexington, MA: Heath, 1985.

Colomb, Gregory C., and Joseph M. Williams. "Perceiving Structure in Professional Prose." *Writing in Nonacademic Settings*. Ed. Lee Odell and Dixie Goswami. New York: Guilford, 1985. 87–128.

Commission on English. *Examining the Examination in English: A Report to the College Entrance Examination Board*. Cambridge, MA: Harvard UP, 1931.

Committee on CCCC Language Statement. *Students' Right to Their Own Language*. spec. issue of *College Composition and Communication* 15 (Fall 1984). 1–32.

Connors, Robert J. "Composition Studies and Science." *College English* 45 (1983): 1–20.

———. "Current-Traditional Rhetoric: Thirty Years of *Writing with a Purpose*." *Rhetoric Society Quarterly* 4 (1981): 208–21.

———. Overwork/Underpay: Labor and Status of Composition Teachers since 1880." *Rhetoric Review* 9 (Fall 1990): 108–26.

———. "Personal Writing Assignments." *College Composition and Communication* 38 (1987): 166–83.

———. "Rhetoric in the Modern University: The Creation of an Underclass." *Politics of Writing Instruction: Postsecondary*. Ed. Richard Bullock and John Trimbur. Portsmouth, NH: Boynton/Cook, 1991. 55–84.

Connors, Robert, Lisa S. Ede, and Andrea Lunsford. "The Revival of Rhetoric in America." *Essays on Classical Rhetoric and Modern Discourse*. Ed. Connors, Ede, and Lunsford. Carbondale, Southern Illinois UP, 1984. 1–15.

Cook, Carole. Rev. of *Paradigms Lost*, by John Simon. *Saturday Review* Aug. 1980:67.

Cooke, Philip. *Back to the Future*. London: Unwin Hyman, 1990.

Cooper, Marilyn M. "Context as Vehicle: Implicatures in Writing." *What Writers Know: The*

Language, Process, and Structure of Written Discourse. Ed. Martin Nystrand. New York: Academic, 1982. 105–28.

———. "The Ecology of Writing." *College English* 48 (1986): 364– 75.

———. "Unhappy Consciousness in First-Year English: How to Figure Things Out for Yourself." *Writing as Social Action.* Ed. Marilyn M. Cooper and Michael Holzman. Portsmouth, NH: Boynton/Cook 1989. 28–60.

Cooper, Marilyn M., and Cynthia L. Selfe. "Computer Conferences and Learning: Authority, Resistance, and Internally Persuasive Discourse." *College English* 52 (1990): 847–69.

Couture, Barbara. "Effect Ideation in Written Text: A Functional Approach to Clarity and Exigence." *Functional Approaches to Writing: Research Perspectives.* Ed. Couture. London: Frances Pinter, 1986. 69–92.

Covino, William. "Making Differences in the Composition Class: A Philosophy of Invention." *Freshman English News* 10 (1981): 1–13.

Coward, Rosalind. *Female Desires: How They Are Sought, Bought, and Packaged.* New York: Grove P, 1985.

Crew, Louie. "The New Alchemy." *College English* 38 (1977): 707–11.

Crowley, Sharon. "Derrida, Deconstruction, and Our Scene of Teaching." *PRE/TEXT* 8 (1987): 169–83.

———. *The Methodical Memory: Invention in Current-Traditional Rhetoric.* Carbondale: Southern Illinois UP, 1990.

Culler, Jonathan. *On Deconstruction: Theory and Criticism after Structuralism.* Ithaca, NY: Cornell UP, 1982.

Daiker, Donald, Andrew Kerek, and Max Morenberg. "Sentence Combining and Syntactic Maturity in Freshman English." *College Composition and Communication* 29 (1978): 36–41.

Daly, Mary. *Gyn/Ecology.* London: The Women's Press, 1979.

D'Angelo, Frank J. "A Generative Rhetoric of the Essay." *College Composition and Communication* 25 (1974): 388–96.

Daniell, Beth. "Against the Great Leap Theory of Literacy." *PRE/TEXT* 7 (1986): 181–93.

Deal, Terrence E., and Allen A. Kennedy. *Corporate Cultures: The Rites and Rituals of Corporate Life.* Menlo Park, CA: Addison-Wesley, 1982.

Debord, Guy. *Society of the Spectacle.* Detroit: Black and Red, 1983.

DeCurtis, Anthony. "'An Outsider in This Society': An Interview with Don DeLillo." *Introducing Don DeLillo.* Ed. Frank Lentricchia. Durham, NC: Duke UP, 1991. 43–66.

Deleuze, Gillès, and Félix Guattari. *Anti-Oedipus: Capitalism and Schizophrenia.* Trans. Robert Hurley, Mark Seem, and Helen R. Lane. New York: Viking, 1977.

DeLillo, Don. *Libra.* New York: Viking, 1988.

———. *Mao II.* New York: Viking, 1991.

———. *White Noise.* New York: Viking, 1985.

Delpit, Lisa D. "The Silenced Dialogue: Power and Pedagogy in Educating Other People's Children." *Harvard Education Review* 58 (1988): 280–98.

de Man, Paul. *Allegories of Reading: Figural Language in Rousseau, Nietzsche, Rilke, and Proust.* New Haven: Yale UP, 1979.

————. *Blindness and Insight: Essays in the Rhetoric of Contemporary Criticism.* New York: Oxford UP, 1971.

Derrida, Jacques. *Of Grammatology.* Trans. Gayatri Chakravorty Spivak. Baltimore: Johns Hopkins UP, 1976.

————. *Speech and Phenomena, and Other Essays on Husserl's Theory of Signs.* Trans. David B. Allison. Evanston: Northwestern UP, 1973.

————. *Writing and Difference.* Trans. Alan Bass. Chicago: U of Chicago P, 1978.

Diederich, Paul B. *Measuring Growth in English.* Urbana: NCTE, 1974.

Dillon, George. *Constructing Texts: Elements of a Theory of Composition and Style.* Bloomington: Indiana UP, 1982.

Donald, James, and Stuart Hall. "Introduction." *Politics and Ideology.* Ed. Donald and Hall. Philadelphia: Milton Keynes, 1986. ix–xx.

D'Souza, Dinesh. *Illiberal Education: The Politics of Race and Sex on Campus.* New York: Free P, 1991.

Eagleton, Terry. "Awakening from Modernity." *Times Literary Supplement* 20 Feb. 1987:194.

————. *Literary Theory: An Introduction.* Oxford: Basil Blackwell, 1983.

Easthope, Anthony. *British Post-Structuralism.* London: Routledge, 1988.

Ede, Lisa, and Andrea Lunsford. *Singular Texts/Plural Authors: Perspectives on Collaborative Writing.* Carbondale: Southern Illinois UP, 1990.

————. "Why Write . . . Together?" *Rhetoric Review* 1 (1983): 57–68.

————. "Why Write Together: A Research Update." *Rhetoric Review* 5 (1986): 71–84.

Ehrenreich, Barbara. *Fear of Falling: The Inner Life of the Middle Class.* New York: Pantheon, 1989.

Elbow, Peter. *Embracing Contraries: Explorations in Learning and Teaching.* New York: Oxford UP, 1986.

————. *Writing without Teachers.* New York: Oxford UP, 1973.

Emig, Janet. *The Compositing Processes of Twelfth Graders.* NCTE Research Report No. 13. Urbana: NCTE, 1971.

Erlanger, Rachel. "Johnny's Teacher Can't Write Either." *The New York Times* 12 June 1991, natl. ed.: A15.

Ewen, Stuart. *All Consuming Images: The Politics of Style in Contemporary Culture.* New York: Basic Books, 1988.

"Executive Pay." *Business Week* 2 May 1988: 50–54.

Fahnestock, Jeanne. "Accommodating Science: The Rhetorical Life of Scientific Texts." *Written Communication* 3 (1986): 275–96.

————. "Semantic and Lexical Coherence." *College Composition and Communication* 34 (1983): 400–16.

Faigley, Lester. "Competing Theories of Process: A Critique and a Proposal." *College English* 48 (1986): 527–42.

————. "The Problem of Topic in Texts." *The Territory of Language: Linguistics, Stylistics, and the Teaching of Composition.* Ed. Donald A. McQuade. Carbondale: Southern Illinois UP, 1986. 123–41.

Faigley, Lester, and Kristine Hansen. "Learning to Write in the Social Sciences." *College Composition and Communication* 36 (1985): 140–49.

Faigley, Lester, and Thomas P. Miller. "What We Learn from Writing on the Job." *College English* 44 (1982): 557–69.

Fairclough, Norman. *Language and Power.* London: Longman, 1989.

Farrell, Thomas J. "IQ and Standard English." *College Composition and Communication* 34 (1983): 470–84.

Fekete, John, ed. *Life After Postmodernism: Essays on Value and Culture.* New York: St. Martin's, 1987.

Ferry, Luc, and Alain Renaut. *Heidegger and Modernity.* Trans. Franklin Philip. Chicago: U of Chicago P, 1990.

Ferry, Michael, and Richard B. Teitelman. "Plain-Language Laws: Giving the Consumer an Even Break." *Clearinghouse Review* 14 (1980): 522–28.

Fiedler, Leslie. *The Collected Essays of Leslie Fiedler.* New York: Stein and Day, 1971.

Fillmore, Charles J. "The Case for Case." *Universals in Linguistic Theory.* Ed. Emmon Bach and Robert T. Harms. New York: Holt, 1968. 1–88.

Firth, J. R. *Papers in Linguistics: 1934–1951.* London: Oxford UP, 1957.

Flax, Jane. "Postmodernism and Gender Relations in Feminist Theory." *Feminism/Postmodernism.* Ed. Linda J. Nicholson. New York: Routledge, 1990. 39–62.

Flesch, Rudolf. *The Art of Readable Writing.* New York: Harper, 1962.

Flower, Linda, and John R. Hayes. "A Cognitive Process Theory of Writing." *College Composition and Communication* 31 (1980): 365–87.

Flynn, Elizabeth. "Composing as a Woman." *College Composition and Communication* 39 (1988): 423–35.

———. "Composition Studies from a Feminist Perspective." *Politics of Writing Instruction: Postsecondary.* Ed. Richard Bullock and John Trimbur. Portsmouth, NH: Boynton/Cook, 1991. 137–54.

Fonda, Jane. *Jane Fonda's Workout Book.* New York: Simon and Schuster, 1981.

Foucault, Michel. *The Archaeology of Knowledge.* Trans. A. M. Sheridan Smith. New York: Harper, 1976.

———. *The Birth of the Clinic.* Trans. A. M. Sheridan Smith. New York: Harper, 1972.

———. *Discipline and Punish: The Birth of the Prison.* Trans. Alan Sheridan. New York: Vintage, 1979.

———. "The Discourse on Language." *The Archaeology of Knowledge.* Trans. A. M. Sheridan Smith. New York: Harper, 1976. 215–37.

———. *The History of Sexuality.* Vol. 1: *An Introduction.* Trans. Robert Hurley. New York: Pantheon, 1978.

———. *The History of Sexuality.* Vol. 2: *The Use of Pleasure.* Trans. Robert Hurley. New York: Random House, 1985.

———. *The History of Sexuality.* Vol. 3: *The Care of the Self.* Trans. Robert Hurley. New York: Random House, 1986.

———. *Language, Counter-Memory, Practice.* Ed. Donald F. Bouchard. Trans. Donald F. Bouchard and Sherry Simon. Ithaca, NY: Cornell UP, 1977.

———. *Madness and Civilization: A History of Insanity in the Age of Reason.* Trans. R. Howard. New York: Vintage, 1973.

———. *Power/Knowledge: Selected Interviews and Other Writings 1972–1977.* Ed. Colin Gordon. New York: Pantheon, 1980.,

———. "The Subject and Power." Afterword to Hubert Dreyfus and Paul Rabinow. *Michel Foucault: Beyond Structuralism and Hermeneutics.* 2nd ed. Chicago: U of Chicago P, 1983. 208–26.

———. "What Is an Author?" *Textual Strategies: Perspectives in Post-Structuralist Criticism.* Ed. and trans. Josué V. Harari. Ithaca, NY: Cornell UP, 1979. 141–60.

———. "What is Enlightenment?" Trans. Catherine Porter. *The Foucault Reader.* Ed. Paul Rabinow. New York: Pantheon, 1984. 32–50.

Fowler, Roger, Robert Hodge, Gunther Kress, and Tony Trew, eds. *Language and Control.* London: Routledge, 1979.

Fowler, Roger, and Gunther Kress. "Critical Linguistics." *Language and Control.* Ed. Roger Fowler, Robert Hodge, Gunther Kress, and Tony Trew. London: Routledge, 1979. 185–213.

Freeman, Donald. "Linguistics and Error Analysis: On Agency." *The Territory of Language: Linguistics, Stylistics, and the Teaching of Composition.* Ed. Donald A. McQuade. Carbondale: Southern Illinois UP, 1986. 165–73.

Freire, Paulo. *Pedagogy of the Oppressed.* Trans. Myra Bergman Ramos. New York: Seabury, 1968.

Friedenberg, Edgar Z. *Coming of Age in America: Growth and Acquiescence.* New York: Random, 1965.

Garson, Barbara. *The Electronic Sweatshop: How Computers Are Transforming the Office of the Future Into the Factory of the Past.* New York: Simon and Schuster, 1988.

Geertz, Clifford. "Deep Play: Notes on the Balinese Cockfight." *The Interpretation of Cultures.* New York: Basic, 1973. 412–53.

———. "Ideology as a Cultural System." *The Interpretation of Cultures.* New York: Basic, 1973. 193–233.

Gere, Anne Ruggles. *Writing Groups: History, Theory, and Implications.* Carbondale: Southern Illinois UP, 1987.

Gibson, Walker. *Tough, Sweet, and Stuffy: An Essay on Modern American Styles.* Bloomington, IN: Indiana UP, 1966.

Giroux, Henry A., David Shumway, Paul Smith, and James Sosnoski. "The Need for Cultural Studies." *Teachers as Intellectuals: Toward a Critical Pedagogy of Learning.* Ed. Henry A. Giroux. Granby, MA: Bergin, 1988. 143–57.

"Good Riddance." *Houston Chronicle.* 6 Feb. 1991: 16A.

Gopen, George D. "The State of Legal Writing: Res Ipsa Loquitur." *Michigan Law Review* 86 (1987): 333–80.

Gorrell, Robert M. "Freshman Composition." *The College Teaching of English.* Ed. John C. Gerber. New York: Appleton-Century-Crofts, 1965. 91–114.

Grady, Michael. "A Conceptual Rhetoric of the Composition." *College Composition and Communication* 22 (1971): 348–54.

Graff, Gerald. *Professing Literature: An Institutional History.* Chicago: U of Chicago P, 1987.

Gragson, Gay, and Jack Selzer. "Fictionalizing the Readers of Scholarly Articles in Biology." *Written Communication* 7 (1990): 25–58.

Gramsci, Antonio. *Selections from the Prison Notebooks of Antonio Gramsci.* Ed. and trans. Quintin Hoare and Geoffrey Nowell Smith. New York: International, 1971.

Greenbaum, Leonard A., and Rudolf B. Schmerl. *Course X: A Left Field Guide to Freshman English*. Philadelphia: Lippincott, 1969.

Greimas, Algirdas Julien. *Structural Semantics: An Attempt at a Method*. Trans. Daniele McDowell, Ronald Schleifer, and Alan Velie: Lincoln: U of Nebraska Press, 1984.

Habermas, Jürgen. "Modernity—An Incomplete Project." *The Anti-Aesthetic: Essays on Postmodern Culture*. Ed. Hal Foster. Port Townsend, WA: Bay P, 1983. 3–15.

————. "Modernity versus Postmodernity." *New German Critique* 22 (Winter 1981): 3–18.

————. *The Philosophical Discourse of Modernity: Twelve Lectures*. Trans. Frederick Lawrence. Boston: MIT P, 1987.

————. *The Theory of Communicative Action*. Vol. 1: *Reason and the Rationalization of Society*. Trans. Thomas McCarthy. Boston: Beacon, 1984.

————. *The Theory of Communicative Action*. Vol. 2: *Lifeworld and System, A Critique of Functionalist Reason*. Trans. Thomas McCarthy. Boston: Beacon, 1987.

Hairston, Maxine C. "Breaking Our Bonds and Reaffirming Our Connections." *College Composition and Communication* 36 (1985): 272–82.

————. "The Winds of Change: Thomas Kuhn and the Revolution in the Teaching of Writing." *College Composition and Communication* 33 (1982): 76–88.

Hall, Stuart. "Cultural Studies and the Centre: Some Problematics and Problems." *Culture, Media, Language*. Ed. Stuart Hall, Dorothy Hobson, Andrew Lowe, and Paul Willis. London: Hutchinson, 1980. 15–47.

————. "On Postmodernism and Articulation: An Interview with Stuart Hall." Ed. Lawrence Grossberg. *Journal of Communication Inquiry* 10:2 (Summer 1986): 45–60.

Hall, Stuart, and Martin Jacques, eds. *New Times: The Changing Face of Politics in the 1990s*. London: Lawrence and Wishart, 1989.

Hall, Stuart, and Frederic Jameson. "Clinging to the Wreckage: A Conversation." *Marxism Today* Sept. 1990: 28–31.

Halliday, M.A.K. *An Introduction to Functional Grammar*. London: Edward Arnold, 1985.

————. "Language and the Order of Nature." *The Linguistics of Writing: Arguments between Language and Literature*. Ed. Nigel Fabb, Derek Attridge, Alan Durant, and Colin MacCabe. Manchester: Manchester UP, 1987. 135–54.

————. *Language as Social Semiotic*. London: Edward Arnold, 1978.

————. *Spoken and Written Language*. Victoria, Australia: Deakin UP, 1985.

Halliday, M.A.K., and Ruqaiya Hasan. *Cohesion in English*. London: Longman, 1976.

Halloran, Michael. "Rhetoric in the American College Curriculum: The Decline of Public Discourse." *PRE/TEXT* 3 (1982): 245–69.

Haraway, Donna. "Situated Knowledges: The Science Question in Feminism and the Privilege of Partial Perspective." *Feminist Studies* 14 (1988): 575–99.

Harris, Joseph. "The Idea of Community in the Study of Writing." *College Composition and Communication* 40 (1989): 11–22.

————. "The Plural Text/The Plural Self: Roland Barthes and William Coles." *College English* 49 (1987): 158–70.

Harris, Zellig. "Discourse Analysis." *Language* 28 (1952): 1–30; 474–94.

Harvey, David. *The Condition of Postmodernity: An Enquiry into the Origins of Cultural Change*. Oxford: Basil Blackwell, 1989.

Hassan, Ihab. "The Culture of Postmodernism." *Theory, Culture, and Society* 2:3 (1985): 119–32.

———. *The Dismemberment of Orpheus: Toward a Postmodern Literature.* Madison: U of Wisconsin P, 1971.

Havelock, Eric A. *Origins of Western Literacy.* Toronto: Ontario Institute of Education, 1976.

———. *Preface to Plato.* Cambridge, MA: Belknap P of Harvard UP, 1963.

Hawisher, Gail E., and Cynthia L. Selfe. "Letter from the Editors." *Papers from the Fifth Computers and Writing Conference.* Spec. issue of *Computers and Composition* 7 (April 1990): 5–14.

Hayakawa, S. I. "Learning to Think and to Write: Semantics in Freshman English." *College Composition and Communication* 13 (1962): 5–8.

Heath, Shirley Brice. "Toward an Ethnohistory of Writing in American Education." *Writing: The Nature, Development, and Teaching of Written Communication.* Vol. 1. Ed. Marcia Farr Whiteman. Hillsdale, NJ: Erlbaum, 1981. 25–45.

———. *Ways with Words: Language, Life, and Work in Communities and Classrooms.* New York: Cambridge UP, 1983.

Hjelmslev, Louis. *Prologomena to a Theory of Language.* Trans. Frans J. Whitfield. Madison: U of Wisconsin P, 1961.

Hochschild, Arlie Russell. *The Managed Heart: Commercialization of Human Feeling.* Berkeley: U of California P, 1983.

Hodge, Robert, and Gunther Kress. *Social Semiotics.* Ithaca, NY: Cornell UP, 1988.

Hodge, Robert, Gunther Kress, and Gareth Jones. "The Ideology of Middle Management." *Language and Control.* Ed. Roger Fowler, Robert Hodge, Gunther Kress, and Tony Trew. London: Routledge, 1979. 81–93.

Hoffer, Eric. *The True Believer: Thoughts on the Nature of Mass Movements.* New York: Harper, 1951.

Holt, Mara. "Towards a Democratic Rhetoric: Self and Society in Collaborative Theory and Practice." *Journal of Teaching Writing* 8 (1989): 99–112.

Holt, Mara, and John Trimbur. "Subjectivity and Sociality: An Exchange." *PRE/TEXT* 11 (1990): 47–56.

hooks, bell. *Talking Back: Thinking Feminist, Thinking Black.* Boston: South End P, 1989.

Hunt, Kellogg W. *Grammatical Structures Written at Three Grade Levels.* NCTE Research Report No. 3. Champaign: NCTE, 1965.

Hutcheon, Linda. *The Politics of Postmodernism.* London: Routledge, 1989.

Huyssen, Andreas. *After the Great Divide: Modernism, Mass Culture, Postmodernism.* Bloomington, IN: Indiana UP, 1986.

Irigaray, Luce. *This Sex Which is Not One.* Trans. Catherine Porter with Carolyn Burke. Ithaca, NY: Cornell UP, 1985.

Jacobs, Jane. *The Life and Death of Great American Cities.* New York: Random House, 1961.

Jacoby, Russell. *The Last Intellectuals: American Culture in the Age of Academe.* New York: Basic, 1987.

Jakobson, Roman. "Linguistics and Poetics." *Style in Language.* Ed. Thomas A. Sebeok. Cambridge, MA: MIT P, 1960. 350–77.

———. *Selected Writings.* Vol. 1: *Phonological Studies.* s'-Gravenhage: Mouton, 1962.

Jameson, Fredric. "Afterword—Marxism and Postmodernism." *Marxism/Jameson/Critique*. Ed. Douglas Kellner. Washington, DC: Maisonneuve, 1989. 369–87.

———. *The Political Unconscious: Narrative as a Socially Symbolic Act*. Ithaca, NY: Cornell UP, 1981.

———. "Postmodernism and Consumer Society." *The Anti-Aesthetic: Essays on Postmodern Culture*. Ed. Hal Foster. Seattle: Bay P, 1983. 111–25.

———. "Postmodernism; or, The Cultural Logic of Late Capitalism." *New Left Review* 146 (July–August 1984): 53–92.

———. *Postmodernism; or, The Cultural Logic of Late Capitalism*. Durham: Duke UP, 1991.

Jarratt, Susan C. "Feminism and Composition Studies: The Case for Conflict." *Contending with Words: Composition and Rhetoric in a Postmodern Age*. Ed. Patricia Harkin and John Schilb. New York: MLA, 1991. 105–23.

———. *Rereading the Sophists: Classical Rhetoric Refigured*. Carbondale: Southern Illinois UP, 1991.

Jencks, Charles A. *The Language of Postmodern Architecture*. New York: Rizzoli, 1977.

Johnson, Richard. "What is Cultural Studies Anyway?" *Social Text* 19 (Winter 1986/87): 38–80.

Jolliffe, David A., ed. *Advances in Writing Research*. Vol. 2: *Writing in Academic Disciplines*. Norwood, NJ: Ablex, 1988.

———. "The Moral Subject in College Composition: A Conceptual Framework and the Case of Harvard, 1865–1900." *College English* 51 (1989): 163–73.

Kellner, Douglas. *Jean Baudrillard: From Marxism to Postmodernism and Beyond*. Stanford: Stanford UP, 1989.

Kenner, Hugh. "Up from Edenism." Rev. of *Paradigms Lost*, by John Simon. *National Review* 32 (17 Oct. 1980): 1272–74.

Kerek, Andrew, Donald Daiker, and Max Morenberg. "Sentence Combining and College Composition." *Perceptual and Motor Skills: Monograph Supplement* 51 (1980): 1059–1157.

Kiesler, Sara, Jane Siegel, and Timothy W. McGuire. "Social Psychological Aspects of Computer-Mediated Communication." *American Psychologist* 39 (1984): 1123–34.

Kimball, Roger. *Tenured Radicals: How Politics Has Corrupted Higher Education*. New York: Harper and Row, 1990.

Kinneavy, James L. *A Theory of Discourse*. New York: Norton, 1980.

Knoblauch, C. H. "Literacy and the Politics of Education." *The Right to Literacy*. Ed. Andrea A. Lunsford, Helene Moglen, and James Slevin. New York: MLA, 1990. 74–80.

———. "Some Observations on Freire's *Pedagogy of the Oppressed*." *Journal of Advanced Composition* 8 (1988): 50–54.

Knoper, Randall. "Deconstruction, Process, Writing." *Reclaiming Pedagogy: The Rhetoric of the Classroom*. Ed. Patricia Donahue and Ellen Quandahl. Carbondale: Southern Illinois UP, 1989. 128–43.

Kolby, Jerry. "The Top-Heavy Economy: Managerial Greed and Unproductive Labor." *Critical Sociology* 15.3 (Fall 1988): 53–69.

Kozol, Jonathan. *Illiterate America*. Garden City: Anchor-Doubleday, 1985.

Kremers, Marshall. "Adams Sherman Hill Meets ENFI: An Inquiry and a Retrospective." *Computers and Composition* 5 (1988): 69–77.

————. "Sharing Authority on a Synchronous Network: The Case for Riding the Beast." *Papers from the Fifth Computers and Writing Conference.* Spec. issue of *Computers and Composition* 7 (April 1990): 33–44.

Kress, Gunther. "Discourses, Texts, Readers and the Pro-Nuclear Arguments." *Language and the Nuclear Arms Debate: Nukespeak Today.* London: Frances Pinter, 1985. 65–87.

Kress, Gunther, and Robert Hodge. *Language as Ideology.* London: Routledge, 1979.

Kristeva, Julia. *Revolution in Poetic Language.* New York: Columbia UP, 1985.

Kroll, Barry M. "Cognitive Egocentrism and the Problem of Audience Awareness in Written Discourse." *Research in the Teaching of English* 12 (1978): 269–81.

Kuhn, Thomas. *The Structure of Scientific Revolutions.* 2nd ed. Chicago: U of Chicago P, 1980.

Labov, William. *Language in the Inner City.* Philadelphia: U of Pennsylvania P, 1973.

Lacan, Jacques. *Ecrits: A Selection.* Trans. Alan Sheridan. London: Tavistock, 1977.

Landow, George P. "Barthes, Hypertext, and the Politics of Reading." MLA Convention. Washington, December 1989.

Lanham, Richard A. *Revising Business Prose.* New York: Scribner's, 1981.

————. *Revising Prose.* New York: Scribner's, 1979.

Lauer, Janice M., and J. William Asher. *Composition Research: Empirical Designs.* New York: Oxford UP, 1988.

Lazere, Donald. "Introduction: Entertainment as Social Control." *American Media and Mass Culture: Left Perspectives.* Ed. Donald Lazere. Berkeley: U of California P, 1987. 1–23.

Leary, William G., and James Steel Smith. *Think Before You Write: A Textbook-Anthology for College English.* New York: Harcourt Brace, 1951.

LeFevre, Karen Burke. *Invention as a Social Act.* Carbondale: Southern Illinois UP, 1987.

Lévi-Strauss, Claude. *Structural Anthropology.* Trans. Claire Jacobson and Brooke Grundfest Schoepf. New York: Penguin, 1972.

Lindemann, Erika. *Longman Bibliography of Composition and Rhetoric: 1984–1985.* New York: Longman, 1987.

Lloyd, Donald J. "An English Composition Course Built Around Linguistics." *College Composition and Communication* 4 (1953): 40–43.

Lodge, David. "After Bakhtin." *The Linguistics of Writing: Arguments between Language and Literature.* Ed. Nigel Fabb, Derek Attridge, Alan Durant, and Colin MacCabe. Manchester: Manchester UP, 1987. 89–102.

Lunsford, Andrea A., and Lisa Ede. "Rhetoric in a New Key: Women and Collaboration." *Rhetoric Review* 8 (1990): 234–41.

Lunsford, Andrea A., Helene Moglen, and James Slevin, ed. *The Right to Literacy.* New York: MLA, 1990.

Lutz, William D. "Making Freshman English a Happening." *College Composition and Communication* 22 (1971): 35–38.

Lyons, Gene. "The Higher Illiteracy." *Harper's.* Sept. 1976. 33–40.

Lyotard, Jean-François. *The Differend: Phrases in Dispute.* Trans. Georges Van Den Abbeele. Minneapolis: U of Minnesota P, 1988.

————. *Peregrinations: Law, Form, Event.* New York: Columbia UP, 1988.

————. *The Postmodern Condition: A Report on Knowledge.* Trans. Geoff Bennington and Brian Massumi. Minneapolis: U of Minnesota P, 1984.

————. "Rules and Paradoxes and Svelte Paradox." *Cultural Critique* 5 (1986-87): 209–19.

————. "Universal History and Cultural Differences." Trans. David Macey. *The Lyotard Reader*. Ed. Andrew Benjamin. Oxford: Basil Blackwell, 1989. 314–23.

Lyotard, Jean-François, and Jean-Loup Thébaud. *Just Gaming*. Trans. Wlad Godzich. Minneapolis: U of Minnesota P, 1985.

MacIntyre, Alasdair. *After Virtue: A Study in Moral Theory*. Notre Dame, IN: U of Notre Dame P, 1981.

Macrorie, Ken. "To Be Read." *English Journal* 57 (1968): 686–92.

Malinowski, Bronislaw. *The Language of Magic and Gardening*. 1935. Bloomington, IN: Indiana UP, 1967.

Malveaux, Julianne. "Changes in the Labor Market Status of Black Women." A *Report of the Study Group on Affirmative Action to the Committee on Education and Labor*. U. S. 100th Cong., 1st sess. H. Rept. 100-L. Washington: GPO, 1987. 213–55.

Marcus, Stephen. "Computers in Thinking, Writing, and Literature." *Writing at Century's End*. Ed. Lisa Gerrard. New York: Random, 1987. 131–40.

Marcuse, Herbert. *One-Dimensional Man: Studies in the Ideology of Advanced Industrial Society*. Boston: Beacon, 1964.

Marvin, Carolyn. *When Old Technologies Were New: Thinking About Electronic Communication in the Late Nineteenth Century*. New York: Oxford, 1988.

Marx, Karl, and Friedrich Engels. *The German Ideology*. Pts. I, III. Ed. R. Pascal. New York: International, 1947.

Mauss, Marcel. "A Category of the Human Mind: The Notion of Person; The Notion of Self." Trans. W. D. Halls. *The Category of the Person: Anthropology, Philosophy, History*. Ed. Michael Carrithers, Steven Collins, Steven Lukes. Cambridge: Cambridge UP, 1985.

McCarney, Joseph. "For and Against Althusser: Rev. of Gregory Elliot, *Althusser: The Detour of Theory*." *New Left Review* 178 (July/Aug. 1989): 115–28.

McCloskey, Donald. *The Rhetoric of Economics*. Madison: U of Wisconsin P, 1985.

McCrimmon, James M. *Writing with a Purpose*. 1st ed. Boston: Houghton Mifflin, 1950.

McCrimmon, James M., with Susan Miller and Webb Salmon. *Writing with a Purpose*. 7th ed. Boston: Houghton Mifflin, 1980.

McCrimmon, James M., Joseph F. Trimmer, and Nancy I. Sommers. *Writing with a Purpose*. 8th ed. Boston: Houghton Mifflin, 1984.

McLuhan, Marshall. *Understanding Media: The Extensions of Man*. New York: 1966.

McQuade, Donald, and Robert Atwan. *Popular Writing in America*. 4th ed. New York: Oxford UP, 1988.

Mead, George Herbert. *Mind, Self, and Society*. Chicago: U of Chicago P, 1934.

Mehan, Hugh. *Learning Lessons*. Cambridge, MA: Harvard UP, 1979.

————. "The Structure of Classroom Discourse." *Handbook of Discourse Analysis*. Ed. Teun A. van Dijk. Vol 3. *Discourse and Dialogue*. London: Academic, 1975. 119–31.

Mellon, John C. "The Role of the Elaborated Dominant Nominal in the Measurement of Conceptual and Syntactic Fluencies in Expository Writing." *Sentence Combining: A Rhetorical Perspective*. Ed. Donald Daiker, Andrew Kerek, and Max Morenberg. Carbondale: Southern Illinois UP, 1985. 1–16.

———. *Transformational Sentence-Combining: A Method for Enhancing the Development of Syntactic Fluency in English Composition.* NCTE Research Report No. 10. Champaign: NCTE, 1969.

Milic, Louis T. "Composition via Stylistics." *The Territory of Language: Linguistics, Stylistics, and the Teaching of Composition.* Ed. Donald A. McQuade. Carbondale: Southern Illinois UP, 1986. 192–203.

Miller, Carolyn R. "Genre as Social Action." *Quarterly Journal of Speech* 70 (1984): 157–78.

Miller, Mark Crispin. *Boxed In: The Culture of TV.* Evanston: Northwestern UP, 1988.

Miller, Susan. "The Feminization of Composition." *Politics of Writing Instruction: Postsecondary.* Ed. Richard Bullock and John Trimbur. Portsmouth, NH: Boynton/Cook, 1991. 39–53.

———. "Is There a Text in This Class?" *Freshman English News* 11 (1982): 20–23.

———. *Rescuing the Subject: A Critical Introduction to Rhetoric and the Writer.* Carbondale: Southern Illinois UP, 1989.

———. *Textual Carnivals: The Politics of Composition.* Carbondale: Southern Illinois UP, 1991.

Mishel, Lawrence, and Jacqueline Simon. *The State of Working America.* Washington, DC: Economic Policy Institute, 1988.

Moffett, James. *Teaching the Universe of Discourse.* Boston: Houghton Mifflin, 1968.

Moi, Toril. *Sexual/Textual Politics.* London: Methuen, 1985.

Murphy, Kathleen. "Gender, Conversation, and Collaborative Groups." Conference on College Composition and Communication. Chicago. March 1990.

Murray, Donald M. "Finding Your Own Voice: Teaching Composition in an Age of Dissent." *College Composition and Communication* 20 (1969): 118–23.

———. "Teach Writing as a Process not Product." *Rhetoric and Composition: A Sourcebook for Teachers and Writers.* Ed. Richard L. Graves. Upper Montclair, NJ: Boynton/Cook, 1984. 89–93.

———. "Writing as Process: How Writing Finds Its Own Meaning." *Eight Approaches to Teaching Composition.* Ed. Timothy R. Donovan and Ben W. McClelland. Urbana: NCTE, 1980. 3–20.

Myers, Greg. "The Pragmatics of Politeness in Scientific Articles." *Applied Linguistics* 10 (1989): 1–35.

———. "Reality, Consensus, and Reform in the Rhetoric of Composition Teaching." *College English* 48 (1986): 154–74.

———. "The Social Construction of Two Biologists' Proposals." *Written Communication* 2 (1985): 219–45.

———. *Writing Biology: Texts in the Social Construction of Scientific Knowledge.* Madison: U of Wisconsin P, 1990.

Naisbitt, John. *Megatrends.* New York: Warner, 1982.

Neel, Jasper. *Plato, Derrida, and Writing.* Carbondale: Southern Illinois UP, 1988.

New University Conference Caucus of CCCC. "Counterstatement." *College Composition and Communication* 20 (1969): 238.

Newmeyer, Frederick J. *Linguistic Theory in America.* 2nd ed. New York: Academic, 1986.

North, Stephen M. *The Making of Knowledge in Composition: Portrait of an Emerging Field.* Upper Montclair, NJ: Boynton/Cook, 1987.

Nystrand, Martin. "Rhetoric's 'Audience' and Linguistics' 'Speech Community': Implications for Understanding Writing, Reading, and Text." *What Writers Know: The Language, Process, and Structure of Written Discourse.* Ed. Nystrand. New York: Academic, 1982. 1–28.

——. "A Social-Interactive Model of Writing." *Written Communication* 6 (1989): 66–85.

——. *The Structure of Written Communication.* New York: Academic, 1987.

Odell, Lee, and Dixie Goswami, eds. *Writing in Nonacademic Settings.* New York: Guilford, 1985.

O'Hare, Frank. *Sentence Combining: Improving Formal Grammar without Formal Grammar Instruction.* NCTE Research Report No. 15. Urbana: NCTE, 1965.

Ohmann, Richard. *English in America: A Radical View of the Profession.* New York: Oxford UP, 1976.

——. "Generative Grammars and the Concept of Literary Style." *Word* 20 (1964): 423–39.

——. *Politics of Letters.* Middletown, CT: Wesleyan UP, 1987.

——. "Use Definite, Specific Concrete Language." *College English* 41 (1979): 390–97.

Olson, Gary A., and Lester Faigley. "Language, Politics, and Composition: A Conversation with Noam Chomsky." *Journal of Advanced Composition* 11 (1991): 1–35.

Ong, Walter J., S. J. *Interfaces of the Word: Studies in the Evolution of Consciousness and Culture.* Ithaca: Cornell UP, 1977.

——. "Literacy and Orality in Our Times." *ADE Bulletin* 58 (September 1978): 1–7.

——. *Orality and Literacy: The Technologizing of the Word.* London: Methuen, 1982.

——. *The Presence of the Word.* New Haven: Yale UP, 1967.

Orwell, George. "Politics and the English Language." *Shooting the Elephant and Other Essays.* London: Secker and Warburg, 1950. 84–101.

Packard, Vance. *The Naked Society.* New York: D. McKay, 1964.

Penney, Alexandra. "How to Keep Your Man Monogamous." *Ladies' Home Journal* July 1989: 70, 74, 78.

Peyton, Joy Kreeft. "Computer Networks for Real-Time Written Interaction in the Writing Classroom: An Annotated Bibliography." *Computers and Composition* 6 (1989): 105–23.

——. "Technological Innovation Meets Institution: Birth of Creativity or Murder of a Great Idea?" *Papers from the Fifth Computers and Writing Conference.* Spec. issue of *Computers and Composition* 7 (April 1990): 15–32.

Phelps, Louise Weatherbee. "Dialectics of Coherence: Toward an Integrative Theory." *College English* 47 (1985): 12–29.

Pitkin, Will. "Hierarchies and the Discourse Hierarchy." *College English* 38 (1977): 648–59.

Porter, James E. "Developing a Postmodern Ethics of Rhetoric and Composition." *Toward Defining New Rhetorics.* Ed. Theresa Enos and Stuart Brown. Beverly Hills, CA: Sage, in press.

Poster, Mark. *The Mode of Information: Poststructuralism and Social Context.* Chicago: U of Chicago P, 1990.

Pratt, Mary Louise. "Linguistic Utopias." *The Linguistics of Writing: Arguments between Language and Literature.* Ed. Nigel Fabb, Derek Attridge, Alan Durant, and Colin MacCabe. Manchester: Manchester UP, 1987. 48–66.

Raban, Jonathan. *Soft City*. London: Hamilton, 1974.

Rabinow, Paul, and William M. Sullivan. "The Interpretive Turn: Emergence of an Approach." *Interpretive Social Science: A Reader*. Ed. Rabinow and Sullivan. Berkeley: U of California P, 1979. 1–21.

Raskin, Victor, and Irwin Weiser. *Language and Writing: Applications of Linguistics to Rhetoric and Composition*. Norwood, NJ: Ablex, 1987.

Readings, Bill. *Introducing Lyotard: Art and Politics*. London: Routledge, 1991.

Reither, James A., and Douglas Vipond. "Writing as Collaboration." *College English* 51 (1989): 855–67.

Rich, Adrienne. "Notes Toward a Politics of Location." *Blood, Bread, and Poetry: Selected Prose 1979–1985*. New York: Norton, 1985. 210–31.

———. "Power and Danger: Works of a Common Woman." *On Lies, Secrets and Silence: Selected Prose 1966–78*. New York: Norton, 1979. 247–58.

———. "Taking Women Students Seriously." *On Lies, Secrets and Silence: Selected Prose 1966–78*. New York: Norton, 1979. 237–45.

Richardson, Kay. "Critical Linguistics and Textual Diagnosis." *Text* 7 (1987): 145–63.

Rodgers, Paul, Jr. "A Discourse-Centered Rhetoric of the Paragraph." *College Composition and Communication* 17 (1966): 2–11.

Rohman, D. Gordon, and Alfred O. Wlecke. "Pre-Writing: The Construction and Application of Models for Concept Formation in Writing." U.S. Department of Health, Education, and Welfare Cooperative Research Project No. 2174. East Lansing: Michigan State U, 1964.

Rorty, Richard. *Philosophy and the Mirror of Nature*. Princeton: Princeton UP, 1979.

Rose, Mike. *Lives on the Boundary: The Struggles and Achievements of America's Underprepared*. New York: Free P, 1989.

———. *Writer's Block: The Cognitive Dimension*. Carbondale: Southern Illinois UP, 1984.

Roth, Audrey J. "Secretary's Report No. 61." *College Composition and Communication* 20 (1969): 268–72.

Sandel, Michael. *Liberalism and the Limits of Justice*. Cambridge: Cambridge UP, 1982.

Saussure, Ferdinand de. *Course in General Linguistics*. Trans. Wade Baskin. Ed. Charles Bally and Albert Sechehaye. New York: Philosophical Library, 1959.

Schafer, John C. "The Linguistic Analysis of Spoken and Written Texts." *Exploring Speaking-Writing Relationships: Processes of Differentiation*. Ed. Barry M. Kroll and Robert J. Vann. Urbana: NCTE, 1981. 1–31.

Schilb, John. "Comment on James Berlin, 'Rhetoric and Ideology in the Writing Class.'" *College English* 51 (1989): 769–70.

———. "Composition and Poststructuralism: A Tale of Two Conferences." *College Composition and Communication* 40 (1989): 422–43.

———. "Cultural Studies, Postmodernism, and Composition." *Contending with Words: Composition and Rhetoric in a Postmodern Age*. Ed. Patricia Harkin and John Schilb. New York: MLA, 1991. 173–88.

———. "Deconstructing Didion: Poststructuralist Rhetorical Theory in the Composition Class." *Literary Nonfiction: Theory, Criticism, Pedagogy*. Ed. Chris Anderson. Carbondale: Southern Illinois UP, 1989. 262–86.

————. "Ideology and Composition Scholarship." *Journal of Advanced Composition* 8 (1988): 22–29.

Schnapp, Alain, and Pierre Vidal Naquet. *The French Student Uprising: November 1967–June 1968.* Trans. Maria Jolas. Boston: Beacon Press, 1971.

Scholes, Robert. *Textual Power: Literary Theory and the Teaching of English.* New Haven: Yale UP, 1985.

Schriner, Delores K., and William C. Rice. "Computer Conferencing and Collaborative Learning: A Discourse Community at Work." *College Composition and Communication* 40 (1989): 472–78.

Schwartz, Nina. "Conversations with the Social Text." *Reclaiming Pedagogy: The Rhetoric of the Classroom.* Ed. Patricia Donahue and Ellen Quandahl. Carbondale: Southern Illinois UP, 1989. 60–71.

Selfe, Cynthia L. "An Apprehensive Writer Composes." *When a Writer Can't Write.* Ed. Mike Rose. New York: Guilford, 1985. 83–95.

————. "Technology in the English Classroom: Computers Through the Lens of Feminist Theory." *Computers and Community: Teaching Composition in the Twenty-First Century.* Ed. Carolyn Handa. Portsmouth, NH: Boynton/Cook, 1990. 118–39.

Sheils, Merrill. "Why Johnny Can't Write." *Newsweek* 8 Dec. 1975:58–65.

Shaughnessy, Mina P. *Errors and Expectations: A Guide for the Teacher of Basic Writing.* New York: Oxford UP, 1977.

Shor, Ira. *Critical Teaching in Everyday Life.* Boston: South End P, 1980.

————. *Culture Wars: School and Society in the Conservative Restoration, 1969–1984.* Boston: Routledge, 1986.

Simon, John. *Paradigms Lost.* New York: Penguin, 1980.

Simons, Herbert W. *Rhetoric in the Human Sciences.* London: Sage, 1989.

Sirc, Geoff. "Further Thoughts on the Marginalized." MegaByte University Electronic Discussion Group. Texas Tech U, Lubbock. 19 June 1989.

Slatin, John M. "Reading Hypertext: Order and Coherence in a New Medium." *College English* 52 (1990): 870–83.

Sledd, James. "In Defense of the *Students' Right.*" *College English* 45 (1983): 667–75.

————. "Layman and Shaman; or, Now About that Elephant Again." *The English Language Today.* Ed. Sidney Greenbaum. Oxford: Pergamon, 1985. 327–42.

Slevin, James F. "Depoliticizing and Politicizing Composition Studies." *Politics of Writing Instruction: Postsecondary.* Ed. Richard Bullock and John Trimbur. Portsmouth, NH: Boynton/Cook, 1991. 1–21.

————. "Genre Theory, Academic Discourse, and Writing Within Disciplines." *Audits of Meaning: A Festschrift in Honor of Ann E. Berthoff.* Ed. Louise Z. Smith. Portsmouth, NH: Boynton/Cook, 1988. 3–16.

Smith, Barbara Herrnstein. *Contingencies of Value: Alternative Perspectives for Critical Theory.* Cambridge, MA: Harvard UP, 1988.

Smith, Paul. *Discerning the Subject.* Minneapolis: U of Minnesota P, 1988.

————. "Pedagogy and the Popular-Culture-Commodity-Text." *Popular Culture, Schooling, and Everyday Life.* Ed. Henry A. Giroux and Roger I. Simon. Granby, MA: Bergin, 1989. 31–46.

Sommers, Nancy I. "Responding to Student Writing." *College Composition and Communication* 33 (1982): 148–56.

Sontag, Susan. *Against Interpretation*. New York: Dell, 1966.

Soper, Kate. "Postmodernism, Subjectivity, and the Question of Value." *New Left Review* 186 (March/April 1991): 120–28.

Spellmeyer, Kurt. "Foucault and the Freshman Writer: Considering the Self in Discourse." *College English* 51 (1989): 715–29.

Spender, Dale. *Man Made Language*. 2nd ed. London: Routledge, 1985.

Spitzer, Michael. "Computer Conferencing: An Emerging Technology." *Critical Perspectives on Computers and Composition Instruction*. Ed. Gail Hawisher and Cynthia L. Selfe. New York: Teachers College P, 1989. 187–200.

Spivak, Gayatri Chakravorty. *The Post-Colonial Critic: Interviews, Strategies, Dialogues*. Ed. Sarah Harasym. New York: Routledge, 1990.

Spradley, James P. *Participant Observation*. New York: Holt, Rinehart, and Winston, 1980.

Spradley, James P., and Brenda J. Mann. *The Cocktail Waitress: Woman's Work in a Man's World*. New York: Wiley, 1974.

Spring, Joel. *The American School: 1642–1985*. New York: Longman, 1986.

Stephanson, Anders. "Interview with Cornel West." *Universal Abandon? The Politics of Postmodernism*. Ed. Andrew Ross. Minneapolis: U of Minnesota P, 1988. 269–86.

———. "Regarding Postmodernism—A Conversation with Fredric Jameson." *Universal Abandon? The Politics of Postmodernism*. Ed. Andrew Ross. Minneapolis: U of Minnesota P, 1988. 3–30.

Stewart, Donald C. "Collaborative Learning and Composition: Boon or Bane?" *Rhetoric Review* 7 (1988): 58–83.

Stuckey, J. Elspeth. *The Violence of Literacy*. Portsmouth, NH: Boynton/Cook, 1991.

Students for a Democratic Society. "The Port Huron Statement." *Individualism: Man in Modern Society*. Ed. Ronald Gross and Paul Osterman. New York: Dell, 1971. 233–40.

"Survey of College Freshmen Finds a Shift in Priorities." *New York Times* 29 Jan. 1991, natl. ed. A12.

Tate, Gary, ed. *Teaching Composition: 10 Bibliographic Essays*. Fort Worth: Texas Christian UP, 1976.

Therborn, Göran. *The Ideology of Power and the Power of Ideology*. London: Verso, 1980.

Thompson, John B. *Studies in the Theory of Ideology*. Cambridge: Polity, 1984.

Tibbetts, Charlene, and A. M. Tibbetts. "How Are English Teachers Reacting to Declining College Entrance Scores?" *English Journal* 66.9 (Dec. 1977): 13–16.

Toffler, Alvin. *The Third Wave*. New York: Morrow, 1980.

Toulmin, Stephen. *The Uses of Argument*. New York: Cambridge UP, 1964.

Trachsel, Mary. *Institutionalizing Literacy: The Historical Role of College Entrance Examinations in English*. Carbondale: Southern Illinois UP, 1992.

Treece, Marla. *Communication for Business and the Professions*. 3rd ed. Boston: Allyn and Bacon, 1986.

Trew, Tony. "Theory and Ideology at Work." *Language and Control*. Ed. Roger Fowler, Robert Hodge, Gunther Kress, and Tony Trew. London: Routledge, 1979. 94–116.

Trimbur, John. "Consensus and Difference in Collaborative Learning." *College English* 51 (1989): 602–16.

———. "Cultural Studies and Teaching Writing." *Focuses* 1.2 (Fall 1988): 5–18.

———. "Literacy and the Discourse of Crisis." *Politics of Writing Instruction: Postsecondary.* Ed. Richard Bullock and John Trimbur. Portsmouth, NH: Boynton/Cook, 1991. 277–95.

———. "Response." *College English* 52 (1990): 696–700.

Trimmer, Joseph F., and James N. McCrimmon. *Writing with a Purpose.* 9th ed. Boston: Houghton Mifflin, 1988.

Tuman, Myron. "Class, Codes, and Composition: Basil Bernstein and the Critique of Pedagogy." *College Composition and Communication* 39 (1988): 42–51.

Urban, Greg. "The 'I' of Discourse." *Semiotics, Self, and Society.* Ed. Benjamin Lee and Greg Urban. Berlin: Mouton de Gruyter, 1989. 27–51.

Van Dijk, Teun A., ed. *Handbook of Discourse Analysis.* 4 vols. London: Academic, 1985.

———. *Macrostructures: An Interdisciplinary Study of Global Structures in Discourse, Interaction, and Cognition.* Hillsdale, NJ: Erlbaum, 1980.

Vande Kopple, William. "Functional Sentence Perspective, Composition, and Reading." *College Composition and Communication* 33 (1982): 50–63.

Venturi, Robert, Denise Scott Brown, and Steven Izenour. *Learning from Las Vegas.* Cambridge, MA: MIT, 1972.

Vitanza, Victor J. "Three 'Counter'-Theses; or, A Critical In(ter)vention into Composition Theories and (Pedagogies)." *Contending with Words: Composition and Rhetoric in a Postmodern Age.* Ed. Patricia Harkin and John Schilb. New York: MLA, 1991. 139–72.

Voloshinov, V. N. *Freudianism: A Marxist Critique.* Trans. I. R. Titunik. New York: Academic, 1976.

Vygotsky, Lev. *Thought and Language.* Trans. Eugenia Hanfman and Gertrude Vakar. Cambridge, MA: MIT P, 1962.

Wallis, Claudia. "Abortion, Ethics and the Law." *Time* 6 July 1987:82–83.

Weaver, Richard. *The Ethics of Rhetoric.* Chicago: Henry Regnery, 1953.

White, Edward. "Post-Structural Literary Criticism and the Response to Student Writing." *College Composition and Communication* 35 (1984): 186–95.

Whyte, William H. *The Organization Man.* New York: Simon and Schuster, 1956.

Will, George F. "Radical English." *Washington Post* 16 Sept. 1990: B7.

Williams, Joseph M. "On Defining Complexity." *College English* 40 (1979): 595–609.

———. *Style: Ten Lessons in Clarity and Grace.* 3rd ed. Glenview, IL: Scott, 1989.

Williams, Raymond. *Keywords: A Vocabulary of Culture and Society.* New York: Oxford, 1976.

Wilson, Sloan. *The Man in the Gray Flannel Suit.* New York: Simon and Schuster, 1955.

Winterowd, W. Ross, ed. *Contemporary Rhetoric: A Conceptual Background with Readings.* New York: Harcourt, Brace, Jovanovich, 1975.

———. "The Grammar of Coherence." *College English* 31 (1970): 828-35.

Witte, Stephen P. "Topical Structure and Revision: An Exploratory Study." *College Composition and Communication* 34 (1983): 313–41.

"Workshop Reports: Annual Meeting, Miami Beach, Florida, April 17–19, 1969." *College Composition and Communication* 20 (1969): 242–65.

Young, Art. "Considering Values: The Poetic Function of Language." *Language Connections*. Ed. Toby Fulwiler and Art Young. Urbana: NCTE, 1982. 77–97.

Young, Iris Marion. *Justice and the Politics of Difference*. Princeton, NJ: Princeton UP, 1991.

Young, Richard E. "Paradigms and Problems: Needed Research in Rhetorical Invention." *Research on Composing: Points of Departure*. Ed. Charles R. Cooper and Lee Odell. Urbana: NCTE, 1978. 29–47.

Young, Richard E., and Alton L. Becker. "Toward a Modern Theory of Rhetoric: A Tagmemic Contribution." *Harvard Education Review* 35 (1965): 450–68.

Zavarzadeh, Mas'ud, and Donald Morton. "Theory, Pedagogy, Politics: The Crisis of 'The Subject' in the Humanities." *Boundary 2* 15 (Fall 1986/Winter 1987): 1–22.

Zemelman, Steven. "The Debate on a CCCC Language Statement Concluded at Last (At Least for Now)." CLAC 11 (Winter 1984): 7–9.

Zuboff, Shoshana. *In the Age of the Smart Machine*. New York: Basic, 1988.

Index

279

Pittsburgh Series in Composition, Literacy, and Culture